Charles Spurgeon, 1854

the LOST SERMONS *of*
C. H. SPURGEON

the LOST SERMONS *of*
C. H. SPURGEON

His Earliest Outlines and Sermons Between 1851 and 1854   *Vol.5*

General Editor JASON G. DUESING • *Volume Editor* GEOFFREY CHANG

NASHVILLE, TENNESSEE

The Lost Sermons of C. H. Spurgeon, Volume 5
Copyright © 2021 by Spurgeon's College
Published by B&H Academic
Nashville, Tennessee

All rights reserved.

Standard Edition ISBN: 978-1-5359-2368-2
Collector's Edition ISBN: 978-1-5359-2370-5

Dewey Decimal Classification: 252
Subject Heading: SPURGEON, CHARLES H. / SERMONS / CHRISTIAN LIFE--SERMONS

Special thanks to Spurgeon's College, spurgeons.ac.uk

Scripture quotations are taken from the King James Version.

The web addresses referenced in this book were live and correct at the time of the book's publication but may be subject to change.

The marbled paper for the cover of the collector's edition was created by Lesley Patterson-Marx, lesleypattersonmarx.com

Printed in China
1 2 3 4 5 6 7 8 9 10 RRD 26 25 24 23 22 21

To

Hinson Baptist Church,
for her commitment
to the gospel
and
to raising up
gospel preachers.

CONTENTS

Foreword..xiii
Editor's Preface..xv
Project Research Team....................................xvii
Abbreviations..xix

PART 1: *Introduction* 1

PART 2: *The Sermons: Notebook 5 (Sermons 233–284)* ...17

Opening Page of Notebook 5		18
Blank Page		20
Skeletons from 233 to 284		22
Sermon 233	The Cherubim—Ezek 1:5	28
Sermon 234	Comfort for the Persecuted—2 Kgs 19:4	40
Sermon 235	The Great Conflagration—2 Pet 3:10–11	46
Sermon 236	The Nail in a Sure Place—Isa 22:23–24	58
Sermon 237	The Faith of Simon Magus—Acts 18:13, 21	68
Sermon 238	Text for Little Children—Matt 21:16	82
Sermon 239	Text for Boys and Girls	86
Sermon 240	Text for Young Believers	90
Sermon 241	What Doth Hinder Me to Be Baptized[?]—Acts 8:36	94
Sermon 242	Brand Plucked from the Fire—Zech 3:2	104
Sermon 243	Christ Our Surety—Ps 119:122	110
Sermon 244	He Was Speechless—Matt 22:12	120
Sermon 245	The Grain of Mustard Seed—Matt 13:31–32	132
Sermon 246	The Stronghold of Refuge—Zech 9:12	136
Sermon 247	Vision of the Holy Waters—Ezek 47:1–12	146
Sermon 248	The Coming of Spring—Song 2:10–13	156
Sermon 249	The Zeal of Thine House Hath Eaten Me Up—Ps 69:9	164
Sermon 250	The New Song on Mount Zion—Rev 14:1–3	168

CONTENTS

Sermon 251	Ask, and It Shall Be Given You—Matt 7:7	178
Sermon 252	Spiritual Decline—Hos 7:9	186
Sermon 253	No Night in Heaven—Rev 22:5	198
Sermon 254	All Ful[l]ness in Jesus—Col 1:19	212
Sermon 255	"He That Believeth Shall Not Make Haste"—Isa 28:16	226
Sermon 256	Vision of the Man with the Inkhorn—Ezekiel 9	236
Sermon 257	Art Thou for Us or for Our Adversaries[?]—Josh 5:13	246
Sermon 258	I Have Been Young and Now Am Old Etc.—Ps 37:25	252
Sermon 259	Can That Which Is Unsavoury Be Eaten Without Salt, Etc.[?]—Job 6:6	262
Sermon 260	"The Holy Ghost Saith Today"—Heb 3:7	266
Sermon 261	Consider Your Ways—Hag 1:5	274
Sermon 262	The Spirits of Bondage and Adoption—Rom 8:15	280
Sermon 263	Job the Perfect Man—Job 1:1	286
Sermon 264	What Have They Seen in Thy House[?]—2 Kgs 20:15	290
Sermon 265	Making Ones-Self Rich Yet Having Nothing—Prov 13:7	294
Sermon 266	Let Us Not Sleep As Do Others—1 Thess 5:6	298
Sermon 267	The Believer[']s Certain Salvation—Rom 5:10	304
Sermon 268	A Righteousness Better Than the Pharisees—Matt 5:20	314
Sermon 269	Blessed Are the Peacemakers—Matt 5:9	320
Sermon 270	"Beware"—Job 36:18	328
Sermon 271	Not Slothful in Business Etc.—Rom 12:11	338
Sermon 272	Prayer for Jesus—Ps 72:15	342
Sermon 273	Man Dieth and Where Is He?—Job 14:10	354
Sermon 274	The Parent and Child of Sin—Jas 1:14	364
Sermon 275	A Crook in Every Lot—Eccl 7:13	368
Sermon 276	Baptism—John 3:23	376
Sermon 277	The Table of the Lord Not Contemptible—Mal 1:7	394
Sermon 278	The Rechabites—Jer 35:18–19	402
Sermon 279	A Fountain Opened—Zech 13:1	408
Sermon 280	The Telling of the Flocks—Jer 33:13	416
Sermon 281	The Far-Off Made Nigh—Eph 2:13	422
Sermon 282	Walk in Love—Eph 5:2	426
Sermon 283	Fishers of Men—Matt 4:19	446
Sermon 284	Less Than the Least—Eph 3:8	456

CONTENTS

The Lord Is My Banner 462
Inside Back Cover of Notebook 5 466
Back Cover of Notebook 5 468
About the Project at Midwestern Seminary .471
About Spurgeon's College 473
Scripture Index 475
Subject Index 489

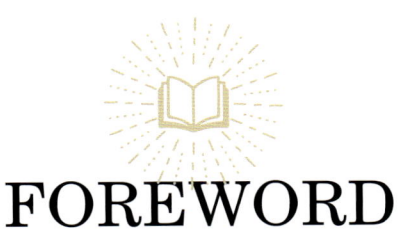

FOREWORD

Monday mornings, for Charles Spurgeon, were normally spent editing. Once he moved to London in 1855 and commenced his thirty-seven-year pastorate at New Park Street Baptist Church/Metropolitan Tabernacle, most of Spurgeon's sermons were published the same week they were preached. It was through those printed sermons that Spurgeon preached, and has continued to preach, to most who have ever heard of him.

Charles Spurgeon was baptized on May 3, 1851 at Isleham, Cambridgeshire, just several weeks before his seventeenth birthday. He had grown up in a minister's home and had been converted about six months earlier. Soon after Charles was converted as a teenager, he was preaching. His autobiography retells the story of his first sermon, in a cottage at Taversham, a village outside of Cambridge, England. On that occasion, Spurgeon picked his text and spoke without notes. As far as this author knows, no further record of that message is left to us.

In between Spurgeon's beginning as a preacher and his London ministry, there were three years of his being the preacher at the Baptist Chapel in Waterbeach (just north of Cambridge). During these few years (1852–1854) his sermons were not published, but we do have more record of his messages than we have of that earliest cottage sermon in Taversham. In fact, twelve notebooks of Charles's own sermon notes from these years have only lately come to light and are now being republished. The book you now hold is volume 5 in that set.

Careful readers of Spurgeon have known of these notebooks. Charles himself mentioned them and gave some examples from them in a few chapters of his autobiography. But the outlines themselves—much less a full set of them—have been unavailable.

In this volume you'll find sermons preached on passages as diverse as Ezekiel and Ephesians. For most of these sermons, Spurgeon's notes consist only of the main points and then, under those, some main points of application. But usually these applications go unnoticed, trapped as they are in this series of notebooks. These volumes are bringing to light sermons that heretofore have been forgotten. Echoes of his ministry as a teenage pastor in Waterbeach are here heard again for the first time.

FOREWORD

In these notebooks we see that Charles kept a record of each time he preached, so that he knew the number of each sermon. One can feel something of the weighty privilege he felt each occasion to be. He recounted anxiety about these messages as they were preached, and especially about whether he was the instrument of anyone's conversion through them.

The church in the village became the college of the preacher. God's providence prevented Charles from attaining more formal education. But God had prepared him specially for his calling, and it was the preaching of God's Word through these sermons that God used to set many of the characteristics that would flower in Spurgeon's later ministry.

Spurgeon tended to preach from a single text. He would often preach from the Old Testament; in fact, almost as often as the New. His sermons would have a few points ("heads" he called them) and would be applied searchingly and brought home with power. Phrases of hymns snatched from memory filled his messages. He would have homely, memorable, and often humorous illustrations. He would never prepare a manuscript of a sermon beforehand, but rather study, pray, and write down an outline, trusting God to provide the words in due time. All of these characteristics began and developed in the sermons we read here in outline form.

Throughout his preaching—as throughout his entire ministry—Spurgeon mixed humor with wisdom. Both can be seen here. Few things seemed to give him more pleasure than to deal with Wesleyans who thought they had reached sinless perfection! As one old preacher said to him after hearing the young preacher, "You are the sauciest dog that ever barked in a pulpit!" (*Autobiography* 1:272).

I pray that through this new publication, many more will hear and be encouraged.

MARK DEVER
Capitol Hill Baptist Church
Washington, DC
September 2019

EDITOR'S PREFACE

In a way, these sermons exist because of a mistake. On February 2, 1852, Charles Spurgeon was to meet with Joseph Angus, the tutor of Stepney College, to discuss the prospect of attending the college. Though Spurgeon had been the pastor of Waterbeach Chapel since the previous October, some of his advisors were encouraging him to pursue an education in order to increase his usefulness. But the meeting never happened. The servant who greeted both men accidentally placed them in separate rooms and never connected them.

Leaving that place, Charles was disappointed and frustrated. But upon further reflection, he called to mind God's words from Jeremiah 45:5: "Seekest thou great things for thyself? Seek them not."[1] He sensed God's call to remain as a pastor at Waterbeach. Writing many years later, Charles recounted:

> I remembered the poor but loving people to whom I ministered, and the souls which had been given me in my humble charge; and, although at that time I anticipated obscurity and poverty as the result of the resolve, yet I did there and then solemnly renounce the offer of College instruction, determining to abide for a season at least with my people, and to remain preaching the Word so long as I had the strength to do it.[2]

A few weeks later, Charles shared this resolve with his father: "I had better not go to College *yet*, at least not just now.... The people at W----- would not like to get even a hint of my leaving them. I do not know why they love me, but they do; it is the Lord's doing."[3]

Charles was not denying his need of training and growth; he planned to go to college eventually. But in the meantime, he saw his pastorate at Waterbeach as his training ground: "I have many opportunities of improvement now; all I want is more

---

[1] *Autobiography* 1:242.
[2] *Autobiography* 1:242.
[3] *Autobiography* 1:244–45, italics in the original.

time. . . . I have plenty of practice; and do we not learn to preach by preaching? . . . I hope you will excuse my scrawl, for, believe me, I am fully employed. Last night, I thought of writing; but was called out to see a dying man, and I thought I dare not refuse."[4] Far from limiting his usefulness, Spurgeon's time at Waterbeach was preparing him for a much wider sphere of ministry.

This volume of sermons, then, begun a year later, provides a closer look at his ministerial preparation. In them the reader sees Spurgeon's careful study of Puritan theologians and Bible commentators such as John Gill, Matthew Henry, and William Greenhill, his deepening knowledge of the Bible, and his growth as a preacher of the gospel. One also sees Spurgeon's pastoral training as he cares for his congregation through various struggles and challenges. Facing antinomianism and opposition, disunity and deaths, Charles shepherded his congregation through these sermons and saw God work mightily in the small village of Waterbeach. But Charles would likely have de-emphasized these observations. Most importantly, he would have wanted these sermons to point readers to the glory of God in the gospel. This is, after all, what he prayed for his own congregation.

In God's providence, Charles ended up not attending college. In 1854, New Park Street Chapel in London called this nineteen-year-old village preacher to be their pastor. From there, Charles would go on to have a ministry that impacted the world and continues to have far-reaching influence today. For those who are familiar with his story, Spurgeon's giftedness and ministry can seem almost incredible. But these sermons reveal God's ordinary means of preparation and growth in the life of one of his servants.

GEOFFREY CHANG
Volume Editor
August 2019

---

[4] *Autobiography* 1:244–45.

PROJECT RESEARCH TEAM

General Editor

Jason G. Duesing

Volume Editor

Geoff Chang

Project Coordinator

Phillip Ort

Spurgeon Library
Research Assistants

Timothy Gatewood
Ronni Kurtz
Ed Romine
Adam Sanders
Devin Schlote
Garrett Skrbina

With Special Thanks To

Jason K. Allen, President, Midwestern Baptist Theological Seminary
The Spurgeon Library

Midwestern Baptist Theological Seminary
Kansas City, Missouri

Spurgeon's College
London, England

ABBREVIATIONS

ARM	*An All-Round Ministry, Addresses to Ministers and Students.* London: Passmore & Alabaster, 1900. Reprint: Pasadena, TX: Pilgrim Publications, 1983.
Autobiography	*C. H. Spurgeon's Autobiography. Compiled from His Diary, Letters, and Records, by His Wife, and His Private Secretary.* 4 vols. London: Passmore & Alabaster, 1899–1900. The Spurgeon Library.
Lectures	*Lectures to My Students: A Selection from Addresses Delivered to the Students of the Pastors' College, Metropolitan Tabernacle.* London: Passmore & Alabaster, 1893. The Spurgeon Library.
LS	*The Lost Sermons of C. H. Spurgeon.* 9 vols. Nashville, TN: B&H Academic, 2016–.
MTP	*The Metropolitan Tabernacle Pulpit: Sermons Preached and Revised by C. H. Spurgeon.* Vols. 7–63. London: Passmore & Alabaster, 1861–1917. Reprint: Pasadena, TX: Pilgrim Publications, 1970–2006.
Notebook	*Spurgeon Sermon Outline Notebooks.* 11 vols. Heritage Room, Spurgeon's College, London. K1/5, U1.02.
NPSP	*The New Park Street Pulpit: Containing Sermons Preached and Revised by the Rev. C. H. Spurgeon, Minister of the Chapel.* 6 vols. London: Passmore & Alabaster, 1855–1860. Reprint: Pasadena, TX: Pilgrim Publications, 1970–2006.
ST	*The Sword and the Trowel: A Record of Combat with Sin and Labour for the Lord.* 37 vols. London: Passmore & Alabaster, 1865–1902. The Spurgeon Library.
TD	*The Treasury of David: Containing an Original Exposition of the Book of Psalms; A Collection of Illustrative Extracts from the Whole Range of Literature; A Series of Homiletical Hints Upon Almost Every Verse; And Lists of Writers Upon Each Psalm.* 7 vols. London: Passmore & Alabaster, 1869–1885. The Spurgeon Library.

INTRODUCTION

WHO IS CHARLES SPURGEON?[1]

---

[1] This section was originally written by Phillip Ort for The Spurgeon Library as "Who Is Charles Haddon Spurgeon?" available from https://www.spurgeon.org/.

Known as the "Prince of Preachers," this Victorian, Calvinistic, Baptist minister testified as a powerful gospel witness in his time, but his influence endures today. So much so that Carl F. H. Henry, the dean of twentieth-century evangelical theologians, once called Spurgeon "one of evangelical Christianity's immortals."[2]

But what makes Charles Haddon Spurgeon immortal? Born on June 19, 1834 in Kelvedon, Essex to John and Eliza Spurgeon, he was the firstborn of seventeen children, although unfortunately only eight survived adolescence.[3] A boy who loved books, he quickly became fascinated with John Bunyan's *Pilgrim's Progress*. However, Spurgeon did not lose his own burden at the foot of the cross until January 6, 1850. Soon thereafter, he moved to Cambridge, joined St. Andrews Street Baptist Church, and began his ministry as an itinerant preacher. In October of 1851 Spurgeon accepted the pastorate of his first church, Waterbeach Chapel, and soon thereafter moved to New Park Street Chapel in Southwark, London in April of 1854. In 1861 the Metropolitan Tabernacle opened and Charles's ministry exploded, resulting in the founding of sixty-six parachurch

---

[2] Carl F. H. Henry quoted in Lewis Drummond, *Spurgeon: Prince of Preachers* (3rd ed.; Grand Rapids, MI: Kregel, 1992), 11.

[3] Photograph of genealogical record, "Pedigree of the Spurgeon (Spurgen, Spurgin, Spirgon, Spirjon, Etc.) Family of Halstead, Co., Essex," cited with permission by David Spurgeon, in Christian T. George, *The Man and His Times: Charles H. Spurgeon in Context* (A graphic timeline displayed at The Spurgeon Library at Midwestern Baptist Theological Seminary, Kansas City, MO). Elsewhere Charles recorded the names of the eight surviving children: Charles Haddon, Eliza, James Archer, Emily, Louisa, Charlotte, Eva, and Flora (*Autobiography* 1:10).

ministries.[4] His remarkable ministry in London would last thirty-eight years before his death on January 31, 1892 in Menton, France.

Spurgeon lived during the Victorian age where "progress" was the prized virtue of the day. Though born in the country, when the nineteen-year-old Charles moved to London in 1854, he was entering the largest and most powerful city in the world. However, in London Spurgeon found himself on the *south side* of the river, Southwark borough. According to Helen Douglas-Irvine's work, *History of London*, Southwark enjoyed "the infamous distinction of a pre-eminently evil reputation"[5] and a "meanness which proceeds from extreme poverty and decay."[6] To complicate matters, when Spurgeon arrived at New Park Street Chapel, the dwindling congregation could not pay him a salary; rather, he was paid by the fluctuating and meagre seat rent.[7] When the congregation—and the giving!—revived after three months of his ministry, he declared, "I will pay for the cleaning and lighting myself."[8] And from that day to his death, he covered all the incidental expenses of New Park Street Chapel and the Metropolitan Tabernacle.[9]

But Spurgeon did more than cover the "incidentals." By the age of twenty-seven, the young pastor had donated approximately $1,325,378 of the required $3,690,913

[4] See the following list of the sixty-six ministries reproduced from ST July 1884:373 on the occasion of Spurgeon's Jubilee, celebrated on June 18, 1884 (see also, Marianne Farningham, *Spurgeon: The People's Preacher* [London: Walter Scott, n.d.], 251–52): The Almshouses; the Pastors' College; the Pastors' College Society of Evangelists; the Stockwell Orphanage; the Colportage Association; Mrs. Spurgeon's Book Fund, and Pastors' Aid Fund; the Pastors' College Evening Classes; the Evangelists' Association; the Country Mission; the Ladies Benevolent Society; the Ladies Maternal Society; the Poor Ministers' Clothing Society; the Loan Tract Society; Spurgeon's Sermons Tract Society; the Evangelists' Training Class; the Orphanage Working Meeting; the Colportage Working Meeting; the Flower Mission; the Gospel Temperance Society; the Band of Hope; the United Christian Brothers' Benefit Society; the Christian Sisters' Benefit Society; the Young Christians' Association; the Mission to Foreign Seamen; the Mission to Policemen; the Coffee-House Mission; the Metropolitan Tabernacle Sunday School; Mr. Wigney's Bible Class; Mr. Hoyland's Bible Class; Miss Swain's Bible Class; Miss Hobbs's Bible Class; Miss Hooper's Bible Class; Mr. Bowker's Bible Class for Adults of Both Sexes; Mr. Dunn's Bible Class for Men; Mrs. Allison's Bible Class for Young Women; Golden Lane and Hoxton Mission (Mr. Orsman's); Edbury Mission and Schools, Pimlico; Green Walk Mission and Schools, Haddon Hall; Richmond Street Mission and Schools; Flint Street Mission and Schools; North Street, Kennington, Mission and Schools; Little George Street Mission, Bermondsey; Snow's Fields Mission, Bermondsey; the Almshouses Missions; the Almshouses Sunday Schools; the Almshouses Day Schools; the Townsend Street Mission; the Townley Street Mission; the Deacon Street Mission; the Blenheim Grove Mission, Peckham; the Surrey Gardens Mission; the Vinegar Yard Mission, Old Street; the Horse Shoe Wharf Mission and Schools; the Upper Ground Street Mission; the Thomas Street Mission, Horsleydown; The Boundary Row Sunday School, Camberwell; the Great Hunter Street Sunday School, Dover Road; the Carter Street Sunday School, Walworth; the Pleasant Row Sunday Schools, Kennington; the Westmoreland Road Sunday Schools, Walworth; the Lansdowne Place Sunday School; Miss Emery's Banner Class, Brandon Street; Miss Miller's Mothers' Meeting; Miss Ivimey's Mothers' Meeting; Miss Francies' Mothers' Meeting.
[5] Helen Douglas-Irvine, *History of London* (New York: James Pott, 1912), 364.
[6] Douglas-Irvine, 364.
[7] *Autobiography* 2:123.
[8] *Autobiography* 2:123.
[9] *Autobiography* 2:123–24.

INTRODUCTION

toward the construction of the Metropolitan Tabernacle.[10] He earned this money from speaking fees and from the sale of his wildly popular sermons and books. He didn't even take a salary from his new megachurch.

Charles Spurgeon was a truly unique instrument of the Lord Jesus Christ. One of the most remarkable aspects of his life and legacy is that he holistically exemplified Christian virtue in his ministry. With respect to evangelistic zeal, Spurgeon's passion for evangelism is seen in every Christ-centered facet of his life, ministry, and especially his sermons. During his lifetime he preached the gospel to more than a million people and personally baptized 15,000 new believers converted under his ministry. Furthermore, his sermons were translated into nearly *forty* languages including Arabic, Armenian, Bengali, Bulgarian, Castilian, Chinese, Congolese, Czech, Dutch, Estonian, French, Gaelic, German, Hindi, Russian, Serbian, Syriac, Tamil, Telugu, Urdu, and Welsh.[11]

Called a "nine-days wonder"[12] by *The Sheffield and Rotherham Independent*, this "boy preacher of the fens" took the world by storm when he arrived in London in 1854. The young preacher was a force to be reckoned with and provoked polarized reactions. *The Ipswich Express* said that his sermons were "redolent of bad taste" and "vulgar and theatrical."[13] On the other hand, Elymas L. Magoon—Spurgeon's first biographer—said that when the young preacher arrived in London, "A burning and shining light has

---

10 *Autobiography* 3:12 records that on January 22, 1862 the Building Committee of the Metropolitan Tabernacle Church finished their audit and presented the final expense report to the church with a total cost of £31,332 4s. 10d. ($3,630,913.30). Among the list of receipts the following entries are made: "collectors' accounts, £7,258 5s. 2d. [$841,117.82]; donations and subscriptions, £9,034 19s. 2d. [$1,047,009.38]; per Pastor C. H. Spurgeon £11,253 15s. 6d. [$1,304,135.34]" (*Autobiography* 3:13). However, this number must be considered alongside the testimony of deacon William Olney, who testified on the 25th anniversary of Spurgeon's ministry that "During those three years [of construction] Mr. Spurgeon paid over to the treasury of the church, for the building of this Tabernacle, just upon £5,000 [$579,424.28], all of which belonged to himself" (*Autobiography* 2:124). However, this too must be weighed carefully as Olney's remarks refer to the seat rent collected during the building/fundraising years of the metropolitan Tabernacle. Thus, it is possible that the difference of £6,253 15s. 6d. [$724,714.06] was contributed by Charles from the sale of his sermons and books. With this in mind, the emphasis on "per Pastor C. H. Spurgeon" implies Spurgeon donated the entire £11,253 15s. 6d. [$1,304,135.34]. Even if the difference of £6,253 15s. 6d. [$724,714.06] was funded through gifts, these gifts would have been understood as having to pass through Charles' hands personally. Additionally, the numbers above have been calculated using the following equation: (GBP(RPI-1984)/(RPI-Year)) x (GBP-USD-1984(RPI-2016)). Here January 1, 1984 has been chosen as the control date for conversion from GBP to USD with the original GBP adjusted for inflation and the subsequent USD adjusted for inflation as of September 2016 when the equation was formulated. The following online sources were used for the calculation: https://www.parliament.uk/briefing-papers/RP99-20.pdf (February 23, 1999); http://www.tradingeconomics.com/united-kingdom/currency (accessed May 31, 2019); http://www.usinflationcalculator.com/inflation/consumer-price-index-and-annual-percent-changes-from-1913-to-2008/ (accessed May 31, 2019).

11 *Autobiography* 4:291.

12 *Autobiography* 2:55.

13 *Autobiography* 2:44.

suddenly burst upon the moral world."[14] His voice was "full, sweet, and musical,"[15] and the massive crowds that he drew by open-air preaching led Magoon to title his biography of Spurgeon *The Modern Whitfield* [sic].[16]

But how was Spurgeon viewed by the people, the "least of these" whom he ministered to in his blighted community? In 1855 one anonymous writer, *Vox Populi*, the "voice of the people," wrote that "Mr. Spurgeon institutes a new era, or more correctly revives the good old style of Bunyan, Wesley, and Whitefield, – men whose burning eloquence carried conviction to the hearts of their hearers, – men who cared naught for the applause of their fellow-mortals, but did all for God's glory."[17] Indeed, Spurgeon gave fresh voice to the stream of rich theology that flowed through Calvin, Owen, Bunyan, Edwards, Wesley, and Whitefield. Charles knew that Christ had not commanded him to "feed my giraffes" but rather to "feed my sheep."[18] Thus, in preaching he insisted, "We must not put the fodder on a high rack by our fine language, but use great plainness of speech."[19] And Charles did speak plainly and often upon his favorite theme, "Jesus Christ and him crucified." Indeed, it is for his richly theological, exceptionally vivid, and dogmatically Christocentric preaching for which Charles Spurgeon is known.

But Spurgeon was not just a preacher—he was also a college president. In 1856 he founded the Pastors' College, a free seminary designed to help "rough and ready" ministers sharpen their skills for the ministry. Within the seminary's first twenty years of operation, Charles's students planted fifty-three new Baptist churches in London, not counting missions around the world or across England.[20]

But Spurgeon also serves as an example of theological integrity. Near the end of his life, in 1887, the Downgrade Controversy erupted as the theological decay of Britain was exposed. At that time, many had abandoned the authority, inspiration, and inerrancy of the Scriptures. Furthermore, others began to reject the bodily resurrection of Jesus Christ.[21] Spurgeon saw this decay in the Baptist Union and called for a direct

---

14   E. L. Magoon, *Sermons of the Rev. C. H. Spurgeon, of London; With Additional Discourses, and an Introduction and Biographical Sketch. First Series—Twentieth Edition* (New York: Sheldon, n.d.), v.
15   Magoon, x.
16   E. L. Magoon, *"The Modern Whitefield." Sermons of the Rev. C. H. Spurgeon, of London; With an Introduction and Sketch of His Life* (New York: Sheldon, Blakeman, 1857).
17   *Autobiography* 2:50–51.
18   C. H. Spurgeon, *The Salt-Cellars: Being a Collection of Proverbs, Together with Homely Notes Thereon. A. – L.* (New York: A. C. Armstrong and Son, 1889), 56.
19   Spurgeon, 1:56.
20   *ST Annual Report of the Pastors' College 1877–78*, 1878:240–63.
21   "A new religion has been initiated, which is no more Christianity than chalk is cheese....The Atonement is scouted, the inspiration of Scripture is derided, the Holy Spirit is degraded into an influence, the punishment of sin is turned into a fiction, and the resurrection into a myth" (*ST* August 1887:397).

response—the drafting of an evangelical statement of faith.[22] However, his call was not heeded, nor was a statement drafted. In the end, Spurgeon submitted his letter of resignation to the Baptist Union on October 28, 1887,[23] only to find himself censured by the same body a few months later.[24] Prophetically, Charles said, "I am quite willing to be eaten of dogs for the next 50 years; but the more distant future shall vindicate me."[25] And today his prophecy rings true.

Finally, Charles Spurgeon exemplified the Christian virtue which David Bebbington has termed "activism," the passionate belief that the gospel must be expressed in action.[26] In addition to the Pastors' College, Spurgeon also founded a ministry to prostitutes, a ministry to policemen, two orphanages, and seventeen almshouses for widows. Research conducted at The Spurgeon Library has shown that a *conservative* estimate of Spurgeon's net worth ran about $50 million, and yet when he died, only about $250,000 was left in his bank account. What does one do with $49,750,000? For Charles Spurgeon the answer was simple: invest it in God's kingdom. Orphans had to be fed, the houses of widows subsidized, and the Home Rescue Society for women suffering from domestic abuse had to be funded somehow.

Any one of these qualities—evangelistic zeal, theological integrity, or evangelical activism—would have been sufficient to earn Spurgeon recognition as an exemplary Christian man. Yet God was pleased to work all these things through his chronically depressed, arthritic, and gout-smitten servant, Charles Haddon Spurgeon. It was not Spurgeon who made Spurgeon great. It was God who made Spurgeon great, or rather, God who magnified his greatness through Spurgeon's weakness. In his words, it was "all of grace." Faithfulness to the Lord Jesus Christ above all other things was the chief goal.

Spurgeon's Sincere and Pure Devotion to Christ[27]

When thinking how best to assess and categorize the life of Charles Haddon Spurgeon, a phrase used by the apostle Paul in 2 Corinthians 11:3 comes to mind.

---

22   *Autobiography* 4:263.
23   G. Holden Pike, *The Life and Work of Charles Haddon Spurgeon* (London: Cassell and Company Lim., n.d.) 6:287.
24   Spurgeon's censorship occurred in two stages, first privately among the council of the Baptist Union (*ST* February 1888:81) and second by the Union as a whole (*Autobiography* 4:254).
25   *ST* August 1889:420.
26   See Phillip Ort, Timothy Gatewood, and Ed Romine, "Charles Spurgeon: The Quintessential Evangelical," in *Midwestern Journal of Theology* 18:1 (Spring 2019), 104–25.
27   Portions of this section originally published by Jason G. Duesing, "The Conversion of C. H. Spurgeon: A Lecture," in *Midwestern Journal of Theology* 17:2 (Fall 2018), 77–84.

For the totality of his life as a Christian, Spurgeon had "a sincere and pure devotion to Christ." His sight was set on Jesus Christ from the moment he "looked" to him in his conversion.

As a young boy, Charles remained close to his grandparents. His grandfather, an Independent minister, had a study in his home filled with books. Thus, reading filled much of Spurgeon's young life. When other children were outside, Charles was always with books. This relationship with written words found further reinforcement at home. Charles's mother regularly gathered the children on Sunday evenings to explain Scripture, read books aloud, and pray. In his *Autobiography*, Charles recounted:

> Yet I cannot tell how much I owe to the solemn words of my good mother. It was the custom, on Sunday evenings, while we were yet little children, for her to stay at home with us, and then we sat round the table, and read verse by verse, and she explained the Scripture to us. After that was done, then came the time of pleading; there was a little piece of Alleine's *Alarm*, or of Baxter's *Call to the Unconverted*, and this was read with pointed observations made to each of us as we sat round the table; and the question was asked, how long it would be before we would think about our state, how long before we would seek the Lord.[28]

Often Spurgeon's mother would pray: "Now, Lord, if my children go on in their sins, it will not be from ignorance that they perish, and my soul must bear a swift witness against them at the day of judgment if they lay not hold of Christ."[29] This thought of his mother standing against him was unbearable and caused him to seek the Lord. Spurgeon would later say:

> Fathers and mothers are the most natural agents for God to use in the salvation of their children. I am sure that, in my early youth, no teaching ever made such an impression upon my mind as the instruction of my mother; neither can I conceive that, to any child, there can be one who will have such influence over the young heart as the mother who has so tenderly cared for her offspring. A man with a soul so dead as not to be moved by the sacred

---

28   *Autobiography* 1:68.
29   *Autobiography* 1:68.

INTRODUCTION

name of "mother" is creation's blot. Never could it be possible for any man to estimate what he owes to a godly mother.[30]

His mother's prayers were answered when Charles was fifteen. At this time Charles was experiencing deep conviction of sin, saying, "I do speak of myself with many deep regrets of heart. I hid as it were my face from Him, and I let the years run round."[31] But soon the Holy Spirit would press the conviction of sin upon Spurgeon's soul:

> My heart was fallow, and covered with weeds; but, on a certain day, the great Husbandman came, and began to plough my soul. Ten black horses were His team, and it was a sharp ploughshare that he used, and the ploughshare made deep furrows.[32]

Here Charles described his young heart as "fallow" and "covered with weeds." But one day the "great Husbandman" began to plow Spurgeon's soul with a team of "ten black horses," one for each commandment under which Charles stood condemned.

In this state, Charles sank lower and saw himself to be nothing but "rottenness, a dunghill of corruption."[33] While he would later acknowledge that "A spiritual experience which is thoroughly flavoured with a deep and bitter sense of sin is of great value to him that hath had it," it was overwhelming for young Spurgeon.[34] In late 1849, Charles visited different churches in and around Colchester, but without much relief or encouragement. He explained:

> From chapel to chapel I went to hear the Word preached, but never a gospel sentence did I hear; but this one text preserved me from what I believe I should have been driven to, —the commission of suicide through grief and sorrow. It was this sweet word, "Whosoever shall call upon the name of the Lord shall be saved."[35]

When Spurgeon was in the "hand of the Holy Spirit" and experiencing a "clear and sharp sense of the justice of God," he could not believe in *substitution*, the "sum and

---

30 *Autobiography* 1:69.
31 *Autobiography* 1:67–68.
32 *Autobiography* 1:75.
33 *Autobiography* 1:93.
34 *Autobiography* 1:76.
35 *Autobiography* 1:95.

substance of the gospel."[36] For Spurgeon, the central question was, "Who would or could have thought of the just Ruler dying for the unjust rebel?"[37] Yet, while Charles did not then believe that "it was possible that *my* sins could be forgiven," soon the "Great Change" would take place.[38]

During this period, Charles was employed as an usher for a private school in Newmarket. As an usher Charles was both student and tutor, paying for his tuition by his work. When the school closed temporarily in December due to an outbreak of fever, Charles returned home to Colchester.

On one Sunday morning Colchester was hit with a substantial snowstorm. Charles, while en route, stumbled into a private Methodist church hidden in a back alley.[39] The regular minister was unavailable that morning, and an unidentified lay preacher took the pulpit. By Spurgeon's account, this person spoke quite ineloquently for about ten minutes on the passage, "Look unto me, and be ye saved, all the ends of the earth" (Isa 45:22).[40]

Thanks to the providence of a snowstorm, Spurgeon found himself subject to the preaching of a man who he claimed was "really stupid" and "did not even pronounce the words rightly."[41] Nevertheless, the message from this crude preacher effectually struck a chord in Spurgeon's anguished soul, for at the end of the service the preacher looked squarely at Spurgeon and said, "Young man, you look very miserable." Spurgeon recounted his thoughts:

> Well, I did but I had not been accustomed to have remarks made from the pulpit about my personal appearance before. However, it was a good blow, struck right home.
>
> He continued, "and you will always be miserable—miserable in life and miserable in death—if you don't obey my text; but if you obey now, this moment, you will be saved." Then lifting his hands, he shouted, as only a

---

36   *Autobiography* 1:98, 113.
37   *Autobiography* 1:98.
38   *Autobiography* 1:97, 103.
39   In recent years, three pews from this Primitive Methodist Chapel on Artillery Street, Colchester, where Charles was converted, were kindly donated by the current congregation of Artillery Street Evangelical Church to The Spurgeon Library at Midwestern Seminary. Visitors to the library can see an artist's depiction of the scene described here as well as the actual pews on which many people of this era sat to hear preaching like Charles heard on that day.
40   *Autobiography* 1:105.
41   *Autobiography* 1:105–6.

INTRODUCTION

Primitive Methodist could do, "Young man, look to Jesus Christ. Look! Look! Look! You have nothing to do but to look and live."

I had been waiting to do fifty things, but when I heard that word, "Look!" what a charming word it seemed to me! Oh! I looked until I could almost have looked my eyes away. There and then the cloud was gone, the darkness had rolled away, and that moment I saw the sun; and I could have risen that instant, and sung with the most enthusiastic of them, of the precious blood of Christ, and the simple faith which looks alone to Him.[42]

And at that moment Spurgeon "saw at once the way of salvation." He *looked* to Jesus Christ and *lived*. From that moment Spurgeon knew he was no longer under the "frown of God," but could now say, "my Father smiles." The joy of that day was "utterly indescribable" as the teenage Spurgeon rejoiced, "I am forgiven, I am forgiven, I am forgiven!"[43] Spurgeon would later say:

When I first received everlasting life I had no idea what a treasure had come to me. I knew that I had obtained something very extraordinary, but of its superlative value I was not aware. I did but look to Christ in the little chapel, and I received eternal life. I looked to Jesus, and He looked on me, and we were one forever. That moment my joy surpassed all bounds, just as my sorrow had before driven me to an extreme of grief. I was perfectly at rest in Christ, satisfied with Him, and my heart was glad, but I did not know that this grace was everlasting life till I began to read in the Scriptures, and to know more fully the value of the jewel which God had given me.[44]

What Spurgeon discovered on January 6, 1850, was the "sum and substance of the gospel . . . *Substitution*."

If I understand the gospel, it is this: I deserve to be lost forever; the only reason why I should not be damned is, that Christ was punished in my stead, and there is no need to execute a sentence twice for sin. On the other hand, I know I cannot enter Heaven unless I have a perfect righteousness; I am absolutely certain I shall never have one of my own, for I find I sin

---

42 *Autobiography* 1:106.
43 *Autobiography* 1:108–10.
44 *MTP* 31:395.

everyday; but then Christ had a perfect righteousness, and He said, "There, poor sinner, take My garment, and put it on; you shall stand before God as if you were Christ, and I will stand before God as if I had been the sinner; I will suffer in the sinner's stead, and you shall be rewarded for works which you did not do, but which I did for you."

    I find it very convenient everyday to come to Christ as a sinner, as I came at the first. "You are no saint," says the devil. Well, if I am not, I am a sinner, and Jesus Christ came into the world to save sinners. Sink or swim, I go to Him; other hope I have none. By looking to Him, I received all the faith which inspired me with confidence in His grace; and the word that first drew my soul — "Look unto Me," — still rings its clarion note in my ears. There I once found conversion, and there I shall ever find refreshing and renewal.[45]

That morning Charles Haddon Spurgeon looked to Jesus Christ and was saved. He found the joy of Christ, and as he put it, "I could have danced."

Interestingly, Charles returned to that same chapel the next week and took issue with the pastor's preaching on Romans 7.

The next Sunday I went to the same chapel, as it was very natural that I should. But I never went afterwards, for this reason, that during my first week the new life that was in me had been compelled to fight for its existence, and a conflict with the old nature had been vigorously carried on. This I knew to be a special token of the indwelling of grace in my soul, but in that same chapel I heard a sermon upon "O wretched man that I am! Who shall deliver me from the body of this death?" [v. 24] And the preacher declared that Paul was not a Christian when he had that experience. Babe as I was, I knew better than to believe so absurd a statement.

    What but divine grace could produce such a sighing and crying after deliverance from indwelling sin? I felt that a person who could talk such nonsense knew little of the life of a true believer. I said to myself, "What! Am I not alive because I feel a conflict within me? I never felt this fight when I was an unbeliever. When I was not a Christian I never groaned to be set free from sin. This conflict is one of the surest evidences of my new birth, and yet this man cannot see it, he may be a good exhorter to sinners,

---

[45] *Autobiography* 1:113.

INTRODUCTION

but he cannot feed believers." I resolved to go into that pasture no more, for I could not feed therein. I find that the struggle becomes more and more intense, each victory over sin reveals another army of evil tendencies, and I am never able to sheathe my sword, nor cease from prayer and watchfulness.[46]

On May 3, 1850, Charles received baptism in the River Larke. As his family were Congregationalists, his mother was saddened to learn that her son would pursue believer's baptism. She had said to him that while she prayed for his conversion, she did not pray he would become a Baptist. Charles responded, "Ah, mother! the Lord has answered your prayer with His usual bounty, and given you exceeding abundantly above what you asked or thought."[47]

By August 1850, Charles preached his first sermon and then was called, in 1851, as pastor in Waterbeach, a village near Cambridge. For the next three years he would hone his craft and record his sermons in nine notebooks. These notebooks were lost to publishing history until now, with the publication of these volumes as *The Lost Sermons of C. H. Spurgeon*.

While lecturing on Spurgeon, Andrew Atherstone, of Wycliffe Hall, Oxford, made a very helpful observation about that sermon Spurgeon heard in Colchester and how God used it in his conversion. He recounted that there are three key elements of Spurgeon's conversion. First, God's sovereignty over the circumstances of it. Second, God's powerful Word that convicted him. Third, God's use of Christ-centered preaching.[48] Atherstone observed that all of these would remain the key components of Spurgeon's ministry throughout his life—God's sovereignty, God's Word, and Christ-centered preaching.

From his conversion in the chapel on Artillery Street, Spurgeon kept his gaze set on his "sincere and pure devotion to Christ." As such, much like that preacher, Spurgeon pointed many others to "look" as well. It is our hope that *The Lost Sermons of C. H. Spurgeon* will further Spurgeon's pointing and direct the gaze of all readers to Jesus Christ.

---

46 *MTP* 31:395–96.
47 *Autobiography* 1:69.
48 Andrew Atherstone, "Andrew Atherstone on C H Spurgeon," at the 2018 Evangelical Ministry Conference. Available from http://acl.asn.au/andrew-atherstone-on-c-h-spurgeon/.

Sources and Method of *The Lost Sermons*

The publication of volume 4 of *The Lost Sermons of C. H. Spurgeon* marked a change in the general editor of this series as well as a refocusing of the editorial task and method for the remaining volumes. The introduction to volume 1 of the *Lost Sermons* projected the series to run to twelve total volumes.[49] However, as that was a reflection of a large endeavor just embarking, the work and reception of the first three volumes allowed the project's research team to refine the total scope to a new total of nine volumes. Within that space the entirety of Spurgeon's earliest unpublished sermons, totaling 400, will still appear.[50]

To that end, the remaining volumes of *The Lost Sermons of C. H. Spurgeon* are still committed to finishing what Spurgeon left unfinished. As his wife, Susannah, shared in the *Autobiography*:

> Mr. Spurgeon had himself intended, long ago, to publish a selection from [his first outlines]; in the Preface to *The New Park Street Pulpit* for 1857, he announced that he hoped shortly to issue a volume of his earliest Sermons, while Pastor at Waterbeach, but this was prevented by the pressure of his rapidly-increasing work.[51]

In an effort to continue what Spurgeon started, Volumes 4–9 follow the same research method and consultation of sources as Volumes 1–3 with only a few adaptations.[52] The overall aim is still to offer the reader "a critical work that can be accessed by academics and laity alike."[53] In sum, the remaining volumes will:

- Continue to consult primary and secondary sources in addition to the Notebooks themselves. These include, in part, the books Spurgeon owned that now make up the collection of The Spurgeon Library at Midwestern Baptist Theological Seminary in Kansas City, Missouri.[54]
- Continue to minimize any technical adjustments to preserve Spurgeon's original voice. However, simple typographical errors or

---

49 LS 1:22.
50 What remains for a future project is the analysis and presentation of Notebooks 10–12, which contain non-sermonic material.
51 *Autobiography* 1:213.
52 See "Sources and Method," LS 1:29–33.
53 LS 1:31.
54 See https://www.spurgeon.org/.

INTRODUCTION

misspellings are corrected and occasional punctuation added to aid in reading and comprehension. Moreover, whereas every ink smear or page discoloration was noted in Volumes 1–3, the editorial work of the remaining volumes has refrained from highlighting such minutiae unless it bears a significant contribution to the content.
- Continue to provide definitions of words likely unfamiliar to a modern audience using Spurgeon's personal copy of Samuel Johnson's dictionary.
- Continue to provide explanation for cultural references using contemporary secondary literature.
- Continue to mark any connection between Spurgeon's earliest sermons and those preached later, recorded in *The New Park Street Pulpit* and *The Metropolitan Tabernacle Pulpit* series.
- Continue to cite Scripture references from Spurgeon's personal copy of the King James Bible.[55]
- Continue to provide references to Scripture when the editor concludes that Spurgeon was directly or indirectly citing specific passages or related doctrines from the Bible.

Finally, here is a representation of the contents of the sermon notebooks housed in the Heritage Room Archives at Spurgeon's College in London that form the substance of *The Lost Sermons of C. H. Spurgeon* project:

Notebook 1: 90 total pages
(81 pages of sermon text, 4 blank pages, and 5 miscellaneous pages)

Notebook 2: 140 total pages
(135 pages of sermon text, 2 blank pages, and 3 miscellaneous pages)

Notebook 3: 140 total pages
(135 pages of sermon text, 2 blank pages, and 3 miscellaneous pages)

Notebook 4: 123 total pages
(114 pages of sermon text, 7 blank pages, and 2 miscellaneous pages)

---

55 See *The Illustrated Family Bible* (London: Fisher, Son, n.d., The Spurgeon Library).

Notebook 5: 123 total pages
(115 pages of sermon text, 5 blank pages, and 3 miscellaneous pages)

Notebook 6: 128 total pages
(120 pages of sermon text, 6 blank pages, and 2 miscellaneous pages)

Notebook 7: 125 total pages
(113 pages of sermon text, 11 blank pages, and 1 miscellaneous page)

Notebook 8: 178 total pages
(167 pages of sermon text, 11 blank pages, and 0 miscellaneous pages)

Notebook 9: 164 total pages
(147 pages of sermon text, 17 blank pages, and 0 miscellaneous pages)

As *The Lost Sermons of C. H. Spurgeon* finally see their publication, we join Susannah Spurgeon in her assessment that these earliest sermons "are valuable, not only because of their intrinsic merits, but also as the first products of the mind and heart which afterwards yielded so many discourses to the Church and the world, for the glory of God and the good of men."[56]

JASON G. DUESING
General Editor

PHILLIP ORT
Project Coordinator

---

56 *Autobiography* 1:213.

THE SERMONS

NOTEBOOK 5 (SERMONS 233–284)

OPENING PAGE OF NOTEBOOK 5

OPENING PAGE OF NOTEBOOK 5

$$\mathrm{V}^{1}$$

1. The Roman numeral V indicates that this is the fifth Notebook in the series. Given the differences in styling from Charles's original notation in Notebooks 1 and 2, this writing was likely not original to Charles but a later cataloger. For an account of similar inscriptions in each Notebook, see *LS* 1:51; 3:28.

BLANK PAGE

BLANK PAGE

[blank]
[Imprint from art on opposite page]

SKELETONS FROM 233 TO 284

[Extremely detailed full-page drawing. It is a goose with interconnected lines and feathers crossed at the bottom]

1. This page shares the same art as the art page from Notebook 4, which perhaps explains how the cataloger mistook Notebook 5 for Notebook 4.

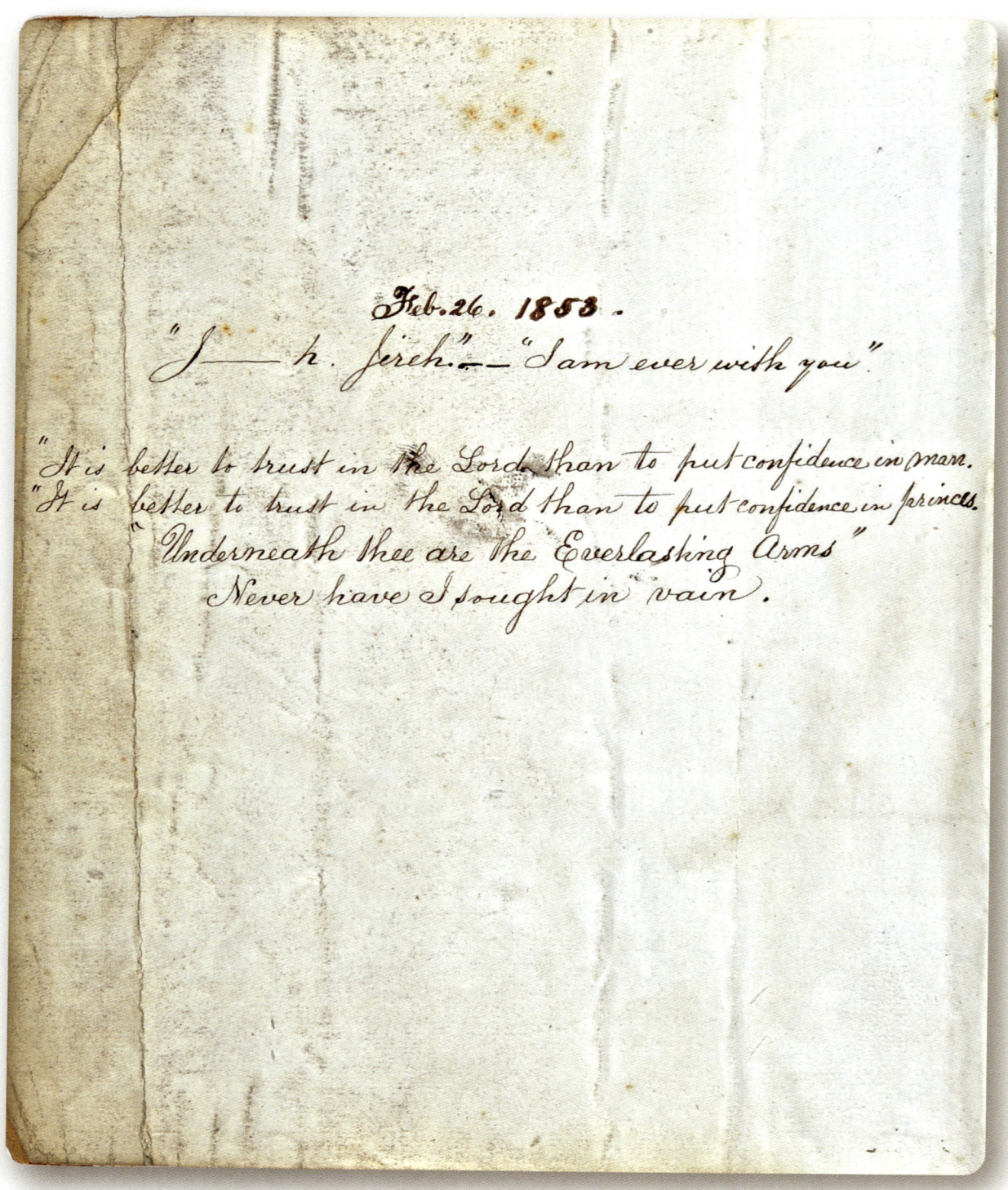

Feb. 26. 1853.
"J——h. Jireh."—"I am ever with you"

"It is better to trust in the Lord than to put confidence in man."
"It is better to trust in the Lord than to put confidence in princes."
"Underneath thee are the Everlasting Arms"
Never have I sought in vain.

Feb. 26. 1853.[1]

"J-----h. Jireh."[2] — —"I am ever with you"[3]

"It is better to trust in the Lord than to put confidence in man.
"It is better to trust in the Lord than to put confidence in princes.[4]
"Underneath thee are the Everlasting Arms"[5]
Never have I sought in vain.[6]

1. This note by Charles was likely written at the commencement of Notebook 5. He finished Notebook 2 on June 19, 1852, close to his eighteenth birthday. *Autobiography* 1:222; *LS* 2:503. While Charles overlapped the composition of his volumes to a degree, it is likely that he completed both Notebooks 3 and 4 by this date. However, it must be remembered that he continued to preach sermons from previous Notebooks while composing new ones.

2. Cf. Gen 22:14. This is the name which Abraham gave to Mount Moriah, the place of his sacrifice of Isaac. Modern Bibles often translate this as "the Lord will provide."

3. Cf. Jer 42:11; Hag 1:13, 2:4; Matt 28:20.

4. Cf. Ps 118:8–9.

5. Cf. Deut 33:27.

6. Cf. Isa 45:19.

Ezekiel. I. 5.   The Cherubim.

The river Chebar was a river running into the Euphrates & by its banks Ezekiel was entranced. We will go and see this great sight — that we may learn how God's will is done in heaven & get a glimpse of those beings who are ministering spirits to us, & whom one day we shall equal.

I. Let us witness the prelude of the vision. The entrance of the sublime company —

1. First comes a whirlwind — to herald the coming of the chariot of God — to clear away the mists & fogs of earth & leave a clear arena for the scene — A great & cutting wind for it came from the north. —

We have much need of a whirlwind to drive away our wandering thoughts, our lusts, our cares & cloudiness — else we shall never discern anything aright. God blesseth us by storms.

2. Then a great cloud — Clouds & darkness are round about him — this was the chariot itself. This shewed the prophet that though all the mists of his nature were gone yet he could not comprehend God. This great cloud saved Ezekiel from death through its veiling the splendour of God.

3. Behind that a fire. This shewed forth the glory of God which would consume us if too nearly approached; this same fire makes him so terrible in wrath.   This fire

THE CHERUBIM
Ezekiel 1:5[1]

"Also out of the midst thereof came the likeness of four living creatures. And this was their appearance; they had the likeness of a man."

The river Chebar was a river running into the Euphrates and by its banks Ezekiel was entranced.[2] We will go and see this great sight that we may learn how God's will is done in heaven and get a glimpse of those beings who are ministering spirits[3] to us, and whom one day we shall equal.[4]

I. LET US WITNESS THE PRELUDE OF THE VISION. THE ENTRANCE OF THE SUBLIME COMPANY.[5]

1. First comes a whirlwind to herald the coming of the chariot of God, to clear away the mists and fogs of earth and leave a clear arena for the scene. A great and cutting wind for it came from the north.

    We have much need of a whirlwind to drive away our wandering thoughts, our lusts, our cares and cloudiness, [or] else we shall never discern anything aright.[6] God blesseth us by storms.[7]

2. Then a great cloud. Clouds and darkness are round about him. This was the chariot itself. This shewed the prophet that though all the mists of his nature were gone, yet he could not comprehend God. This great cloud saved Ezekiel from death through its veiling the splendour of God.[8]

3. Behind that a fire. This shewed forth the glory of God which would consume us if too nearly approached.[9] This same fire makes him so terrible in wrath.[10] This fire

infolded itself so doth God's mercy infold his justice, his truth weaves itself into his love. Yea all his attributes infold each other.

4. Though in great part concealed by the cloud, yet there was a brightness of the most intense kind. God, even to our partial view is full of brightness. Brighter than the noonday sun.

II. The Prophet takes a hasty glance let us examine his outline —

1. Out of the fire & cloud came these creatures so even angels are God's workmanship.

2. The likeness was all he saw angels being Spirits cannot be seen; he saw a likeness which taught him something.

3. Four was their number though God hath myriads — yet four were seen to show that they are engaged in all corners of the earth.

4. Even at first sight he saw that they were living creatures — full of activity & vigour. not subject to death. So in heaven the word "immortal" is written on every brow. here men are idle, weak & dying —

III. The Prophet regards them more closely — let us imitate him

1. They were like a man — so angels are not unlike us in nature. An angel is a high style of man. We shall find them fit companions. If not we could not associate in

infolded[11] itself. So doth God's mercy infold his justice. His truth weaves itself into his love. Yea all his attributes infold each other.[12]

4. Though in great part concealed by the cloud, yet there was a brightness of the most intense kind. God, even to our partial view, is full of brightness.[13] Brighter than the noonday sun.

II. THE PROPHET TAKES A HASTY GLANCE. LET US EXAMINE HIS OUTLINE.

1. Out of the fire and cloud came these creatures.[14] So even angels are God's workmanship.[15]

2. The likeness was all he saw. Angels, being spirits, cannot be seen.[16] He saw a likeness which taught him something.

3. Four was their number though God hath myriads.[17] Yet four were seen to show that they are engaged in all corners of the earth.[18]

4. Even at first sight he saw that they were living creatures, full of activity and vigour, not subject to death. So in heaven the word "immortal" is written on every brow. Here men are idle, weak, and dying.

III. THE PROPHET REGARDS THEM MORE CLOSELY. LET US IMITATE HIM.

1. They were like a man. So angels are not unlike us in nature. An angel is a high style of man. We shall find them fit companions. If not, we could not associate in

heaven. But in intelligence, consciousness &c in all but our frailties they are like us.

2. They superior to us — in that they have four faces & four wings. Four times the honour & intelligence & four times the strength & swiftness. They are never deceived, — can see many things at once — & have thus more reach & compass of mind. As to wings we have not even one pair, they have two.

3. Their feet — are straight feet. Solid, unbending able to sustain any burden or run on any service. The soles we round — no front, no back able to run all ways, whereas our foot must go forward in one direction. Any way is in their front. — Their feet too were swift.

4. There was such sparkling about them that the prophet needed no other light to see them by. So God hath made an angel complete in himself, he is not in need of food, clothing, house furniture — but he is all in himself. So in heaven we shall be independent of all extraneous help. God will satisfy us from ourselves. So that in a desert we should have all within. —

IV. The Prophet now ventures to gaze more fully still — let us do likewise —

1. Hands he discovers beneath their wings. These glorious beings let not the right-hand know what the left hand doeth. They boast not of their own performances but the contrary. They hide their hands under their wings as being only unprofitable

heaven. But in intelligence, consciousness, etc., in all but our frailties they are like us.[19]

2. They [are] superior to us in that they have four faces and four wings.[20] Four times the honour and intelligence and four times the strength and swiftness. They are never deceived, can see many things at once, and have thus more reach and compass of mind.[21] As to wings we have not even one pair. They have two.

3. Their feet are straight feet.[22] Solid, unbending, able to sustain any burden or run on any service. The soles we[re] round, no front, no back, able to run all ways, whereas our foot must go forward in one direction. Any way is in their front. Their feet too were swift.

4. There was such sparkling about them that the prophet needed no other light to see them by. So God hath made an angel complete in himself. He is not in need of food, clothing, house, furniture, but he is all in himself.[23] So in heaven we shall be independent of all extraneous help. God will satisfy us from ourselves.[24] So that in a desert we should have all within.

IV. THE PROPHET NOW VENTURES TO GAZE MORE FULLY STILL. LET US DO LIKEWISE.

1. Hands he discovers beneath their wings.[25] These glorious beings let not the right-hand know what the left hand doeth.[26] They boast not of their own performances but the contrary. They hide their hands under their wings as being only unprofitable

servants. These hands wipe off tears, fight devils, bring comforts, keep our bones &c &c –

2. Their wings being joined, I understand not.
3. Their direct, undeviating, onward motion teaches us a lesson most clearly.
4. Their four faces are indices of their character.
   Face of a man – wisdom, religion, thought
   Face of a Lion – courage, might, grandeur.
   Face of an ox – diligence, strength, obedience
   Face of an eagle – swiftness, lightness, clearness of sight
5. Wings upward, in readiness, showing also their dependance on divine aid.
   Wings over their bodies – conceal them from us & show their need of covering before God.
6. They obeyed the Spirit. & were supported by the Burning lamp of the Holy Ghost. How wondrous his influence see. verse. 13.
7. How quickly they moved – they returned for a fresh errand. Like Lightening. How different we are. But one day we too shall flash like they. — —
   Lord give us something from this.
                                    Amen

389.

servants.²⁷ These hands wipe off tears, fight devils, bring comforts, keep our bones etc. etc.²⁸

2. Their wings being joined, I understand not.²⁹
3. Their direct, undeviating, onward motion teaches us a lesson most clearly.
4. Their four faces are indices of their character.³⁰

    Face of a man – wisdom, religion, thought.

    Face of a lion – courage, might, grandeur.

    Face of an ox – diligence, strength, obedience.

    Face of an eagle – swiftness, lightness, clearness of sight.

5. Wings upward, in readiness, showing also their dependance on divine aid. Wings over their bodies conceal them from us and show their need of covering before God.³¹
6. They obeyed the Spirit and were supported by the Burning lamp of the Holy Ghost.³² How wondrous his influence. See verse 13.
7. How quickly they moved. They returned for a fresh errand. Like Lightening.³³ How different we are. But one day we too shall flash like they.³⁴

Lord give us something from this.

<u>Amen</u>

389.

SERMON 233

1. It appears Charles did not preach another sermon on the text of Ezek 1:5.

2. Cf. Ezek 1:1–3.   3. Cf. Heb 1:14.

4. Cf. Luke 20:36.   5. Cf. Ezek 1:4.

6. Charles's exposition of Ezekiel 1 may have been influenced by William Greenhill's work, *An Exposition of the Prophet Ezekiel*. Greenhill wrote, "The northern winds are very piercing; and if we respect the prophet in this whirlwind, it was to purge the air, that the visions might be clearer and more conspicuous to his eyes, and himself better disposed to the reception of them." William Greenhill, *An Exposition of the Prophet Ezekiel*, 3rd ed. (London: Henry G. Bohn, 1846, The Spurgeon Library), 22. Charles would later commend this work to his students: "We always get something out of Greenhill whenever we refer to him. He had not, of course, the critical skill of the present day, but his spiritual insight was keen. He rather commented on a passage than expounded it." *Lectures* 4:125.

7. "Love letters from heaven are often sent in black-edged envelopes. The cloud that is black with horror is big with mercy. We may not ask for trouble, but if we were wise we should look upon it as the shadow of an unusually great blessing. Dread the calm, it is often treacherous, and beneath its wing the pestilence is lurking. Fear not the storm, it brings healing in its wings, and when Jesus is with you in the vessel the tempest only hastens the ship to its desired haven." *MTP* 27:373.

8. Cf. Exod 19:16–18; 33:20; Isa 6:4–5; Mark 9:7.

9. Cf. Deut 4:24; Heb 12:29.

10. Greenhill wrote, "There being a globe of fire within, it sent forth beams which produced an answerable brightness; which brightness (the cloud being thick and dark of itself) was a window to let in the prophet's eye to see what was in the cloud. By this brightness is shadowed out unto us, the terrible majesty and glory of the divine presence, putting itself forth in the punishment of sinners. As fire begets a splendour round about where it is; so do the judgments of God set out to the world his glory, justice, holiness, Psal. ix. 16. The glory of his judgment in punishing ill-doers, is a solid, constant, spreading glory; as that brightness was not flashy in the cloud, occasioned by the lightning, but fixed, certain, and on every side." Greenhill, *An Exposition of the Prophet Ezekiel*, 25.

11. "To involve; to inwrap; to inclose with involutions." Johnson's *Dictionary*, s.v. "To Infold."

12. "All the attributes of God are well balanced: like himself, they are infinite, and no one of them entrenches upon or dims the lustre of another. He is infinitely just, yet infinitely good; infinitely powerful, yet infinitely tender." *MTP* 20:542.

13. Cf. 1 Cor 13:12; 1 Tim 6:15–16.

14. Cf. Ezek 1:5.

15. Cf. Gen 2:1; Neh 9:6.

16. Cf. 2 Kgs 6:16–17; Heb 13:2. Greenhill wrote, "The prophet saw not these cherubims, or angels, or living creatures, but the likeness of them. For the nature of spirits is invisible; no soul, no angel, neither God himself, can be seen. How then is their likeness presented to the prophet? It is no bodily likeness, but a likeness in life, quality, and motion. But the text saith, 'They had the likeness of a man,' that is, not in his nature and essence, but in some qualities; they had the face, hands, thighs, and legs of a man, all which set out some choice qualities in the angels." Greenhill, *An Exposition of the Prophet Ezekiel*, 27.

17. Cf. Ezek 1:8, 10; Rev 4:6–8; 5:11.

18. Cf. Ezek 7:2; Rev 7:1.

19. Charles believed that angels and mankind were both created in the image of God. Commenting on Psalm 8, Charles wrote, "At all events, we can be sure that nothing higher could be affirmed of the angels, than that they were made in the image of God. If, then, they had originally superiority over man, it must have been in the degree of resemblance. The angel was made immortal, intellectual, holy, powerful, glorious, and in these properties lay their likeness to their Creator. But were not these properties given also to man? Was not man made immortal, intellectual, holy, powerful, glorious? And if the angel excelled the man, it was not, we may believe, in the possession of properties which had no counterpart in the man; both bore God's image, and both therefore had lineaments of the attributes which centre in Deity." *TD* 1:102.

20. Cf. Ezek 1:6.

21. Greenhill wrote, "The angels are in all quarters of the world, taking notice of men's words, works, and ways they go; I had almost said, of their very thoughts; and that they do, if discovered by some sign. Angels can be present at all times, know what devils or other men can know of us; any voice, any act they are privy to; yea, by outward expressions they may gather what is within; they, being spirits, can insinuate far into our hearts and natures, though not immediately know our thoughts." Greenhill, *An Exposition of the Prophet Ezekiel*, 28.

22. Cf. Ezek 1:7.

23. Charles attributed self-sufficiency to God alone. He wrote, "God is independent -- the only being who is so. We must find food with which to repair the daily wastes of the body; we are dependent upon light and heat, and innumerable external agencies, and above all and primarily dependent upon the outgoings of the divine power towards us. But the I AM is self-sufficient and all-sufficient." *MTP* 16:495. Here, Charles extended a limited form of self-sufficiency to angels, in that angels do not require food, clothing, etc. Unlike humans, they are not dependent on temporal, earthly items for survival.

24. Cf. Rev 7:16–17; 21:23. Again, Charles was not denying that God alone is ultimately self-sufficient. Rather, he was making the point that, like the angels, the glorified believer will one day no longer need temporal, earthly items for survival.

25. Cf. Ezek 1:8.   26. Cf. Matt 6:3–4.

27. Cf. Matt 25:30; Luke 17:10. Greenhill wrote, "Angels, that are agents for God, have their hands under their wings; their actions are seen, but not their hands. . . . Angels are jealous of God's glory, and had rather conceal their hands and names, than God should lose the least degree of his glory . . . It is wisdom to muffle up ourselves, and to hold forth God as much as may be: Matt. v. 16, 'Let your light so shine before men, that they may see your good works,' he doth not say, that they may see you, but see your good works, and glorify your Father, not you." Greenhill, *An Exposition of the Prophet Ezekiel*, 37.

28. This list resembles Greenhill's description of the roles angels serve including: to inform, to oppose enemies of Christ, to execute judgments of God, to defend

the godly, to guide and lead the godly, and to comfort. Greenhill, *An Exposition of the Prophet Ezekiel*, 29–30.

29. Cf. Ezek 1:9.

30. Cf. Ezek 1:10. Charles summarized Greenhill on these points but did not strictly commit to Greenhill's wording. Greenhill wrote, "The face of a man represents to use the understandings of angels, and that their administrations are with knowledge and equity.... The face of a lion signifies the strength of angels.... [The face of an ox] shows the willing obedience, faithfulness, patience, and usefulness of angels in their ministrations; for an ox accustomed to the yoke is very tractable, not stubborn, as untamed heifers are.... The last face is of an eagle, and in it, as in a glass, we may see the perspicaciousness, swiftness, and vivacity of the angels." Greenhill, *An Exposition of the Prophet Ezekiel*, 31–32.

31. Greenhill wrote, "In this covering of their bodies, God propounds them as a pattern of chastity and modesty unto us: those parts are hid, which might, uncovered, argue disreverence of God, or concupiscence in them, or be offensive unto men. God loves chaste spirits, and chaste behaviours: the angels are very chaste, and would not have any indecent thing objected to divine view, whose authority and majesty they adore." Greenhill, *An Exposition of the Prophet Ezekiel*, 35.

32. Cf. Ezek 1:13. Greenhill wrote, "Angels are led, and easily led by the Spirit.... The Spirit is so infinitely wise, holy, and good, that even angels do freely and fully submit to the conduct of it; and therefore it is that they go straight forward, and that there is no crookedness in their works." Greenhill, *An Exposition of the Prophet Ezekiel*, 41.

33. Cf. Ezek 1:14. Charles spelled this with an unnecessary "e." Johnson did note this about "lightning": "[It is] from *lighten, lightening, lightning.*" Johnson's *Dictionary*, s.v. "Lightning."

34. Cf. Matt 13:43.

II Kings. XIX. 4.   Comfort for the persecuted.

Hezekiah had too much faith to live without trials, too much piety to be loved by the world, & too much reliance on God ever to yield. The Lord's people in all times have been opposed & illtreated & even thus was the heir of all things. So now are we.

I. How does the world now oppose.
Not by persecuting us by tortures & death, nor forbidding our worship —
 1. But some openly avow & propagate infidelity.
 2. Others slander our character.
 3. Some deny charity to poor saints.
 4. Many laugh outright at us.

II. How their opposition is overruled for good.
 1. Some are inclined to regard the illtreated with favour, from natural sympathy
 2. It tends to make us more cautious in walk
 3. It makes us value this world less & so makes us strangers & foreigners.
 4. It endears to us the sweet things of religion, makes us prize our doctrines more.
 5. It often drives us more fervently to prayer.
Out of the Lion cometh honey —

III. How may we comfort ourselves in it.
 1. By the thought that you do not deserve it

COMFORT *for the* PERSECUTED
2 Kings 19:4[1]

"It may be the Lord thy God will hear all the words of Rabshakeh, whom the king of Assyria his master hath sent to reproach the living God; and will reprove the words which the Lord thy God hath heard: wherefore lift up thy prayer for the remnant that are left."

Hezekiah had too much faith to live without trials, too much piety to be loved by the world, and too much reliance on God ever to yield. The Lord's people in all times have been opposed and illtreated and even thus was the heir of all things.[2] So now are we.

I. HOW DOES THE WORLD NOW OPPOSE[?]

Not by persecuting us by tortures and death, nor [by] forbidding our worship:

1. But some openly avow[3] and propagate infidelity.
2. Others slander our character.
3. Some deny charity to poor saints.
4. Many laugh outright at us.[4]

II. HOW THEIR OPPOSITION IS OVERRULED FOR GOOD.

1. Some are inclined to regard the illtreated with favour, from natural sympathy.
2. It tends to make us more cautious in walk.
3. It makes us value this world less and so makes us strangers and foreigners.[5]
4. It endears to us the sweet things of religion, & makes us prize our doctrines more.[6]
5. It often drives us more fervently to prayer. Out of the Lion cometh honey.[7]

III. HOW MAY WE COMFORT OURSELVES IN IT[?]

1. By the thought that you do not deserve it.[8]

2. By the remembrance of God's omniscience.
3. Think of Jesus' sympathy.
4. Take encouragement & hope that in you there is the same spirit as brought others into suffering.
5. Have an eye to the recompense

IV. How should the persecuted behave.
1. Give none offence by harsh religion, or by unseasonable denunciations.
2. Answer not again.
3. Return good for evil.
4. Pray more for yourself & them.
5. Yield not, but maintain your ground.

V. A word to persecutors.
1. If you reject Christ let others have him.
2. True religion is an evident benefit — why oppose?
3. You cannot stop our progress — why try?
4. All you do to us, is done to our Master.
5. We love you & pray for you that you may become a Christian — why then give us evil for good?

390.   Bless. of Jesus.

COMFORT FOR THE PERSECUTED—2 Kings 19:4

    2. By the remembrance of God's omniscience.[9]

    3. Think of Jesus'[s] sympathy.[10]

    4. Take encouragement and hope that in you there is the same Spirit as brought others into suffering.[11]

    5. Have an eye to the recompense.[12]

IV. HOW SHOULD THE PERSECUTED BEHAVE[?]

    1. Give none offence by harsh religion, or by unseasonable denunciations.[13]

    2. Answer not again.[14]

    3. Return good for evil.[15]

    4. Pray more for yourself and them.[16]

    5. Yield not, but maintain your ground.[17]

V. A WORD TO PERSECUTORS.

    1. If you reject Christ let others have him.

    2. True religion is an evident benefit. Why oppose?

    3. You cannot stop our progress. Why try?[18]

    4. All you do to us is done to our Master.[19]

    5. We love you and pray for you that you may become a Christian. Why then give us evil for good?

390.   <u>Bless. Oh Jesus</u>

1. It appears that Charles did not preach from 2 Kgs 19:4 at any other point in his ministry.

2. Cf. Isa 53:3–7; Acts 2:36; Heb 1:2.

3. "To declare with confidence; to justify; not to dissemble." Johnson's *Dictionary*, s.v. "To Avow."

4. During his pastorate at Waterbeach, Charles regularly faced ridicule as a preacher for his youthfulness. See *Autobiography* 1:271, 298.

5. Cf. Heb 11:13.

6. Charles's insight here illumines his future encounters with theological controversy. Rather than tempting him to abandon his doctrines, opposition made him cherish them more, strengthening him to stand firmly in his position.

7. Cf. Judg 14:8–9, 14.   8. Cf. 1 Pet 2:19–20.

9. Cf. 2 Pet 3:1–10.   10. Cf. Heb 4:15.

11. Cf. Matt 5:11–12; Mark 1:12–13.

12. Cf. 2 Cor 4:17–18.

13. "The act of denouncing; the proclamation of a threat; a publick menace." Johnson's *Dictionary*, s.v. "Denunciation." Charles's reference to "unseasonable" likely alluded to Col 4:6, that the believer's speech should always be seasoned with grace.

14. Cf. 2 Tim 2:14, 23.   15. Cf. Rom 12:17–21; 1 Pet 3:9.

16. Cf. Matt 5:43–44.   17. Cf. Gal 1:8–9; Jude 3.

18. Throughout his ministry, Charles remained optimistic about the work of the church because of his confidence that Christ would be glorified. "Some narrow-minded bigots think that heaven will be a very small place, where there will be a very few people, who went to their chapel or their church. I confess, I have no wish for a very small heaven, and love to read in the Scriptures that there are

many mansions in my Father's house. How often do I hear people say, 'Ah! strait is the gate and narrow is the way, and few there be that find it. There will be a very few in heaven; there will be most lost.' My friend I differ from you. Do you think that Christ will let the devil beat him? That he will let the devil have more in hell than there will be in heaven? No: it is impossible. For then Satan would laugh at Christ. There will be more in heaven than there are among the lost. God says, that 'there will be a number that no man can number who will be saved;' but he never says that there will be a number that no man can number that will be lost. There will be a host beyond all count who will get into heaven. What glad tidings for you and for me! For if there are so many to be saved why should not I be saved? Why should not you?" *NPSP* 1:303.

19. "You know what mysterious, yet real union exists between Christ the head and all his members. It came out clearly in the case of Paul, when [Christ] said to him, 'Why persecutest thou me?' [Paul] was persecuting only a few poor people in Jerusalem, or in Damascus, whom he despised, but Christ said, 'Why persecutest thou me?' because persecuting the saints was persecuting Christ – Christ suffering in his members. Christ suffering on the cross was the head suffering, but when his people were rent to pieces in the amphitheatre, when they were burned at Smithfield, and when to-day they are hooted and made a jest of, it is Christ suffering, still suffering in his members, and when any child of God suffers in any righteous cause, whenever affliction comes upon a saint in any form, Christ sympathises with him. Rest assured: -- 'In every pang that rends the heart, The Man of sorrows bears his part.' In all their affliction he was afflicted. A finger never suffers without the brain participating and no humble member of the true Church of Christ ever suffers without Christ, the glorious head, suffering in sympathy therewith." *MTP* 61:4.

II Pet III. 10.11 — The Great Conflagration.

We should take heed of prying too deeply into mysteries. Unrevealed things belong not to us — & even what of futurity is revealed must not too much occupy our minds to the exclusion of weightier matters.

Certain scoffers in Peter's day as now in ours said that God did not come, did not act, but allowed all things to go on independently — from this there is a short step to broad atheism. Peter points to the flood as an instance of divine interposition & foretels another change by fire soon to come

I. I would make some remarks upon Peter's description of the final conflagration.

1. The Conflagration here spoken of is literal, not figurative — else it would be no answer to the scoffers, nor would there be any similarity between it & Noah's flood. besides the words are plainly literal.

2. It will come unexpectedly — when men shall not look for it — True religion will be dominant but still there will be sin & sinners. These will be unprepared. It cometh "as a thief in the night"

3. This fire will melt but not annihilate the globe. Elements, — rocks &c shall melt & the whole mass shall be in a blazing state. This molten earth shall then become a new earth & a new heaven shall be its canopy. But yet all the buildings, books &c, works of

THE GREAT CONFLAGRATION

2 Peter 3:10–11[1]

> *"But the day of the Lord will come as a thief in the night; in the which the heavens shall pass away with a great noise, and the elements shall melt with fervent heat, the earth also and the works that are therein shall be burned up. Seeing then that all these things shall be dissolved, what manner of persons ought ye to be in all holy conversation and godliness."*

We should take heed of prying too deeply into mysteries. Unrevealed things belong not to us,[2] and even what of futurity is revealed must not too much occupy our minds to the exclusion of weightier matters.[3]

Certain scoffers in Peter's day, as now in ours, said that God did not come, did not act, but allowed all things to go on independently. From this there is a short step to broad atheism.[4] Peter points to the flood as an instance of divine interposition and foretells another change by fire soon to come.

I. I WOULD MAKE SOME REMARKS UPON PETER'S DESCRIPTION OF THE FINAL CONFLAGRATION.

1. The Conflagration here spoken of is literal, not figurative — else it would be no answer to the scoffers, nor would there be any similarity between it and Noah's flood.[5] Besides[,] the words are plainly literal.

2. It will come unexpectedly when men shall not look for it. True religion will be dominant but still there will be sin and sinners.[6] These will be unprepared. It cometh <u>"as a thief in the night."</u>[7]

3. This fire will melt but not annihilate the globe.[8] Elements, rocks, etc. shall melt and the whole mass shall be in a blazing state. This molten earth shall then become a new earth, and a new heaven shall be its canopy.[9] But yet all the buildings, books, etc., works of

man shall be utterly consumed. Earth & what stands on it, with the surrounding atmosphere shall be wrapt in flames.

4. There are some things this flame will not touch. not God's people who will be caught up into the air. nor the book of life, nor the covenant, nor the inheritance. these are safe

II. I would offer some proof of the doctrine of the general conflagration of our globe.

1. I argue its possibility from the fact of one destruction by water which was (in human thought) more unlikely to be brought about than the one by fire yet to come. If by water far more likely by fire.

2. I argue its possibility from several partial miraculous burnings — Sodom & Gomorrah. Nadab & Abihu. Korah & his company. Elijah's sacrifice & fire coming on the captains of fifty. Job's sheep destroyed — surely he who could do these could do the one here spoken of.

3. Lightening & thunder are mighty orators on this subject. I have wondered often that anything escaped amid such awful displays of power.

4. The earth is doubtless in a melted state at about 100 miles depth. Volcanoes are warm disputers & hot springs are enough to convince the coolest intellect —

THE GREAT CONFLAGRATION—2 *Peter 3:10–11*

man shall be utterly consumed.[10] [The] Earth and what stands on it, with the surrounding atmosphere[,] shall be wrapt in flames.

4. There are some things this flame will not touch. Not God's people who will be caught up into the air,[11] nor the book of life,[12] nor the covenant,[13] nor the inheritance.[14] These are safe.

II. I WOULD OFFER SOME PROOF OF THE DOCTRINE OF THE GENERAL CONFLAGRATION OF OUR GLOBE.

1. I argue its possibility from the fact of one destruction by water[,][15] which was (in human thought) more unlikely to be brought about than the one by fire yet to come. If by water far more likely by fire.[16]

2. I argue its possibility from several partial miraculous burnings. Sodom and Gomorrah.[17] Nadab and Abihu.[18] Korah and his company.[19] Elijah's sacrafice[20] and fire coming on the captains of fifty.[21] Job's sheep destroyed.[22] Surely he who could do these could do the one here spoken of.

3. Lightening[23] and thunder are mighty orators on this subject. I have wondered often that anything escaped amid such awful displays of power.[24]

4. The earth is doubtless in a melted state at about 100 miles depth.[25] Volcanoes are warm disputers and hot springs are enough to convince the coolest intellect.

5. Scripture however is our main guide
Psal. 50. 3. Describes God coming with fire & tempest.
Psal. 97. 2-5. Is a grand view of the scene.
Isa. 56. 15.16. "By fire & sword will the Lord plead.
Nahum. 1. 3.4.5. Strikingly agrees with the text.
2 Thess. I. 7. 8. with several other New Testament prophecies
are amply sufficient.

III. I would endeavour to make some remarks on Peter's practical inference.
1. From the sublimity & dread mystery of futurity we should be led to tremble & search, in order that we may be prepared.
2. From the dissolution of terrestrial objects learn not to set our affections on a doomed earth.
3. From the uncertainty of the hour, let us learn the duty of continued watchfulness.
4. From the safety of the righteous amid the wreck of matter — let us gather subjects for grateful song to grace divine.
5. From the dreadful doom of the ungodly to be consumed in this fire, & then in a worse let us learn to pity & pray for them & labour for their conversion.

    Father. Help. Help. through Jesus.

397-

THE GREAT CONFLAGRATION—2 Peter 3:10-11

5. Scripture however is our main guide.[26]

Psal. 50. 3.[27] Describes God coming with fire and tempest.

Psal. 97. 2-5.[28] Is a grand view of the scene.

Isa. 56. 15.16.[29] "By fire and sword will the Lord plead."

Nahum. 1. 3.4.5.[30] Strikingly agrees with the text.

2 Thess. I. 7. 8.[31] With several other New Testament prophecies are amply sufficient.[32]

III. I WOULD ENDEAVOUR TO MAKE SOME REMARKS ON PETER'S PRACTICAL INFERENCE.

1. From the sublimity[33] and dread[34] mystery of futurity we should be led to tremble and search, in order that we may be prepared.

2. From the dissolution[35] of terrestrial objects learn not to set our affections on a doomed earth.[36]

3. From the uncertainty of the hour, let us learn the duty of continued watchfulness.[37]

4. From the safety of the righteous amid the wreck[38] of matter, let us gather subjects for grateful song to grace divine.

5. From the dreadful doom of the ungodly to be consumed in this fire, and then in a worse [fire] let us learn to pity and pray for them and labour for their conversion.

Father, Help, Help, through Jesus.

397.

SERMON 235

1. Charles preached a later sermon on this text, "The World on Fire" (*MTP* 19, Sermon 1125). Charles's later sermon contains a significant amount of overlapping material and was likely influenced by this earlier one. Additionally, the Roman numeral divisions of the later sermon are the same except that in Charles's original, the first two Roman numerals have been condensed into one. The overlapping content is noted below.

2. Cf. Deut 29:29.

3. Charles once dedicated an entire sermon to this concept: "Witnessing Better Than Knowing the Future" (*MTP* 39, Sermon 2330). He wrote, "What would you be the better if you could make a map of all that is yet to be? Suppose it were revealed to you to-night, by an angel, in what respect would it alter your conduct for to-morrow? In what way would it help you to perform the duties which your Master has enjoined upon you? I believe that it would be to you a very dangerous gift; you would be tempted to set yourself up as an interpreter of the future . . . it would distract your attention from the great things of which you have to think. It is enough for your mind to dwell upon the cross and the coming glory of your Lord. Keep these two things distinctly before you, and you need not puzzle your brains about the future." *MTP* 39:495.

4. Cf. 2 Pet 3:3–7. Charles's contention here was that if God is seen as an absentee Creator (deism), then it is much easier to not believe in him at all (atheism).

5. Cf. Genesis 6.

6. Charles's optimism regarding the future of the church led many to categorize him as a postmillennialist. Charles, however, denied this: "If I read the word aright, and it is honest to admit that there is much room for difference of opinion here, the day will come, when the Lord Jesus will descend from heaven with a shout, with the trump of the archangel and the voice of God. Some think that this descent of the Lord will be post-millennial -- that is, after the thousand years of his reign. I cannot think so. I conceive that the advent will be premillennial; that he will come first; and then will come the millennium as the result of his personal reign upon the earth. But whether or no, this much is the fact, that Christ will suddenly come, come to reign, and come to judge the earth in righteousness." *MTP* 11:249.

THE GREAT CONFLAGRATION — *2 Peter 3:10-11*

7. Cf. 1 Thess 5:2; 2 Pet 3:10.

8. "1. To reduce to nothing; to put out of existence. 2. To destroy, so as to make the thing otherwise than it was. 3. To annul; to destroy the agency of any thing." Johnson's *Dictionary*, s.v. "To Annihilate." By this definition, Charles rejected annihilationism, not only for the created world but for the human soul. He wrote, "Do not have the edge of this truth taken off by those who suggest a hope that though you may be punished for a time in the next world you will ultimately be destroyed and annihilated. Now nothing in nature ever has been annihilated yet, and it would be a new thing if you should be. . . . I dare not, however, hold out to you the hope of annihilation while the Bible contains such words as these. 'These shall go away into everlasting punishment,' -- everlasting! The word is precisely the same as that which is applied to heaven, and though I shall be told that this is an old argument, I reply that this is the very reason why I use it." *MTP* 12:17.

9. Cf. 2 Pet 3:11–13; Rev 21:1–2.

10. "We gather also from our text that this fire will burn up all the works existing upon the earth – everything which man has constructed shall perish. We have heard architects speak of building for eternity! Aha! Aha! They have built but for an hour, and their noblest fabrics will disappear like children's castles of sand upon the sea beach. Down will go vast cathedrals and the towering palaces, in one common crash; whole cities will flame upon earth's funeral pyre, while forests and melting mountains blend their smoke. The pride of power, the pomp of wealth, the beauty of art, the cunning of skill – all, all, must go; the sea of flame will overwhelm and devour everything without exception. The massive masonry, and rock-like foundations of our vast engineering works shall run like wax in the tremendous heat. So fierce will be the flames that everything capable of being burned will be utterly consumed, and the elements, or the solid portions of the earth shall be liquified by the intense heat." *MTP* 19:435.

11. Cf. 1 Thess 4:17.

12. Cf. Rev 20:12, 15.

13. Cf. Heb 8:6–13.

14. Cf. 1 Pet 1:3–5.

15. Cf. Genesis 6–8.

16. Charles likely borrowed this idea from Gill: "... all OR [A]ll the works of nature, wicked men, cattle, trees, &c. And all the works of men, cities, towns, houses, furniture, utensils, instruments of arts of all sorts, will be burnt by a material fire, breaking out of the earth, and descending from heaven, for which the present heavens and earth are reserved: this general conflagration was not only known to the Jews, but to the heathens, to the poets, and Platonist and Stoic philosophers, who frequently speak of it in plain terms." John Gill, *An Exposition of the New Testament, In Three Volumes: In Which the Sense of the Sacred Text is Given; Doctrinal and Practical Truths Are Set in a Plain and Easy Light, Difficult Places Explained, Seeming Contradictions Reconciled; and Whatever is Material in the Various Readings, and the Several Oriental Versions, Is Observed. The Whole Illustrated with Notes Taken from the Most Ancient Jewish Writings*, vol. 1 (London: printed for the author, and sold by Aaron Ward, 1746, The Spurgeon Library), 573. Hereafter, *An Exposition of the New Testament*. Charles saw evidence for this conflagration in volcanic activity: "We may here note that the prophecy that the earth will thus be consumed with fervent heat, is readily to be believed, not only because God says it, but because there are evidently the means at hand for the accomplishment of the prophecy. Pliny was wont to say that it was a miracle that the world escaped burning for a single day, and I do not wonder at the remark, considering the character of the district in which he spent much of his time. In visiting the country around Naples, the same thought constantly occurred to me, Yonder is Vesuvius ready at any moment to vomit fire, and continually sending up clouds of smoke. Ascend the mountain side, clambering over ashes and masses of lava; all beneath you is glowing; thrust in your staff and it is charred." *MTP* 19:436.

17. Cf. Gen 19:24.

18. Cf. Lev 10:1–2.

19. Cf. Num 16:27–33.

20. Cf. 1 Kgs 18:37–38. Charles misspelled "sacrifice."

21. Cf. 2 Kgs 1:9–12.

22. Cf. Job 1:16.

23. Here a light pencil mark appears to cross out the "e" in "lightening." This editorial activity indicates that Charles revised this sermon to some extent.

THE GREAT CONFLAGRATION—2 Peter 3:10–11

24. Charles loved thunderstorms because he saw in them a display of God's power. During these early years of ministry, he enjoyed walking through the countryside to various preaching engagements during a storm. "I always feel ashamed to keep indoors when the thunder shakes the solid earth, and the lightnings flash like arrows from the sky. Then God is abroad, and I love to walk out in some wide space, and to look up and mark the opening gates of heaven, as the lightning reveals far beyond, and enables me to gaze into the unseen. I like to hear my Heavenly Father's voice in the thunder." *Autobiography* 1:205.

25. Charles was referring to the earth's mantle. "According to the belief of many geologists, the whole centre of the earth is a mass of molten matter, and we live upon a thin crust which has cooled down, and is probably not so much as one hundred miles thick. When the miner descends no further than forty-five feet, he finds that the heat has increased one degree Fahrenheit, so that it is easy to see how a small distance down the solid shell extends. There is no known rock which would not be entirely liquified by the heat produced at sixty miles depth." *MTP* 19:436.

26. While external arguments can be helpful, Charles believed that Scripture derives authority from itself. "We accept it as the very word of the living God, every jot and tittle of it, not so much because there are external evidences which go to show its authenticity—a great many of us do not know anything about those evidences, and probably never shall—but because we discern an inward evidence in the words themselves. They have come to us with a power that no other words ever had in them, and we cannot be argued out of our conviction of their superlative excellence and divine authority." *MTP* 18:618–19.

27. Psalm 50:3, "Our God shall come, and shall not keep silence: a fire shall devour before him, and it shall be very tempestuous round about him."

28. Psalm 97:2–5, "Clouds and darkness are round about him: righteousness and judgment are the habitation of his throne. A fire goeth before him, and burneth up his enemies round about. His lightnings enlightened the world: the earth saw, and trembled. The hills melted like wax at the presence of the Lord, at the presence of the Lord of the whole earth."

29. Here Charles misquoted his text. Isaiah 56:15–16 does not exist. Rather, the fifty-sixth chapter of Isaiah ends with verse 12. The text Charles intended to

cite is Isa 66:16, "For by fire and by his sword will the Lord plead with all flesh: and the slain of the Lord shall be many."

30. Nahum 1:3–5, "The Lord is slow to anger, and great in power, and will not at all acquit the wicked: the Lord hath his way in the whirlwind and in the storm, and the clouds are the dust of his feet. He rebuketh the sea, and maketh it dry, and drieth up all the rivers: Bashan languisheth, and Carmel, and the flower of Lebanon languisheth. The mountains quake at him, and the hills melt, and the earth is burned at his presence, yea, the world, and all that dwell therein."

31. Second Thessalonians 1:7–8, "And to you who are troubled rest with us, when the Lord Jesus shall be revealed from heaven with his mighty angels, in flaming fire taking vengeance on them that know not God, and that obey not the gospel of our Lord Jesus Christ."

32. Cf. Matt 3:12; 13:40; Acts 2:19; 2 Pet 3:7; Rev 8:5–8; 9:17–18; 16:8.

33. "1. Height of place; local elevation. 2. Height of nature; excellence. 3. Loftiness of style or sentiment." Johnson's *Dictionary*, s.v. "Sublimity."

34. "Terrible; frightful. . . . Awful; venerable in the highest degree." Johnson's *Dictionary*, s.v. "Dread."

35. "Destruction of any thing by the separation of its parts. . . . Destruction." Johnson's *Dictionary*, s.v. "Dissolution."

36. "Now our life ought to be like that of Noah. Look around on the beauties of nature, and when you enjoy them say to yourself, 'All these are to be dissolved and melt with fervent heat.' Look up into the clear blue and think that yonder sky itself shall shrivel like a scroll, and be rolled up like a garment that has seen its better days and must be put aside. Look on your fellow-men, your own children, and your household, and those you pass in the street or meet with in transacting business, and say 'Alas, alas, unless these men, women, and children, fly to Jesus and are saved in him, they will be destroyed with the earth on which they dwell, for the day of the Lord is surely coming, and judgment awaits the ungodly.' This should make us act in a spirit the opposite of those who now say, 'Go to, let us buy and sell and get gain; let us heap together treasure; let us live for this world; let us eat and drink and be merry.'" *MTP* 19:439.

37. "Once more, he meant us to feel that the suddenness of all this ought to keep us on our watchtower. This conflagration will come with no signs to herald it which the ungodly will observe. Ye who are on the watch will observe them; ye will see the tokens of his coming; ye will rejoice to go forth to meet him; but to the ungodly his coming will be as much unawares as was his first advent, which happened in the night, when all the world was wrapped in sleep. Men will still be buying and selling, and getting gain, and thinking of nothing so little as of the last advent; and then the Lord will appear. Christian, let not that day come upon you as a thief. Stand ever watching." *MTP* 19:443.

38. "Dissolution by violence.... Ruin; destruction." Johnson's *Dictionary*, s.v. "Wreck."

236. Isa. XXII. 23. 24. The nail in a sure place

Eliakim was raised by God to be the glory of his family, the ruler of the people & the sole dependance of his friends — — So long as he remained fast; his friends were safe, he sustained them all but even he passed away like other mortals.

Thanks be unto God, we have a safer trust than this, even an everlasting nail.

Jesus Christ, even him crucified.

I. "I will fasten him as a nail in a sure place."
 1. The nail. Some nails will break, and are not strong but this nail will never be strained. The Godhead of Jesus puts iron into his office. He is a good nail.
 2. The fastener. Some nails are not well driven in & therefore fall out. But God has driven this well. His sufferings were blows which fixed him firmly. The hammers of Law & Inexorable Justice beat on him.
 3. The sure place. Some nails are in rotten wood & therefore break out. Jesus is secured in the covenant of the Triune God. In the solemn oath & mighty love of his father. So it is sure.

II. "He shall be for a glorious throne to his father's house."
 1. Jesus is the glory of his "father's house". The

THE NAIL IN A SURE PLACE—*Isaiah 22:23–24*

THE NAIL *in a* SURE PLACE
Isaiah 22:23–24[1]

"And I will fasten him as a nail in a sure place; and he shall be for a glorious throne to his father's house. And they shall hang upon him all the glory of his father's house, the offspring and the issue, all vessels of small quantity, from the vessels of cups, even to all the vessels of flagons."

Eliakim was raised by God to be the glory of his family, the ruler of the people, and the sole dependance of his friends.[2] So long as he remained fast; his friends were safe, he sustained them all[,] but even <u>he</u> passed away like other mortals.[3] Thanks be unto God, we have a safer trust than this, even an everlasting nail.

Jesus Christ, even him crucified.[4]

I. "<u>I will fasten him as a nail in a sure place</u>."

   1. The nail. Some nails will break, and are not strong, but this nail will never be strained. The Godhead of Jesus puts iron into his office.[5]

      He is a good nail.

   2. The fastener. Some nails are not well driven in and therefore fall out. But God has driven this [nail in] well.[6] His sufferings were blows which fixed him firmly.

      The hammers of Law and Inexorable Justice beat on him.[7]

   3. The sure place. Some nails are in rotten wood and therefore break out. Jesus is secured in the covenant of the Triune God. In the solemn oath and mighty love of his father.[8] So it is sure.[9]

II. "<u>HE SHALL BE FOR A GLORIOUS THRONE TO HIS FATHER'S HOUSE</u>."

   1. Jesus is the <u>glory</u> of his "<u>father's house</u>."[10] The

whole of the family derive honour from his glorious exaltation. Jesus is the boast of his brethren.

2. He is the <u>ruler</u> of "his father's house". He is indeed Lord over all but this is his favorite dominion. The Queen may reign over Hindostan or the Cape, but England and Englishmen are her original subjects. So are the elect our Lord's peculiar treasure.

3. He is the <u>Safeguard</u> of "his father's house". The brazen wall, the massive bulwark of our safety is the throne of Jesus.

4. He will be the <u>means of conquest</u> for "his father's house". By him each one shall win a crown & sit on a glorious throne. By him we conquer.

III. <u>"They shall hang on him all the glory of his father's house."</u> — Blessings great & small, cups & flagons come from him. Unto him belongeth all "worthy the Lamb!" Every doctrine derives glory from him.

<u>Election</u> — we are elect in **him** as our Head.
<u>Redemption</u> — we are purchased by **his** blood.
<u>Justification</u> — a righteousness we find in **him**.
<u>Perseverance</u> — is ~~solely~~ mainly through **his** intercession.
<u>Resurrection</u> — is after the model of **his** resurrection.
<u>Judgment</u> — **He** will judge both quick & dead.
<u>Glory</u> — would be no glory without **him**
<u>All in all</u> he is. Alpha & Omega

whole of the family derive honour from his glorious exaltation. Jesus is the boast of his brethren.[11]

2. He is the <u>ruler</u> of "<u>his father's house</u>." He is indeed Lord over all[,][12] but this is his favorite dominion. The Queen may reign over Hindostan[13] or the Cape,[14] but England and Englishmen are her original subjects.

So are the elect our Lord's peculiar treasure.[15]

3. He is the <u>safeguard</u> of "<u>his father's house</u>." The brazen wall, the massive bulwark of our safety, is the throne of Jesus.[16]

4. He will be the <u>means of conquest</u> for "<u>his father's house</u>." By him each one shall win a crown and sit on a glorious throne.[17] By him we conquer.[18]

III. "THEY SHALL HANG ON HIM ALL THE GLORY OF HIS FATHER'S HOUSE."
— Blessings great and small, cups and flagons come from him. Unto him belongeth all "worthy the Lamb!"[19] Every doctrine derives glory from him.

<u>Election</u> – we are elect in <u>him</u> as our Head.[20]

<u>Redemption</u> – we are purchased by <u>his</u> blood.[21]

<u>Justification</u> – a righteousness we find in <u>him</u>.[22]

<u>Perseverance</u> – is ~~solely~~[23] mainly through <u>his</u> intercession.[24]

<u>Resurrection</u> – is after the model of <u>his</u> resurrection.[25]

<u>Judgment</u> – <u>He</u> will judge both quick and dead.[26]

<u>Glory</u> – would be no glory without <u>him</u>.[27]

<u>All in all</u> he is. <u>Alpha and Omega</u>.[28]

IV. All — both cups & flagons hang on him
1. Great Saints & Small ones alike hang on him
2. Great Sinners & Little sinners may trust in him.
3. Great troubles & cup troubles we may cast on him for he will sustain all.

~ ~ ~ ~ ~ ~ ~ ~ ~ ~ ~ ~ ~ ~

1. Do I believe on him — if so let me trust on him more & more.
2. Are you trusting elsewhere. Remember all else are "refuges of lies". —
3. Are you afraid because of great sin. Remember he will bear the "flagons" A world of sin would be a dust on him. Like a gnat on the horn of a bull of Bashan. — He can save to the Uttermost & who knows the measure of that word. As far as hell is from heaven will that one word reach —

Forgive past follies & help anew.
Oh my Lord.

398.

THE NAIL IN A SURE PLACE—*Isaiah 22:23-24*

IV. ALL – BOTH CUPS AND FLAGONS HANG ON HIM.[29]
1. Great Saints and Small ones alike hang on him.
2. Great Sinners and Little sinners may trust in him.
3. Great troubles and cup troubles we may cast on him for he will sustain all.

~ ~ ~ ~ ~ ~ ~ ~ ~ ~ ~ ~ ~

1. Do I believe on him—if so let me trust on him more and more.
2. Are you trusting elsewhere[?] Remember all else are "refuges of lies."[30]
3. Are you afraid because of great sin[?] Remember he will bear the "flagons." A world of sin would be a dust on him. Like a gnat on the horn of a bull of Bashan. He can save to the Uttermost[31] and who knows the measure of that word. As far as hell is from heaven will that one word reach.[32]

Forgive past follies and help anew.
Oh My Lord.

398.

1. Charles preached a later sermon on this text, "The Nail in a Sure Place" (*MTP* 60, Sermon 3402). Charles's later sermon contains enough overlapping material to indicate possible influence by the earlier sermon. The overlapping content is noted below.

2. Cf. Isa 22:20–24.   3. Cf. Isa 22:25.

4. "It has been generally propounded and admitted by commentators and expositors that Eliakim is a type of our Lord Jesus Christ. While this passage literally refers to Eliakim himself, it may, with very great instructiveness, be used as applicable to the Lord Jesus, and so I use it." *MTP* 60:182.

5. "The Lord knew what he was doing when he appointed the Only Begotten to be the sinner's pillar of strength, upon which he might lean. He knew that Jesus could not fail; that as God he was all-sufficient, that as perfect man he would not turn aside; that as a bleeding surety, having paid all the debt of our sin upon Calvary, he was able to save to the uttermost all them that come unto God by him." *MTP* 60:184–85.

6. Cf. Isaiah 53:10; Acts 2:23; 4:27–28.

7. "The reliance of a really saved soul is upon the person, the work, and righteousness of Jesus Christ only. This dependence is warranted by God's *appointment*. . . . what God does lasts for ever. Dost thou, dear hearer, rest thy soul's salvation alone upon Jesus? Then, mark thee, he can never fail thee, for if he do, then it would be true that God has been mistaken. 'Twere blasphemy to think it. If the Lord appoints Jesus Christ to be a propitiation for sin, and yet he doth not make that propitiation, then there is a mistake somewhere. If God bids me lean my whole weight upon his Son, and I do so lean, and yet am not sustained, then there is a great mistake, not on my part only, but on the part of Infinite Wisdom. But we cannot suppose that." *MTP* 60:184, italics in the original.

8. Charles held that Christ had pledged himself as the surety for God's covenant and solemn oath to elect and save a people. Charles was likely influenced by a number of authors in this view; however, John Gill seems to have been especially formative. Gill commented on this passage, "And I will fasten him as a nail in a sure place. . . . In a strong part of the wall or timber, where it shall not fail, or

be removed, or cut down, and so let drop what is hung upon it: it denotes the stability and continuance of [Christ's] government, and of the strength and support he should be of unto others; and well agrees with Christ his antitype; see Zech. x.14 and is expressive of the strength of Christ, as the mighty God; and as the man of God's right hand, made strong for himself; and as the able Saviour, and mighty Redeemer; and of the stability of his person, he is unchangeable, the same today, yesterday, and for ever; and of his office, as Mediator, Head, and Surety of the covenant; whose priesthood passes not from one to another, and whose kingdom is an everlasting one, and his truths and ordinances unshaken and immovable: the sure place in which he is fixed is both his church, where he is the everlasting Head, Husband, and Saviour of it; and heaven, where he is, and will be retained, until the time of the restitution of all things." John Gill, *An Exposition of the Books of the Prophets of the Old Testament. Both Larger and Lesser, viz. Isaiah, Jeremiah, Lamentations, Ezekiel, Daniel, Hosea, Joel, Amos, Obadiah, Jonah, Micah, Nahum, Habakkuk, Zephaniah, Haggai, Zechariah, and Malachi. In Two Volumes. In Which it Is Attempted to Give an Account of the Several Books, and the Writers of Them; A Summary of Each Chapter; And the Genuine Sense of Every Verse. And Throughout the Whole, The Original Text and Various Versions are Inspected and Compared; Interpreters of the Best Note, Both Jewish and Christian, Consulted; and the Prophecies Shewn Chiefly to Belong to the Times of the Gospel, and a Great Number of Them to Time yet to Come*, vol. 1 (London: printed for the author and sold by G. Keith and by J. Robinson, 1757, The Spurgeon Library), 117. Hereafter, *An Exposition of the Books of the Prophets of the Old Testament*.

9. "Moreover, the believer's dependence *is of God's sustaining*, for note, 'I will fasten him as a nail in a sure place, and he shall be for a glorious throne to his father's house.' God ensure the future – that Christ shall always be to his people their glory and their defence, . . . here, if nowhere else, here in the gospel we have a name in which we may trust, the name of the thrice-holy God that cannot lie, and he declares that he will sustain his Son as the Saviour of his people. Need I urge any rational spirit to depend where God pledges his word? . . . if you have God's word for it, cast yourselves unreservedly upon his Word. You shall not find him fail you; you shall rejoice as in heaven you sing the faithfulness of the God that spake, and the everlasting righteousness with which he fulfills every word he has spoken." *MTP* 60:185, italics in the original.

10. Cf. Heb 3:1–6.   11. Cf. 1 Cor 1:31; Eph 2:8–10.

12. Cf. Psalm 110; Phil 2:9–11.

13. Charles was referring to the then British Colonial province of India. According to the *Encyclopædia Britannica*, the name "Hindustan" is of Persian origin and was adopted by early European explorers. *Encyclopædia Britannica*, 11th ed. (1910), s.v. "India."

14. Charles's reference to "the Cape" was a reference to Cape Colony, or the Cape of Good Hope as it was alternatively known. In Charles's time, Cape Colony had been officially incorporated as a British colony, although it was sometimes referred to as a province. *Encyclopædia Britannica*, 11th ed. (1910), s.v. "Cape Colony."

15. Cf. 1 Pet 2:9–10.   16. Cf. Isa 26:1–4; Heb 4:16.

17. Cf. 2 Tim 4:7–8; Jas 1:12; Rev 3:21.

18. Cf. Rom 8:35–37.   19. Cf. Rev 5:12.

20. Cf. Eph 1:3–5; 5:23; Col 1:18.

21. Cf. Acts 20:28; Eph 1:7; Col 1:14.

22. Cf. Rom 3:22–24; Phil 3:9.

23. Charles struck through the word "solely" and added the superscripted word "mainly." Originally this line read, "Perseverance – is solely through his intercession." This change reflected Charles's dual commitment to God's grace in Christ as the primary cause for perseverance and yet the necessity of human working, as a result of faith, within God's working. During this time, Charles had to deal with the teaching of antinomians, who removed the necessity of effort and obedience in the Christian life. He wrote, "In my first pastorate, I had often to battle with Antinomians, — that is, people who held that, because they believed themselves to be elect, they might live as they liked. I hope that heresy has to a great extent died out, but it was sadly prevalent in my early ministerial days." *Autobiography* 1:258.

24. Cf. Rom 8:34; Heb 7:25.

25. Cf. Rom 6:5; 1 Cor 15; Phil 3:10–11; 1 Pet 1:3.

26. Cf. Rom 14:10; 2 Cor 5:10.

27. Cf. Rom 15:7; 2 Cor 3:18; 4:6.

28. Cf. Rev 1:8; 21:6; 22:13.

29. "All Christians are not alike capacious vessels of grace. Some can receive much; they are full of knowledge, zeal, hope, joy, faith. Others will never be anything but little vessels. They have believed, but their faith is mixed with unbelief. They can do but little; they have but few talents; their knowledge is obscured; their progress in divine life is but small. Still, for all that, they rest on nothing less than Christ, nor can they rest on anything more. The little cup is quite as safe, for it hangs on the nail, as the flagon does. Truly, one might be ambitious to be a flagon, to hold a deeper draught for its Lord's pleasure, but the littleness of the tiniest vessel does not affect its safety. The safety of all that hang there lies in the fastness of the pin, the strength and security of the nail. Not in the littleness of the one, nor the greatness of the other, is there either safety or danger, but all rests on that pin. So is it with the whole Church of God. We are all hanging upon the finished work of Jesus Christ." *MTP* 60:186–87.

30. Cf. Isa 28:17.   31. Cf. Heb 7:25.

32. Cf. Ps 103:12; 139:8, Jonah 2:2.

Acts. VIII. 13 & 21. — The faith of Simon Magus.   237

There are many points of interest in this narrative ....
Here is a preaching deacon — Philip one of the 7 chosen to oversee their secular affairs, yet he preaches. From this it would be wrong to argue that all deacons should be preachers or that ex officio the ministry is theirs — If Stephen & Philip were preachers that will not prove that all our deacons should do the same. It only proves that any gifted member of a church may preach & that no office in the church excludes a man from preaching or justifies him in holding his peace if really qualified for the work. It is worthy of note that the first martyr & the first missionary were both deacons.

Philip was successful because (God blessing him) he preached Christ: he is called an "evangelist" because he was very full of true gospel.
....

Here are believers of whom it is said "the Holy Ghost was not yet fallen on them." Now by this is not intended that they were destitute of the divine grace of the Holy Spirit but of his extraordinary & miraculous operations. This was communicated to some of them by the laying on of hands of the apostles. which could not be, if the converting power

THE FAITH *of* SIMON MAGUS
Acts 8:13, 21[1]

"Then Simon himself believed also: and when he was baptized, he continued with Philip, and wondered, beholding the miracles and signs which were done. . . . Thou hast neither part nor lot in this matter: for thy heart is not right in the sight of God."

There are many points of interest in this narrative.

. . . .

Here is a preaching deacon–Philip, one of the 7 chosen to oversee their secular affairs,[2] yet he preaches. From this it would be wrong to argue that all deacons should be preachers or that *ex officio*[3] the ministry is theirs. If Stephen and Philip were preachers that will not prove that all our deacons should do the same. It only proves that any gifted member of a church may preach and that no office in the church excludes a man from preaching or justifies him in holding his peace if really qualified for the work.[4]

It is worthy of note that the first martyr and the first missionary were both deacons.

Philip was successful because (God blessing him) he preached Christ:[5] he is called an "evangelist" because he was very full of true gospel.

. . . .

Here are believers of whom it is said "the Holy Ghost was not yet fallen on them." Now by this is not intended that they were destitute of the divine grace of the Holy Spirit[,] but of his extraordinary and miraculous operations.[6] This was communicated to some of them by the laying on of hands of the apostles. Which could not be, if the converting power of the Holy One be meant — Laying on of hands by ministers in ordination derives no support from this since no apostles are to be found & no gifts give — Nor does Confirmation get any help here since these were all professed, baptized believers, they rec'd the Holy Ghost, & apostles did it — —

Now we will look at Simon Magus.

I Let us see the man loose & wild.

1. He was an impostor — He pretended some say to be the Messiah, at any rate he thought to pass for some great prophet. This is gross sin indeed — to play with souls. —

2. He was a sorcerer — In order to maintain his imposture he either practised juggling tricks or really was in league with Satan. In those days Satan was abroad, unclean spirits were common, but now times are changed & such black arts cannot be really performed. However he did.

3. He was a licentious man, according to Josephus who says he persuaded Drusilla to leave her husband to live with Felix & he led about a bad woman whom he called Mother of All. This was after his warning by Peter —

THE FAITH OF SIMON MAGUS—*Acts 18:13, 21*

of the Holy one be meant. Laying on of hands by ministers in ordination derives no support from this since no apostles are to be found and no gifts given.[7] Nor does Confirmation get any help here since these were all professed, baptized believers,[8] they recd[9] the Holy Ghost, and [the] apostles did it.[10]

Now we will look at Simon Magus.

I. LET US SEE THE MAN LOOSE AND WILD.

1. He was an impostor. He pretended some say to be the Messiah[.][11] [A]t any rate he thought to pass for some great prophet. This is gross sin indeed–to play with souls.

2. He was a sorcerer. In order to maintain his imposture he either practised juggling tricks or really was in league with Satan.

    In those days Satan was abroad, unclean spirits were common, but now times are changed and such black arts cannot be really performed. However[,] he did.

3. He was a licentious man, according to Josephus[,] who says he persuaded Drusilla to leave her husband to live with Felix.[12] And he led about a bad woman whom he called Mother of All. This was after his warning by Peter.[13]

II. Let us see the man muzzled & bound.
When Philip first came he doubtless opposed him — as all went to hear so did he. He then saw himself outstripped by real wonders, he feared his own downfall & could not help seeing the reality of Philip's acts. He comes out, confesses faith, is baptized & remains a reformed & wondering man.

He believed. —
1. Because there was much reasonable in the gospel, & much pleasing to him.
2. He believed because there was an excitement, others did & so did he.
3. He believed because there was the most chance of gain that way.
4. He feared & therefore believed, he was convinced (temporarily) that he was wrong, truth terrified him & he believed.

III. Let us see the man's heart.
We cannot do this in other cases; let us then make the more use of this.
From his love of fame & greed of gain, we can see or guess all is not right —
1. He & his money were under a curse.
2. He had neither part nor lot in the matter, not a grain of true grace.
3. His heart was untouched & there all the mischief lay —

THE FAITH OF SIMON MAGUS—*Acts 18:13, 21*

II. LET US SEE THE MAN MUZZLED AND BOUND.

When Philip first came [Simon] doubtless opposed him. As all went to hear [Philip] so did he. [Simon] then saw himself outstripped by real wonders[.][14] [H]e feared his own downfall and could not help seeing the reality of Philip's acts. He comes out, confesses faith, is baptized and remains a reformed and wondering man.[15]

He believed:

1. Because there was much reasonable[16] in the gospel, and much pleasing to him.
2. He believed because there was an excitement[.] [O]thers did and so did he.[17]
3. He believed because there was the most chance of gain that way.
4. He feared and therefore believed, he was convinced (temporarily) that he was wrong. Truth terrified him and he believed.

III. LET US SEE THE MAN'S HEART.

We cannot do this in other cases; let us then make the more use of this.

From his love of fame and greed of gain we can see or guess [that] all is not right.

1. He and his money were under a curse.[18]
2. He had neither part nor lot in the matter, not a grain of true grace.[19]
3. His heart was untouched and there all the mischief lay.[20]

4. He had not repented & faith without repentance is worthless.
5. He was in the gall of bitterness - the most hopeless state of all.
6. He was fast bound & it was next to impossible he could be saved. Yet he exhorted him to repent & pray.

IV. Let us find some parrallel cases.
1. In the Baptist denomination - some are found sound in faith - rotten in heart. They know but do not feel aright.
2. In the Wesleyan & Primitive Methodist bodies are men professing to be converted worked upon by excitement, noise & earnestness - but they soon turn again.
3. In the Establishment there are Simons in shoals. Simonian parsons, Simonite Bishops, Simonite Squires, Simonite Poor. But let each man look at home. If there be a Simon here, may God detect him & save him.
Help. Help. Amen

411.

THE FAITH OF SIMON MAGUS—*Acts 18:13, 21*

4. He had not repented and faith without repentance is worthless.[21]
5. He was in the gall of bitterness,[22] the most hopeless state of all.
6. He was fast bound and it was next to impossible [that] he could be saved. Yet [Peter] exhorted him to repent and pray.[23]

IV. LET US FIND SOME PARALLEL CASES.

1. In the Baptist denomination some are found sound in faith [but] rotten in heart. They know but do not feel alright.
2. In the Wesleyan and Primitive Methodist bodies are men professing to be converted[,] worked upon by excitement, noise[,] and earnestness—but they soon turn again.
3. In the Establishment[24] there are Simons in shoals.[25] Simonian parsons.[26] Simonite Bishops,[27] Simonite Squires, [and] Simonite Poor.

But let each man look at home. If there be a Simon here, may God detect him and save him.

                Help. Help.   <u>Amen</u>

411.

SERMON 237

1. It appears that Charles did not preach another sermon on the text of Acts 8:13, 21.

2. Cf. Acts 6:1–7. Charles commended his deacons at Waterbeach: "The Church owes an immeasurable debt of gratitude to those thousands of godly men who study her interests day and night, contribute largely of their substance, care for her poor, cheer her ministers, and in times of trouble as well as prosperity, remain faithfully at their posts. Whatever there may be here and there of mistake, infirmity, and even wrong, I am sure, from wide and close observation, that the most of our deacons are an honor to our faith, and we may style them, as the apostle did his brethren, 'the glory of Christ.' The deacons of my first village pastorate were in my esteem the excellent of the earth, in whom I took great delight. Hard-working men on the week-day, they spared no toil for their Lord on the Sabbath; I loved them sincerely, and do love them still." *Autobiography* 1:255–56.

3. *Ex officio* is a Latin term that conveys the sense of "by virtue of one's position or status." Charles was saying that it would be wrong to argue from Philip's example that all deacons are required or obligated to preach by virtue of their diaconal office.

4. For Charles, the evangelistic fervor behind this remark was also the impetus for the Pastors' College. In his autobiography, Charles recalled the founding of the college in this way: "When, in early days, God's Holy Spirit had gone forth with my ministry at New Park Street, several zealous young men were brought to a knowledge of the truth; and among them some whose preaching in the street was blessed of God to the conversion of souls. Knowing that these men had capacities for usefulness, but laboured under serious disadvantage of having no education, and were, moreover, in such circumstances that they would not be likely to obtain admission into any of our Colleges, it entered into my heart to provide them with a course of elementary instruction, which might, at least, correct their inaccuracies of speech, and put them in the way of obtaining further information by reading." *Autobiography* 2:147. Thus, the Pastors' College was born. Charles made it clear that "We never dreamed of making men preachers, but we desired to help those whom God had already called to be such." *Autobiography* 2:148. For Charles, it was the call of God, evidenced in fruitfulness, that fundamentally qualified a man to preach regardless of office.

5. Cf. Acts 8:5–8. "We must preach Christ only. With Paul, every true minister ought to be able to say to his hearers, 'I determined not to know anything among you, save Jesus Christ, and him crucified.' The preacher must never mix up anything else with the gospel. Every time he preaches, he must still have the same old theme, 'Jesus Christ, and him crucified.' Christ is the Alpha of the gospel, and he is the Omega too; the first letter of the gospel alphabet, and the last letter, and all the letters in between. It must be Christ, Christ, CHRIST from beginning to end." *MTP* 56:489.

6. It is possible that Charles received this interpretation from John Gill. Gill explained Acts 8:15–16 by writing, "They had received [the Holy Ghost] as a spirit of illumination and sanctification, and as a spirit of conversion and faith; they had been regenerated, enlightened, and sanctified by him; and were converted by him, and brought to believe in Christ, and live by faith upon him; they were baptized believers, and no more; as yet, none of them had gifts qualifying them for the ministry; and still less could any of them speak with tongues, or prophesy, or work miracles; the Holy Ghost had not yet descended on them for such purposes." Gill, *An Exposition of the New Testament* (1747) 2:197.

7. Gill wrote, "[The apostles] were directed unto by the Spirit of God; whom he had designed, and now would qualify for the work of the ministry, that so this new church might be supplied with proper officers, pastors, and teachers, to feed them with knowledge and with understanding; and who might not only have ministerial gifts to qualify them for preaching the Gospel, but extraordinary ones, which would serve for the confirmation of it; and for this purpose the apostles, *both* of them, as the Arabic version reads, laid their hands on them: for it will not seem probably, that they laid their hands upon the women, on such an account; and it will hardly be received, that they should lay their hands on *Simon Magus*, otherwise he would have received the Holy Ghost too; so that it seems a plain case, that imposition of hands was not used to them all: *and they received the Holy Ghost*; that is they received the gifts of the Holy Ghost; for so that they could prophesy and speak with tongues, and heal diseases, and do other wonderful works: and since now these effects have ceased, the rite and ceremony which was peculiar to the apostles as such, it should seem should cease likewise." Gill, *An Exposition of the New Testament*, 2:197, italics in the original. Charles did not recognize ordination as a biblical practice and was never ordained, even though ordination was extended to him on multiple occasions (cf. Sermon 283, note 2).

8. According to the *Encyclopædia Britannica*, confirmation "in the Christian sense" is "the initiatory rite of laying on of hands, supplementary to and completing baptism, and especially connected with the gift of the Holy Ghost to the candidate." In Charles's day, this was a ritual associated particularly with churches that practiced infant baptism. *Encyclopædia Britannica*, 11th ed. (1910), s.v. "Confirmation."

9. Charles abbreviated the word "received."

10. Cf. Acts 8:14–17.

11. Gill mentioned this extrabiblical idea: "He is commonly called *Simon Magus*, for he was a magician, who had learned diabolical arts, and used enchantments and divinations, as *Balaam* and the magicians of Egypt did: *and bewitched the people of Samaria*; or rather astonished them, with the strange feats he performed; which were so unheard of and unaccountable, that they were thrown into an exstasy (sic.) and rapture; and were as it were out of themselves, through wonder and admiration, at the amazing things that were done by him: *giving out that himself was some great one*: a divine person, or an extraordinary prophet, and it may be the Messiah; since the Samaritans expected the Messiah, as appears from *John iv. 25* and which the *Syriac* version seems to incline to, which renders the words thus, *and he said, I am that great one*; that great person, whom *Moses* spake of as the seed of the woman, under the name of *Shiloh*, and the character of a prophet." Gill, *An Exposition of the New Testament* 2:196, italics in the original.

12. Josephus wrote, "For the marriage of Drusilla with Azizus, it was in no long time afterward dissolved upon the following occasion: While Felix was procurator of Judea, he saw this Drusilla, and fell in love with her; for she did indeed exceed all other women in beauty; and he sent to her a person whose name was Simon*, one of his friends, a Jew he was, and by birth a Cypriot, and one that pretended to be a magician, and endeavoured to persuade her to forsake her present husband and marry him; and promised, that if she would not refuse him, he would make her a happy woman. Accordingly she acted ill, and because she was desirous to avoid her sister Bernice's envy, for she was very ill treated by her on account of her beauty, was prevailed upon to transgress the laws of her forefathers, and to marry Felix; and, when he had had a son by her, he named him Agrippa." William Whiston, trans., *The Works of Flavius Josephus, The Learned and Authentic Jewish Historian, and Celebrated Warrior. To Which Are Added, Three*

Dissertations Concerning Jesus Christ, John the Baptist, James the Just, God's Command to Abraham, etc., with an Index to the Whole. In Four Volumes, vol 3. (London: printed for William Allason and J. Maynard, 1818, The Spurgeon Library), 174–75. Whiston, the translator of this passage, inserted a footnote pointing out that the Simon in Josephus's passage is a Jew from Cyprus, while the one in Acts 8 is a Samaritan from Samaria, as also attested by early church documents. In this case, Whiston believed that unless Josephus was mistaken about Simon's background, Simon was likely "a different person from the other." Whiston, *The Works of Flavius Josephus*, 174–75. It would seem that Charles either rejected this footnote or overlooked its information. Modern scholarship affirms that the Simon from Acts 8 was from Samaria, which would distinguish him from the Simon in Josephus. See Eckhard J. Schnabel, *Acts*, Zondervan Exegetical Commentary on the New Testament, ed. Clinton Arnold (Grand Rapids: Zondervan, 2012), 407; Craig Keener, *Acts: An Exegetical Commentary*, vol. 2 (Grand Rapids: Baker, 2013), 1508–11; and Ben Witherington III, *The Acts of the Apostles: A Socio-Rhetorical Commentary* (Grand Rapids: Eerdmans, 1998), 282–84. Therefore, it is likely that Charles was incorrect on this point, and the Simon Magus of Acts neither persuaded Drusilla to leave her husband nor led a woman he called "Mother of All."

13. Cf. Acts 8:20–24.
14. Cf. Acts 8:6–8.

15. Cf. Acts 8:13.

16. "1. Having the faculty of reason; endued with reason. 2. Acting, speaking, or thinking rationally. 3. Just, rational; agreeable to reason. 4. Not immoderate. Tolerable; being in mediocrity." Johnson's *Dictionary*, s.v. "Reasonable."

17. Throughout his ministry, Charles was careful to distinguish between emotionalism and true belief. "Do not aim at sensation and 'effect.' Flowing tears and streaming eyes, sobs and outcries, crowded after-meetings and all kinds of confusions may occur, and may be borne with as concomitants of genuine feeling; but pray do not plan their production. It very often happens that the converts that are born in excitement die when the excitement is over." C. H. Spurgeon, *The Soul Winner* (Pasadena, TX: Pilgrim Publications, 2007), 16.

18. Cf. Acts 8:20.
19. Cf. Acts 8:21.

20. Cf. Acts 8:21; Ezek 36:26.

21. Cf. 2 Cor 7:10. "There never was in this world such a thing as an impenitent believer in Jesus Christ, and there never can be. Faith and repentance are born in a spiritual life together, and they grow up together. The moment a man believes he repents, and while he believes he both believes and repents, and until he shall have done with faith he will not have done with repenting. If thou hast believed, but hast never repented of thy sins, then beware of thy believing." MTP 60:567.

22. Cf. Deut 29:18; Acts 8:23. Charles often associated "the gall of bitterness" with the condition of those who are outwardly religious but inwardly lost in sin. "They are church members, they are baptized persons, they have passed the rubicon; what do they want more? You can do little for them. I do tremble for these. For my most hard-hearted hearers I weep before God; but for these people I need to have four eyes to weep with. For who can make an impression upon them, when they are firmly persuaded that they are right, and have had the seal of the church that they are right, though notwithstanding that they are deceiving themselves and others, and are still 'in the gall of bitterness and in the bond of iniquity.' My young friends, I do not want to check any of you in joining a church; but I do say to you, make sure work of it before you make a profession." NPSP 3:149.

23. Cf. Acts 8:22.

24. That is, the Church of England. Charles often warned his hearers against finding assurance in their church associations rather than in a genuine work of the Spirit through Christ. "My hearer, dost thou belong to the church? For out of the church there is no salvation. But mark what the church is. It is not the Episcopalian, Baptist, or Presbyterian: the church is a company of men who have received the Spirit. If thou canst not say thou hast the Spirit, go thy way and tremble; go thy way and think of thy lost condition; and may Jesus by his Spirit so bless thee, that thou mayest be led to renounce thy works and ways with grief, and fly to him who died upon the cross, and find a shelter there from the wrath of God." NPSP 4:24.

25. "A crowd; a great multitude; a throng." Johnson's *Dictionary*, s.v. "Shoal."

26. One example of a "Simonian parson" whom Charles could have had in mind was Dr. Edward Drax Free. Although Dr. Free was a brilliant student, he was assigned to the small village of Sutton in 1808 in what might have been an attempt to contain his infamy. He was accused of a litany of offenses such as skipping service, extorting the townspeople for baptism and burials, and having fathered three illegitimate children with three different housekeepers. R. B. Outhwaite, *The Rise and Fall of English Ecclesiastical Courts, 1500–1860* (Cambridge: Cambridge University Press, 2006), 133–34.

27. An example of a scandalous bishop was Lancelot Blackburne (1658–1743), who became archbishop of York in 1724. According to tradition, he had been a pirate in his youth, would sometimes refresh himself in his vestry with "tobacco and liquor," and was rumored to have fathered an illegitimate child whose later ecclesiastical career he advanced. Mary A. De Morgan, ed., *Threescore Years and Ten: Reminiscences of the Late Sophia Elizabeth De Morgan. To Which are Added Letters to and from Her Husband the Late Augustus De Morgan, and Others* (London: Richard Bentley and Son, 1895), xx.

Matt. XXI. 16. Text for little Children. — 238.

I. In heaven a great part of God's praise comes from the mouths of babes & sucklings. —
Of such is the Kingdom of heaven.
Think of your baby brothers & sisters in heaven, you would wish to see them. Then

II. On Earth you little children should sing Jesus Christ's praises. —
Young Children just accountable are in hell, & if they are old enough to be lost, they are old enough to be saved by grace. — Many very little ones have learned to love Jesus early. —
Jesus accepts your songs & loves to hear them. You should love him —
1. For house & home, health, father & mother — &c.
2. For a bible, Sunday, teacher — &c.
3. For dying for you.

III. Question them.
1. As to their sins & the way of pardon.
2. As to their hearts & way of cure.
3. As to heaven & hell & salvation. —
showing from each that they should trace all to Jesus & love him very much.
Father perfect praise in them amen

413

TEXT *for* LITTLE CHILDREN
Matt 21:16[1]

"And said unto him, Hearest thou what these say? And Jesus saith unto them, Yea; have ye never read, Out of the mouth of babes and sucklings thou hast perfected praise?"

I. IN HEAVEN A GREAT PART OF GOD'S PRAISE COMES FROM THE MOUTHS OF BABES AND SUCKLINGS.

Of such is the Kingdom of heaven.[2]

Think of your baby brothers and sisters in heaven.[3] You would wish to see them. Then[:]

II. ON EARTH YOU LITTLE CHILDREN SHOULD SING JESUS CHRIST'S PRAISES.

Young children just accountable are in hell, and if they are old enough to be lost, they are old enough to be saved by grace.[4] Many very little ones have learned to love Jesus early.

Jesus accepts your songs and loves to hear them. You should love him:

1. For house and home, health, father and mother, etc.
2. For a Bible, Sunday, teacher, etc.
3. For dying for you.

III. QUESTION THEM.[5]

1. As to their sins and the way of pardon.
2. As to their hearts and way of cure.
3. As to heaven and hell and salvation, showing from each that they should trace all to Jesus and love him very much.

Father perfect praise in them.

Amen

413.

SERMON 238

1. Charles preached a later sermon on this text, "The Children and Their Hosannas" (*MTP* 30, Sermon 1785). However, the latter sermon does not appear to contain any overlapping content and does not appear to have been influenced by the former.

2. Cf. Matt 19:14.

3. Throughout Charles's ministry he made his opinions regarding infant salvation abundantly clear. He wrote, "I rejoice to know that the souls of all infants, as soon as they die, speed their way to paradise." *NPSP* 3:28. Charles went so far as to suggest that infants will make up the majority of the elect in heaven. In a sermon dedicated to the matter, "Infant Salvation" (Sermon 411), he wrote, "All Scripture seems to teach that heaven will not be a narrow world, that its population will not be like a handful gleaned out of a vintage, but that Christ shall be glorified by ten thousand times ten thousand, whom he hath redeemed with his blood. . . . I do not see it possible, unless indeed the millennium age should soon come, and then far exceed a thousand years; I do not see how it is possible that so vast a number should enter heaven, unless it be on the supposition that infant souls constitute the great majority." *MTP* 7:509. However, Charles was careful to teach that this salvation was applied to infants only through Christ, the same as every other believer: "Some ground the idea of the eternal blessedness of the infant upon its innocence. We do no such thing; we believe that the infant fell in the first Adam. . . . On what ground, then, do we believe the child to be saved? We believe it to be as lost as the rest of mankind, and as truly condemned by the sentence which said, 'In the day that thou eatest thereof thou shalt surely die.' It is saved because it is elect. . . . They are saved, too, because they were redeemed by the precious blood of Jesus Christ. . . . They are saved, again, not without regeneration. . . . No doubt, in some mysterious manner the Spirit of God regenerates the infant soul, and it enters into glory made meet to be a partaker of the inheritance of the saints in light. . . . By election, by redemption, by regeneration, the child enters into glory, by the selfsame door by which every believer in Christ Jesus hopes to enter, and in no other way." *MTP* 7:506–7.

4. Charles clearly believed that the benefits of infant salvation cease to apply to older children, but his opinions regarding the age of accountability are not as clear. As shown through the reference of this note, he believed that there comes

a time when children are held accountable before God, but Charles did not feel the need to speculate on a specific age of accountability.

5. Charles's encouragement to parents to question their children as to their state of grace was likely influenced by his mother's early ministry to her children. "It was the custom, on Sunday evenings, while we were yet little children, for her to stay at home with us, and then we sat round the table, and read verse by verse, and she explained the Scripture to us. After that was done, then came the time of pleading; there was a little piece of Alleine's *Alarm*, or Baxter's *Call to the Unconverted*, and this was read with pointed observation made to each of us as we sat around the table; and the question was asked, how long it would be before we would think about our state, how long before we would seek the Lord." *Autobiography* 1:68. This formative experience for Charles affirmed his later view that "fathers and mothers are the most natural agents for God to use in the salvation of their children." *Autobiography* 1:68.

239

Text for Boys & Girls.

413

239

TEXT *for* BOYS *and* GIRLS[1]

[blank]

1. At first glance it is unclear why Charles left this sermon blank. Previously, Charles has left only four sermons blank: "Son, Be of Good Cheer" (Notebook 4, Sermon 225); "He Filleth the Hungry with Good Things" (Notebook 4, Sermon 226); "He Will Bring Every Work into Judgment" (Notebook 4, Sermon 228); and "As One Whom His Mother Comforteth" (Notebook 4, Sermon 229). Additionally, up to this point Charles has only outlined and preached two sermons with no Scripture text: "Regeneration" (Notebook 1, Sermon 7) and "The Seven Cries on the Cross" (Notebook 3, Sermon 142). A likely explanation for this blank sermon and the following one, "Text for Young Believers" (Sermon 240), is that they both appear to be directed toward children, as was the previous one, "Text for Little Children" (Sermon 238). It is possible that Charles began sketching a number of possible outlines for a single occasion before selecting "Text for Little Children" (Sermon 238). The repetition of "413" as the preaching occurrence number also appears to indicate that the outlines likely originated together and then one was selected, as there is no evidence that Charles preached this sermon or the one following.

Text for young Believers. 240

413.

240

TEXT *for* YOUNG BELIEVERS[1]

[blank]

413.[2]

SERMON 240

1. See Sermon 239, note 1.

2. Cf. Gal 1:8–9; Jude 3. Also, As noted above, the repetition of the preaching occurrence number "413" likely indicates that this outline, or at least its title, was composed at the same time as the two prior sermons, "Text for Little Children" (Sermon 238) and "Text for Boys and Girls" (Sermon 239). Since only the outline for "Text for Little Children" (Sermon 238) was completed, it is likely that Charles intended to preach one sermon for children and chose between three possible titles.

241. Acts VIII. 36. What doth hinder me to be baptized.
This chapter is a "desperately baptistical one", it is full of water; & cannot be coaxed out of it. May there be some spiritual profit arising to each of us out of it. —

I. Who ought to be baptized?
II. What does being baptized mean?
III. Why are not you baptized?

I. Who ought to be baptized? To the Law & to the testimony. —
1. Matt. III. 6. Those who confessed their sins.
 "   " 13. Jesus & therefore all his followers.
2. Mark. XVI. 16. All Believers. —
3. Luke. VII. 29. 30. Justifiers of God.
4. John. IV. 1. — Disciples.
5. Acts II. 41 — Glad Receivers of the word.
  Acts VIII. 12 — Men & women Believing.
  "   " 37 — Heart Believers.
  Acts XVI. 33. 34 — The Believing Household.
6. Rom. VI. 3. 4 — Those who walk in newness of life
7. 1 Cor. XII. 13 — Receivers of the Spirit.
8. Gal III. 27 — Those who put on Christ.
9. Eph. IV. 5 — Those who have a Lord & a faith.
10. Col. II. 12 — Those who dead with him

WHAT DOTH HINDER ME *to* BE BAPTIZED[?]

Acts 8:36[1]

"And as they went on their way, they came unto a certain water: and the eunuch said, See, here is water; what doth hinder me to be baptized?"

This chapter is a "<u>desperately baptistical one</u>."[2] It is full of water, and cannot be coaxed out of it. May there be some spiritual profit arising to each of us out of it.

I. WHO OUGHT TO BE BAPTIZED?

II. WHAT DOES BEING BAPTIZED MEAN?

III. WHY ARE NOT YOU BAPTIZED?

I. WHO OUGHT TO BE BAPTIZED? TO THE LAW AND TO THE TESTIMONY.[3]

    1. Matt. III. 6.[4] Those who confessed their sins.
       "   " 13.[5] – Jesus and therefore all his followers.

    2. Mark. XVI. 16[6,7] – All Believers.

    3. Luke. VII. 29. 30.[8] – Justifiers of God.

    4. John. IV. 1.[9] – Disciples.

    5. Acts. II. 41[10] – Glad Receivers of the word.
       Acts VIII. 12[11] – Men and women Believing.
       "   " 37[12] – Heart Believers.
       Acts XVI .33. 34[13] – The Believing Household.

    6. Rom. VI. 3. 4[14] – Those who walk in newness of life.

    7. I Cor. XII. 13[15] – Receivers of the Spirit.

    8. Gal. III. 27[16] – Those who put on Christ.

    9. Eph. IV. 5[17] – Those who have a Lord and a faith.

    10. Col. II. 12[18] – Those who died[19] with him.

Surely here is enough to prove that Believers only ought to be baptized.

II. What does Baptism mean?

A thousand conflicting answers are given by Pædobaptists but only one by Scripture.

It is the rite whereby we in formâ unite ourselves to Jesus & his cause.

& immersion is a most excellent mode of setting this forth —

1. It is a representation of our likeness to Jesus in that we are buried & rise again.
2. It well sets forth pardon of sin which we trust we have enjoyed.
3. It pledges us to sanctification.

It is a solemn thing to be baptized, it may not be neglected, it may not be lightly entered upon.

III. What doth hinder thee?

Babe. Thy want of understanding, repentance, faith the word of God & common sense hinder <u>thee</u>

But *Adult* what hinders you?

1. Sin constantly indulged in.
2. Self Righteousness. —

But Christian what hindereth thee

1 Is it shame — art thou afraid to own thy Lord? dost thou blush at his name?

Surely here is enough to prove that Believers only ought to be baptized.

II. WHAT DOES BAPTISM MEAN?

A thousand conflicting answers are given by Pædobaptists but only one by Scripture.

It is the rite whereby we ~~pr~~ *in forma*[20] unite ourselves to Jesus and his cause.

And immersion is a most excellent mode of setting this forth[:]

1. It is a representation of our likeness to Jesus in that we are buried and rise again.[21]
2. It well sets forth pardon of sin which we trust we have enjoyed.[22]
3. It pledges us to sanctification. It is a solemn thing to be baptized.[23] It may not be neglected. It may not be lightly entered upon.

III. WHAT DOTH HINDER THEE?

Babe. Thy want of understanding, repentance, faith, the word of God, and common sense hinder <u>thee</u>.[24] But **Adult**, what hinders you?

1. Sin constantly indulged in.
2. Self Righteousness.

    But Christian, what hindereth thee[?]

1. Is it shame–art thou afraid to own thy Lord? Dost thou blush at his name?

2. It is perhaps want of Self Denial.
3. Is it fear of the Church or the gazing throng?
4. Is it a sense of your own imperfections?
5. Is it thy sense of weakness?
Come poor soul come on. come on.
Not fit to be baptized? ⸻ ⸻ ⸻
Not a believer! ⸻ not fit to die!!
Not fit for heaven!! Then what is there?
A fearful looking for of judgment!!!
  Brethren pray for conversions,
labour for conversions, look for conversions,
  Father open thou my mouth.

2. Is it perhaps want of Self Denial?
3. Is it fear of the Church[25] or the gazing throng?
4. Is it a sense of your own imperfections?
5. Is it thy sense of weakness?

Come poor soul. Come on. Come on.

Not fit to be baptized! - - - - - - - - - -
Not a believers! Not fit to die!! Not fit for heaven!! Then what is there? A fearful looking for of judgment!!![26]

Brethren pray for conversions.
Labour for conversions. Look for conversions.

Father open thou my mouth.

1. It appears that Charles did not preach another sermon on the text of Acts 8:36, though he did preach a sermon on Acts 8:35, "All at It" (*MTP* 34, Sermon 2044), and Acts 8:37, "Who Should Be Baptized?" (*MTP* 47, Sermon 2737). However, neither of those other sermons contained sufficient overlap to suggest that they had been influenced by this sermon.

2. "Relating to baptism; baptismal." Worcester's *Dictionary*, s.v. "Baptistical." This phrase was often used in Charles's day to criticize Baptists who were too eager to promote Baptist doctrines and causes. For example, see Joseph Foulkes Winks, ed., *The Baptist Reporter, and Missionary Intelligencer 1846* (London: Simpkin, Marshall, n.d.), 179; and *MTP* 7:231.

3. Cf. Isa 8:20. Charles frequently referred to the entirety of Scripture as "the law and the testimony."

4. Matthew 3:6, "And were baptized of him in Jordan, confessing their sins."

5. Matthew 3:13, "Then cometh Jesus from Galilee to Jordan unto John, to be baptized of him."

6. Mark 16:16, "He that believeth and is baptized shall be saved; but he that believeth not shall be damned."

7. Cf. Gal 1:8–9; Jude 3.

8. Luke 7:29–30, "And all the people that heard him, and the publicans, justified God, being baptized with the baptism of John. But the Pharisees and lawyers rejected the counsel of God against themselves, being not baptized of him."

9. John 4:1, "When therefore the Lord knew how the Pharisees had heard that Jesus made and baptized more disciples than John, . . ."

10. Acts 2:41, "Then they that gladly received his word were baptized: and the same day there were added unto them about three thousand souls."

11. Acts 8:12, "But when they believed Philip preaching the things concerning the kingdom of God, and the name of Jesus Christ, they were baptized, both men and women."

12. Acts 8:37, "And Philip said, If thou believest with all thine heart, thou mayest. And he answered and said, I believe that Jesus Christ is the Son of God."

13. Acts 16:33–34, "And he took them the same hour of the night, and washed their stripes; and was baptized, he and all his, straightway. And when he had brought them into his house, he set meat before them, and rejoiced, believing in God with all his house."

14. Romans 6:3–4, "Know ye not, that so many of us as were baptized into Jesus Christ were baptized into his death? Therefore we are buried with him by baptism into death: that like as Christ was raised up from the dead by the glory of the Father, even so we also should walk in newness of life."

15. First Corinthians 12:13, "For by one Spirit are we all baptized into one body, whether we be Jews or Gentiles, whether we be bond or free; and have been all made to drink into one Spirit."

16. Galatians 3:27, "For as many of you as have been baptized into Christ have put on Christ."

17. Ephesians 4:5, "One Lord, one faith, one baptism . . ."

18. Colossians 2:12, "Buried with him in baptism, wherein also ye are risen with him through the faith of the operation of God, who hath raised him from the dead."

19. Charles originally miswrote "dead" instead of "died."

20. "*In forma*" related to the legal concept of "*in forma pauperis*" meaning "in the character or manner of a pauper." Charles wrote, "Cast yourself upon the mercy of the court and ask for mercy, free mercy, undeserved mercy, gratuitous favour: this is what you must ask for, and as in law they have a form of suing called *in forma pauperis*, that is, in the form of a pauper, do you adopt the method, and as a man full of necessities do you beg for favour at the hands of God, *in forma pauperis*, and it shall be bestowed upon you." *MTP* 23:178. It is unclear what the "pr" word that Charles struck through would have been.

21. Cf. Rom 6:4.

22. Charles rejected the idea of baptismal regeneration or any other conception of baptism that made it a condition of salvation. Rather, baptism portrays ("sets forth") the forgiveness of the believer, which he has already enjoyed. For further information on Charles's contention against baptismal regeneration, see "Baptismal Regeneration" (*MTP* 10, Sermon 573).

23. Charles's own baptism was marked by solemnity and joy. He wrote, "I can never forget the 3rd of May, 1850; it was my mother's birthday, and I myself was within a few weeks of being sixteen years of age. I was up early, to have a couple of hours for quiet prayer and dedication to God. Then I had some eight miles to walk, to reach the spot where I was to be immersed into the Triune Name according to the sacred command. What a walk it was! What thoughts and prayers thronged my soul during that morning's journey! It was by no means a warm day, and therefore all the better for the two or three hours of quiet foot-travel which I enjoyed. The sight of Mr. Cantlow's smiling face was a full reward for that country tramp. . . . The wind blew down the river with a cutting blast, as my turn came to wade into the flood; but after I had walked a few steps, and noted the people on the ferry-boat, and in boats, and on either shore, I felt as if Heaven, and earth, and hell, might all gaze upon me; for I was not ashamed, there and then, to own myself a follower of the Lamb. My timidity was washed away; it floated down the river into the sea, and must have been devoured by the fishes, for I have never felt anything of the kind since. Baptism also loosed my tongue, and from that day it has never been quiet. I lost a thousand fears in that River Lark, and found that "in keeping His commandments there is great reward." *Autobiography* 1:151–52.

24. Here, Charles admitted that infants lack the repentance and faith to be baptized. But children are a different matter. In later years, Charles was open to baptizing children and bringing them into church membership. Charles wrote, "We have never as a church thought that a certain number of years must have passed over a child before it can confess its faith in Christ and be received into the church. It is sometimes said that we teach adult baptism. We do nothing of the sort. We practise believer's baptism, and baptize all who confess faith in the Lord Jesus Christ, whether they are children or adults. Our enquiry as to fitness does not refer to age, but to faith. The number of the fewness of days or years is no consideration whatever with us. Our question is, 'Dost thou believe in the Lord Jesus Christ?' If that be fairly answered we say at once, 'What doth hinder you to be baptized?'

However young a believer may be he should make an open confession of his faith, and be folded with the rest of the flock of Christ." *MTP* 28:568.

25. Like other Baptists, Charles held baptism and church membership together. To be baptized was to be brought into the membership and accountability of the church. At the same time, Charles did not want to make the membership process a hindrance to making a profession of faith through baptism. He wrote, "May God grant that our church may never be terrible to young converts by moroseness and uncharitableness. Whenever I hear of candidates being alarmed at coming before our elders, or seeing the pastor, or making confession of faith before the church, I wish I could say to them: 'Dismiss your fears, beloved ones; we shall be glad to see you, and you will find your intercourse with us a pleasure rather than a trial.' So far from wishing to repel you, if you really do love the Saviour, we shall be glad enough to welcome you. If we cannot see in you the evidence of a great change, we shall kindly point out to you our fears, and shall be thrice happy to point you to the Saviour; but be sure of this, if you have really believed in Jesus, you shall not find the church terrible to you." *MTP* 17:198–99.

26. Cf. Heb 10:26–27.

Zech. III. 2 — Brand plucked from the fire.

Suggested by a firebrand falling on the hearth —

I. Remarks on the wording of the text.
"Brand" — Saints by nature like others "brands"
"out of the fire" — not away from it — to show the great danger.
"plucked" — by mighty grace & omnipotence

II. Instances of plucking from the burning —
1. The narrow escapes saints have had from death — before conversion
2. The old age of some.
3. The natural depravity of the heart
4. Evil habits into which they had fallen
5. Temptations & trials after conversion
6. The spirituality of the law.
7. The immense price of our ransom

III. How can I tell if I am one
1. Can you remember the plucking.
2. Do you hate the fire —
3. Do you love other plucked brands —
4. Do you love to adore divine free grace.

412. 415. 416. 418. 438. 560. 566.

BRAND PLUCKED *from the* FIRE
Zechariah 3:2[1]

"And the Lord said unto Satan, The Lord rebuke thee, O Satan; even the Lord that hath chosen Jerusalem rebuke thee: is not this a brand plucked out of the fire?"

Suggested by a firebrand[2] falling on the hearth.[3]

I. REMARKS ON THE WORDING OF THE TEXT.

"Brand" – Saints by nature like others, "brands."[4]

"out of the fire" – not away from it, to show the great danger.

"plucked" – by mighty grace and omnipotence.[5]

II. INSTANCES OF PLUCKING FROM THE BURNING.

1. The narrow escapes saints have had from death before conversion.
2. The old age of some.[6]
3. The natural depravity of the heart.[7]
4. Evil habits into which they had fallen.[8]
5. Temptations and trials after conversion.
6. The spirituality of the law.[9]
7. The immense price of our ransom.

III. HOW CAN I TELL IF I AM ONE[?]

1. Can you remember the plucking[?][10]
2. Do you hate the fire[?]
3. Do you love other plucked brands[?]
4. Do you love to adore divine, free grace[?]

412. 415. 416. 418. 438. 560. 566.

SERMON 242

1. It appears that Charles preached a later sermon on this text, "God's Firebrands" (*MTP* 57, Sermon 3233), and another on Zech 3:1–5, "Zechariah's Vision of Joshua the High Priest" (*MTP* 11, Sermon 611). While the latter sermon does not appear to have any overlapping material, the introduction to "God's Firebrands" (*MTP* 57, Sermon 3233) corresponds closely to Charles's first Roman numeral here. The overlapping content is noted below.

2. Johnson listed an entry for "brand" but not "firebrand": "A stick lighted, or fit to be lighted, in the fire." Johnson's *Dictionary*, s.v. "Brand."

3. In his autobiography, Charles recounted the incident behind this sermon:

> On another occasion, I had a trouble of quite a different character. I had preached on the Sunday morning, and gone home to dinner, as was my wont, with one of the congregation. The afternoon sermon came so close behind the morning one, that it was difficult to prepare the soul, especially as the dinner was a necessary but serious inconvenience where a clear brain was required. By a careful measuring of diet, I remained in an earnest, lively condition; but, to my dismay, I found that the pre-arranged line of thought was gone from me. I could not find the trail of my prepared sermon; and press my forehead as I might, the missing topic would not come. Time was brief, the hour was striking, and in some alarm I told the honest farmer that I could not for the life of me recollect what I had intended to preach about.
>
> "Oh!" he said, "never mind; you will be sure to have a good word for us." Just at that moment, a blazing block of wood fell out of the fire upon the hearth at my feet, smoking into my eyes and nose at a great rate. "There," said the farmer, "there's a text for you, sir. 'Is not this a brand plucked out of the fire?'"
>
> "No," I thought, "it was not plucked out, for it fell out of itself." Here, however, was a text, an illustration, and a leading thought as a nest-egg for more. Further light came, and the discourse was certainly not worse than my more prepared effusions; it was better in the best sense, for one or two came forward declaring themselves to have been aroused and converted through that afternoon's sermon. I have always considered that it was a happy circumstance that I had forgotten the text from which I had intended to preach. *Autobiography* 1:266.

4. "Nothing can be more suitable to burn in the fire than a brand. . . . And what does this indicate but man's natural heart, which is so congenial to the fire of sin? Our heart is like the tinder, and Satan has but to strike the spark, and how readily does the spark find a nest within our bosom! As the firebrand fits the fire, so does the sinner fit in with sin. . . . Not to go a step without a particular application, it will be well for us all to understand that we are ourselves like the brands; there is a fitness between us and sin; if we burn in the fire of sin, it is no wonder; with our fallen nature, it is no greater marvel that we should be instigated by sin than that the firebrand should kindle in the flame." MTP 57:26.

5. "Still, the force of the passage seems to lie in the words, '*plucked out of.*' . . . [The Christian] does not escape by his own free will. He is plucked out of it. To be plucked out, there needs a hand quick and to rescue. You know that pierced hand, and how it burnt itself when it was thrust into the hot coals to pluck us out like brands from the burning. It was no use waiting till we dropped out, for we should never have done so; there was no hope of that. With all the appliances of grace and of judgment, the two together could not bring us out. But effectual vocation did it, when the Spirit of the living God took the firebrand in his hand, and without asking it whether it would or not, by the sweet and irresistible compulsions of divine grace plucked the brand out of the fire." MTP 57:26–27, italics in the original.

6. "There have been instance of persons converted at the most advanced age. There was one who went, I believe, to hear Mr. Toplady preach the very day when he was aged a hundred. He had been a constant neglecter of the house of God, but when he arrived at the age of a hundred, attracted by the fame of Mr. Toplady, who was an exceedingly popular, as he certainly was a highly evangelical preacher, and happened to be preaching in the town where the man lived, he said he would go on that day to hear him, that he might recollect his birthday. He went, and that day God in his grace met with him. . . . Just as he was on the borders of the tomb, he was made to enter into eternal life." MTP 57:29.

7. Cf. Jer 17:9. "Out of the state of our natural depravity we have been plucked, so that every man who is delivered from its sway may well say, 'Am not I a brand plucked out of the fire?' Each Christian, knowing his own heart, and having a special acquaintance with his own peculiar besetting sin, feels as if the conquest

of his own will by the grace of God were a more illustrious trophy of that grace than the conquest of a thousand others." *MTP* 57:28.

8. In "God's Firebrands," Charles expounded on the sins of drunkenness, blasphemy, greed, and other gross transgressions from which sinners are rescued. And then he reflected, "Oh! when such are saved—and there are scores, and scores, and scores, to our knowledge, now rejoicing in Christ, who have found peace in this house, though once the chief of sinners—when such are saved, we say of each one of them, 'Is not this a brand plucked out of the fire?'" *MTP* 57:30–31.

9. Charles was likely referring to the danger of self-righteousness and trusting in outward religion, rather than understanding the spiritual nature of God's law. He said, "They are double-distilled in their refinement, they are unutterably holy and free from hypocrisy, their heart all the while loathing the plan of salvation, and rejecting the grace of God, because they believe that they are as good as they need be. To talk to them of crying, 'God be merciful to me a sinner,' is to insult them. Have they not been baptized? Have they not been confirmed? Have they not gone through all the means? All must be right with them, they are so good; who could think of finding fault with them? Now, if ever such people as these are saved from this terrible disease of self-righteousness, we should have to, say indeed, "Is not this a brand plucked out of the fire?" *MTP* 57:31–32.

10. "It is God's design that his wonderful works should be remembered.... Do you remember your conversion, beloved friend? Peradventure, you were a great and open sinner, and the change in you was so remarkable that you can easily recollect the time when it occurred, and it would not be possible for Satan himself to make you doubt that such a change did happen to you. You remember, my brother, when the load of your guilt was removed from your burdened heart. I can imagine that I could forget my own name, and that I could forget my own sons, but I think I never could, under any circumstances, forget the day when I began to sing to my dear Lord and Saviour." *MTP* 49:445–46.

243.   Ps. 119. 122.   Christ our Surety.

The 27th verse of Heb. 7th Supplies a comment on this text. These are the only two places in which a surety between God & man is mentioned — but though spoken of sparingly it is none the less important.

I. Consider wherein Christ is a Surety.
II. What as a surety he engaged to do.
III. What benefits flow to us through his suretyship.

× ×

I   Consider in what sense Jesus is a Surety.

1. Not for his Father — to us — For God is so true, his word & oath so firm that unbelief need not wish for a surety, & indeed it would not be an assistance to our faith since he who who doubts the Father would doubt the Son. —

2. Not as promising in our behalf. He is not bound to see that we perform obligations. Nor bound with us to help. For he knows well enough that we cannot pay a farthing, even if we would —

3. But he is our surety by taking all our debts upon himself — standing in our stead. Promising to do what we ought to have done we will illustrate it — from instances in ~~Scripture~~ the world. A Son about to set up in business has little money, but his father says — set the goods to my account, let him have the goods & send me the bill.

CHRIST OUR SURETY
Psalm 119:122[1]

"Be surety for thy servant for good: let not the proud oppress me."

The 22nd verse of Heb. 7th [s]upplies a comment on this text.[2] These are the only two places in which a surety between God and man is mentioned. But though spoken of sparingly it is none the less important.

I. CONSIDER WHEREIN CHRIST IS A SURETY.[3]

II. WHAT AS A SURETY HE ENGAGED TO DO.

III. WHAT BENEFITS FLOW TO US THROUGH HIS SURETYSHIP.

x x x x x x x x x x x x x x x x x x x x x x x x x x x x x x x x x x x x x

I. CONSIDER IN WHAT SENSE JESUS IS A SURETY.

1. Not for his Father, [but] to us.[4] For God is so true, his word and oath so firm, that unbelief need not wish for a surety.[5] And indeed, it would not be an assistance to our faith since he who doubts the Father would doubt the Son.[6]

2. Not as promising in our behalf. He is not bound to see that we perform obligations, nor bound with us to help.[7] For he knows well enough that we cannot pay a farthing,[8] even if we would.

3. But he is our surety by taking all our debts upon himself. Standing in our stead.

   Promising to do what we ought to have done.[9] We will illustrate it — from instances in ~~Scripture~~ the world.

   A son about to set up in business has little money, but his father says, ["]Set the goods to my account. Let him have the goods and send me the bill.["][10]

A poor man is in prison for debt & must ever lie there unless some one pay it — A Howard comes in & bids his creditor loose him & accept him as his surety for his debt. —

Damon in prison must die, he wishes to see his children — Pythias is chained for him & engages to die in his stead if he does not return.

II. What as a Surety he engaged to do.
Not more than he could do — for he is God
Not more than he will do — for he is faithful.

1. He has promised to give the law a perfect righteousness. This was our debt — but he has taken it away, cancelled it for ever.

2. He promised to satisfy justice for our debt of punishment. Just as Paul said to Philemon concerning Onesimus. Set it to my account. This he has done for all believers.

3. He has engaged to bear all the elect to glory. Judah said he would bear the blame if he did not bring back Benjamin. Jacob had to be responsible for the sheep. So Jesus is bound by covenant to save every believer.

III. What blessings flow to us through his Suretyship.

1. Complete Pardon — for the punishment is now transferred from us to him — we are as if we had passed the whole measure of pain in hell & were therefore free.

A poor man is in prison for debt and must ever lie there unless some one pay[s] it.[11] A Howard[12] comes in and bids his creditor loose him and accept him as his surety for his debt.

Damon in prison must die. He wishes to see his children. Pythias is chained for him and engages to die in his stead if he does not return.[13]

II. WHAT AS A SURETY HE ENGAGED TO DO.

Not more than he could do–for he is God. Not more than he will do–for he is faithful.

1. He has promised to give the law a perfect righteousness.[14] This was our debt but he has taken it away, cancelled it for ever.

2. He promised to satisfy justice for our debt of punishment.[15] Just as Paul said to Philemon concerning Onesimus. Set it to my account.[16] This [Christ] has done for all believers.

3. He has engaged to bear all the elect to glory.[17] Judah said he would bear the blame if he did not bring back Benjamin.[18] Jacob had to be responsible for the sheep.[19] So Jesus is bound by covenant to save every believer.

III. WHAT BLESSINGS FLOW TO US THROUGH HIS SURETYSHIP.

1. Complete Pardon. For the punishment is now transferred from us to him.[20] We are as if we had passed the whole measure of pain in hell and were therefore free.

2. Complete justification. What he does for us is counted ours so that now, we are not only considered as sinless but as meritorious.
3. Freedom from fear — Peace — No bailiff can arrest us — 'tis paid — we have no ground for despondency or terror —
4. Everlasting security — for now we are safe for ever if the whole is gone.

How foolish not to seek this surety. — How dangerous to delay, lest death come and God demand his due & we nothing to pay. Eternity of woe will not pay it, a Life of Holiness cannot pay it. Tears, groans & prayers cannot pay it.
Faith looks at Jesus & desires no other means of paying — — Trust him then.
    Lord aid me

419.

CHRIST OUR SURETY—*Psalm 119:122*

2. Complete Justification. What he does for us is counted ours, so that now we are not only considered as sinless but as meritorious.[21]

3. Freedom from fear. Peace. No bailiff can arrest us. 'Tis paid. We have no ground for despondency or terror.

4. Everlasting security. For now we are safe for ever if the whole is gone.

How foolish not to seek this surety. How dangerous to delay, lest death come and God demand his due and we [have] nothing to pay. [An] Eternity of woe will not pay it. A life of Holiness cannot pay it. Tears, groans, and prayers cannot pay it.

Faith looks at Jesus and desires no other means of paying. Trust him then.

Lord aid me.

419.

1. It appears that Charles did not preach another sermon on the text of Ps 119:122.

2. Hebrews 7:22, "By so much was Jesus made a surety of a better testament."

3. In writing this sermon, Charles was likely influenced by John Gill. See Gill's chapter, "Of Christ the Surety of the Covenant," in John Gill, *A Body of Doctrinal Divinity; Or, A System of Evangelical Truths, Deduced from the Sacred Scriptures. In Two Volumes*, vol. 1 (London: printed for the author and sold by George Keith, 1769, The Spurgeon Library), 383–89. Hereafter, *BDD*. For an additional time where Charles referred to Christ as the surety of the covenant, see "The Nail in a Sure Place" (Sermon 236).

4. Gill wrote, "[Christ] is not the Surety for his Father, to his people, engaging that the promises made by him in covenant shall be fulfilled. . . . Such is the faithfulness of God that has promised, that there needs no surety for him; his faithfulness is sufficient, which he will not suffer to fail; he is God, that cannot lie, nor deny himself; there is no danger of his breaking his word, and not fulfilling his promise, which may be depended on. And strongly confided in." Gill, *BDD* 1:383–84.

5. Cf. Heb 6:13–18.   6. Cf. John 14:9–11; 1 John 2:23.

7. Gill wrote, "Now none of these things are to be supposed in Christ's suretyship. -- 1. He is not a mere accessory to the obligation of his people for payment of their debts; he and they are not engaged in one joint-bond for payment; he has taken their whole debt upon himself, as the apostle *Paul* did in the case of *Onesimus*; and he has paid it off, and entirely discharged it alone. -- 2. Nor was any such condition made in his suretyship-engagements for his people, that they should pay if they were able; for God the Father, to whom Christ became a Surety, knew, and he himself, the Surety, knew full well, when this suretyship was entered into, that they were not able to pay, and never would be; yea, that it was impossible for them, in their circumstances, ever to pay." Gill, *BDD* 1:384, italics in the original.

8. "1. The fourth of a penny; the smallest English coin. 2. Copper money. 3. It is used sometimes in a sense hyperbolical: as, it is not worth a *farthing*; or proverbial." Johnson's *Dictionary*, s.v. "Farthing," italics in original.

9. Gill wrote, "Christ is in such sense a Surety . . . one that promises out and out, absolutely engages to pay another's debt; takes another's obligation, and transfers it to himself, and by this act dissolves the former obligation, and enters into a new one . . . so that the obligation no longer lies on the principal debtor, but he is set free, and the Surety is under the obligation, as if he was the principal debtor, or the guilty person." Gill, *BDD* 1:385.

10. Charles illustrated the role of a surety during a sermon on Psalm 10, "The man is so deeply in debt that he cannot pay his creditors even a farthing in the pound; but here is someone who can pay everything that the debtor owes, and he says to him, 'I will stand as security for you; I will be bondsman for you; I will give full satisfaction to all your creditors, and discharge all your debts.' There is no person who is thus deeply in debt, who would not be glad to know of such a surety, both able and willing to stand in his stead, and to discharge all his responsibilities. If the surety said to this poor debtor, 'Will you make over all your liabilities to me? Will you sign this document, empowering me to take all your debts upon myself, and to be responsible for you? Will you let me be your bondsman and surety?' 'Ah!' the poor man would reply, 'that I will, most gladly.' That is just what spiritually poor men have done to the Lord Jesus Christ, -- committed their case, with all their debts and liabilities, into the hands of the Lord Jesus Christ, and he has undertaken all the responsibility for them." *MTP* 53:472.

11. Charles was referring to the former practice under British law that permitted a debtor to be imprisoned in jail until either a surety was provided for, the sentence was served, or the debt itself was paid. On this point, the *Encyclopædia Britannica* acknowledges the "evils" of the practice, which "have been so graphically described by Dickens," and notes with a tone of approval the passing of the Debtors Act 1869, which essentially eliminated the institution. *Encyclopædia Britannica*, 11th ed. (1910), s.v. "debt."

12. This sermon was included in Charles's autobiography but "a Howard" was substituted with "A philanthropist, like John Howard." *Autobiography* 1:278. John Howard was a Christian philanthropist who worked for prison reform. Charles referenced Howard in a few of his sermons, once paraphrasing Howard's diary: "John Howard spent his time in visiting the gaols [jails] and going from one haunt of fever to another[;] he was asked how he could find any ground of happiness when he was living in miserable Russian villages, or dwelling in discomfort

in an hospital or a gaol. Mr. Howard's answer was very beautiful. 'I hope,' said he, 'I have sources of enjoyment which depend not upon the particular spot I inhabit. A rightly cultivated mind, under the power of divine grace and the exercise of a benevolent disposition affords a ground of satisfaction that is not to be affected by *heres* and *theres.*'" *MTP* 10:185, italics in the original. The actual quote can be found in Thomas Taylor's biography of John Howard, which resides in Charles's personal library. Thomas Taylor, *Memoirs of John Howard, ESQ., F.R.S., the Christian Philanthropist* (London: John Hatchard and Son, 1836, The Spurgeon Library), 398. In 1875, Charles wrote, "Everyone who gives up self for God's glory is Jesus in miniature. Look at John Howard going about among the dungeons of Europe, spying out poor prisoners to do them good. Is not that Christ over again, with glad tidings for the captives?" *MTP* 21:454. Clearly, Howard served as a fitting example of Christian service in Charles's eyes.

13. Charles was probably referring to the Greek legend of Damon and Pythias. According to *Encyclopædia Britannica*, Damon was a Pythagorean along with his friend Pythias. In the story, Pythias had been "[c]ondemned to death by Dionysius the Elder (or younger) of Syracuse." However, Damon pledges his life as a surety for Pythias so that he can see to his family first. Pythias returns before the time of execution and "to express his admiration of their fidelity, [Dionysius] released both the friends and begged to be admitted into their friendship." *Encyclopædia Britannica*, 11th ed. (1910), s.v. "Damon."

14. Cf. Heb 7:18–22. Gill wrote, "There is a twofold debt paid by Christ, as the Surety of his people; the one is a debt of obedience to the law of God; this he engaged to do, when he said, *Lo, I come to do thy will; thy law is within my heart;* and accordingly he was made under the law, and yielded perfect obedience to it, by which his people are made righteous." Gill, *BDD* 1:387, italics in the original.

15. Gill wrote, "The other is a debt of punishment, incurred through failure of obedience in them; the curse of the law he has endured, the penalty of it, death; and by paying both these debts, the whole righteousness of the law is fulfilled in his people, considered in him their Head and Surety." Gill, *BDD* 1:387.

16. Cf. Phlm 18–19.

17. Gill wrote, "Another thing which Christ as a Surety engaged to do, was to bring all the elect safe to glory; this may be illustrated by *Judah's* suretyship for *Benjamin*;

thus expressed to his father, *I will be surety for him; of my hand shalt thou require him; if I bring him not unto thee, and set him before thee, then let me bear the blame for ever*, Gen. xliii. 9. And thus Christ became a Surety to his divine Father, for his beloved *Benjamins*, the chosen of God, and precious; as he asked them of his Father, and they were given into his hands, to be preserved by him, that none of them might be lost." Gill, *BDD* 1:388, italics in the original.

18. Cf. Gen 43:8–10.

19. Cf. Gen 30:31–33. Gill continued, "Christ engaged to *bring* his people to his Father; this was the work proposed to him, and which he agreed to do; *to bring Jacob again to him, and to restore the preserved of Israel*, Isa. xlix. 5, 6. to recover the lost sheep, to ransom them out of the hands of him that was stronger than they." Gill, *BDD* 1:388, italics in the original.

20. Cf. Isa 53:5–6; 1 Pet 2:24; 3:18.

21. Cf. 2 Cor 5:21. Charles believed in a double imputation that takes place in our justification. "Picture the saint in Christ, robed in Christ's righteousness, wearing Christ's nature, bearing Christ's palm of victory, sitting on Christ's throne, wearing Christ's crown. And yet this is our privilege! He wore my crown of thorns; I wear his crown, the crown of glory. He wore my dress, nay, rather, he wore my nakedness when he died upon the cross, I wear his robes, the royal robes of the King of kings. He bore my shame; I bear his honor. He endured my sufferings to this end that my joy may be full, and that his joy may be fulfilled in me. He laid in the grave that I might rise from the dead and that I may dwell in him, and all this he comes again to give me, to make it sure to me and to all that love his appearing, to show that all his people shall enter into their inheritance." *NPSP* 6:195.

Matt. XXII. 12.   He was speechless.

This man had gained admittance into the outer church but had not the necessary inward qualification. None could discover him but the King, he can see where the worm is, he discerns the hypocrite.

He was no doubt as good by nature as any of the others, perhaps his clothes were better, but he could talk away fast enough & perhaps knew more than any one at the table, but when the King came in — that one question so staggered him that he was speechless.

What made him speechless? By God's help this shall be our question.

1. The Question staggered him —

When Adam & Eve sinned they had something to say when accused, it was worse than nothing however — they had however a different kind of question proposed, It was about their nakedness by fallen nature — & they knew nothing of the wedding garment, moreover that was on earth.

Cain too was impudent — but that was on earth & the question different —

Matt. VII. 22. Some said Lord, Lord &c. but these thought they had the robe, had this question been asked — silence would have prevented an answer.

In the three parables Matt. XXV. all of them answered but this question had never been

HE WAS SPEECHLESS[1]
Matthew 22:12[2]

"And he saith unto him, Friend, how camest thou in hither not having a wedding garment? And he was speechless."

This man had gained admittance into the outer church but had not the necessary inward qualification.[3]

None could discover him but the king. He can see where the worm is. He discerns the hypocrite. [The man] was no doubt as good by nature as any of the others, perhaps his clothes were better. ~~but~~ He could talk away fast enough and perhaps knew more than any one at the table, but when the king came in, that one question so staggered him that he was speechless.

What made him speechless? By God's help this shall be our question.

1. THE QUESTION STAGGERED HIM.

When Adam and Eve sinned they had something to say when accused.[4] It was worse than nothing however. They had however a different kind of question proposed. It was about their nakedness by fallen nature and they knew nothing of the wedding garment.[5] [M]oreover[,] that was on earth.

Cain too was impudent, but that was on earth and the question different.[6]

Matt. VII. 22.[7] Some said ["]Lord, Lord["] etc. but these thought they had the robe, had this question been asked, silence would have prevented an answer.

In the three ~~chapters~~ parables [from] Matt. XXV. all of them answered but this question had never been put to them else they had been silent too.

2. His real reasons he dare not mention. Either he thought himself good enough without this robe — his coat was good, in fact very grand, he was a gentleman, but he dare not tell the King this.

Or he despised the robe, laughed at it's shape & material & thought it degrading to wear it — he dare not say this to the King.

Or he had come in out of bravado, to see whether the King would notice & punish him, this he dare not say.

Or he meant to have put it on but the King came in unexpectedly, but as he had had time enough. this he dare not say.

3. Fear Silenced him — the awful bearing majestic carriage & dread look of the King quite terrified him — So at the judgment day — the scene shall be so grand, so awful, so terrific, that no strength shall be left in the wicked. The judge shall appear so gloriously dreadful that impiety once so brave shall shake as a leaf. Heaven, Hell, Angels, Devils, Judgment, God are no trifling matters.

put to them[,][8] [or] else they [would have] been silent too.

2. HIS REAL REASONS HE DARE NOT MENTION.

Either he thought himself good enough without this robe—his coat was good, in fact very grand, he was a gentleman, but he dare not tell the king this.[9]

Or he despised the robe, laughed at its shape and material, and thought it degrading to wear it. He dare not say this to the king.

Or he had come in out of bravado, to see whether the king would notice and punish him. This he dare not say.

Or he meant to have put it on but the king came in unexpectedly. But as he had had time enough, this he dare not say.[10]

3. FEAR SILENCED HIM.

The awful bearing[,][11] majestic carriage[,][12] and dread look of the king quite terrified him.[13] So at the judgment day, the scene shall be so grand, so awful, so terrific, that no strength shall be left in the wicked. The judge shall appear so gloriously dreadful that impiety[,] once so brave[,] shall shake as a leaf.[14] Heaven, Hell, Angels, Devils, Judgment, [and] God are no trifling matters.

4. His many iniquities must silence him or at least it will do at the judgment all sinners.

He now saw his vileness, raggedness & beggarly condition, while the whiteness of the robe shone out most wondrously. —   So will sinners see their own state at last. They do not believe it now, but then it will come before them. Memory will be so strengthened that sins now forgotten will have a resurrection.

If a man is not guilty in one point, he will be in another — crimes wave on wave will overwhelm his excuses.

The sins of his youth, manhood, age, will haunt him like spectres.

The enormity of sin will appear & its desert of hell will be as clear as noonday.

Millions on Millions will rise up in his memory of sins of various hues & colours.

The Commandments discharging themselves at him crying Damn him! Damn him!

Well may his tongue refuse her office.

5. The many witnesses in court will shut his mouth.

The murderer shall see the murdered & the bloody knife — the night, the grove shall all be clear before him. —

The thief shall have no way of hiding

HE WAS SPEECHLESS—*Matthew 22:12*

4. **HIS MANY INIQUITIES MUST SILENCE HIM OR AT LEAST IT WILL DO [SO] AT THE JUDGMENT [OF] ALL SINNERS.**

   He now saw his vileness, raggedness, and beggarly condition while the whiteness of the robe shone out most wondrously. So will sinners see their own state at last. They do not believe it now, but then it will come before them. Memory will be so strengthened that sins now forgotten will have a resurrection.

   If a man is not guilty in one point he will be in another. Crimes[,] wave on wave[,] will overwhelm his excuses.

   The sins of his youth, manhood, [and] age will haunt him like spectres.[15] The enormity of sin will appear and its desert of hell will be as clear as noonday.

   Millions on Millions will rise up in his memory of sins of various hues and colours.

   The Commandments discharging[16] themselves at him crying, ["]Damn him! Damn him!["]

   > Well may his tongue refuse her office.[17]

5. **THE MANY WITNESSES IN COURT WILL SHUT HIS MOUTH.**

   The murderer shall see the murdered and the bloody knife. The night, the grove shall all be clear before him.

   The thief shall have no way of hiding

the crime shall be so clearly laid before him that his conscience must admit it.
Angels will be no mean witnesses against the ungodly for they doubtless see much.
Devils too tempt men & lead them astray & then anxious to see men condemned they will turn loud accusers.
Bad Men & Women will accuse each other in the vain hope of pardon as King's evidence or in hatred since all evil love like sweet milk turns sour in lightning storms.
Parents who prayed for their children Teachers who taught them the way. Ministers who warned them all will be witnesses. & say Amen to their condemnation — while
God himself will witness secret things.
Remember.
6. The man was changed.
Memory was strengthened. Judgment & Reason had sway. Conscience is wakened. Perceptions are clear. Knowledge is great
Lord. Lord Help. Help for Jesus sake

420.

the crime. [It] shall be so clearly laid before him that his conscience must admit it.

Angels will be no mean witnesses against the ungodly for they doubtless see much.[18]

Devils too tempt men and lead them astray. And then anxious to see men condemned they will turn [into] loud accusers.

Bad Men and Women will accuse each other in the vain hope of pardon as King's evidence, or in hatred since all evil love[,] like sweet milk[,] turns sour in lightning storms.[19]

Parents who prayed for their children.

Teachers who taught them the way.

Ministers who warned them all will be witnesses and say Amen[20] to their condemnation, while

God himself will witness secret things.

>Remember:

6. THE MAN WAS CHANGED.

Memory was strengthened. Judgment and Reason had sway. Conscience is wakened. Perceptions are clear. Knowledge is great.[21]

>Lord. Lord Help. Help for Jesus['s] sake.

420.

1. Charles originally misspelled this title, writing "He Was Speecless" instead of "He Was Speechless." However, it appears that Charles caught the error in a later editorial review of this Notebook because the *h* was correctly added in pencil with a caret.

2. It appears that Charles preached two later sermons on this verse and its context: "The Wedding Garment" (*MTP* 17, Sermon 976) and "What Is the Wedding Garment?" (*MTP* 34, Sermon 2024). However, there does not appear to be significant overlap in the structure of the later sermons. Thus, while the content of the parable itself is repeated, the later sermons do not appear to have been influenced by this sermon.

3. Charles believed that membership in the local church was no guarantee of the genuineness of a person's salvation. Rather, the professing believer should look for signs of inward change, evidenced by outward works of holiness and love for God. This was the wedding garment in Charles's later sermons. "What is that which we must have in connection with our Lord's marriage or be cast out for ever? I think I may say plainly that it must signify a distinguishing mark of grace. . . . True members of the church of God wear a distinguishing mark. If you are not different from other people, you have no right in the church of God. . . . Is there, then, a something about you which the Lord in love has given you? Do you differ from others, not in natural attainments, but in spiritual grace? Does the difference mainly lie in what God himself has done for you? That is the question involved in the symbol of the wedding garment. Do you differ from what you used to be[?] Do you differ from what you were years ago? Do you differ from those with whom you used to associate, so that you seek other company and turn aside from those who once were charming fellows to you? If so, you have on the wedding garment. It is a distinguishing mark." *MTP* 34:282–83. See also *MTP* 17:98–100.

4. Cf. Gen 3:12–13.

5. Cf. Gen 3:11.

6. Cf. Gen 4:9.

7. Matthew 7:22, "Many will say to me in that day, Lord, Lord, have we not prophesied in thy name? And in thy name have cast out devils? And in thy name done many wonderful works?"

8. Cf. Matthew 25. Charles was referring to the parables of the ten virgins (vv. 1–13), the three servants (vv. 14–30), and the sheep and the goats (vv. 31–46).

9. Charles extended the clothing metaphor to illustrate different excuses people might give for rejecting Christ's righteousness, including self-righteousness, a low view of Christ's righteousness, defiance of God's commands, and delayed obedience. But all these excuses simply leave the man speechless before the King.

10. "The reason why he was speechless was because, even if he could have spoken and been free from terror, there was nothing to be said. He could not cry, 'Lord, I did not know it.' He saw all the rest with wedding garments on. He could not say, 'Lord, I could not get a wedding garment': each one had received a garment gratis, and he might have received the same. He could not say, 'Lord, I was pushed in here by somebody else.' No, he had willingly chosen to come, and to defy the rule." *MTP* 34:287.

11. "Gesture; mien; behavior." Johnson's *Dictionary*, s.v. "Bearing."

12. "Behaviour; personal manners. . . . Conduct; measures; practices." Johnson's *Dictionary*, s.v. "Carriage."

13. "But why was the man speechless? I answer once more, because it was the king himself who spoke to him. Ah! if I speak to you, what am I but flesh and blood? You do not mind me! But if the King himself were here today, and he said to any one of you, 'Friend, how camest thou in hither not having a wedding garment?' the tone of his voice, the glory of his presence, would flash in upon your hearts, you would be obliged to feel it, and you could not invent an answer." *MTP* 34:287.

14. Cf. Rev 19:11–16.

15. "Apparition; appearance of persons dead." Johnson's *Dictionary*, s.v. "Spectre."

16. Here this likely means something akin to these definitions in Johnson: "To throw off any thing collected or accumulated; to give vent to any thing; to let fly. It is used of any thing violent or sudden" or "To unload a gun." Johnson's *Dictionary*, s.v. "To Discharge."

17. Cf. Rom 3:19.

18. Concerning Matt 22:13, Gill wrote, "*Then said the king to his servants*, . . . by whom are meant . . . the angels, who will bind up the tares in bundles, and burn them, and gather out of Christ's kingdom, all that offend and do iniquity; and sever the wicked from the just, and tie them in the manner here directed to." Gill, *An Exposition of the New Testament* 1:229, italics in the original.

19. Charles's note about lightning storms curdling milk was based on anecdotal evidence. For example, the 1861 *Friends' Intelligencer* noted: "Distant thunder, for instance, will curdle milk and stop the fermentation of brewer's yeast, while active lightning putrefies the fresh meat hanging on a butcher's stall." An Association of Friends, ed., *Friends' Intelligencer* (Philadelphia: William W. Moore, 1861), 249.

20. Cf. Acts 20:26.

21. In this final point, Charles was likely calling for any who were experiencing conviction of sin, characterized by these effects, to respond with repentance. "Have I any one here in such a condition of heart, that while he has been sinning by making a false profession, and knows it, yet he sullenly refuses to confess his fault? Yield thee, man! Yield at once. Fall at the King's feet at once. Even if you are not a hypocrite, if you have any suspicion that you are, fall down and say, 'My King, make me sincere; I submit myself to thy will, and am ready to put on the wedding badge; if there is any method by which I can honor thy Son, I cavil not at it; let me wear his colors, and be known by all men to be truly a lover of the great Prince.'" *MTP* 17:106.

Matt XIII. 31.32. The grain of mustard seed.
By this parable is represented the growth of Christ's
kingdom in the world & in the heart.
The Last sense I will dwell upon. & remark

I. That the work of grace is small at first.
  Faith, is at first weak & tottering.
  Hope, is not yet matured into confidence.
  Courage, as yet is but in the bud.
  Knowledge, consists of only the elements.

II. Though small there are signs of its reality.
1. It is seed, there is life & vitality in it.
2. It is seed sown by the man Jesus & him alone.
3. It is in prepared soil, ploughing, convictions &c.

III. There are means for promoting growth.
1. The sweet air of the Spirit.
2. The waterings out of the Bible.
3. Diggings by troubles & providences.
4. Sprouting in prayer is caused by heat of love.

IV. It grows into a tree. The birds
of Faith, Hope, charity, humility &c come
& lodge in the branches & sweet praise
ascends to God on High. —

422. 423. 521.

THE GRAIN *of* MUSTARD SEED
Matthew 13:31–32[1]

> "Another parable put he forth unto them, saying, The kingdom of heaven is like to a grain of mustard seed, which a man took, and sowed in his field: Which indeed is the least of all seeds: but when it is grown, it is the greatest among herbs, and becometh a tree, so that the birds of the air come and lodge in the branches thereof."

By this parable is represented the growth of Christ's kingdom in the world and in the heart.[2]

The Last sense I will dwell upon and remark[:]

I. THAT THE WORK OF GRACE IS SMALL AT FIRST.

<u>Faith</u>, is at first weak and tottering.[3]

<u>Hope</u>, is not yet matured into confidence.

<u>Courage</u>, as yet is but in the bud.

<u>Knowledge</u>, consists of only the elements.

II. THOUGH SMALL THERE ARE SIGNS OF ITS REALITY.

1. It is seed, there is life and vitality in it.[4]
2. It is seed sown by <u>the man</u> Jesus and him alone.
3. It is in prepared soil, ploughing, convictions etc.[5]

III. THERE ARE MEANS FOR PROMOTING GROWTH.[6]

1. The sweet air of the Spirit.
2. The waterings out of the Bible.[7]
3. Diggings by troubles and providences.
4. Sprouting in prayer is caused by heat of love.[8]

IV. IT GROWS INTO A TREE.

The birds of Faith, Hope, charity, humility etc.[9] come and lodge in the branches and sweet praise ascends to God on High.

422. 423. 521.

1. It appears that Charles did not preach another sermon on the text of Matt 13:31–32.

2. Matthew Henry, who may have inspired Charles on this point, believed that the sign of the presence of the kingdom of God in this world is the church, the community of people who know God's work of grace in their hearts. Henry wrote, "The scope of this parable is to show, that the beginnings of the gospel *would be small, but that its latter end would greatly increase.* In this way the gospel church, the kingdom of God among us, would be *set up in the world*; in this way the work of grace in the heart, *the kingdom of God within us*, would be carried on in particular persons." Matthew Henry, *An Exposition of the New Testament,* vol. 1 (London: Thomas C. Jack, n.d., The Spurgeon Library), 298, italics in the original. In this sermon, Charles focused not on the growth of the church but on God's work of grace in the heart of the believer.

3. Charles's autobiographical account of his conversion is full of confidence and joy in the saving work of Christ (*Autobiography* 1:105–15). However, his personal letters reveal his personal struggles following his conversion. Writing to his father a few weeks after his conversion, Charles confessed, "Now I see Him, I can firmly trust to Him for my eternal salvation. Yet soon I doubt again; then I am sorrowful; again faith appears, and I become confident of my interest in Him." *Autobiography* 1:117. Charles similarly described his spiritual struggles to his mother in another letter: "I have been in the miry Slough of Despond. . . . I pray as if I did not pray, hear as if I did not hear, and read as if I did not read, – such is my deadness and coldness." *Autobiography* 1:118–19.

4. In his exposition on the Gospel of Matthew, Charles wrote, "The results of the divine life in the soul are by no means little; but great graces, great projects, and great deeds are produced by it. . . . We know not to what our own inner life will come. It has an expanding power within it, and it will burst every bond, and grow to a thing which will cast shadow, yield fruit, and lend shelter. If the Lord has planted the incorruptible seed within, its destiny is a great one. Good Master, hasten this blessed development. We have seen nearly enough of the mustard seed; now let us see the tree." Charles Spurgeon, *The Gospel of the Kingdom: A Popular Exposition of The Gospel According to Matthew* (London: Passmore and Alabaster, 1893), 104.

5. Cf. Matt 13:8–9; Mark 4:8–9; Luke 8:8. Charles mixed parables on this point, drawing on the parable of the Sower. Remarking on this parable in another sermon, Charles described how God prepares soil: "Of the good soil as you will, mark, we have but one in four. Ah! Would to God there were one in four of us here, with well-prepared hearts to receive the Word. The ground was good; not that it was good by nature, but it had been made good by grace. God had ploughed it; he had stirred it up with the plough of conviction, and there it lay in ridge and furrow as it should be. And when the Gospel was preached, the heart received it, for the man said, 'That's just the Christ I want. Mercy!' . . . So that the preaching of the gospel was THE thing to give comfort to this disturbed and ploughed soil." *NPSP* 6:179–80.

6. Against the antinomianism prevalent in his congregation, Charles was careful to emphasize the use of means for spiritual growth.

7. "*The Lord's people usually get this watering through instrumentality.* God does not speak to us out of heaven with his own voice—perhaps the thunder might appal us; he doth not write texts of Scripture with his own finger in letters of fire across the sky, but he waters us by instrumentality, by his Word written and his Word preached, or otherwise uttered by his servants." *MTP* 11:231, italics in the original.

8. "Prayer comes spontaneously from those who abide in Jesus, even as certain oriental trees, without pressure, shed their fragrant gums. Prayer is the natural outgushing of a soul in communion with Jesus. Just as the leaf and the fruit will come out of the vine-branch without any conscious effort on the part of the branch, but simply because of its living union with the stem, so prayer buds, and blossoms, and fruits out of souls abiding in Jesus." *MTP* 34:14–15.

9. Cf. 1 Cor 13:13; Gal 5:22–23.

246. Zech. IX. 12. — The Stronghold of Refuge.

The cities of refuge were so often and solemnly mentioned by God to the Jews that none can doubt their spiritual signification. This passage in Zechariah clearly relates to the cities of Refuge. —

I. The Exhortation is to "prisoners of hope."
"Prisoners." condemned to die, lying in the dungeon, bound hand & foot by your own depravity, locked in by the law & Satan — trembling, groaning, dying. "of Hope" despair not, there is a lattice in the dungeon, look through it! — whom see you? Jesus breaks the doors, opens them wide & setting you at large cries. "Turn ye to the Stronghold" Let me exhort you to flee — Listen.

II. Some talk about the City of Refuge.
1. As the cities of Refuge were appointed by God, so is Jesus the Saviour, set apart as our Refuge.
2. As the cities were built on Hills or had high towers — so is Jesus exalted on high.
3. As the gates were open night & day so are Jesus' arms ever ready to receive sinners.
4. As foreigners or jews were alike received so are all coming men welcome.
5. As the very suburbs were safe. — so if thou touch the hem of his garment, thou shalt be saved. —

THE STRONGHOLD *of* REFUGE
Zechariah 9:12[1]

"Turn you to the strong hold, ye prisoners of hope: even to day do I declare that I will render double unto thee."

The cities of refuge were so often and solemnly mentioned by God[2] to the Jews that none can doubt their spiritual signification. This passage in Zechariah clearly relates to the cities of Refuge.[3]

I. THE EXHORTATION IS TO *"prisoners of hope."*

"Prisoners." Condemned to die, lying in the dungeon, bound hand and foot by your own depravity,[4] locked in by the law and Satan[5] – trembling, groaning, dying.

"of Hope" despair not, there is a lattice in the dungeon. Look through it! Whom see you? Jesus breaks the doors, opens them wide, and setting you at large cries, "Turn ye to the Stronghold."

Let me exhort you to flee. Listen.

II. SOME TALK ABOUT THE CITY OF REFUGE.

1. As the cities of Refuge were appointed by God,[6] so is Jesus the Saviour set apart as our Refuge.[7]
2. As the cities were built on hills or had high towers, so is Jesus exalted on high.[8]
3. As the gates were open night and day, so are Jesus'[s] arms ever ready to receive sinners.[9]
4. As foreigners or jews were alike received[10] so are all coming men welcome.[11]
5. As the very suburbs[12] were safe, so if thou touch the hem of his garment, thou shalt be saved.[13]

II. Some remarks on the privileges of the city.
1. The greatest privilege in its charter is that the manslayer cannot be touched there — in the old city the guilty were tried & condemned but in this you will be made innocent, even though guilty.
2. For company you will have the Levites who may teach and instruct you, the servants of God.
3. You will be housed, nourished, & satisfied all at free cost — Jesus shall feed you.
4. You will enjoy perfect peace for no weapon may be made in any city of refuge.
5. You will recover your lost inheritance through the death of the High-priest.
III. Some information as to the Road.
1. It is not far off — a man could run there in half a day — the word is nigh thee.
2. The road is easy — the road was carefully mended, made very smooth — very wide, bridges made over rivers, hills levelled &c — what doth hinder?
3. The direction is clear — The Bible like a handpost points ☞ Refuge. Refuge — all difficulties it answers & ministers are willing to guide you.
4. It is away from your sins; not in your sins — Repentance & Faith are the road he that runneth is safe. —

THE STRONGHOLD OF REFUGE—*Zechariah 9:12*

III. SOME REMARKS ON THE PRIVILEGES OF THE CITY.

1. The greatest privilege in its charter is that the manslayer cannot be touched there.[14] In the old city the guilty were tried and condemned but in this [city] you will be made innocent, even though guilty.[15]

2. For company you will have the Levites who may teach and instruct you,[16] the servants of God.[17]

3. You will be housed, nourished, and satisfied all at free cost. Jesus shall feed you.[18]

4. You will enjoy perfect peace for no weapon may be made in any city of refuge.[19]

5. You will recover your lost inheritance through the death of the High-priest.[20]

III. SOME INFORMATION AS TO THE ROAD.

1. It is not far off. A man could run there in half a day. The word is nigh [unto] thee.[21]

2. The road is easy. The road was carefully mended, made very smooth, very wide bridges made over rivers, hills levelled etc. What doth hinder?[22]

3. The direction is clear. The Bible like a handpost points: ☞ **Refuge. Refuge.**[23] All difficulties it answers[,] and ministers are willing to guide you.

4. It is away <u>from</u> your sins, not <u>in</u> your sins. Repentance and Faith are the road. He that runneth is safe.

IV. I would urge you to run.
1. Even to-day — for the avenger pursues, he is perhaps nigh at hand run then.
2. To-day — for he is swift of foot & you need a good start lest he overtake you.
3. God promises to give you *double* for all the pains of running — when indeed it is for your advantage — not his — yet he will give you double for your trouble.
4. Double for all you leave you shall receive — if it be pleasure or profit, you shall have double. aye. a thousand fold.

A Word of Warning. If you do not run you will rue it.
A Word of Advice. Run at once.
A Word of Comfort. Fear not exclusion.
A Word of Encouragement. God will help.

Oh may I & all my hearers.
find a Miklat in thee
Oh Jesus —

428

IV. I WOULD URGE YOU TO RUN.

1. <u>Even to day</u> for the avenger pursues,[24] he is perhaps nigh at hand[,] run then.
2. <u>To day</u>, for he is swift of foot and you need a good start lest he overtake you.
3. God promises to give you <u>double</u> for all the pains of running, when indeed it is for your advantage, not his. Yet he will give you double for your trouble.[25]
4. <u>Double</u> for all you leave you shall receive.[26] If it be pleasure or profit, you shall have double. Aye, a thousand fold.[27]

   A Word of Warning. If you do not run you will rue[28] it.

   A Word of Advice. Run at once.

   A word of comfort. Fear not exclusion.

   A word of encouragement. God will help.

   Oh may I and all my hearers find a Miklat[29] in thee.

   Oh Jesus.

428

1. It appears that Charles preached three later sermons on the text of Zech 9:11–12: "'Prisoners of Hope'" (*MTP* 49, Sermon 2839), "Prisoners Delivered" (*MTP* 50, Sermon 2883), and "Freedom Through Christ's Blood" (*MTP* 54, Sermon 3106). However, none of these sermons appears to contain enough overlapping content to indicate influence from this earlier sermon. Notably, it is only in this sermon that Charles spiritualized the city of refuge as a type of Christ, making it distinct from the later three.

2. Cf. Num 35:1–29.

3. Charles was not alone in this interpretation of Zech 9:12. John Gill also believed that this passage referenced Christ by means of the cities of refuge. Gill wrote: "*To turn to the strong hold*: by which is meant, not Judea, nor Jerusalem, nor the temple in it, nor the church of God; but rather the blessed God . . . and indeed a divine person is intended, even the Messiah, who is a strong hold for refuge, and was typified by the cities of refuge, whither the man-slayer fled, and was safe; to which the allusion may well be thought to be, since one of the names of the cities of refuge was Bezer, which signifies a fortress, or strong-hold; and comes from the same root as the word here used; and such who are enabled and encouraged to flee to Christ for refuge, are safe from vindictive justice, which is fully satisfied by the blood, righteousness, and atoning sacrifice of Christ." Gill, *An Exposition of the Books of the Prophets of the Old Testament* 2:690, italics in the original.

4. "It is a terrible mystery that man should be so great a fool, so mad a creature as to be held by cords apparently so feeble as the cords of his own sins. To be bound by reason is honourable; to be held by compulsion, if you cannot resist it, is at least not discreditable; but to be held simply by sin, by sin and nothing else, is a bondage which is disgraceful to the human name. It lowers man to the last degree, to think that he should want no fetter to hold him but the fetter of his own evil lusts and desires." *MTP* 16:91–92.

5. Cf. Gal 3:23–25; Eph 2:1–3.

6. Cf. Num 35:29.

7. Cf. Heb 6:18. This sermon seems to have been heavily influenced by Matthew Henry's work concerning the cities of refuge. Henry wrote, "The protection

which the man-slayer found in the city of refuge, was not owing to the strength of its walls, or gates, or bars, but purely to the divine appointment, so it is the word of the gospel that gives souls safety in Christ; *for him hath God the father sealed.*" Matthew Henry, *An Exposition on the Old and New Testament, Wherein Each Chapter Is Summed Up in its Contents; The Sacred Text Inserted at Large in Distinct Paragraphs; Each Paragraph Reduced to its Proper Heads; The Sense Given; and Largely Ilustrated with Practical Remarks and Observations. Forming the Most Complete Family Bible Ever Published*, vol. 1 (London: W. and J. Stratford, n.d., The Spurgeon Library), Num XXXV, italics in the original.

8. Cf. Acts 2:33; Phil 2:9–11.

9. Cf. Isa 60:11; Luke 15.

10. Cf. Num 35:15.

11. Cf. John 6:37. Henry wrote, "Even strangers and sojourners, though they were not native Israelites, might take benefit of these cities of refuge, *ver.* 15. So in Christ Jesus no difference is made between Greek and Jew, even the *sons of the stranger* that by faith fly to Christ shall be safe in him." Henry, *An Exposition on the Old and New Testament* 1: Num XXXV, italics in the original.

12. "1. Building without the walls of a city. 2. The confines; the outpart." *Johnson's Dictionary*, s.v. "Suburb."

13. Cf. Matt 9:20–22. Henry wrote, "Even the suburbs or borders of the city were a sufficient security to the offender, ver.26, 27. So there is virtue, even in the hem of Christ's garment, for the healing and saving of poor sinners." Henry, *An Exposition on the Old and New Testament* 1: Num XXXV.

14. Cf. Num 35:12.   15. Cf. Rom 4:5.

16. Henry wrote, "They were Levites' cities: it was a kindness to the poor prisoner, that though he might not go up to the place where the ark was, yet he was in the midst of Levites who would teach him the good knowledge of the Lord, and instruct him how to improve the providence he was now under: It might also be expected, that the Levites would comfort and encourage him, and bid him welcome; so it is the work of gospel-ministers to bid poor sinners welcome to

Christ, and to assist and counsel those that through grace are in him." Henry, *An Exposition on the Old and New Testament* 1: Num XXXV.

17. Charles was likely comparing the work of God's servants in Christ, either the pastors and elders or the congregation, to the work of the Levites.

18. Cf. Isa 55:1–3; John 6:35.

19. Cf. Isa 2:4; Matt 5:9.

20. Cf. Num 35:25–28; Heb 9:11–12. Henry wrote, "The high priest was to be looked upon as so great a blessing to his country, that when he died, their sorrow upon that occasion should swallow up all other resentments. The cities of refuge being all of them Levites' cities, and the high priest being the head of that tribe, and consequently having a peculiar dominion over those cities, those that were confined to them might properly be looked upon as his prisoners, and so his death must be their discharge; it was, as it were, at his suit that the delinquent was imprisoned, and therefore at his death it fell." Henry, *An Exposition on the Old and New Testament* 1: Num XXXVI.

21. Cf. Num 35:14; Rom 10:8–9. Charles originally wrote, "The word is nigh thee." For clarity, and also to preserve the style of Charles's English, the preposition "unto" has been added in the transcription.

22. Cf. Matt 11:28; John 14:6. Gill likely also influenced Charles in his study of the cities of refuge. Gill wrote, "The cities of refuge were of God's appointing; so Christ, as a Savior, and rock of refuge . . . they were open for all, at all times, as Christ is for all sinners . . . all impediments were removed out of the way of them, and plain directions to them given, as are in the gospel, and by ministers of it." John Gill, *An Exposition of the Old Testament, In which Are Recorded the Original of Mankind, of the Several Nations of the World, and of the Jewish Nation in Particular: The Lives of the Patriarchs of Israel; The Journey of the People from Egypt through the Wilderness to the Land of Canaan, and Their Settlement in that Land; Their Laws Moral, Ceremonial, and Judicial; Their Government and State under Judges and Kings; Their Several Captivities, and Their Sacred Books of Devotion. In the Exposition of which, It Is Attempted to Give an Account of the Several Books, and the Writers of Them; a Summary of Each Chapter; and Genuine Sense of Every Verse; and Throughout the Whole, the Original Text, and the Versions of it Are Inspected*

and Compared; Interpreters of the Best Note, Both Jewish and Christ, Consulted; Difficult Places at Large Explained; Seeming Contradictions Reconciled, and Various Passages Illustrated and Confirmed by Testimonies of Writers, as Well Gentile as Jewish, vol. 1 (London: printed for the author and sold by George Keith, 1763, The Spurgeon Library), 807. Hereafter *An Exposition of the Old Testament*.

23. In the manuscript, Charles drew the aforementioned "handpost" (signpost) with a hand. Additionally, he bolded the text "Refuge. Refuge." for greater emphasis.

24. Cf. Num 35:19.

25. Cf. Isa 40:2.

26. Cf. Num 35:28; Isa 61:7.

27. Cf. Matt 19:27–29; Mark 10:28–31; Luke 18:28–30.

28. "To grieve for; to regret; to lament." Johnson's *Dictionary*, s.v. "To Rue."

29. "Miklat" is a transliteration of the Hebrew "מִקְלָת" found in Num 35:12, which Charles frequently referenced in this sermon. Alone it means "asylum" or "refuge" but was often used in the phrase "cities of refuge." Edward Robinson, trans., *A Hebrew and English Lexicon of the Old Testament, Including the Biblical Chaldee. Translated from the Latin of William Gesenius* (Boston: Crocker and Brewster; New York: Leavitt, Lord & Co.; Andover, MA: Gould and Newman, 1836, The Spurgeon Library), 612.

Ezek. XLVII. 1–12.   Vision of the Holy Waters.   247.

The visions of Ezekiel are sublime, often very difficult to understand but always profitable, yielding a rich harvest to a careful student.

The river here spoken of is one often mentioned in the Bible, the streams thereof make glad the city of God. It is the water of Life. The Gospel of the grace of God.

1. The source of the river demands notice.
The house of God at Jerusalem became the starting point of the gospel, out of it went the apostles.

God's covenant & love are the source of grace. Jesus the door, the despised threshold, became the source of a living stream when from his pierced side came gushing a stream of blood & water. The foundations of the temple supplied the stream, the part immediately under the altar — so does grace spring from the very foundations of Jehovah's glory in his purposes in connection with the great atonement of the Son.

2. The increase of the stream is remarkable.
The church was small at the beginning a mere rill — the 3000 converts swelled it & soon by other additions it was made a brook — now it is knee deep — soon it will be up to our loins & in the latter days so deep that one may swim in it. —

VISION *of the* HOLY WATERS
Ezekiel 47:1–12[1]

The visions of Ezekiel are sublime, often very difficult to understand but always profitable, yielding a rich harvest to a careful student.[2]

The river here spoken of is one often mentioned in the Bible,[3] the streams thereof make glad the city of God.[4] It is the water of Life.

The Gospel of the grace of God.[5]

1. ## THE SOURCE OF THE RIVERS DEMANDS NOTICE.

    The house of God at Jerusalem became the starting point of the gospel.[6] Out of it went the apostles.

    God's covenant and love are the source of grace. Jesus the door,[7] the despised threshold, became the source of a living stream when from his pierced side came gushing a stream of blood and water.[8]

    The foundations of the temple supplied the stream, the part immediately under the altar.[9] So does grace spring from the very foundations of Jehovah's glory in his purposes in connection with the great atonement of the Son.[10]

2. ## THE INCREASE OF THE STREAM IS REMARKABLE.

    The Church was small at the beginning[,] a mere rill.[11] The 3000 converts[12] swelled it and soon by other additions it was made a brook. Now it is knee deep. Soon it will be up to our loins[,] and in the latter days so deep that one may swim in it.[13]

So in personal religion — the sea grows gradually deeper — little brooks sink all at once from the bank, true grace is not so precipitate — we just go in up to the ankles — God washeth our feet from sin. It swells to our knees we become mighty in prayer. It goeth to the loins, the whole heart is covered & at last we are carried wholly away.

3. The direction in which the river ran.
(1) Like all other rivers it sought the lowlands. Mountains rivers will not climb. The proud are had in derision but the humble shall receive supplies — (2) But look nearer. It ran to the desert, not to plains rejoicing in verdure but to deserts. Here is grace. Surely I was a desert but he came to me. — (3) More wonderful still it flowed towards the Dead Sea of Sodom — to show that it will visit even the vilest places. Where sin hath abounded grace doth much more abound.

4. The healing power of the water.
It is no common river; it flows not in vain. It heals. Even Sodom's sulphureous lake loses its killing power & nauseous taste for it is healed. Far superior to Bath springs it never fails in curing the worst disease whether internal, external, or both. It makes the dead live, sweetens bitters,

VISION OF THE HOLY WATERS—*Ezekiel 47:1-12*

So in personal religion, the sea grows gradually deeper. Little brooks sink all at once from the bank. True grace is not so precipitate.[14] We just go in up to the ankles. God washeth our feet from sin. It swells to our knees[.] [W]e become mighty in prayer. It goeth to the loins, the whole heart is covered[,] and at last we are carried wholly away.[15]

3. THE DIRECTION IN WHICH THE RIVER RAN.

(1) Like all other rivers it sought the lowlands. Mountains rivers will not climb. The proud are had in derision[,] but the humble shall receive supplies. (2) But look nearer. It ran to the desert, not to plains rejoicing in verdure,[16] but to deserts. Here is grace. Surely I was a desert but he came to me.[17] (3) More wonderful still it flowed towards the Dead Sea of Sodom,[18] to show that it will visit ~~all~~ even the vilest places. Where sin hath abounded grace doth much more abound.[19]

4. THE HEALING POWER OF THE WATER.

It is no common river; it flows not in vain. It heals.[20] Even Sodom's sulphureous lake loses its killing power and nauseous taste for it is healed.[21] Far superior to Bath springs,[22] it never fails in curing the worst disease whether internal, external, or both.

It makes the dead live,[23] sweetens bitters,[24]

revives the faint, restores the barren.
But the miry places, the marshes receive no benefit — hypocrites, professors merely, half-bred Christians, mongrel-religionists — are left salt, they are made worse; it is a savour of death unto death.

5. The life caused by the water. —
Fish will swarm where once there were none. A few were dead, floating on the backs in the Salt Sea but this stream turns them right they increase & multiply. — So that the stream is well stocked. — "Very great multitudes" are made alive by it — & these not little sprats but as the fish of the great sea — whales of sinners, leviathan rebels shall swarm.

6. The verdure on the banks.
On the banks of the river are the precious trees of promises. — All varieties to suit both old & young, weak and strong. Many of them to keep up a plenteous supply — Unfading never losing their beauty. Never stripped. Ever new. Made so by this sanctuary water. The fruit is the meat of God's people — the leaves are for medecine — or rather as the margin says for bruises & sores. These are heal-all plaisters —

1. Have we ever tasted the water of this river,

427.

VISION OF THE HOLY WATERS—*Ezekiel 47:1-12*

revives the faint,[25] [and] restores the barren.[26]

But the <u>miry places</u>, the marshes[,] receive no benefit – Hypocrites, professors merely, half-bred Christians, mongrel-religionists – are left salty.[27] They are made worse; it is a savour of death unto death.[28]

5. **THE LIFE CAUSED BY THE WATER.**

Fish will swarm where once there were none.[29] A few were dead, floating on the[ir] backs in the Salt Sea[,][30] but this stream turns them right. They increase and multiply, so that the stream is well stocked. "Very great multitudes" are made alive by it, and these not [as] little sprats[,][31] but as the fish of the great sea[.] [W]hales of sinners, leviathan rebels[,] shall swarm.

6. **THE VERDURE ON THE BANKS.**

On the banks of the river are the precious trees of promises.[32] All varieties to suit both old and young, weak and strong. Many of them to keep up a plenteous supply. Unfading never losing their beauty. Never stripped. Ever new. Made so by this sanctuary water. The fruit is the meat of God's people. The leaves are for medicine,[33] or rather as the margin says[,] for bruises and sores.[34] These are heal-all plaisters.[35]

   1. Have we ever tasted the water of this river?[36]

427.

SERMON 247

1. It appears that Charles did not preach another sermon on the text of Ezek 47:1–12. However, he did preach a later sermon on Ezek 47:5, "'Waters to Swim In'" (*MTP* 18, Sermon 1054), and on Ezek 47:8, "The Modern Dead Sea, and the Living Waters" (*MTP* 31, Sermon 1852). While some similarities can be noted, neither sermon contains enough overlapping material to indicate significant influence from this earlier sermon.

2. Charles recommended several commentaries to enrich one's study of Ezekiel. Some of his favorites included: Henry Cowles, *Ezekiel and Daniel with Notes, Critical, Explanatory, and Practical*, 8 vols. (New York: D. Appleton & Co., 1867); Patrick Fairbairn, *Ezekiel: Exposition with New Translation*, 8 vols. (Edinburgh: T&T Clark, 1851); William Greenhill, *Exposition of Ezekiel*, 5 vols. (London: Nisbet, 1863); Ebenezer Henderson, *Ezekiel with Commentary*, 8 vols. (London: Hamilton, 1855); John Peter Lange, *A Commentary on the Holy Scriptures: Critical, Doctrinal, and Homiletical, with Special Reference to Ministers and Students. Translated from the German, and Edited, with Additions, Original and Selected by Philip Schaff. Vol. XIII. of the Old Testament: Containing Ezekiel and Daniel* (New York: Charles Scribner's Sons, 1876); cf. *Lectures* 4:125–26.

3. Charles saw the river Chebar in Ezekiel as a type of the "river of water of life" in John's vision. Cf. Ezek 1:1, 3; 3:15, 23; 10:15, 20, 22; 43:3; Rev 22:1–2, 17.

4. Cf. Ps 46:4.

5. Charles seems to have returned to William Greenhill, one of his favorite commentators concerning the book of Ezekiel. Greenhill wrote, "We may take the gospel, with the gifts and graces of the Spirit, to be these waters; for the gospel is the ministration of the Spirit. . . . And the Spirit, with the graces and gifts, are oft compared to water, as well as the gospel." William Greenhill, *An Exposition of the Prophet Ezekiel*, 815. Greenhill went on to list seven examples of imagery linking the gospel to water.

6. Cf. Acts 1:12ff. Greenhill wrote, "The waters of the gospel, the fits and graces of the Spirit, do flow from Zion, from Jerusalem, where Ezekiel had his vision. . . . Yet Christ himself was the fountain and original of them; they came from the door and threshold of the house. All spiritual water is in him, all heavenly doctrine, all gifts and graces. When the Spirit moved holy men to speak, as

it is 2 Pet. 1.21, it received of Christ, and showed unto them, John xvi. 14; and all the waters which flowed from the apostles they received from Christ. The Spirit was given them to fill their vessels, and fitted them to carry these living waters from Jerusalem to all parts. Acts ii.8; and Christ sent them forth to preach the gospel." Greenhill, *An Exposition of the Prophet Ezekiel*, 816.

7. Cf. Ezek 47:1; John 10:7–9.   8. Cf. John 19:34.

9. Cf. Exod 29:12; Lev 8:15.   10. Cf. Eph 1:3–5.

11. "A small brook; a little streamlet." Johnson's *Dictionary*, s.v. "Rill."

12. Cf. Acts 2:41.   13. Cf. Hab 2:14.

14. "1. Steeply falling. 2. Headlong; hasty; rashly hasty. 3. Hasty; violent." Johnson's *Dictionary*, s.v. "Precipitate."

15. Cf. Ezek 47:3–5. "It is quite certain that there are degrees in the development of grace. You will surely not say that the young man, who has been converted only for the last few months, knows as much of grace, understands as much about it, and has as much faith, and as much love, as the man who has for the last twenty or thirty years been earnestly engaged in his Master's service. . . . It is true, they are not more loved of God than others are, and not more justified, nor more accepted, for in that respect we all stand on a level, and there is no difference; but as to the development of grace in our souls, and the display of grace in our lives, everyone must admit that there is a difference between different saints." *MTP* 46:531.

16. "Green; green colour." Johnson's *Dictionary*, s.v. "Verdure."

17. Cf. Ezek 47:8; Isa 43:19–20.

18. Greenhill wrote, "Galilee was eastward from Jerusalem, and in it was Lacus Asphaltites, the lake of Sodom, or Dead sea, so called because no fish could live in it, nor birds fly over it, but died, so deadly were the waters and vapours thereof." Greenhill, *An Exposition of the Prophet Ezekiel*, 820.

19. Cf. Rom 5:20.   20. Cf. Ezek 47:8–11.

21. Cf. Exod 15:23–26; 2 Kgs 2:21–22; Ezek 47:8–9.

SERMON 247

22. Charles was referring to the medical properties of the natural springs in Bath, England. The springs at Bath were so renowned that Dr. Julius Braun of Rehme Oeynhausen was recorded expressing his astonishment at their neglect in recent years and his opinion that "with the abundance of hot water in Bath, a military sanitorium for rheumatic and gouty patients or those who suffer from the effects of wounds and accidents, should not have been established." Henry William Freeman, *The Thermal Baths of Bath: Their History, Literature, Medical and Surgical Uses and Effects. Together with the Aix Massage and Natural Vapor Treatment* (London: Hamilton, 1888), 244. Ironically, these same conditions would plague Charles throughout his later ministry.

23. Cf. Eph 2:5–6; 1 Thess 4:13–18.

24. "A liquid, or a spirituous liquor, containing an infusion of bitter herbs or roots." Worcester's *Dictionary*, s.v. "Bitters." Cf. Exod 15:23–26.

25. Cf. Isa 40:29–31.

26. Greenhill wrote, "The waters of the sanctuary, the doctrine of the gospel, doth powerfully and speedily beget and bring men to God. . . . The waters of the gospel turn thorns and thistles into vine and fig trees, and make an orchard for God where none was. This was foretold by Isaiah. . . . The meaning is God would cause the gospel to be preached in dry and barren places, and there should some of all sorts come in, believe, and grow up like trees of God." Greenhill, *An Exposition of the Prophet Ezekiel*, 820–21.

27. Greenhill wrote, "People without the gospel are like unto the Dead sea, that lake of Sodom, into which, by our apostasy from God, we have cast ourselves. The Dead sea in a spiritual sense is the lake of our sins, where all things are loathsome, dead, and deadly; whence nothing but corrupt and pestilent vapours do flow." Greenhill, *An Exposition of the Prophet Ezekiel*, 821.

28. Cf. 2 Cor 2:16.   29. Cf. Ezek 47:9–10.

30. Greenhill referred to this body of water as the Dead sea or the Salt sea. Greenhill wrote, "Hither the sanctuary waters came, and they went down also into the desert, that is, say some expositors, into the Mediterranean sea, which was in the west; suitable to which interpretation seems that in Zech. xiv. 8, where living

waters are said to go out from Jerusalem, 'half of them toward the former sea,' that is, the Salt or Dead sea, 'and half of them toward the hinder sea,' that is, the Mediterranean sea." Greenhill, *An Exposition of the Prophet Ezekiel*, 820.

31. "A small sea fish." *Johnson's Dictionary*, s.v. "Sprat."

32. Cf. Ezek 47:12.   33. Cf. Rev 22:2.

34. Charles was referring to the marginal note in his Bible. Following the phrase "and the leaf thereof," the alternate reading "for bruises and sores" is provided. George D'Oyly and Richard Mant, arr., *The Holy Bible, According to the Authorized Version; with Notes, Explanatory and Practical; Taken Principally from the Most Eminent Writers of the United Church of England and Ireland: Together with Appropriate Introductions, Tables, Indexes, Maps, and Plans: Prepared and Arranged by the Rev. George D'Oyly, B D. and the Rev. Richard Mant, D. D. Domestick Chaplains to His Grace the Lord Archbishop of Canterbury. Under the Direction of The Society for Promoting Christian Knowledge. For the Use of Families. Vol. 1. Part. II* (Oxford: printed for the Society at the Clarendon Press by Binsely, Cooke, and Collingwood, 1817, The Spurgeon Library), Ezekiel 47:12.

35. Johnson listed this without the "i": "A glutinous or adhesive salve." *Johnson's Dictionary*, s.v. "Plaster."

36. This is an uncommon and abrupt ending for Charles. While he did end other sermons with a question to the congregation, it was unusual for him to leave a dangling subpoint with a question headed by an Arabic numeral. The immediate reason is not clear, but it is possible that he was cut short in his preparation time or that he originally intended to have more questions, but then found his initial question to be sufficient.

248. Cant. II. 10-13... The coming of Spring.
Spring is a delightful season, especially if it succeeds a severe winter —
Some expressions in this description arise from the county in which Solomon dwelt.

I. Let us think on the winter experienced by every child of God — He has many wintry seasons but one above all others deserves this name it is the season of unregeneracy — We are in that state uncomfortable & unfruitful. & when God awakens us by conviction we have stormy weather — our own coals cannot warm us. the wind howls into our warmest room & our rags are blown off by the wind just at the very moment when we hoped to make them our covering. This we cannot forget.

II. But spring came in due season, not warmth by means of a fire of our own making but a spring from heaven. The sun turned his rein & cheered us by his near approach. Some sermon, portion of Scripture, prayer, or train of thought were the apparent means. Many can recollect the very day when spring dawned on them but more though they know not days or months yet they have enjoyed the season. & will never forget it —

THE COMING *of* SPRING
Song of Solomon 2:10–13[1]

"My beloved spake, and said unto me, Rise up, my love, my fair one, and come away. For, lo, the winter is past, the rain is over and gone; the flowers appear on the earth; the time of the singing of birds is come, and the voice of the turtle is heard in our land; the fig tree putteth forth her green figs, and the vines with the tender grape give a good smell. Arise, my love, my fair one, and come away."

Spring is a delightful season, especially if it succeeds a severe winter.

Some expressions in this description arise from the country in which Solomon dwelt.

I. LET US THINK ON THE WINTER EXPERIENCED BY EVERY CHILD OF GOD.

He has many wintry seasons, but one above all others deserves this name[.] [I]t is the season of unregeneracy.[2] We are in that state uncomfortable and unfruitful. And when God awakens us by conviction we have stormy weather, our own coals cannot warm us.[3] The wind howls into our warmest room and our rags[4] are blown off by the wind just at the very moment when we hoped to make them our covering. This we cannot forget.

II. BUT SPRING CAME IN DUE SEASON.

Not warmth by means of a fire of our own making but a spring from heaven.

The sun turned his rein and cheered us by his near approach. Some sermon, portion of Scripture, prayer, or train of thought [was] the apparent means. Many can recollect the very day when spring dawned on them[.] [B]ut more[,] though they know not days or months[,] yet they have enjoyed the season and will never forget it.

III. There are signs of spring for which we must look —

The flowers appear on earth — the teardrop supplies the place of the snow-drop as a billet announcing springs approach
The violet of humility begins to blow — the lilly of the valley, heart's ease & Rose of Sharon shall follow —
The singing of birds. Songs come from the warm heart the lark of hope mounts upward carolling — the nightingale gives songs in the night. Joy comes.
The voice of the dove. The Holy Spirits comforts & warnings
The fruits come, barren no longer, fruit appears. though as yet "green" & "tender"

IV. The duties of spring time.
"Arise" — we should not sleep in spring — we must awake, rejoice, watch, enjoy our privileges.
"Come away", from sin & sinners, from cares & troubles, from self & sense — — to Jesus, to his church, his Baptism, his table.
Hark he calls thee his love, his fair one Fear not, Blush not, he who has given thee a spring will help thee to improve it.

Pray for spring —
Look for its evidences —
Rejoice in hope of summer —

425. 426. 430.

THE COMING OF SPRING—*Song of Solomon 2:10–13*

III. THERE ARE SIGNS OF SPRING FOR WHICH WE MUST LOOK.

<u>The flowers appear on earth.</u>[5] The tear drop supplies the place of the snow-drop as a billet[6] announcing spring[']s approach.

The violet of humility begins to blow.[7] The lily of the valley,[8] heart's ease,[9] and Rose of Sharon[10] shall follow.

<u>The singing of birds.</u> Songs come from the warm heart. The lark of hope mounts upward caroling. The nightingale gives songs in the night.[11] Joy comes.[12]

<u>The voice of the dove.</u> The Holy Spirit[']s comforts and warnings.[13]

<u>The fruits come.</u> Barren no longer, fruit appears, though as yet "<u>green</u>" and "<u>tender</u>."[14]

IV. THE DUTIES OF SPRINGTIME.

"Arise." We should not sleep in spring. We must awake, rejoice, watch, enjoy our privileges.[15]

"Come away" from sin and sinners, from cares and troubles, from self and sense – to Jesus, to his church, his Baptism, his table.[16]

Hark he calls thee his love, his fair one. Fear not. Blush not. He who has given thee a spring will help thee to improve it.[17]

Pray for spring.

Look for its evidences.

Rejoice in hope of summer.

425. 426. 430.

SERMON 248

1. It appears that Charles preached two later sermons on this text: "A Sermon for Spring" (*MTP* 8, Sermon 436) and "The Tender Grapes" (*MTP* 42, Sermon 2480). Neither of the later sermons appear to have enough overlapping content to indicate that they were influenced by this earlier sermon.

2. John Gill, commenting on this passage, wrote, "[The winter and rain] may in general represent the state of God's people both before and after conversion; before conversion it is a time of darkness, coldness, barrenness, and unfruitfulness." Gill, *An Exposition of the Old Testament* (765) 4:602.

3. Charles himself went through such a stormy period from age ten to fifteen: "I, at least, can bear my personal testimony to the fact that grace operates on some minds at a period almost too early for recollection. When but young in years, I felt with much sorrow the evil of sin. My bones waxed old with my roaring all the day long. Day and night God's hand was heavy upon me. I hungered for deliverance, for my soul fainted within me. . . . That misery was sent for this reason, that I might then be made to cry to Jesus. Our Heavenly Father does not usually cause us to seek the Saviour till He has whipped us clean out of all our confidence; He cannot make us in earnest after Heaven till He has made us feel something of the intolerable tortures of an aching conscience, which is a foretaste of hell. I remember, when I used to awake in the morning, the first thing I took up was Alleine's *Alarm*, or Baxter's *Call to the Unconverted*. Oh, those books, those books! I read and devoured them when under a sense of guilt, but it was like sitting at the foot of Sinai. For five years, as a child, there was nothing before my eyes but my guilt; and though I do not hesitate to say that those who observed my life would not have seen any extraordinary sin, yet as I looked upon myself, there was not a day in which I did not commit such gross, such outrageous sins against God, that often and often have I wished I had never been born." *Autobiography* 1:79–80.

4. Cf. Isa 64:6.

5. Gill expounded, "These flowers may be meant either the graces of the Spirit in the saints, which when a winter-time with them seem to be dead, at least are hid; but upon a return of the sun of righteousness, revive and are seen again: or the saints themselves, when in a flourishing condition, and in the exercise of grace; who may be compared to the flowers of the field for the production of them in the spring, which is a kind of re-creation of them." Gill, *An Exposition of the Old*

Testament 4:602. In this point, Charles used the flowers to signify the graces of the Spirit in the saints.

6. "A small paper; a note." Johnson's *Dictionary*, s.v. "Billet."

7. Charles likened the melting "snow-drop" to the teardrop of repentance and pointed to the violet of humility as signs of the Spirit's work in the life of the saint.

8. Cf. Song 2:1. Also Charles spelling of "lily" as "lilly" has been corrected in the transcription.

9. Charlotte Elizabeth described the heart's-ease flower in her book *Chapters on Flowers*: "Sweet flower! Tranquility makes its lowly rest upon its dark green couch; and cheerfulness is legibly written on every clear tint of its glossy petals." Charlotte Elizabeth, *Chapters on Flowers*, new ed. (London: Seeley, 1886, The Spurgeon Library), 21.

10. Cf. Song 2:1. Given the context, Charles's reference for these three flowers was most likely Christ and the peace that comes from knowing him.

11. "It is easy to sing when we can read the notes by daylight; but he is the skillful singer who can sing when there is not a ray of light by which to read, – who sings from his heart and not from a book that he can see, because he has no means of reading. . . . But what does the text mean, when it asserts that God giveth songs in the night? We think we find two answers to the questions. The first is, that usually in the night of a Christian's experience, God is his only song. . . . And yet again, not only does God give the song in the night, because he is the only subject upon which we can sing then, but because *he is the only One who inspires songs in the night*." MTP 44:98–99, italics in the original.

12. Cf. Ps 30:5

13. Cf. John 14:16–18, 26; 16:7–15.

14. Cf. Gal 5:22–23.

15. Cf. 1 Thess 5:4–8.

16. "Make no reserves. Come altogether away from selfishness—from aught which would divide your chaste and pure love to Christ, your soul's husband. Rise up and come away. In this the beginning of your spiritual life, the young dawn of marvellous light, come away from your old habits; avoid the very appearance of

evil; come away from old friendships which may tempt you back to the flesh pots of Egypt. Leave all these things. Come away to higher flights of spirituality than your fathers as yet have known. Come away to private communion. Be much alone in prayer. Come away: be diligent in the study of God's Word. Come away, shut the doors of your chamber, and talk with your Lord Jesus, and have close and intimate dealing with him." *MTP* 8:116.

17. "To advance any thing nearer to perfection; to raise from good to better." Johnson's *Dictionary*, s.v. "To Improve."

249. Ps. 69. 9. The zeal of thine house hath eaten me up. We say a man is eaten up with a thing when he is so fond of it as to make it give way to everything else. —

I. Some men are eaten up with other things —
1. with business, labouring for the meat which perisheth
2. with riches, hoarding, grasping.
3. with learning, — hard study —
4. with love of fame, pride, flattery,
5. with pleasure, sin, licentiousness —

II. Few Men are eaten up with religion
1. Because few believe the truth firmly enough
2. Few love God much, our desires are cold.
3. Most men follow the multitude, or at least others damp their zeal —
4. We do not think enough of eternal things.
5. Our nature opposes our wishes —

III. If we were eaten up with zeal.
1. Persecution would be welcomed.
2. Duties would be cheerfully performed.
3. Services would never lack attendants.
4. Money would come when required —

432. 584.

THE ZEAL OF THINE HOUSE . . . —*Psalm 69:9*

THE ZEAL *of* THINE HOUSE HATH EATEN ME UP
Psalm 69:9[1]

"For the zeal of thine house hath eaten me up; and the reproaches of them that reproached thee are fallen upon me."

We say a man is eaten up with a thing when he is so fond of it as to make it give way to everything else.

I. SOME MEN ARE EATEN UP WITH OTHER THINGS.
  1. With business, labouring for the meat[2] which perisheth.[3]
  2. With riches, hoarding, grasping.[4]
  3. With learning, hard study.[5]
  4. With love of fame, pride, flattery.[6]
  5. With pleasure, sin, licentiousness.[7]

II. FEW MEN ARE EATEN UP WITH RELIGION.
  1. Because few believe the truth firmly enough.
  2. Few love God much, our desires are cold.
  3. Most men follow the multitude, or at least others damp their zeal.[8]
  4. We do not think enough of eternal things.[9]
  5. Our nature opposes our wishes.[10]

III. IF WE WERE EATEN UP WITH ZEAL.
  1. Persecution would be welcomed.[11]
  2. Duties would be cheerfully performed.
  3. Services would never lack attendants.
  4. Money would come when required.[12]

432. 584.

SERMON 249

1. It appears Charles did not preach another sermon on this text.

2. "1. Flesh to be eaten. 2. Food in general." Johnson's *Dictionary*, s.v. "Meat."

3. Cf. John 6:27.

4. Cf. Matt 6:19–21; 19:21–22; Luke 18:15–21; 1 Tim 6:10.

5. Cf. Eccl 12:12.

6. Cf. Prov 8:13; 16:18; Mark 7:21–23; 1 John 2:16. Charles was not afraid to admit his personal struggles with pride. Writing in his diary a few months after his conversion, he confessed, "I have the seeds of all evil in my own heart; pride is yet my darling sin, I cannot shake it off." *Autobiography* 1:146. This could be why Charles was able to describe pride's destructive power so clearly. He wrote, "Nothing proves men so mad as pride. For this they have given up rest, and ease, and repose, to find rank and power among men; for this they have dared to risk their hope of salvation, to leave the gentle yoke of Jesus, and go toiling wearily along the way of life, seeking to save themselves by their own works, and at last to stagger into the mire of fell despair." *NPSP* 2:347.

7. Cf. Rom 13:13; 1 Cor 6:9–10; Gal 5:19–21.

8. "A man will willingly amount to be the slave of sin, because his fellow-man sins after the same fashion. He must do this and that because his neighbors or his comrades do the same. Why should he be singular? Why should he swim against the general current? If others see no harm, feel no compunction, and find it pleasant sport, why should he not join them? Is it not always more lively to follow the multitude? What road is better than the broad road where all sorts of good company may be met with? And, brethren, the less scrupulous men are the more self complacent they become. Mirth, it would seem, extracts the venom from sin, and wit can robe ribaldry in innocence. But be not deceived. The customs you adopt and the habits you cherish combine with the depravity of your own nature to weld a chain, which the strength of Hercules could not snap—a chain that makes the creature an abject slave to the flesh, instead of a liege subject of his adorable Creator." *MTP* 61:266–67.

9. "The apostle warns us not to say, 'We will go into such a city, and continue there a year, and buy and sell, and get gain,' and all that kind of talk. He who

speaks like that has not seen God of late, for he who is much with God thinks of eternal things, and he knows how near they are, and he says to himself, 'I shall soon be gone. This world is not my rest; there is nothing here that is substantial and abiding.' So he is waiting to hear the trumpet sound, 'Boot and saddle! Up and away!' and he stands ready, at his Captain's call, to be gone to another and a better world." *MTP* 48:430.

10. Cf. Gal 5:17.

11. "As before the engagement the captain stimulates his soldiers by reminding them that 'the sterner the warfare the greater the honour;' even so may we nerve our spirits. 'Gentlemen in England now abed will think themselves accursed that they were not here, and hold their valour cheap that went not with us on this glorious day' --so spake the hero; and so let us also welcome persecution and tribulation. We should hold ourselves as being so far impoverished for eternity in being spared affliction upon earth. Up yonder to relate the triumphs of grace in us; to tell of the faithfulness of God in poverty and affliction; to make known to principalities and powers for ever the wonderful and eternal love of God, as we have discovered it in the furnace and amidst the flames; this will be everlasting wealth, for which we may be grateful now that God is putting us in the way of gaining it." *MTP* 14:599.

12. Throughout his ministry, Charles bore witness to the unique providence of God in financial provision for his zealous endeavors for God, from the building of the Metropolitan Tabernacle to funding for his orphanages and the Pastors' College. Several poignant examples can be found in Charles's Monday address given during the testimonial services celebrating his twenty-fifth anniversary in the ministry in London. *Memorial Volume. Sermons and Addresses Delivered in the Metropolitan Tabernacle, Newington, in Connection with the Presentation of a Testimonial to Pastor C. H. Spurgeon, to Commemorate the Completion of the Twenty-Fifth Year of His Pastorate, with Selection of Music Sung on the Occasion* (London: Passmore and Alabaster, 1879), 28–38. For Charles, such providential kindnesses strengthened his conviction that God would provide what was needed and bolstered his confidence in attempting great things for Christ.

Rev. XIV. 1.2.3 — The New Song on Mount Zion.
What scenes have been enacted on Mount Zion
There — or near it Abraham offered Isaac. —
There — the temple, the glory of the earth was placed
& crowds of worshippers continually gathered there.
On that same hill the second temple was raised.
There too came Jesus when a child brought
by his mother — again when in triumph he
rode the streets — & when he chased the dealers.
The army of Titus flamed the fabric & ploughed
mount Zion — but there is a scene to
be witnessed on that hill of which Zion was
a type which shall transcend all these.
I. Let us devoutly gaze upon the subject of
the song — "the Standing Lamb"
Jesus as leader of his people stood in their midst
under the figure of a lamb — which is the
type of patient suffering, atonement, & purity.
The Lamb stood to show that he had triumphed
& gotten the victory — he sits until his foes
are made his footstool — now he lifts his
noble head & stands erect triumphant
Oh for a sight of him by faith & at
last in blest reality. — None but Jesus
is their theme. Not unto us — He is worthy
for he has washed us in his blood.

THE NEW SONG on MOUNT ZION

Revelation 14:1–3[1]

"And I looked, and, lo, a Lamb stood on the mount Zion, and with him an hundred forty and four thousand, having his Father's name written on their foreheads. And I heard a voice from heaven, as the voice of many waters, and as the voice of a great thunder: and I heard the voice of harpers harping with their harps: And they sung as it were a new song before the throne, and before the four beasts, and the elders: and no man could learn that song but the hundred and forty and four thousand, which were redeemed from the earth."

What scenes have been enacted on Mount Zion.

There, or near it, Abraham offered Isaac.[2]

There, the temple, the glory of the earth was placed and crowds of worshippers continually gathered there.[3] On that same hill the second temple was raised.[4]

There too came Jesus when a child brought by his mother,[5] again when in triumph he rode the streets,[6] and when he chased the dealers.[7]

The army of Titus flamed the fabric and ploughed Mount Zion.[8] But there is a scene to be witnessed on that hill of which Zion was a type[9] which shall transcend all these.

I. LET US DEVOUTLY GAZE UPON THE SUBJECT OF THE SONG, "THE STANDING LAMB."

Jesus as leader of his people stood in their midst under the figure of a lamb, which is the type of patient suffering, atonement, and purity.[10]

The Lamb stood to show that he had triumphed and gotten the victory. He sits until his foes are made his footstool.[11] Now he lifts his noble head and stands erect, triumphant[.][12]

Oh for a sight of him by faith and at last in blest reality. ["]None but Jesus["] is their theme, ["]Not unto us. He is worthy for he has washed us in his blood.["][13]

II. Let us notice the singers —

Their number — how great, yet this is only a number representing an innumerable host.

Their number — how complete — all the chosen ones are there, none lacking but all there.

Redeemed ones — they are so called since they are the only persons who derive saving benefit from the redemption of our Lord Jesus.

They had learnt the song — They were a prepared people, none can be so but those who are redeemed & made to differ from the world.

They had the Father's name on their foreheads — not the name of sects, denominations, countries

Not one unregenerate person among them nor one regenerate one absent

III. Let us note their mode of singing.

As the noise of the ocean or thunder the swell of their song arose — not cold, feeble gentle, dull as our songs now but loud solemn, grand, hearty, sublime —

Yet most melodiously were the harpings heard — sweetly harmonious — though rolling grandly like thunder yet sweet as David's seven stringed harps. Oh for a little of such singing — Here are so many

THE NEW SONG ON MOUNT ZION—*Revelation 14:1–3*

II. LET US NOTICE THE SINGERS.

Their number, how great, yet this is only a number representing an innumerable host.[14]

Their number, how complete.[15] All the chosen ones are there, none [are] lacking but all there.

Redeemed ones.[16] They are so called since they are the only persons who derive saving benefit from the redemption of our Lord Jesus.

They had learnt the song. They were a prepared people. None can be so but those who are redeemed and made to differ from the world.

They had the Father's name on their foreheads.[17] Not the name of sects, denominations,[18] [or] countries.

Not one unregenerate person among them[,] nor one regenerate one absent.

III. LET US NOTE THEIR MODE OF SINGING.

As the noise of the ocean or thunder the swell of their song arose. Not cold, feeble, gentle, dull, as our songs now[,] but loud, solemn, grand, hearty, sublime.[19]

Yet most melodiously were the harpings heard, sweetly harmonious, though rolling grandly like thunder[,] yet sweet as David's seven stringed harp. Oh for a little of such singing. There are so many, no wonder they are loud, so perfect, no wonder at the melody — so happy no wonder at its heartiness

IV. Let us note the song —
It was a new song — which we shall know soon. Songs are expressive of joy & triumph — See Miriam's song over Pharoah, Deborah's song on Sisera, & several others, but this shall surpass all —
It will be a new song
1. Because the subject is ever new.
2. Because never did so many sing before
3. Because it will celebrate the completion of the great work now going on.
4. Because we shall have new joys calling for new songs.
5. Because never did such a variety of persons sing before — from Adam to the last, all shall meet, of all denominations, countries &c
6. Because there will not be one hypocrite, or mere vocalist there.
7. Because complete victory will crown every head & this will be their hymn of triumph Jesus has other crown but at this moment the brightest will be on his head.
Like Cromwell & his men at Dunbar we shall sing to him who hath gotten us the victory
&c &c — Friend till we win & sing
Hallelujah. Hallelujah, Hallelujah
Amen

434. 439. 458. 482. 543. 568. 563

THE NEW SONG ON MOUNT ZION—*Revelation 14:1–3*

no wonder they are loud. So perfect, no wonder at the melody. So happy[,] no wonder at its heartiness.

IV. LET US NOTE THE SONG.

It was a new song, which we shall know soon. Songs are expressive of joy and triumph. See Miriam[']s song over Pharaoh.[20] Deborah's song on Sisera.[21] And several others,[22] but this shall surpass all. It will be a new song[:]

1. Because the subject is ever new.
2. Because never did so many sing before.
3. ~~Some of~~ Because it will celebrate the completion of the great work now going on.[23]
4. Because we shall have new joys calling for new songs.
5. Because never did such a variety of persons sing before. From Adam to the last, all shall meet, of all denominations, countries, etc.
6. Because there will not be one hypocrite or mere vocalist there.
7. Because complete victory will crown every head and this will be their hymn of triumph. Jesus has other crown[s,] but at this moment the brightest will be on his head.

Like Cromwell and his men at Dunbar[,] we shall sing to him who hath gotten us the victory.[24]

On, On, Friend till we win and sing.

Hallelujah, Hallelujah, Hallelujah,

<u>Amen</u>

434. 439. 458. 482. 543. 568. 563

SERMON 250

1. It appears that Charles preached a later sermon on this text, "Heavenly Worship" (*NPSP* 3, Sermon 110). Charles's later sermon seems to contain some overlapping material and structural divisions. An outline of this structure appeared in his introduction, where Charles said, "This morning I shall endeavour to show you, first of all, *the object of heavenly worship* – the Lamb in the midst of the throne; in the next place we shall look at *the worshippers themselves*, and note their manner and their character; in the third place we shall listen to *hear their song*, for we may almost hear it; it is like 'the noise of many waters and great thunder;' and then we shall close by noting, that it is a *new song* which they sing, and by endeavouring to mention one or two reasons why it must necessarily be so." *NPSP* 3:25, italics in the original. Additional overlapping content is noted below.

2. Cf. Gen 22:2. Mount Zion was associated with Jerusalem, the Temple Mount.

3. Cf. 1 Kgs 6–8. "[It] was there, too, in commemoration of that great triumph of faith, Solomon built a majestic temple." *NPSP* 3:25.

4. Cf. Ezra 6:14–15.   5.   Cf. Luke 2:41–52.

6. Cf. Matt 21:6–11; Mark 11:4–10; Luke 19:32–38.

7. Cf. Matt 21:12–13; Mark 11:15–17; Luke 19:45–46.

8. Charles was likely referring to Titus, the Roman general responsible for the siege and destruction of Jerusalem. It is possible that Charles learned this story from the works of Josephus. For Josephus's account of the siege of Jerusalem, see his work *The Jewish War* in William Whiston, trans., *The Works of Flavius Josephus, the Learned and Authentic Jewish Historian, and Celebrated Warrior. To Which Are Added, Three Dissertations Concerning Jesus Christ, John the Baptist, James the Just, God's Command to Abraham, etc. With an Index to the Whole. In Four Volumes.* vol. 3 [London: printed for William Allason, 1818, The Spurgeon Library), 246–418, and *The Works of Josephus*, 4:1–279.

9. Charles believed that the Bible could be, and at times should be, interpreted typologically, meaning that Old Testament events, persons, and things foreshadowed their New Testament antitype. While Charles normally focused on Christological typologies, this introduction focused on the typological relationship between the earthly Mount Zion and the heavenly Mount Zion.

10. Cf. Rev 5:6; 14:1. "And now observe *the figure under which Christ is represented in heaven.* . . . Why should Christ in heaven choose to appear under the figure of a lamb, and not in some other of his glorious characters? We reply, because it was as a lamb that Jesus fought and conquered, and therefore as a lamb he appears in heaven. . . . He whom they address is represented in heaven under the figure of a Lamb, to teach us to come close to him, and tell him all our wants, believing that he will not disdain to hear them." NPSP 3:26–27, italics in the original.

11. Cf. Ps 110:1.

12. "And you will further notice that *this Lamb is said to stand.* Standing is the posture of triumph. The Father said to Christ, 'Sit thou on my throne, till I make thine enemies thy footstool.' It is done; they are his footstool, and here he is said to stand erect, like a victor over all his enemies. Many a time the Saviour knelt in prayer; once he hung upon the cross; but when the great scene of our text shall be fully wrought out, he shall stand erect, as more than a conqueror, through his own majestic might." NPSP 3:27, italics in the original.

13. Cf. Ps 115:1; Rev 1:5.

14. Cf. Rev 7:9. "This is a certain number put for an uncertain – I mean uncertain to us, though not uncertain to God. It is a vast number, put for that 'multitude which no man can number,' who shall stand before the throne of God." NPSP 3:27–28.

15. Charles reconciled the innumerable multitude in Rev 7:9 with the 144,000 in this passage by interpreting that number symbolically. The 144,000 represent the complete number of all redeemed ones.

16. "But notice, whilst the number is very large, how very certain it is. By turning over the leaves of your Bible to a previous chapter of this book, you will see that at the 4th verse it is written, that there are one hundred and forty-four thousand saved; not 143,999, and 144,001, but exactly the number that are sealed. Now, my friends may not like what I am going to say; but if they do not like it, their quarrel is with God's Bible, not with me. There will be just as many in heaven as are sealed by God – just as many as Christ did purchase with his blood; all of them, and no more and no less." NPSP 3:28.

17. Cf. Rev 22:4.

18. "'I looked, and lo, a Lamb stood on the Mount Sion, and with him an hundred forty and four thousand.' And who were these people, 'having his Father's name written on their foreheads?' Not *B*s for 'Baptists,' not *W*s for 'Wesleyans,' not *E*s for 'Established Church:' they had their Father's name and nobody else's. What a deal of fuss is made on earth about our distinctions! We think such a deal about belonging to this denomination, and the other. Why, if you were to go to heaven's gates, and ask if they had any Baptists there, the angel would only look at you, and not answer you; if you were to ask if they had any Wesleyans, or members of the Established Church, he would say, 'Nothing of the sort;' but if you were to ask him whether they had any Christians there, 'Ay,' he would say, 'an abundance of them: they are all one now – all called by one name; the old brand has been obliterated, and now they have not the name of this man or the other; they have the name of God, even their Father, stamped on their brow.' Learn then dear friends, whatever the connection to which you belong, to be charitable to your brethren, and kind to them, seeing that, after all, the name you now hold here will be forgotten in heaven, and only your Father's name will be known." *NPSP* 3:29–30, italics in the original.

19. "First, then, singing *how loud*! It is said to be 'like the voice of many waters.' Have you never heard the sea roar, and the fulness thereof? Have you never walked by the sea-side, when the waves were singing, and when every little pebble stone did turn chorister, to make up music to the Lord God of hosts? And have you never in time of storm beheld the sea, with its hundred hands, clapping them in gladsome adoration of the Most High? Have you ever heard the sea roar out his praise[?] . . . You are to suppose ocean piled upon ocean, sea upon sea, – the Pacific piled upon the Atlantic, the Arctic upon that, the Antarctic higher still, and so ocean upon ocean, all lashed to fury, and all sounding with a mighty voice the praise of God. Such is the singing of heaven." *NPSP* 3:30, italics in the original.

20. Cf. Exod 15:1–21.   21. Cf. Judges 5.

22. Cf. Num 21:17–18; 1 Sam 18:6–7; 2 Sam 22:1–50; Ezra 3:11; Rom 11:33–36; Eph 1:3–14; Phil 2:6–11; Col 1:15–20.

23. "They are in heaven now; but the scene of our text is something more than heaven. It refers to the time when all the chosen race shall meet around the throne, when

the last battle shall have been fought, and the last warrior shall have gained his crown. It is not now that they are thus singing, but it is in the glorious time to come, when all the hundred and forty and four thousand – or rather, the number typified by that number – will be safely housed and all secure." NPSP 3:32.

24. Charles seemed to be referring to the historic Battle of Dunbar, fought during the Third English Civil War, where Oliver Cromwell won a decisive upset victory over the Scottish forces led by David Leslie. In one account of the story, when Cromwell saw the sun rising upon the battlefield, "The words of the 117th Psalm sprang from the lips of the enthusiastic conqueror; to his warring hosts it sounded like a hymn of battle. 'O! Praise the Lord, all ye nations; praise him, all ye people!' he cried. 'For his merciful kindness is great towards us; and the truth of the Lord endureth forever. Praise ye the Lord!'" Samuel Harden Church, *Oliver Cromwell: A History. Comprising a Narrative of His Life, with Extracts from His Letters and Speeches and an Account of the Political, Religious, and Military Affairs of England During His Time* (New York; London: G. P. Putnam's Sons, The Knickerbocker Press, 1894), 362. Charles also referenced this piece of history in his later sermon, saying, "There is a story told in the history of brave Oliver Cromwell, which I will use here to illustrate this new song. Cromwell and his Ironsides before they went into battle bowed the knee in prayer, and asked for God's help. Then, with their Bibles in their breasts, and their swords in their hands – a strange and unjustifiable mixture, but which their ignorance must excuse – they cried, 'The Lord of hosts is with us, the God of Jacob is our refuge;' and rushing to battle they sang – 'O Lord our God, arise and let / Thine enemies scattered be, / And let all those that do thee hate / Before thy presence flee.' They had to fight up hill for a time, but at last the enemy fled. The Ironsides were about to pursue them and win the booty, when the stern harsh voice of Cromwell was heard – 'Halt! Halt! now the victory is won, before you rush to the spoil return thanks to God;' and they sang some such song as this – 'Sing unto the Lord, for he has gotten us the victory! Sing unto the Lord.' It was said to have been one of the most majestic sights in that strange, yet good man's history." NPSP 3:32.

251 — Matt VII. 7. Ask, & it shall be given you.

There are a few limitations to be made in this text — It does not mean that God will give us improper things or things contrary to his will — Nor does it say he will give at once, or on the first time of asking — Nor will he always hear prayer, for in the next world prayer cannot be answered. But yet here it stands, Ask & ye shall receive

I. The command — "Ask."
Upon this I would remark.
1. How little God requires of us simply to ask.
2. How reasonable it is that he should require us to ask for such precious mercies.
3. How kind it is of him to let us ask.
4. How well suited to all cases, if it were any other command some could not do it but this the simplest, poorest can do —
5. How little form in it — any ask will do if it come from the heart.
6. Even this he gives us grace to do — for indeed we need help in our least action — he gives it.

II. The promise. "It shall be given you."
Not because you ask, but if you ask. Upon this we may remark.

ASK, *and* IT SHALL BE GIVEN YOU
Matthew 7:7[1]

"Ask, and it shall be given you; seek, and ye shall find; knock, and it shall be opened unto you."

There are a few limitations to be made in this text. It does not mean that God will give us improper things or things contrary to his will. Nor does it say he will give at once, or on the first time of asking. Nor will he always hear prayer, for in the next world prayer cannot be answered. But yet, here it stands. Ask and ye shall receive.[2]

I. THE COMMAND. "<u>Ask</u>."

   Upon this I would remark[:]

   1. How little God requires of us simply to ask.[3]
   2. How reasonable it is that he should require us to ask for such precious mercies.[4]
   3. How kind it is of him to let us ask.
   4. How well suited to all cases. If it were any other command some could not do it but this the simplest, poorest, can do.[5]
   5. How little <u>form</u> [is] in it.[6] <u>Any</u> ask will do if it come from the heart.
   6. Even this he gives us grace to do, for indeed we need help in our least action. He gives it.

II. THE PROMISE. *"It shall be given you."*

   Not because you ask, but if you ask. Upon this we may remark[:]

1. Its positive assertion is clear enough, there is no crack in this bell — It is a _shall_.
2. Its truth has been tested by Abraham, Jacob, Moses, Gideon, David, Elijah, Hezekiah, Manasseh, Jonah, &c &c —
3. Its absence of any condition, or prerequisite save the mere asking, to any character, age &c —
4. Its perpetual standing as long as there are askers is proved by saints daily.
5. Its unfailingness cannot be disputed — for the glorified own it & the damned dare not say they ever sought in vain.

III. The argument from it —
1. That when the church prays more, we shall have more success and our great want is more earnest effectual prayer.
2. That if a man says he has sought his salvation & asked — if he has not received it — he is mistaken.

God will hear all callers — If he answer not there is some wrong in us —
     Father Help —

435. 483.

ASK, AND IT SHALL BE GIVEN YOU—*Matthew 7:7*

1. Its positive assertion is clear enough. There is no crack in this bell. It is a <u>shall</u>.[7]
2. Its truth has been tested by Abraham,[8] Jacob,[9] Moses,[10] Gideon,[11] David,[12] Elijah,[13] Hezekiah,[14] Manasseh,[15] Jonah,[16] etc. etc.
3. Its absence of any condition, or prerequisite save the mere asking, to any character, age etc.
4. Its perpetual standing[,] as long as there are askers[,] is proved by saints daily.
5. Its unfailingness cannot be disputed, for the glorified own it and the damned dare not say they ever sought in vain.

III. THE ARGUMENT FROM IT.

1. That when the church prays more we shall have more success[,] and our great want is more earnest, effectual prayer.[17]
2. That if a man says he has sought his salvation and asked, if he has not received it, he is mistaken.

God will hear all callers. If he answer not[,] there is some wrong in us.[18]

<u>Father. Help.</u>

435. 483.

SERMON 251

1. It appears that Charles did not preach on this passage again, although he later exposited upon it at the end of "'How Good to Those Who Seek!'" (*MTP* 41, Sermon 2436). However, another sermon that he later preached on Matt 7:12, "Knock" (*MTP* 29, Sermon 1723) has notable similarities. It is possible that the later sermon was influenced by this one. The overlapping content has been noted below.

2. "Men get more by asking than by working without prayer. Though I do not discommend working, yet I most highly commend praying. Nothing under heaven pays like prevailing prayer." *MTP* 29:302.

3. "When the text says, '*Knock*, and it shall be opened unto you,' it teaches us that *the way of winning admission to the blessing is simple*, and suitable to common people. If I have to enter in by a door, which is well secured, I shall need tools and science. I confess I do not understand the art; you must send for a gentleman who understands picklocks, 'jemmies,' and all sorts of burglarious instruments: but if I am only told to knock, fool as I am at opening doors, I know how to knock. Any uneducated man can knock if that is all, which is required of him." *MTP* 29:307, italics in the original.

4. "Besides, to make us knock at mercy's gate is *a great blessing to ourselves* upon the spot. It is a going to school for us when we are set to plead with God for awhile without realised success. It makes a man grow more earnest, for his hunger increases while he tarries. If he obtained the blessing when he first asked for it, it might seem dog cheap; but when he has to plead long he arrives at a better sense of the value of the mercy sought." *MTP* 29:305, italics in the original.

5. "Is there a person here who cannot put words together in prayer? Never mind friend; knocking can be done by one who is no orator. Perhaps another cries, 'I am no scholar.' Never mind, a man can knock though he may be no philosopher. A dumb man can knock. A blind man can knock. With a palsied hand a man may knock. He who knows nothing of his book can still lift a hammer and let it fall. The way to open heaven[']s gate is wonderfully simplified to those who are lowly enough to follow the Holy Spirit's guidance, and ask, seek, and knock believingly. God has not provided a salvation which can only be understood by learned men; he has not prepared a gospel which requires half-a-dozen folio volumes to describe it: it is intended for the ignorant, the short-witted, and the

dying, as well as for others, and hence it must be as plain as knocking at a door." *MTP* 29:307.

6. Charles was likely referring to the growing ritualism under Edward Pusey found in the written and read prayers (i.e., formed prayers) of the Church of England. This movement, also known as Puseyism, Tractarianism, or the Oxford Movement, was a subject of concern for Charles in previous sermons. See "Salvation in God Only" (Notebook 1, Sermon 24); "The Fight and the Weapons" (Notebook 1, Sermon 37a); "Justification by Imputed Righteousness" (Notebook 2, Sermon 117); "Come Ye Out from Among Them" (Notebook 2, Sermon 119); "More for Us Than Against Us" (Notebook 3, Sermon 180); "Linsey-Woolsey Forbidden" (Notebook 4, Sermon 210).

7. "'Knock, and it shall be opened unto you.' Observe how plain and positive it is with its glorious 'shall' burning like a lamp in the center of it. In letters of love the inscription shines out amidst all the darkness that surrounds you, and these are its words, 'It shall be opened unto you.' If you knock at the door of the kindest of men you see no such promise set before you, and yet you knock, and knock confidently; how much more boldly should you come to the door of grace when it is expressly declared, 'It shall be opened unto you!'" *MTP* 29:309.

8. Cf. Gen 18:23–33.
9. Cf. Gen 32:24–29.
10. Cf. Exod 33:12–23.
11. Cf. Judg 6:36–40.
12. Cf. 2 Sam 5:17–25; 24:10–25.
13. Cf. 1 Kgs 18:30–38, 41–46.
14. Cf. 2 Kgs 19:14–37; 20:1–11.
15. Cf. 2 Chr 33:12–13.
16. Cf. Jonah 2:1–10.
17. "The Church is never healthy except when she abounds in prayer. . . . Now, what Church can be considered to be as Christ would have her, when her members meet to pray, and they constitute but a handful? I care not if the place is crowded at your other services, the Church is not prosperous if the prayer-meetings be thin. It signifies nothing if that Church has sent up a hundred, or five hundred, or a thousand pounds to the Missionary Society—write 'Ichabod' on her walls, unless the brethren meet together for prayer. The most erudite minister may

instruct the people; the most earnest preacher may plead God's cause with men, but if he hath not with him a band of men who plead man's cause with God, his pleadings will be in vain. Shut up that house in which men have ceased to pray; or if you open it, let your opening be a meeting for hearty and earnest prayer." *NPSP* 6:224.

18. This was an unusual comment from Charles, but he was likely referring to the sinner's own fear, unbelief, and lack of persistence, which causes the sinner to give up seeking.

252. Hos. VII. 9.   Spiritual Decline.

A double figure is here used to set forth the sad state of Israel. Secret robbers had eaten his substance & unnoticed old age was creeping upon him. It may possibly be so with some of us & if not, it will be profitable surely for us to know our own state.—

That Christians may much decline must be admitted by every person who looks either at his own experience or at the church of God. We are often dull, careless — yea wandering ourselves and our friends are sometimes hot & then cold.

Decline in grace is the frost which nips the plant, the locust ravaging all around.

I. What are the causes of decline?

1. Sometimes an unedifying ministry, wanting salt, life, & truth. If our food be adulterated we shall not thrive so well, even though it be given to us in the most elegant or eloquent way. Take heed to go where you can get food.

2. Then far oftener it is neglect of private devotion — Sluggishness in prayer — Seldom reading the word of grace. No meditation upon the great truths contained therein. Here alas the greatest part of declension commences — This is the fountain

SPIRITUAL DECLINE
Hosea 7:9[1]

"Strangers have devoured his strength, and he knoweth it not: yea, gray hairs are here and there upon him, yet he knoweth not."

A double figure is here used to set forth the sad state of Israel.[2] Secret robbers had eaten his substance[,] and unnoticed old age was creeping upon him. It may possibly be so with some of us[,] and if not, it will be profitable surely for us to know our own state.

That Christians may much decline must be admitted by every person who looks either at his own experience or at the church of God.[3] We are often dull, careless, yea wandering ourselves, and our friends are sometimes hot and then cold.

Decline in grace is the frost which nips the plant, the locust ravaging all around.[4]

I. WHAT ARE THE CAUSES OF DECLINE?

1. Sometimes an unedifying ministry, wanting salt, life, and truth.[5] If our food be adulterated we shall not thrive so well,[6] even though it be given to us in the most elegant or eloquent way.[7] Take heed to go where you can get food.

2. Then far oftener it is neglect of private devotion. Sluggishness in prayer.[8] Seldom reading the word of grace.[9] No meditation upon the great truths contained therein. Here alas the greatest part of declension commences. This is the fountain.

3. Too worldly a spirit — too much business, anxiety, desire of gain, discontent, pride with all the train of worldly passions.
4. Evil company, light conversation, &c —
5. Indulgence in known sin, whatever may be our besetting sin if we curb it not we cannot help declining —

There are many other causes, which our experience warns us of let these suffice & now let us enquire whether we are declining & in searching we must endeavour to see.

II. What are the Symptoms of decline?
1. Closet Symptoms. As this is the seat of the evil, it feels it first — There will be a want of life, enjoyment, peace, presence of God & delight in prayer — Is it so with us?
2. Family Symptoms. The man pays less attention to his language & conduct in his house. Family prayer is hurried over, religion seldom broached, children ill taught.
3. Sabbath Symptoms. — Want of appetite, a critical spirit, seldom enjoying the word, the days services a duty more than a delight.
4. Church Symptoms. Want of love to the brethren, forgetfulness of their wants.

SPIRITUAL DECLINE—*Hosea 7:9*

3. Too worldly a spirit. Too much business, anxiety, desire of gain, discontent, pride with all the train of worldly passions.[10]
4. Evil company, light conversation,[11] etc.
5. Indulgence in known sin. Whatever may be our besetting sin[,] if we curb it not[,] we cannot help declining.[12]

    There are many other causes, which our experience warns us of[.] [L]et these suffice and now let us enquire whether we are declining. And in searching we must endeavour to see.

II. WHAT ARE THE SYMPTOMS OF DECLINE?

1. Closet Symptoms. As this is the seat of the evil, it feels it first. There will be a want of life, enjoyment, peace, [the] presence of God[,] and delight in prayer. Is it so with us?
2. Family Symptoms. The man pays less attention to his language and conduct in his house. Family prayer is hurried over, religion seldom broached, [and] children ill taught.[13]
3. Sabbath Symptoms. Want of appetite, a critical spirit, seldom enjoying the word, the day[']s services a duty more than a delight.[14]
4. Church Symptoms. Want of love to the brethren,[15] forgetfulness of their wants,[16]

neglect of visiting the sick — absence from prayer meeting, resting on past doings. Zeal gone, no desire for increase —
5. Week-day Symptoms. Forgetfulness of God, loss of tenderness of conscience, slight sins, conformity to the world — not serving God in business —
<u>III</u>. What are the results of decline?
1. If it continues we may fear that our conversion is not real & we may turn out to be hypocrites.
2. It will bring on us much affliction in getting back to the road.
3. It will spoil our usefulness in the cause of our adorable Lord.
4. It will betray us into gross open sin causing the enemy to blaspheme & the hearts of the brethren to bleed —
    Oh Father recover me & my hearers. Amen

441.

SPIRITUAL DECLINE—*Hosea 7:9*

    neglect of visiting the sick, absence from prayer meeting, resting on past doings. Zeal gone, no desire for increase.

5. Week-day Symptoms. Forgetfulness of God, loss of tenderness of conscience, slight sins, conformity to the world, not serving God in business.

III. WHAT ARE THE RESULTS OF DECLINE?

1. If it continues we may fear that our conversion is not real and we may turn out to be hypocrites.[17]

2. It will bring on us much affliction in getting back to the road.

3. It will spoil our usefulness in the cause of our adorable Lord.[18]

4. It will betray us into gross[,] open sin[,] causing the enemy to blaspheme and the hearts of the brethren to bleed.[19]

    Oh Father recover <u>me</u> and my hearers.

                                          <u>Amen</u>

44I.

SERMON 252

1. It appears that Charles preached this text one other time in his sermon "Grey Hairs" (*MTP* 14, Sermon 830). It is possible that the later sermon was influenced by this one. The overlapping content has been noted below.

2. Charles may have been referring here to the phenomenon of parallelism in Semitic poetry.

3. "Oh, beware of a decline. We were accustomed to use that term years ago to signify the commencement of a consumption, or perhaps the effects of it; and indeed, a decline in the soul often leads on to a deadly consumption. In a spiritual consumption the very life of religion seems to ebb out by little and little. The man does not die by a wound that stabs his reputation, but by a secret weakness within him, which eats at the vitals of godliness and leaves the outward surface fair. God save us from declining." *MTP* 26:152.

4. Cf. Joel 1:4.

5. A few months after his conversion, Charles wrote his mother a letter expressing his concern for the unprofitable preaching under which his family sat: "I often think of you poor starving creatures, following Mr._____ for the bony rhetoric and oratory which he gives you. What a mercy that you are not dependent upon him for spiritual comfort! I hope you will soon give up following that empty cloud without rain, that type-and-shadow preacher, for I don't think there is much substance. But, my dear Mother, why do you not go and hear my friend, Mr. Langford? . . . God can save whom He will, when He will, and where He will, but I think Mr._____'s Mount Sinai roarings are the last things to do it, to all human appearance." *Autobiography* 1:122.

6. Cf. 1 Cor 3:1–3; Heb 5:11–14; 1 Pet 2:2.

7. Charles would later experience such "adulterated" food in the form of the critical theologies that became popular in the second half of the nineteenth century. These theologies, which Charles unequivocally rejected, birthed the Downgrade Controversy that eventually claimed his life. "There is a new theology lately sprung up, which has taken every pea out of the pod, and every kernel out of the shell, and its advocates present us with the empty shucks and shells, and say, 'Do not quarrel with us; we are all brethren; and there is very little difference

between what we hold and what you teach, only we are not so dogmatic and positive as you are.' Yet, all the while, they are throwing doubts upon that which is our very life; and we cannot help feeling that they have learnt the devil's way of dealing with the truth." MTP 45:124–25.

8. "There be some who, if we speak of private prayer, retire into their closets as regularly as others, but yet they never draw near to God in spirit and in truth. How many there be who are as apparently devout in the externals of religion as if they were the children of God, while all the while they are formalists, and Pharisees, without the root of the matter in them. It is the easiest thing in all the world to counterfeit the issues of the mint of heaven; ay, and to pass the spurious coin amongst your fellow creatures, and to make them think that you are richer far than they in gracious things, while all the while your virtue is counterfeit, and your profession a lie. O my hearers, take care of putting formal prayer, sham holiness, and imitation godliness, into the place of the real fruits of the Spirit." MTP 14:508.

9. "Many see not the grey hairs because they do not look into the glass to see them. We cannot very well perceive grey hairs without the use of the mirror, or our sins without the glass of the word. Many professors search not the Scriptures. They will never win the blessing of the first Psalm, for they are not day and night found reading in God's word. They do not come unto this book, which is God's looking-glass, which he hangs up in the chambers of his people, that they may see the natural face, and perceive what manner of men they are. Oh, these unread Bibles! These neglected Bibles, how they cry out against us! What swift witnesses will they be against many professors in the last heart-searching day!" MTP 14:507.

10. "They rise up early, and sit up late, and eat the bread of carefulness, but forget the Lord who alone can build the house. Do not some of you find yourselves falling into this fretful way? There was a time when it was not so. Oh, that hour of prayer, how you enjoyed it, but you clip it very short now! You say you cannot afford the time. Ah, that Thursday night lecture, that evening prayer-meeting, how sweet those used to be! How you went home thanking God that there were such wells in the desert! But you cannot come out to them now you are so pestered with cares, and even on the Sabbath day does your business intrude itself into your thoughts. You have been making calculations in the pew this morning;

you have been worrying yourself about interest and discount, and mortgage and commission. The stockbroker's din and the rate collector's knock have sounded in your ears. The fact is, my friend, you are growing worldly." *MTP* 14:511.

11. "Behaviour; manner of acting in common life." Johnson's *Dictionary*, s.v. "Conversation." Based on the sermon's context, Charles was likely using the word "light" with a negative connotation: "11. Easy to admit any influence; unsteady; unsettled; loose. 12. Gay; airy; wanting dignity or solidity; trifling. 13. Not chaste; not regular in conduct." Johnson's *Dictionary*, s.v. "Light."

12. "Week after week you observe that the general fall of the leaves is drawing nearer, but it is a matter that creeps slowly on. And so with backsliders. They are not put out of the visible church all at once, they do not become open offenders all at once. The heart by slow degrees turns aside from the living God, and then at last comes the outward sin and the outward shame. God save us from falling by little and little! The devil's little strokes have felled many great oaks." *MTP* 14:508.

13. "I esteem [family prayer] so highly that no language of mine can adequately express my sense of its value. The house in which there is no family altar can scarcely expect the divine blessing. If the Lord do not cover our habitation with his wings our family is like a house without a roof; if we do not seek the Lord's guidance our household is a ship without a pilot; and unless guarded by devotion our family will be a field without a hedge. The mournful behaviour of many of the children of professing parents is mainly due to the neglect or the coldness of family worship; and many a judgment has, I doubt not, fallen upon households because the Lord is not duly honoured therein." *MTP* 20:506.

14. "It is a grey hair, too, when we have no delight in listening to the word, or reading it. Time was with some of you when you would cheerfully stand in the aisles with the crowd to listen and were glad, though you had not a place to lean against, if you might catch a good word from the Master. But now it must be a soft cushion if you are to sit easy, and the preacher must mind that he choose out goodly similes and choice words, if he would hold your ear. You are dainty now. When you were hungry, you could eat gospel meat from the bone, cut how it might be; but now it must be daintily carved, or your stomach turns against it. When the appetite fails, the man's health is wrong, and he needs a tonic, and

perhaps the great Physician will ere long send him a bitter draught which will bring him right." *MTP* 14:512–13.

15. "A want of love to believers also is another grey hair. They who love not the Father are not likely to love the children. Many professors seem to be entirely wrapped up in themselves. Their notion of religion is their own salvation, and their idea of zeal is simply seeing after their own prosperity. Brethren, see that ye love one another. 'Little children, love one another,' said John, 'for love is of God;' and if you do not love the poor and needy of Christ's church, and the feeble and the suffering, yea, if your heart doth not go out towards all in whom there is anything of Christ Jesus, depend upon it you are not living so near to God as you should." *MTP* 14:513.

16. "1. Need. 2. Deficiency. 3. The state of not having. 4. Poverty; penury; indigence." Johnson's *Dictionary*, s.v. "Want."

17. "Young people, you joined the church some years ago, and you thought then you felt deep repentance, conviction of sin, and a true faith in Christ; you have had two or three years to try you, how is it with you now? Is not the world getting the upper hand with you? Does not that tempting offer of marriage almost persuade you to break the Lord's command not to be unequally yoked together with unbelievers? Do not the pleasures of the world, which are so congenial to poor evil flesh and blood, do not they begin to fascinate you? Then ask yourselves, 'Am I built on the rock, or is it a sandy foundation? Have I received the grace of God in truth, or am I under some fond delusion, which is lulling my conscience for awhile, and stupefying my reason?' I conjure you by the blessed God, by death and by eternity, make sure work of it; see that you get to Christ and not to a fancied peace; see that you possess true and living faith in a living Savior, and not a confidence based on mere excitement." *MTP* 14:514. See also *LS* 1:339–40 for the story of "Mr. Charles," a church member who initially displayed a dramatic conversion but eventually fell away from the faith.

18. "Next, I beseech you professors, who can honestly feel that you are converted, to remember what will be the result of decays in grace. You cannot keep those decays inward always; even if you could they would be mischievous. They will lose you the company of Christ; they will deprive you of the joy of the Lord; they will mar your prevalence in prayer; they will take away from you much of your usefulness in outward life." *MTP* 14:514.

19. "Do you know what it will come to in the long run, unless grace prevents? Why, these decays will begin to tell upon your outward conduct and conversation. Say not, 'I shall never be an open sinner.' Little dost thou know what thou wilt be. That lip which vows today, 'I will never deny him,' may yet deny Christ with oaths and curses. Who are you that you should be better than Peter? Do not you start at the thought of it? Then start at the sight of these grey hairs. Amend, I pray you, and return to God with grieving and repentance, to think you should already have so much departed from him, or else your last end may be worse than the first." *MTP* 14:514.

Rev. XXII. 5. No night in heaven.

Night on earth is absolutely necessary from its very constitution — the round world cannot have light on its entire surface at once. If he should always shine on us — myriads would never see him. —

Night on earth is no waste of time, it is the season of gathering in fresh strength for the morrows toils. Much is going on in its still hours. The dews are falling. The beasts are prowling, ocean is rolling on & the stars are marching on in their everlasting course.

Night occupies no mean place in the worlds history. — Man's helpmate was fashioned in the hour of night. In night God made or rather confirmed his covenant with Abraham. Twas night that saw the ladder reaching from earth to heaven. Night saw the wrestling angel contending with Jacob. Night was the hour when the red winged angel flew o'er Egypt. At night the fiery pillar was a shield & a sun to Israel when they passed the Red Sea. In the night Gideon saw his foes discomfited. In the night Samson bare away proud Gaza's gates.

NO NIGHT IN HEAVEN
Revelation 22:5[1]

"And there shall be no night there; and they need no candle, neither light of the sun; for the Lord God giveth them light: and they shall reign for ever and ever."

Night on earth is absolutely necessary from its very constitution. The round world cannot have light on its entire surface at once. If he should always shine on us, myriads would never see him.

Night on earth is no waste of time. It is the season of gathering in fresh strength for the morrow[']s toils.[2] Much is going on in its still hours. The dews are falling. The beasts are prowling, [the] ocean is rolling on[,] and the stars are marching on in their everlasting course.

Night occupies no mean place in the world[']s history. Man's helpmate was fashioned in the hour of night.[3] In night God made[,] or rather confirmed[,] his covenant with Abraham.[4] Twas night that saw the ladder reaching from earth to heaven.[5] Night saw the wrestling angel contending with Jacob.[6] Night was the hour when the red winged angel flew o'er Egypt.[7] At night the fiery pillar was a shield[8] and a sun to Israel when they passed the Red Sea.[9] In the night Gideon saw his foes discomfited.[10] In the night Samson bare away proud Gaza's gates.[11]

Let none speak ill of night for in her hours.
1. God has wrought his greatest wonders. —
   First born slain. Egyptians kept at bay near Red Sea.
   Gideon routs the Midianites. Samson in Gaza.
   Sennacherib's army slain. Belshazzar was slain.
   Daniel in Lion's den. Jesus walked on the sea.
   Spoke peace to the storm. Peter released.
   The prison of Paul shaken. &c —
2. God has manifested himself to his people.
   Abraham & the lamps. Jacob's ladder. Peniel.
   Joseph's dreams. Samuel called. Solomon spoken
   to. Eliphaz saw the spirit. Jesus came
   to his own when the doors were shut.
3. God's best gifts have come in the night.
   Woman was given or made at night.
   Jesus became a babe in the night.
   He died in noonday night.
4. Night too has been hallowed.
   By Jacob's prayers. By Nicodemus coming.
   By Jesus prayers all night —
We must remember too the uses of night
as allowing us time for rest.
   We must rest & even the slavedriver's
clotted whip cannot put away night.
Darkness so soft to the eyelids renders it
more easy to sleep — Or if we wake

NO NIGHT IN HEAVEN—*Revelation 22:5*

Let none speak ill of night for in her hours[:]

1. God has wrought his greatest wonders. First born slain,[12] Egyptians kept at bay near Red Sea.[13] Gideon routs the Midianites.[14] Samson in Gaza.[15] Sennacherib's army slain.[16] Belshazzar was slain.[17] Daniel in Lion's den.[18] Jesus walked on the sea.[19] Spoke peace to the storm.[20] Peter released.[21] The prison of Paul shaken.[22] Etc.

2. God has manifested himself to his people: Abraham and the lamps,[23] Jacob's ladder.[24] Peniel.[25] Joseph's dreams.[26] Samuel called.[27] Solomon spoken to.[28] Eliphaz saw the spirit.[29] Jesus came to his own when the doors were shut.[30]

3. God's best gifts have come in the night. Woman was given or made at night.[31] Jesus became a babe in the night.[32] He died in noon-day night.[33]

4. Night too has been hallowed. By Jacob's prayers.[34] By Nicodemus['s] coming.[35] By Jesus['s] prayers all night.[36]

We must remember too the uses of night as allowing us time for rest.

We must rest and even the slavedriver's clotted whip cannot put away night. Darkness so soft to the eyelids renders it more easy to sleep. Or if we wake[,] distant worlds radiant with glory meet our eyes in the clear sky of heaven (night has staid bloodshed)

Let us then bless God for night now, & thank him more that in heaven none is needed and none exists.

I. Night is associated with fatigue — but in heaven they never weary, though with ceaseless song they circle his throne rejoicing. Neither their minds nor their bodies can tire. A heavenly ichor gives perpetual youth, bloom & freshness — They rest, yet rest not.

II. Night is associated with unconsciousness. we are as dead, we know nothing of the great world around us. Save a few light clouds that flit along our empty soul, all is vacuity — but they are never unconscious in glory, they know even as they are known.

III. Night is associated with ignorance. we can then discern but little. we say a dark village, the dark ages &c — Our souls are dark — but rejoice poor ignorant believer in heaven there is no ignorance. Conflicting parties will be no more, no mistakes will arise. We shall wonder at our own extreme ignorance & folly. All things that are to be known we shall

NO NIGHT IN HEAVEN—*Revelation 22:5*

distant worlds radiant with glory meet our eyes in the clear sky of heaven. \Night has staid\ bloodshed. \ Let us then bless God for night <u>now</u>, and thank him more that in heaven none is needed and none exists.

I. NIGHT IS ASSOCIATED WITH FATIGUE.

But in heaven they never weary,[37] though with ceaseless song they circle his throne rejoicing.[38] Neither their minds nor their bodies can tire. A heavenly ichor[39] gives perpetual youth, bloom[,] and freshness. They rest, yet rest not.[40]

II. NIGHT IS ASSOCIATED WITH UNCONSCIOUSNESS.

We are as dead. We know nothing of the great world around us. Save a few light clouds that flit along our empty soul, all is vacuity,[41] but they are never unconscious in glory, they know even as they are known.[42]

III. NIGHT IS ASSOCIATED WITH IGNORANCE.

We can then discern but little. We say a dark village, the dark ages etc. Our souls are dark. But rejoice poor ignorant believer[,] in heaven there is no ignorance.[43] Conflicting parties will be no more. No mistakes will arise. We shall wonder at our own extreme ignorance and folly.

All things that are to be known we shall

know. This is the dispensation of twilight knowledge that the noonday light.

IV. Night is associated with terror. The ignorant then look for sheeted ghosts. Then the thief prowls. The wolf & lion seek their prey. Every trifling noise causes alarm in some minds & even the bravest shake. Dreams scare us, &c But in yon bright worlds fear cannot enter, it is exiled, there is nothing to fear, all is joy & gladness.

V. Night is associated with sin. They that be drunken are drunken in the night, ~~has~~ The mantle of darkness has covered o'er the filthiest crimes. Judas betrayed his master & that master in the seizure of our Saviour was perpetrated 'neath its cover. But in heaven sin cannot breathe. Light is pure & unmingled there. Would to God night could indeed hide man's sin but no — it shall be revealed — Sin is not to be found to worry us there

VI. Night is associated with sorrow. 'Tis sorrow's emblem & the hour she loves

NO NIGHT IN HEAVEN—*Revelation 22:5*

know. <u>This</u> is the dispensation of twilight knowledge[,] <u>that</u> the noonday light.

IV. NIGHT IS ASSOCIATED WITH TERROR.

The ignorant then look for sheeted ghosts. Then the thief prowls. The wolf and lion seek their prey. Every trifling noise causes alarm in some minds[,] and even the bravest shake. Dreams scare us, etc. But in yon bright worlds fear cannot enter, it is exiled. There is nothing to fear, all is joy and gladness.[44]

V. NIGHT IS ASSOCIATED WITH SIN.

They that be drunken are drunken in the night,[45] ~~has~~ The mantle of darkness has covered o'er the filthiest crimes. Judas betrayed his master.[46] And that master sin[,] the seizure of our Saviour[,] was perpetrated 'neath its cover.[47] But in heaven sin cannot breathe. Light is pure and unmingled there. Would to God[48] night could indeed hide man's sin, but no, it shall be revealed.[49] Sin is not to be found to worry us there.[50]

VI. NIGHT IS ASSOCIATED WITH SORROW.

'Tis sorrow[']s emblem and the hour she loves[.]

The hidings of God's face make night in the believers breast — Satan, the world & the flesh do screen the light of heaven — but joy there shall come most pure. A sun of joy sparkling & illuminating our countenance —
"Delighted range th' ethereal plains
"And take our fill of joy.

<u>VII</u>. Night is associated with death. The night cometh. We must die once. The exhalations of life must soon condense into clouds & our sun shall set behind them.

We cannot delight in <u>death</u> itself, although we rejoice at it regarding its consequences too.

In heaven there is no death. There can be none. Immortality is the entail of every heir of grace.

Well may it be that there is no night there. Father give me thine aid &pray

442. 447. 570.

NO NIGHT IN HEAVEN—*Revelation 22:5*

The hidings of God's face make night in the believer[']s breast.[51] Satan, the world, and the flesh[52] do screen the light of heaven, but joy there shall come most pure. A sun of joy sparkling and illuminating our countenance.

> "Delighted range the' ethereal plains["]
>
> "And take our fill of joy.["][53]

VII. NIGHT IS ASSOCIATED WITH DEATH.

The night cometh.[54] We must die once.[55] The exhalations of life must soon condense into clouds and our sun shall set behind them.

We cannot delight in <u>death</u> itself,[56] although we rejoice at it regarding its consequences too.[57]

In heaven there is no death. There can be none.[58] **Immortality is the entail**[59] **of every heir of grace.**

Well may it be that there is no night there.

> Father give me thine aid I pray.

442. 447. 570.

1. It appears that Charles did not preach another sermon on the text of Rev 22:5.

2. Charles dedicated an entire sermon to the value of sleep as a gift from God, "The Peculiar Sleep of the Beloved" (*NPSP* 1, Sermon 12). In this sermon he wrote, "O my friends, how thankful should we be for sleep. Sleep is the best physician that I know of. Sleep hath healed more pains of wearied bones than the most eminent physicians upon earth. It is the best medicine; the choicest thing of all the names which are written in all the lists of pharmacy. There is nothing like to sleep! What a mercy it is that it belongs alike to all! God does not make sleep the boon of the rich man, he does not give it merely to the noble, or the rich, so that they can keep it as a peculiar luxury from themselves; but he bestows it upon all." *NPSP* 1:85–86.

3. Cf. Gen 2:21.

4. Cf. Gen 15:12–21.

5. Cf. Gen 28:12–17.

6. Cf. Gen 32:24–31.

7. Cf. Exod 12:29.

8. Cf. Exod 13:21–22.

9. Cf. Exod 14:19–20.

10. "To defeat; to conquer; to vanquish; to overpower; to subdue; to beat; to overthrow." Johnson's *Dictionary*, s.v. "To Discomfit." Cf. Judg 7:9–22.

11. Cf. Judg 16:2–3.

12. Cf. Exod 12:29.

13. Cf. Exod 14:19–20.

14. Cf. Judg 7:9–22.

15. Cf. Judg 16:2–3.

16. Cf. 2 Kgs 19:35–36.

17. Cf. Dan 5:30.

18. Cf. Dan 6:16–22.

19. Cf. Matt 14:25; Mark 6:48; John 6:17–19.

20. Cf. Matt 8:23–27; Mark 4:37–41; Luke 8:23–25.

21. Cf. Acts 12:6–12.

22. Cf. Acts 16:25–26.

23. Cf. Gen 15:17.

24. Cf. Gen 28:12.

25. Cf. Gen 32:30.   26. Cf. Gen 37:5–11.

27. Cf. 1 Sam 3:1–14.   28. Cf. 1 Kgs 3:5–15.

29. Cf. Job 4:12–21.   30. Cf. John 20:19.

31. Cf. Gen 2:21–22.   32. Cf. Luke 2:6–7.

33. Cf. Matt 27:45–50; Mark 15:33–37; Luke 23:44–46.

34. Cf. Gen 32:9–13, 24–31.   35. Cf. John 3:1–2.

36. Cf. Luke 6:12.   37. Cf. Isa 40:31.

38. Cf. Rev 4:8; 7:15.

39. "A thin watery humour like serum." Johnson's *Dictionary*, s.v. "Ichor."

40. Cf. Heb 4:1–10; Rev 14:13.

41. "1. Emptiness; state of being unfilled. 2. Space unfilled; space unoccupied. 3. Inanity; want of reality." Johnson's *Dictionary*, s.v. "Vacuity."

42. Cf. 1 Cor 13:12.   43. Cf. 1 Cor 13:11–12.

44. Cf. Isa 51:11   45. Cf. 1 Thess 5:7.

46. Cf. John 13:30.   47. Cf. Matt 27:45; Mark 15:33; Luke 23:44.

48. In this context, "Would to God" functioned as an emphatic expression denoting a wish that was not expected to be fulfilled for one reason or another. In modern English, the phrase is quite similar in force to "If only!"

49. Cf. Luke 12:2.   50. Cf. Rev 21:27.

51. "Oh! how transitory is our view of Jesus!! It is only a little while we get a glimpse of Christ, and then he seems to depart from us. . . . But, Christians, there will be no hidings of faces in heaven! Blessed Lord Jesus! there will be no coverings of thine eyes in glory; Is not thine heart a sea of love, where all my passions roll? And there is no ebb-tide of thy sea, sweet Jesus, there. Art thou not everything?

SERMON 253

There will be no losing thee there—no putting thy hand before thine eyes up there; but without a single alteration, without change or diminution, our unwearied, unclouded eyes, shall throughout eternity perpetually behold thee. 'We shall see him as he is!'" *NPSP* 2:65–66.

52. Cf. Eph 2:1–3.

53. Here, Charles appears to be quoting the final verse of Simon Brown's hymn "Frequent the Day of God Returns." *A New Selection of Hymns, Especially Adapted to Public Worship, and Intended as a Supplement to Dr. Watts' Psalms and Hymns*, 4th ed. (London: printed for the proprietors by J. Haddon, 1830), Hymn 325. In full, the verse reads, "Where we, in high seraphic strains, / Shall all our power employ; / Delighted range th' ethereal plains, / And take our fill of joy."

54. Cf. John 9:4.   55. Cf. Heb 9:27.

56. Cf. 1 Cor 15:26.

57. "It is the glow of the Christian religion to have let light into the sepulcher, to have taken the sting away from death, and, in fact, to have made it no more death to die." *MTP* 46:39.

58. Cf. 1 Cor 15:54–55.

59. "1. The estate entailed or settled, with regard to the rule of its descent. 2. The rule of descent settled for any estate." Johnson's *Dictionary*, s.v. "Entail."

254 Col. I. 19.   All fulness in Jesus.

It is one great object of the plan of salvation to glorify Jesus Christ. God will make his son sit preeminent & every Christian desires to see him have the honour & the praise & the power. Every system of divinity should be tried by this touch-stone & every doctrine that does not really magnify Christ must be rejected.

Down goes Popery, Socinianism is abjured, Merit ceases and some Arminian tenets fall.

I. The Fulness — in Christ —

How can we better prepare to meditate on this glorious fact than by considering our own *emptiness* by Adam's fall, by our own sins, by our evil nature &c — But in him there is "fulness".

Put again all our graces & gifts together, (though received from him) how small our united graces, or those of all the elect —; in us in our best estate there is *paucity* but in him there is fulness

There dwells in him as God all the fulness of divinity, of all the attributes of God he has a fulness — whether it be omnipotence, omniscience, eternity

ALL FUL[L]NESS IN JESUS[1]
Colossians 1:19[2]

"For it pleased the Father that in him should all fulness dwell."

It is one great object of the plan of salvation to glorify Jesus Christ. God will make his son sit preeminent and every Christian desires to see him have the honour and the praise and the power.[3] Every system of divinity should be tried by this touchstone[4] and every doctrine that does not really magnify Christ must be rejected.

Down goes Popery, Socinianism is abjured, Merit ceases and some Arminian tenets fall.[5]

I. THE FULNESS. IN CHRIST.

How can we better prepare to meditate on this glorious fact than by considering our own emptiness[?][6] [B]y Adam's fall,[7] by our own sins, by our evil nature etc.[8] But in him there is "fulness."

Put again all our graces and gifts together, (though received from him) how small our united graces, or those of all the elect. In us[,] in our best estate[,] there is paucity[,][9] but in him there is fulness.

There dwells in him as God all the fulness of divinity. Of all the attributes of God he has a fulness – whether it be omnipotence, omniscience, eternity,

infinity, immutability, or selfexistence.
In all his various offices he has a fulness.
He is a <u>Mediator</u>, and he is completely so, no priest
or angel is required, he is in this — <u>fulness</u>.
He is a <u>Councillor</u>, to plead our cause, our advocate who never fails — whatever foe accuses
we are acquitted from harm by his <u>fulness</u>
He is a <u>Substitute</u>, a <u>Redeemer</u>, a <u>Deliverer</u>
a <u>Conqueror</u>, a <u>Captain</u>, a Friend &
in all these he is intensely, superlatively
the <u>fulness</u> of every character.
As <u>Prophet</u>, never has he been equalled.
In depth of knowledge, penetration of character
kindness & firmness, wisdom & love. —
We need not chose any philosopher,
or divine for our leader, <u>he</u> is <u>fulness</u>.
Nor need we look for signs & wonders
or fresh revalations — for Christ is
our <u>fulness</u> & we want none other —
As <u>Priest</u>. He is Melchizedek.
He needs no altar, victim, fire or vestments
he is all in himself — <u>fulness</u>
No type & shadow, symbol or picture
he is the <u>fulness</u> — —
No need of aid from works, or penance
or hosts, or priests, or groans, tears &c —

ALL FUL[L]NESS IN JESUS—*Colossians 1:19*

infinity, immutability, or self-existence.[10]

In all his various offices he has a fulness. He is a <u>Mediator</u>,[11] and he is completely so. No priest or angel is required.[12] He is in this, <u>fulness</u>. He is a <u>Councillor</u>,[13] to plead our cause, our advocate who never fails.[14] Whatever foe accuses, we are acquitted from harm by his <u>fulness</u>.[15] He is a <u>Substitute</u>,[16] a <u>Redeemer</u>,[17] a <u>Deliverer</u>,[18] a <u>Conqueror</u>,[19] <u>a Captain</u>,[20] a Friend[21] and in all these he is intensely, superlatively the <u>fulness</u> of every character.

As <u>Prophet</u>,[22] never has he been equalled. In depth of knowledge, penetration of character, kindness and firmness, wisdom and love. We need not choose any philosopher or divine for our leader, <u>he</u> is <u>fulness</u>.[23] Nor need we look for signs and wonders[,] or fresh revelations, for Christ is our fulness and we want none other.

<u>As Priest</u>.[24] He is Melchizedek.[25] He needs no altar,[26] victim,[27] fire[,][28] or vestments[,][29] he is all in himself,[30] <u>fulness</u>. No type and shadow,[31] symbol or picture[,] he is the fulness.

No need of aid from works, or penance or hosts, or priests, or groans, tears etc.

All is stored in him, the fulness —
Surely as priest he needs to have it if he would pardon us — Scanty mercy will not avail for great sinners but thanks be to God he has fulness.
As King, all power dwells in him. Popes are impostors, Kings or queens who call themselves Heads of the Church are but Usurpers — no tier on tier of rectors deans, prebends, bishops & archbishops. But all power is with him — The government is on his shoulders. He will never lose one of his for lack of power for he has all fulness of Kingly might —

Now stay a moment & admire Jesus Christ in his fulness. Let all mean thoughts of him be gone, banish distrusful fears & mourning thy poverty adore his fulness —

II. The Dwelling —— of the fulness.
He is not as a river swollen at one time & dry at another — nor is this

ALL FUL[L]NESS IN JESUS—*Colossians 1:19*

All is stored in him, the fulness.

Surely as priest he needs to have it if he would pardon us. Scanty[32] mercy will not avail for great sinners[,] but thanks be to God he has <u>fulness</u>.[33]

<u>As King</u>,[34] all power dwells in him. Popes are impostors, kings or queens who call themselves Heads of the Church are but usurpers.[35] No tier on tier of rectors, deans, prebends, bishops[,] and archbishops.[36] But all power is with him. The government is on his shoulders.[37]

He will never lose one of his for lack of power[,][38] for he has all fulness of kingly might.

Now stay a moment and admire Jesus Christ in his fulness. Let all mean[39] thoughts of him be gone, banish distrustful fears[,] and[,] mourning thy poverty, adore his fulness.

II. THE <u>DWELLING.</u> OF THE FULNESS.

He is not as a river swollen at one time and dry at another.[40] Nor is this fulness like the foliage of summer but on him it dwells — Aaron laid aside his vests at death but this man never. The prophets sometimes were but as one of the people, he has it dwelling in him, we have varying graces his ever dwells they cannot be transferred. The same yesterday, to-day & for ever —

Remember then poor soul though thou dost change, he does not, it dwells in him.

III. The Choice — made by the Father. It is the Father's will that all fulness should be in Jesus — & that

1. Because thus all honour comes to him.
2. There is none other so fitting as he Adam has failed once, he will not do — Priests would turn monopolizers or sell to the rich alone, — we ourselves cannot be trusted, we should soon undo ourselves if set up with the largest stock of capital.
3. He alone (by his Godhead) can possibly contain all the fulness — & preserve it for ever —

May we each receive of his fulness, and grace for grace.

448.461.

fulness like the foliage of summer[,] but on him it dwells. Aaron laid aside his vests at death[,][41] but this man <u>never</u>. The prophets sometimes were but as one of the people,[42] he has it dwelling in him.

We have varying graces, his ever dwell. They cannot be transferred. The same yesterday, to-day[,] and for ever.[43]

Remember then poor soul[,] though thou dost change, he does not. It <u>dwells</u> in him.

III. THE CHOICE. MADE BY THE FATHER.[44]

It is the Father's will that all fulness should be in Jesus. And that[:]

1. Because thus[,] all honour comes to him.[45]
2. There is none other so fitting as he.[46]

    <u>Adam</u> has failed once. He will not do.[47]

    <u>Priests</u> would turn monopolizers or sell to the rich alone.

    <u>We</u> ourselves cannot be trusted. We should soon undo ourselves if set up with the largest stock of capital.

3. He alone (by his Godhead) can possibly contain all the fulness. And preserve it for ever.[48]

    May we each receive of his fulness.

          And grace for grace.[49]

448. 461.

SERMON 254

1. Charles spelled "fullness" with only one "l" throughout this sermon, which matches the King James Bible spelling.

2. It appears that Charles preached two later sermons on this text: "All Fulness in Christ" (*MTP* 17, Sermon 978) and "The Fulness of Christ the Treasury of the Saints" (*MTP* 20, Sermon 1169). Notably, both sermons share overlapping general thematic material, but this is likely due to the nature of the text that Charles preached. However, "All Fulness in Christ" (*MTP* 17, Sermon 978) contains a significant amount of overlapping content. Further, the structural division of the sermon indicates that it was possibly influenced by this earlier sermon. The overlapping content has been noted below.

3. Cf. Ps 110:1; Col 1:18. "The preacher is under no difficulties this morning as to the practical object to be aimed at in his discourse. . . . Read the words of the immediately preceding text, and you find it declared that our Lord Jesus is in all things to have pre-eminence. We would seek by this text to yield honour and glory to the ever-blessed Redeemer, and enthrone him in the highest seat in our hearts. O that we may all be in an adoring frame of mind, and may give him the pre-eminence in our thoughts, beyond all things or persons in heaven or earth." *MTP* 17:121.

4. Cf. "1. Stone by which metals are examined. 2. Any test or criterion." Johnson's *Dictionary*, s.v. "Touchstone."

5. In his critique of Arminianism, Charles was careful not to reject it entirely (as he did Popery and Socinianism). At the same time, he believed that "some Arminian tenets" do not "really magnify Christ." On another occasion, Charles wrote, "I do not wonder that a man who believes Arminian doctrine, for instance, has little peace. There is nothing in the doctrine to give him any. It is a bone without marrow; it is a religion that seems to me to be cold, sapless, marrowless, fruitless--bitter and not sweet. There is nothing about it but the whip of the law; there are no grand certainties--no glorious facts of covenant love, of discriminating grace, of Almighty faithfulness, and suretyship engagements. I will never quarrel with the man that can live on such stones and scorpions as conditional election, haphazard redemption, questionable perseverance, and unavailing regeneration. There may be some, I suppose, who can live on this dry meat. If they can live on it, be it so; but I believe many of our doubts and fears arise from doctrinal ignorance." *NPSP* 6:115.

6. "In us there is a lack of all merit, an absence of all power to procure any, and even an absence of will to procure it if we could. In these respects human nature is a desert, empty, and void, and waste, inhabited only by the dragon of sin, and the bittern of sorrow." *MTP* 17:122.

7. Cf. Genesis 3.

8. "You, sinner, are all emptiness and death; you, saint, would be so if it were not for the 'all fulness' of Christ which you have received; therefore both to saint and sinner the words are full of hope. There is joy in these words to every soul conscious of its sad estate, and humbled before God." *MTP* 17:122.

9. "1. Fewness; smallness of number. 2. Smallness of quantity." Johnson's *Dictionary*, s.v. "Paucity."

10. "When John saw the Son of Man in Patmos, the marks of Deity were on him. 'His head and his hairs were white like wool, as white as snow'—here was [the Son of Man's] eternity; 'His eyes were as a flame of fire'—here was his omniscience; 'Out of his mouth went a sharp two-edged sword'—here was the omnipotence of his word; 'And his countenance was as the sun shineth in his strength'—here was his unapproachable and infinite glory. [Jesus] is the Alpha and Omega, the beginning and the end, the first and the last. Hence nothing is too hard for him. Power, wisdom, truth, immutability, and all the attributes of God are in him, and constitute a fulness inconceivable and inexhaustible. The most enlarged intellect must necessarily fail to compass the personal fulness of Christ as God." *MTP* 17:123.

11. Cf. Heb 9:14–15. "Fulness, moreover, dwells in our Lord not only intrinsically from his nature, but as the result of his mediatorial world. He achieved by suffering as well as possessed by nature a wondrous fulness. He carried on his shoulders the load of our sin; he expiated by his death our guilt, and now he has merit with the Father, infinite, inconceivable, a fulness of desert." *MTP* 17:124.

12. Cf. Heb 1:4–14; 9:6–10.

13. Cf. Isa 9:6.   14. Cf. 1 John 2:1–2.

15. Cf. Rom 8:34. "All fulness towards God and—I mean all that God requires of man; all that contents and delights the eternal mind, so that once again with

complacency he may look down on his creature and pronounce him 'very good.' The Lord looked for grapes in his vineyard, and it brought forth wild grapes, but now in Christ Jesus the great Husbandman beholds the true vine which bringeth forth much fruit. The Creator required obedience, and he beholds in Christ Jesus the servant who has never failed to do the Master's will." *MTP* 17:124.

16. Cf. Isa 53:4–6; Mark 10:45; John 10:11; Rom 5:6; 2 Cor 5:21; 1 Pet 2:23–25.

17. Cf. Luke 1:68; 1 Cor 1:30; 7:23; Gal 3:13–14; Eph 1:7; Col 1:13–14.

18. Cf. Ps 18:2; Gal 1:4; 1 Thess 1:10.

19. Cf. Rom 8:37; Rev 19:11.

20. Cf. Heb 2:10.   21. Cf. John 15:15.

22. Cf. Deut 18:15; Acts 3:22–23.

23. "Let it be noted here, however, very carefully, that while fulness is treasured up in Christ, it is not said to be treasured up in the doctrines of Christ; though they are full and complete, and we need no other teachings when the Spirit reveals the Son in us; nor is it said to be treasured up in the commands of Christ, although they are amply sufficient for our guidance; but it is said, 'It pleased the Father that in him,' in his person, 'should all fulness dwell.' In him, as God incarnate dwelleth in all the fulness of the godhead bodily; not as a myth, a dream, a thought, a fiction, but as a living, real personality. We must lay hold of this." *MTP* 17:128.

24. Cf. Heb 6:20; 9:26–27; 10:12.

25. Cf. Heb 7:11–28.   26. Cf. Lev 17:6; Deut 12:27.

27. Charles here was referring to the sacrifice. Cf. Num 6:10–11, 14; 15:27; 29:11.

28. Cf. Lev 6:13.   29. Cf. Exod 28.

30. Cf. Heb 10:8–14.

31. "Types may instruct, but they cannot actually save. The patterns of the things in the heavens are too weak to serve our turn, we need the heavenly things

themselves. No bleeding bird nor slaughtered bullock, nor running stream, nor scarlet wool and hyssop, can take away our sins." *MTP* 17:122.

32. "1. Narrow; small; wanting amplitude; short of quantity sufficient. 2. Small; poor, not copious; not ample." Johnson's *Dictionary*, s.v. "Scanty."

33. "Here is exactly what our desperate estate demands for its recovery. Had the Saviour only put out his finger to help our exertions, or had he only stretched out his hand to perform a measure of salvation's work, while he left us to complete it, our soul had for ever dwelt in darkness. In these words, 'all fulness,' we hear the echo of his death-cry, 'It is finished.' We are to bring nothing, but to find all in him, yea, the fulness of all in him: we are simply to receive out of his fulness grace for grace." *MTP* 17:123.

34. Cf. John 12:15; 18:37; 1 Tim 6:15; Rev 17:14; 19:16. "I know that the fulness dwells in him officially as Prophet, Priest, and King—but the fulness lies not in the prophetic mantle, nor in the priestly ephod, nor in the royal vesture, but in the person that wears all these." *MTP* 17:128–29.

35. Throughout his ministry, Charles was vigorously opposed to the state sponsorship of the Church of England. In his view, the kingship of the Church belonged to Christ, and no earthly monarch could merit the title "head of the church." Charles once remarked on the text of Isa 49:20–23, saying, "There is no headship of the Church here, nothing of that sort; the kings are to be at the feet of the Church, and that is what the State ought to do, submit itself to God, and obey his commands, and give full liberty to the preaching of the gospel. This is all the true Church of Christ asks, and all she can ever fairly take if she is loyal to her Lord." *MTP* 46:576.

36. "Go to your dupes who know not Christ, those who possess the exceeding riches of Christ's grace bow not to you. We are 'complete in Christ' without you, O hierarchy of bishops; without you, ye conclave of cardinals; and without you, O fallible infallible, unholy Holiness of Rome. He who has all in Christ would be insane indeed if he looked for more, or having fulness craved for emptiness. This text drives us from all confidence in men, ay, or even in angels, by making us see that everything is treasured up in Jesus Christ." *MTP* 17:126.

37. Cf. Isa 9:6.   38. Cf. John 10:28–29.

39. "1. Wanting dignity; of low rank or birth. 2. Low-minded; base; ungenerous; spiritless. 3. Contemptible; despicable. 4. Low in the degree of any good quality; low in worth; low in power." Johnson's *Dictionary*, s.v. "Mean."

40. Charles may have had in mind the wadis of the Middle East. Charles wanted to highlight the permanence of the fullness of God dwelling in Christ: "While the expression '*dwell*' indicates perpetuity, does it not indicate *constancy and accessibility*? A man who dwells in a house is always to be found there, it is his home. The text seems to me to say that this fulness of grace is always to be found in Christ, ever abiding in him." *MTP* 17:131, italics in original.

41. Cf. Num 20:27–28.   42. Cf. 1 Kgs 19:19; Amos 1:1.

43. Cf. Heb 13:8. "Above all, here we see immutability. All fulness dwells in Christ – that is to say, it is never exhausted or diminished. . . . He is to-day as great a Saviour as when Magdalen was delivered from seven devils. Till time shall be no more he will exercise the same infinite power to forgive, to renew, to deliver, to sanctify, to perfectly save souls. Shall not all this make us praise Christ, since all fulness is permanent in him?" *MTP* 17:131.

44. "III. The third question is, WHY? '*It pleased the Father.*' That is answer enough. He is a sovereign, let him do as he wills. Ask the reason for election, you shall receive no other than this, 'Even so, Father, for so it seemed good in thy sight.'" *MTP* 17:129, italics and capitals in the original.

45. Cf. John 5:22–23. "This is the very crown and glory of being saved, that our being saved will bring honour to Christ. It is delightful to think that Christ will have the glory of all God's grace; it were shocking if it were not so. Who could bear to see Jesus robbed of his reward? We are indignant that any should usurp his place, and ashamed of ourselves that we do not glorify him more. No joy ever visits my soul like that of knowing that Jesus is highly exalted, and that to him 'every knee shall bow and every tongue confess that Jesus Christ is Lord, to the glory of God the Father.'" *MTP* 17:130.

46. Cf. Rev 5:11–14.   47. Cf. Rom 5:12–21; 1 Cor 15:20–28.

48. "Where else could all fulness have been placed? There was wanted a vast capacity to contain 'all fulness.' Where dwells there a being with nature capacious enough to compass within himself all fulness?... To [Christ] only could it belong to contain 'all fulness,' for he must be equal with God, the Infinite." *MTP* 17:127.

49. Cf. John 1:16.

255. Isa XXVIII. 16. "He that believeth shall not make haste."

It is almost a pity to have to leave the first part of the verse but indeed time would fail to do it justice —

Jesus our crucified Lord is here promised as one laid in Zion for her sons to build on for a foundation. A stone, no wood but something solid, a tried stone which has never failed though it has often been tried — a precious (more than diamonds) corner stone. Like as if one of the great stones of Stonehenge, were laid along the side of a building so as to have its ends at the corners & knit the building together. A sure foundation, nor arminian quicksand, moving about but sure to all the seed. Have we found Jesus to be truly these to us —

But now to the text. —
It has been misunderstood by some who say they must not make haste to be baptized or join the church. Now the text means no such thing

"HE THAT BELIEVETH SHALL NOT MAKE HASTE"
Isaiah 28:16[1]

"Therefore thus saith the Lord God, Behold, I lay in Zion for a foundation a stone, a tried stone, a precious corner stone, a sure foundation: he that believeth shall not make haste."

It is almost a pity to have to leave the first part of the verse[,] but indeed time would fail to do it justice.

Jesus our crucified Lord is here promised as one laid in Zion for her sons to build on for a foundation.[2] A stone, no wood but something solid, a tried stone which has never failed though it has often been tried. A precious (more than diamonds) corner stone. Like as if one of the great stones of Stonehenge were laid along the side of a building so as to have its ends at the corners and knit the building together. A <u>sure</u> foundation, no[t] Arminian quicksand, moving about but <u>sure</u> to all the seed.[3]

Have we found Jesus to be truly these to us?

But now to the text.

It has been misunderstood by some who say they must not make haste to be baptized or join the church. Now the text means no such thing.[4]

David says in Ps. CXIX. 60. I made haste & delayed not to run in the ways of thy commandments.
The Jailor was baptized the very night & hour in which he was ~~baptized~~ converted. Why tarriest thou? The Eunuch received it since he believed with all his heart.
But you say then what does it me.

I. It means that believers will not be impatient. If the promise tarry they will wait for it. In troubles they will wait their Maker's will. They will be content to <u>wait</u> for their portion. They will pray if no sign of an answer comes.

II. It means that believers will be calm in danger trusting in their God. When others are running to hills for shelter their stronghold makes them secure. Nothing can make them afraid.

III. It means (I think) that true believers will not be flitting but enduring ones. Not as the field flower, the meteor, the cataract, These are hasty things, they soon disappear; but a Christian casts forth his roots like Lebanon's cedars or as the majestic oak.

Mark this enduring calm stability is promised to b<u>elievers</u>, not to <u>workers</u>. <u>Workers</u> by all their toils shall gather gall & not honey — They are slaves, they are never certain of salvation but true

"HE THAT BELIEVETH SHALL NOT . . ."—Isaiah 28:16

David sings in Ps. CXIX. 60. ["]I made haste and delayed not to run in the ways of thy commandments.["]⁵ The Jailor was baptized the very night and hour in which he was ~~baptized~~ converted.⁶ Why tarriest thou? The Eunuch received it since he believed with all his heart.⁷

But you say then what does it me[an?]

I. IT MEANS THAT BELIEVERS WILL NOT BE IMPATIENT.

If the promise tarry they will wait for it. In troubles they will wait [for] their Maker's will. They will be content to <u>wait</u> for their portion. They will pray if no sign of an answer comes.

II. IT MEANS THAT BELIEVERS WILL BE CALM IN DANGER[,] TRUSTING IN THEIR GOD.

When others are running to hills for shelter[,] their stronghold makes them secure.

Nothing can make them afraid.⁸

III. IT MEANS (I THINK)⁹ THAT TRUE BELIEVERS WILL NOT BE FLITTING¹⁰ BUT ENDURING ONES.

Not as the field flower,¹¹ the meteor, the cataract.¹² These are hasty things, they soon disappear; but a Christian casts forth his roots like Lebanon's cedars¹³ or as the majestic oak.

Mark this enduring[,] calm stability is promised to <u>believers</u>, not to <u>workers</u>.

<u>Workers</u> by all their toils shall gather gall¹⁴ and not honey.¹⁵ They are slaves,¹⁶ they are never certain of salvation but true

believers can talk with certainty of security.

God has not promised it to workers, lest men should boast — faith is the only grace which could comport with free grace & whole glory to God —

To believe is to trust in Jesus alone for salvation, it must be accompanied with repentance & be productive of fruit otherwise it is of no true use.

Before a man will believe on Jesus alone — he must see the need of a Saviour then he must see the emptiness of every other way of salvation & at last as a guilty one must cast himself on the mercy & love of Jesus Christ.

God will then supply fresh oil to his lamp so that it shall not be quenched for ever —

He that believeth shall not make haste. God of love — help me. I pray —

449

"HE THAT BELIEVETH SHALL NOT . . ."—*Isaiah 28:16*

believers can talk with certainty of security.[17]

God has not promised it to workers, lest men should boast.[18] Faith is the only grace which could comport with free grace and whole glory to God.[19]

To believe is to trust in Jesus alone for salvation[.] [I]t must be accompanied with repentance and be productive of fruit[,] otherwise it is of no true use.

Before a man will believe on Jesus alone, he must see the need of a Saviour. Then he must see the emptiness of every other way of salvation[,] and at last, as a guilty one[,] must cast himself on the mercy and love of Jesus Christ.[20]

God will then supply fresh oil to his lamp so that it shall not be quenched for ever.[21]

He that believeth shall not make haste.

God of love, help me. I pray.

449

SERMON 255

1. It appears that Charles did not preach another sermon on the text of Isa 28:16.

2. Cf. 1 Pet 2:4–6. John Gill wrote, "Christ, who is frequently spoken of, under the simile of a stone, Genesis xlix. 24, and may be compared to one for his usefulness in the spiritual building, being both foundation and cornerstone, and for his great strength and durableness; and this is a stone of the Lord's laying, which he had been laying in his eternal purposes and decrees, as the Mediator, Saviour, and Redeemer of his people; and whom he was about to lay, by sending him forth, in the fulness of time, to be incarnate, suffer, and die for them: and whom he lays as the foundation in the effectual calling of his people, to build their faith and hope upon; and this is done in Zion, in the church, which is built upon him, and where he is revealed and made known to be what he is, and as here described: a tried stone; by the Old Testament saints, and by saints in all ages, who have ventured their souls on him, and laid the whole stress of their salvation upon him, and have been saved by him." Gill, *An Exposition of the Books of the Prophets of the Old Testament* 1:148.

3. "I do not know how some people, who believe that a Christian can fall from grace, manage to be happy. It must be a very commendable thing in them to be able to get through a day without despair. If I did not believe the doctrine of the final perseverance of the saints, I think I should be of all men the most miserable, because I should lack any ground of comfort. I could not say, whatever state of heart I came into, that I should be like a well-spring of water, whose stream fails not; I should rather have to take the comparison of an intermittent spring, that might stop on a sudden, or a reservoir, which I had no reason to expect would always be full. I believe that the happiest of Christians and the truest of Christians are those who never dare to doubt God, but who take His Word simply as it stands, and believe it, and ask no questions, just feeling assured that if God has said it, it will be so." *Autobiography* 1:173.

4. See *LS* 5, Sermon 241, where Charles urged professing believers to be baptized.

5. Cf. Ps 119:60.

6. Cf. Acts 16:25–34.

7. Cf. Acts 8:26–39.

8. Cf. Psalm 91.

9. Here, Charles made use of parentheses to indicate that his application of the text was somewhat uncertain. Charles's qualification might have been due to his

spiritualization of the passage. His unique use of parentheses here reveals that he was thoughtful about how he spiritualized the text.

10. "To fly away.... To be flux or unstable." Johnson's *Dictionary*, s.v. "To Flit."

11. Cf. Isa 40:8.

12. "A fall of water from on high; a shoot of water; a cascade." Johnson's *Dictionary*, s.v. "Cataract."

13. The cedars of Lebanon are known in Scripture to be massive trees. Cf. Judg 9:15; 1 Kgs 5:6–9; 2 Kgs 14:9.

14. Cf. Jer 23:15; Acts 8:23.   15. Cf. Rom 6:23.

16. Cf. Rom 6:16.   17. Cf. 1 John 5:11–13.

18. Cf. Eph 2:8–10.

19. "A believer never claims merit or honor on account of his faith. Faith is a self-denying grace, and never dares to boast. Where is the great credit of simply believing the truth, and humbly trusting Christ to save you? Faith glorifies God, and so our Lord has chosen it as the means of our salvation." *MTP* 25:597.

20. "So you want to be saved, do you? The way of salvation is, 'Believe in the Lord Jesus Christ.' 'But,' you say, 'I cannot understand it.' Yet it is very simple; no hidden meaning lies in the words: you are simply bidden to trust Jesus. If, however, you feel as if you could not do that, let me urge you to go to God in secret and own the sin of this unbelief; for a great sin it is. Humble yourself. Do not try to make out that you are good. That will be fatal, for it will be a falsehood, which will shut the gate of grace. Confess that you are guilty. When a man is clearly and manifestly guilty, it is of no use his standing before the judge and beginning to urge his own merit: his best course is to cast himself upon the mercy of the court. It is your only course, dear soul, the only one that can avail you." *MTP* 29:430.

21. Cf. Matt 25:1–13. Charles's affinity for John Bunyan's *The Pilgrim's Progress* is well documented. As such, Charles may also have had Bunyan in mind when he wrote this conclusion. In his book, Bunyan recorded a conversation between his

protagonist, Christian, and his guide, Interpreter, regarding the fire of grace in a Christian's life: "Then I saw in my Dream, that the *Interpreter* took *Christian* by the hand, and led him into a place, where was a Fire burning against a Wall and one standing by it always, casting much Water upon it to quench it: Yet did the Fire burn higher and hotter. *Then said* Christian, *What means this?* The *Interpreter* answered, This fire is the work of Grace that is wrought in the heart; he that casts Water upon it, to extinguish and put it out, is the Devil: but in that thou seest the fire notwithstanding burn higher and hotter, thou shalt also see the reason of that: So he had him about to the back side of the Wall, where he saw a Man with a Vessel of Oyl in his hand, of the which he did also continually cast (but secretly,) into the fire. Then said *Christian, What means this?* The *Interpreter* answered, This is *Christ*, who continually with the Oyl of his Grace, maintains the work already begun in the heart; By the means of which, notwithstanding what the Devil can do, the souls of his People prove gracious still. And in that thou sawest, that the Man stood behind the Wall to maintain the fire; this is to teach thee, that it is hard for the tempted to see how this work of Grace is maintained in the soul." John Bunyan, *The Pilgrim's Progress* (London: printed for the Society by J. Haddon, 1847, The Spurgeon Library), 31–32.

Ezek. IX. Vision of the man with the inkhorn. 256.

This is a vision concerning the ruin of Jerusalem by the Babylonians, it follows hard upon the revelation of the enormous crimes of Israel & thus shows the punishment of their sin.

The scene is sublime, the prophet views Jerusalem beneath his feet, he sees six fierce men, at the loud voice of God, come in at the north gate. Their swords are drawn for death but ere they fall to the bloody work they wait a command from the Master & stand waiting at the brazen altar.

One man, uncalled, stands in their midst clothed in linen with a writers inkhorn, to him a commission is given to seal the mourners, then comes the bloody work.

The prophet at his own safety & intercedes but in vain — the sentence is gone forth.

The man in linen reports the matter. He could say It is finished. —

Let us here note.

I. A dreadful slaughter.
II. A glorious salvation.
III. The character saved.
IV. The feelings caused by the salvation

May it be profitable to us for many purposes through the gracious Spirit.

VISION *of the* MAN *with the* INKHORN
Ezekiel 9[1]

This is a vision concerning the ruin of Jerusalem by the Babylonians.[2] It follows hard upon the revelation of the enormous crimes of Israel and thus shows the punishment of their sin.[3]

The scene is sublime, the prophet views Jerusalem beneath his feet, he sees six fierce men, at the loud voice of God, come in at the north gate.[4] Their swords are drawn for death[,] but ere[5] they fall to the bloody work they wait a command from the Master and stand waiting at the brazen altar.[6]

One man, uncalled, stands in their midst clothed in linen with a writer[']s inkhorn[.] [T]o him a commission is given to seal the mourners,[7] then comes the bloody work.

The prophet [is] at his own safety and intercedes[,] but in vain.[8] The sentence is gone forth.

The man in linen reports the matter. He could say, ["]It is finished.["][9]

Let us here note[:][10]

    I. A DREADFUL SLAUGHTER.

    II. A GLORIOUS SALVATION.

    III. THE CHARACTER SAVED.

    IV. THE FEELINGS CAUSED BY THE SALVATION.

May it be profitable to us for many purposes through the gracious Spirit.

I. A most dreadful slaughter.
A loud voice told the prophet that something direful was about to be done. "Six men", came, one for every gate — all to be thus cut off — Two destroyed Sodom here are six — Each man armed, all foes. Their swords drawn to set out speedy death. By the higher gate, they came, our pride will let in our own ruin.

They were to spare none, impartial justice shall destroy all the rebels — No pity was to come from their lips or hands.

All ages & sexes fall. The sanctuary is no refuge — the ancient men, the hypocrites receive the first blow. Heaps on heaps are piled the slain. The streets are filled, vengeance has its due, destruction reigns.

May God spare us so dread a sight and save us from this deserved wrath.

II. A most glorious salvation:
one man is the author of it.
our Jesus, clothed in the linen robes of a priest. A sapphire girdle & an inkhorn He goes himself & seals the foreheads of his children & suffers not the executioners

VISION OF THE MAN WITH THE INKHORN—*Ezekiel 9*

I. A MOST DREADFUL SLAUGHTER.

A loud voice told the prophet that something direful was about to be done.

"Six men" came, one for every gate. All hope [was] thus cut off. Two destroyed Sodom[,][11] here are six. Each man armed, all foes. Their swords drawn to set out speedy death. By the higher gate, they came, our pride will let in our own ruin.

They were to spare none, impartial justice shall destroy all the rebels. No pity was to come from their lips or hands.

All ages and sexes fall.[12] The sanctuary is no refuge. The ancient men, the hypocrites receive the first blow.[13] Heaps on heaps are piled the slain. The streets are filled, vengeance has its due, destruction reigns.

May God spare us so dread a sight and save us from this deserved wrath.

II. A MOST GLORIOUS SALVATION.

One man is the author of it.[14]

Our Jesus, clothed in the linen robes of a priest. A sapphire girdle and an inkhorn. He goes himself and seals the foreheads of his children and suffers not the executioners so much as to come near the sealed ones. This seal is the divine work of the Spirit, it is prominent & may be seen, for it is on their foreheads. — It does not tell us here how this man had power to save but we know that his mighty work & precious ransom gave him the authority.

He came & said he had done all & so shall Jesus be a complete Saviour to the elect.

<u>III</u>. The character of the saved.

Oh that we might discern ourselves here as in a glass, then we may rejoice.

They did not participate in the sin of the people or they would have shared their doom.

They sighed & mourned over the sins of the people, they acted as intercessors on their behalf and pleaded for them.

Can we say we do this.

These men were a remnant according to the election of grace & were made to differ by sovereign grace alone.

<u>IV</u>. The feelings of the saved.

Wonder — when others fall that we are safe. "Prayer for others" which we trust will be availing, but at last we shall see our godless relations damned without being able to plead or prevail on their behalf.

Lord — may I warn the sinners.

454.

so much as to come near the sealed ones.[15] This seal is the divine work of the Spirit.[16] It is prominent and may be seen, for it is on their foreheads. It does not tell us here how this man had power to save[,] but we know that his mighty work and precious ransom gave him the authority.[17] He came and said he had done all[,] and so shall Jesus be a complete Saviour to the elect.

III. THE CHARACTER OF THE SAVED.

Oh that we might discern ourselves here as in a glass, then we may rejoice.

They did not participate in the sin of the people or they would have shared their doom.

They sighed and mourned over the sins of the people.[18] They acted as intercessors on their behalf and pleaded for them.

>Can we say we do this[?]

These men were a remnant according to the election of grace and were made to differ by sovereign grace alone.

IV. THE FEELINGS OF THE SAVED.

Wonder. When others falls, that we are safe.[19] "Prayer for others" which we trust will be availing, but at last we shall see our godless relations damned without being able to plead or prevail on their behalf.[20]

>Lord, may I warn the sinner.

454.

SERMON 256

1. It appears that Charles preached from Ezekiel 9 on three other occasions during his later ministry, although never from the entire chapter. Of the three later sermons, the first two—"The Evil and Its Remedy" (*NPSP* 4, Sermon 223) and "Spared!" (*MTP* 48, Sermon 2807)—indicate some influence from this earlier sermon. However, the third one, "The Greatest Wonder of Grace" (*MTP* 59, Sermon 3377), contains overlapping content and similarity in structure, indicating the significant influence of this sermon. The overlapping content will be noted below.

2. Cf. 2 Kgs 25:1–21.

3. Cf. Ezek 8. "Read the story of the gross idolatry of the people of Jerusalem, as recorded in the eighth chapter of Ezekiel's prophecy, and you will not wonder at the judgment with which the Lord at length overthrew the city." *MTP* 59:505.

4. Cf. Ezek 9:2.

5. "Before; sooner than." Johnson's *Dictionary*, s.v. "Ere."

6. Cf. Ezek 9:2, 5–7.   7. Cf. Ezek 9:2–4.

8. Cf. Ezek 9:8–10.   9. Cf. Ezek 9:11.

10. Charles's later sermon, "The Greatest Wonder of Grace" (*MTP* 59, Sermon 3377), was structured around three general points: "*the character of the doom*"; "*the persons who are privileged to escape the destruction*"; and "*the emotions which the escaped feel.*" *MTP* 59:506, italics in the original. Respectively, these three points correspond structurally to Roman numerals I. and II., III., and IV.

11. Cf. Gen 19:1–25.

12. "After the executioners had begun at the sanctuary, it is to be observed that they did not spare any, except those upon whom was the mark. Old and young, men and women, priests and people, all were slain who had not the sacred sign; and so in the last tremendous day all sinners who have not fled to Christ will perish. . . . There will be no sparing of one man because he was rich, nor of another because he was learned, nor of a third because he was eloquent, nor of a fourth because he was held in high esteem." *MTP* 59:509–10.

VISION OF THE MAN WITH THE INKHORN—*Ezekiel 9*

13. "The first thing the slaughtermen did was to slaughter the ancient men which were before the temple, even the seventy elders of the people, for they were secret idolaters.... Elders of our churches, ministers of Christ, judgment will begin with us; we must not expect to find more lenient treatment than others at the last great assize [court]; nay, rather, if there shall be a specially careful testing of sincerity, it will be for us who have taken upon ourselves to lead others to the Savior. For this cause let us see well to it that we be not deceived or deceivers, for we shall surely be detected in that day." *MTP* 59:509.

14. Cf. Heb 12:2.

15. Cf. Ezek 9:4–6; Rev 7:2–3. "Next, this judgment was placed in the Mediator's hands.... Observe that, according to the chapter, there was no slaughter done, except where the man with the writer's inkhorn led the way.... When God no longer deals with men in Christ, his wrath burns like fire, and he commissions the ambassador of mercy to be the messenger of wrath. The very man who marked with his pen the saved ones threw burning coals upon the city, and led the way for the destruction of the sinful.... Think of it, ye careless ones: the very Christ who died on Calvary is he by whom you will be sentenced. God will judge the world by this man Christ Jesus." *MTP* 59:508.

16. Cf. Eph 1:13–14.

17. In his latter sermon, Charles saw the sacrificial work of Christ in the glory of God shining out from the cherub, that is, the ark of the covenant (see Ezek 9:3): "God's glory of old shone forth between the cherubim[,] that is to say, over the place of propitiation and atonement, and as long as that glow of light remained, no judgment fell on Jerusalem, for God in Christ condemns not." *MTP* 59:508.

18. "We do not read that the devouring sword passed by those quiet people who never did anybody any harm: no mention is made of such an exemption. Neither does the record say that the Lord saved those professors who were judicious, and maintained a fair name and repute until death. No; the only people that were saved were those who were exercised in heart, and that heart-work was of a painful kind: they sighed and cried because of abounding sin. They saw it, protested against it, avoided it, and, last of all, wept over it continually." *MTP* 59:510.

19. "He saw men falling right and left, and he himself stood like a lone rock amidst a sea of blood; and he cried in wonder, 'And I was left.' . . . Indeed, each saved man is a marvel to himself. Nobody here wonders more at divine grace in his salvation than I do myself. Why was I chosen, and called, and saved? I cannot make it out, and I never shall; but I will always praise, and bless, and magnify my Lord for casting an eye of love upon me. Will you not do the same, beloved, if you feel that you by grace are left? Will you not fall on your face and bless the mercy which makes you to differ?" *MTP* 59:512–13.

20. "Oh, beloved friends, if you are left while others perish, I beseech you, by the mercies of God, by the bowels of compassion which are in Christ Jesus, by the bleeding wounds of the dying Son of God, do love your fellow-men, and sigh and cry about them if you cannot bring them to Christ. If you cannot save them, you can weep over them. If you cannot give them a drop of cold water in hell, you can give them your heart's tears while yet they are in this body." *MTP* 59:514.

257. Josh. V. 13. Art thou for us or for our adversaries

I see so many of my hearers undecided & so many negligent of making a profession. I desire therefore to ply this question as closely as I can. Oh Blessed Spirit give me thoughts and utterances.

I will throw my remarks into three observations —

I. That there are some ostensibly for us who are not for us in the sense meant.

Some are for us as <u>Men</u>, they like our ministry, they think us good company, they respect us as honest, respectable men.

Some are for us as <u>Dissenters</u>, they dislike the Established Church and as we protest against it, they approve of it.

Some are for us as <u>Baptists</u>, they read their bibles and they see nothing about babies or sprinkling there & therefore they join with us in the matter.

Some are with us as <u>Calvinists</u>, they love to hear free grace extolled, they love election, effectual calling & perseverance, they love a consistent ministry & in this are for us.

ART THOU *for* US *or for* OUR ADVERSARIES[?]

Joshua 5:13[1]

"And it came to pass, when Joshua was by Jericho, that he lifted up his eyes and looked, and, behold, there stood a man over against him with his sword drawn in his hand: and Joshua went unto him, and said unto him, Art thou for us, or for our adversaries?"

I see so many of my hearers undecided and so many negligent of making a profession.

I desire therefore to ply[2] this question as closely as I can. Oh Blessed Spirit[,] give me thoughts and utterances.

I will throw my remarks into three observations.

I. THAT THERE ARE SOME OSTENSIBLY FOR US [WHO] ARE NOT FOR US IN THE SENSE MEANT.

Some are for us as <u>Men</u>. They like our ministry. They think us good company. They respect us as honest, respectable men.[3]

Some are for us as <u>Dissenters</u>. They dislike the Established Church and as we protest against it, they approve of it.

Some are for us as <u>Baptists</u>. They read their bibles and they see nothing about babies or sprinkling there and therefore they join with us in the matters.

Some are with us as <u>Calvinists</u>. They love to hear free grace extolled. They love election, effectual calling[,] and perseverance. They love a consistent ministry and in this are for us.

But how few are with us as the humble followers of Jesus Christ whithersoever he goeth — They divide on some point or other. They are not with us in prayer, nor praise, nor holy living — They go to the feast, they drink — th Father forgive the

II. That if any man is for us, he has experienced a great change.

we are not born for God but against him. If we are for him it is because he wrought a new heart & right spirit in us.

Let every man's conscience say whether he is a changed character or no.

III. That every man is either for or against.
1. In every other thing men are one or the other.
2. The blessings of religion are such that a man must either have them or not have them.
3. All figures of speech whereby religion is set forth require one or the other to be true. new birth, quickening, out of darkness, &c —

Now my friends are you for or against. Why turn your back on our Master's table

455. 479.

But how few are with us as the humble followers of Jesus Christ whithersoever[4] he goeth. They divide on some point or other. They are not with us in prayer, nor praise, nor holy living. They go to the feast, they drink.[5] Oh Father forgive them.[6]

II. THAT IF ANY MAN~~Y~~ IS FOR US, HE HAS EXPERIENCED A GREAT CHANGE.

We are not born for God but against him.[7] If we are for him it is because he wrought a new heart and right spirit in us.[8]

Let every man's conscience say whether he is a changed character or no.

III. THAT EVERY MAN IS EITHER FOR OR AGAINST.

1. In every other thing men are one or the other.
2. The blessings of religion are such that a man must either have them or not have them.[9]
3. All figures of speech whereby religion is set forth require one or the other to be true.[10] New birth,[11] quickening,[12] out of darkness,[13] etc.

Now my friends are you for or against[?] Why turn your back on our Master's table[?]

455. 479.

SERMON 257

1. It appears that Charles preached a later sermon on this text, "Joshua's Vision" (*MTP* 14, Sermon 795). However, Charles's later sermon does not appear to contain any notable overlapping content.

2. "To work on any thing closely and importunately." Johnson's *Dictionary*, s.v. "Ply."

3. Charles told of a notorious man who came to hear him early on in his Waterbeach ministry. This man professed a dramatic conversion, but in the end fell away. Looking back on that experience, Charles concluded, "He sat there, and fell in love with me; I think that was the only conversion that he experienced, but he professed to be converted." *Autobiography* 1:238; see also *LS* 1:339–40.

4. "To whatsoever place." Johnson's *Dictionary*, s.v. "Whithersoever."

5. This was likely a reference to a member of Charles's church who attended one of the ill-reputed feasts at Waterbeach, a situation which Charles recounted in his autobiography: "While I was Pastor at Waterbeach, a certain young man joined the church. We thought he was a changed character, but there used to be in the village, once a year, a great temptation in the form of a feast; and when the feast came round, this foolish fellow was there in very evil company. He was in the long room of a public house in the evening, and when I heard what happened, I really felt intense gratitude to the landlady of that place. When she came in, and saw him there, she said, 'Halloa, Jack So-and-so, are you here? Why, you are one of Spurgeon's lot, yet you are here; you ought to be ashamed of yourself. This is not fit company for you. Put him out of the window, boys.' And they did put him out of the window on the Friday night, and we put him out of the door on the Sunday, for we removed his name from our church-book." *Autobiography* 1:260.

6. Cf. Luke 23:34. The previous note recounts a time when Charles spoke with firmness about the discipline of a member of his church. Here, however, he revealed his tenderness toward those struggling with sin.

7. Cf. Ps 51:5.

8. Cf. Ps 51:10; Ezek 36:26–27.

9. "There are in this world nowhere any other sort of people beside those who are dead in sin and those who are alive unto God. There is no state between. A man either lives or is dead; you cannot find a neutral condition. A man may be in a swoon, or he may be asleep, but he is alive; no state is there that is not

within the boundary of either life or death. Is not this clear enough? There is no state between being converted and unconverted—between being quickened and being dead in sin. There is no condition between being pardoned and having our sins upon us." *MTP* 21:279–80.

10. Cf. Matt 6:24; John 8:34–36; Eph 5:8; 1 Pet 2:10.

11. Cf. John 3:2–6.

12. "To become alive: as, a woman quickens with child." Johnson's *Dictionary*, s.v. "Quickening." Cf. Rom 8:11.

13. Cf. Col 1:13; 1 Pet 2:9.

258. Ps. XXXVII. 25. I have been young & now am old &c

Good men have been divided as to the exact meaning of this verse as a whole. —

Some have said that this verse is a promise to be understood literally & that it will be literally fulfilled — Adam Clarke declares that he though grayheaded had never seen one of the seed of the righteous begging.

But I think this is not always true, for we think we know instance of sons of pious parents turning out ill & at last coming to poverty. — —

Some to get over this say it should be translated "although his seed may beg bread". but I see no authority for this.

Some again think the word "seed" refers to a man's family as long as they are with him at home & they say that after that time the children are plants, not seeds, but this I think is idle — for the word "seed" in the Bible means a man's children whether old or young; & to any numbers of generations

The difficulties would vanish if we look at it as a declaration made by David as the result of a whole

I HAVE BEEN YOUNG
and NOW AM OLD ETC.
Psalm 37:25[1]

*"I have been young, and now am old; yet have I not seen the
righteous forsaken, nor his seed begging bread."*

Good men have been divided as to the exact meaning of this verse as a whole.

Some have said that this verse is a promise to be understood literally and that it will be literally fulfilled. Adam Clarke declares that he[,] though grayheaded[,] had never seen one of the seed of the righteous begging.[2]

But I think this is not always true, for we think we know instance[s] of sons of pious parents turning out ill[3] and at last coming to poverty.[4]

Some to get over this say it should be translated "although his seed may beg bread,"[5] but I see no authority for this.

Some again think the word "seed" refers to a man's family as long as they are with him at home and they say that after that time the children are plants, not seeds, but this I think is idle.[6] For the word "seed" in the Bible means a man[']s children whether old or young; and to any number of generations.[7]

The difficulties would vanish if we look at it as a declaration made by David as the result of a whole

SERMON 258

life of observation. —

David had never seen the righteous forsaken nor his seed begging bread.

On this we may remark that David's times were not times of persecution — though David was persecuted by Saul & had to beg bread of the priest. Yet Saul was not a general persecutor, nor could there be any persecution in his own reign ——— Had David lived in other days he would not have seen the righteous forsaken but he might have seen both them and their children perishing of hunger, cold & nakedness.

The first part as just hinted will ever be literally true in every case — no righteous man will ever be truly forsaken.

What then is to be learned from this declaration of the Psalmist. —

I. That we rarely see good men brought absolutely to want for bread.

They are often poor, but God provides, they are sometimes in great straits, but in some way deliverance comes. Hardly ever do we see a good man begging — if we ever do — let it be our pleasure at once to relieve his wants and raise him from poverty.

II. That in most cases the blessing of God will rest on the seed of the righteous.

Though sometimes they turn out ill, a mother's prayers will usually be heard

I HAVE BEEN YOUNG AND NOW AM OLD ETC.—*Psalm 37:25*

life of observation.

David had never seen the righteous forsaken[,] nor his seed begging bread.

On this we may remark that David's times were not times of persecution – though David was persecuted by Saul[8] and had to beg bread of the priest.[9] Yet Saul was not a general persecutor, nor could there be any persecution in his own reign.[10] ---
Had David lived in other days he would not have seen the righteous forsaken but he might have seen both them and their children perishing of hunger, cold[,] and nakedness.[11]

The first part as just hinted will ever be literally true in every case. No righteous man will ever be truly forsaken.[12]

What then is to be learned from this declaration of the Psalmists[?]

I. THAT WE RARELY SEE GOOD MEN BROUGHT ABSOLUTELY TO WANT FOR BREAD.

They are often poor, but God provides. They are sometimes in great straits, but in some way deliverance comes.[13] Hardly ever do we see a good man begging. If we ever do, let it be our pleasure at once to relieve his wants and raise him from poverty.[14]

II. THAT IN MOST CASES THE BLESSING OF GOD WILL REST ON THE SEED OF THE RIGHTEOUS.

Though sometimes they turn out ill, a mother's prayers will usually be heard.[15]

Seed sown in infancy takes deep root, habits of devotion, morality, &c become strong & every parent has a promise that his endeavours will have some success.

In temporal matters, habits of economy, order, temperance & religion will in ally cases give a man decided advantage over his ungodly and wicked neighbour.

III. That we see Godliness is profitable for both worlds —

In this it saves a man from many diseases, it gives us lessons of prudence, it spares us many a bitter regret, it helps us to die well, yea & blesses our seed after us.

In the next world it stands by us at judgment, it saves us from hell, it lifts us to eternal glory —

May we ever seek this righteousness to which such blessings are attached.

   Give me th great one - words
    to speak in thy name.

462

I HAVE BEEN YOUNG AND NOW AM OLD ETC.—*Psalm 37:25*

Seed sown in infancy takes deep root, habits of devotion, morality, etc. become strong and every parent has a promise that his endeavours will have some success.[16] In temporal matters, habits of economy, order, temperance and religion will in ~~most~~ all[17] cases give a man decided advantage over his ungodly and wicked neighbour.

III. THAT WE SEE GODLINESS IS PROFITABLE FOR BOTH WORLDS.[18]

In this it saves a man from many diseases, it gives us lessons of prudence, it spares us many a bitter regret, it helps us to die well, yea and blesses our seed after us.

In the next world it stands by us at judgment, it saves us from hell, it lifts us to eternal glory.

May we ever seek this righteousness to which such blessings are attached.[19]

> Give me, oh great one, words
> to speak in thy name.

462

SERMON 258

1. It appears that Charles did not preach another sermon on the text of Ps 37:25.

2. Adam Clarke wrote, "I believe this to be literally true in all cases. I am now grey-headed myself; I have travelled in different countries, and have had many opportunities of seeing and conversing with religious people in all situations in life; and I have not, to my knowledge, see one instance to the contrary. I have seen no righteous man forsaken, nor any children of the righteous begging their bread. God puts this honour upon all that fear him; and thus careful is he of them, and of their posterity." Adam Clarke, *The Holy Bible, Containing the Old and New Testaments with a Commentary and Critical Notes*, vol. 3 (London: William Tegg, 1854, The Spurgeon Library), 2051. Next to Clarke's commentary on this verse is a small penciled checkmark, most likely scribbled by Charles. Charles also quoted Clarke in his commentary on this verse in the *Treasury of David* (see *TD* 2:211).

3. "1. Bad in any respect; contrary to good, whether physical or moral; evil. 2. Wickedness; depravity; contrariety to holiness." Johnson's *Dictionary*, s.v. "Ill."

4. "It is not my observation just as it stands, for I have relieved the children of undoubtedly good men, who have appealed to me as common mendicants. But this does not cast a doubt upon the observation of David. He lived under a dispensation more outward, and more of this world than the present rule of personal faith. Never are the righteous forsaken; that is a rule without exception. Seldom indeed do their seed beg bread; and although it does occasionally occur, through dissipation, idleness, or some other causes on the part of their sons, yet doubtless it is so rare a thing that there are many alive who never saw it." (*TD* 2:195).

5. Charles may have first come across this unusual rendering in Gill: "In an ancient Midrash, or exposition of the Jews, the sense is thus given: 'Although his seed and his sons are begging bread, yet I have not seen the righteous man, their father forsaken, because of his fear of the blessed God.'" Gill, *An Exposition of the Old Testament* (1765) 3:639.

6. "4. Useless; vain; ineffectual. . . . 6. Trifling; of not importance: as, an idle story." Johnson's *Dictionary*, s.v. "Idle."

7. The Hebrew word to which Charles referred here is זֶרַע (zerah), which was defined in his Hebrew lexicon as "a) i. q. *children, offspring, posterity* . . . b) i. q. *a race, stock, family*." William Gesenius, *A Hebrew and English Lexicon of the Old Testament*,

Including the Biblical Chaldee (Boston: Crocker and Brewster, 1836), s.v. "זֶרַע," italics in the original.

8. Cf. 1 Sam 18:8–9; 19:10–11; 23:7–8.

9. Cf. 1 Sam 21:1–6.

10. The long dash marks an aside where Charles recognized that David did experience persecution and poverty before his kingship, but this was not characteristic of David's entire life.

11. Cf. Ruth 1:1; 2 Kgs 6:25; 8:1; 25:3; Lam 5:1–21; Heb 11:35–38.

12. Cf. Ps 94:14; Rom 8:35–39; Heb 13:5.

13. Charles was himself quite destitute in the early years of his ministry. In his autobiography, he told this amusing story: "When I became Pastor at Waterbeach, the people could do very little for my support, and therefore I was an usher in a school at Cambridge at the same time. After a while, I was obliged to give up the latter occupation, and was thrown on the generosity of the people. They gave me a salary of £45 [about $5,443 in today's currency] a year, but as I had to pay 12s. [about $73] a week for two rooms which I occupied, my income was not sufficient to support me; but the people, though they had not money, had produce, and I do not think there was a pig killed by any one of the congregation without my having some portion of it, and one or other of them, when coming to the market at Cambridge, would bring me bread, so that I had enough bread and meat to pay my rent with, and I often paid my landlady in that fashion." *Autobiography* 1:253; see also *LS* 2:3.

14. Despite earning tremendous wealth over the course of his lifetime, Charles died poor because of his remarkable generosity. At one point in his autobiography, he described his daily struggle to meet all the needs that he encountered: "I have only one grievance, and that is, being asked for loans and gifts of money when I have none to spare. Under the impression that I am a very rich man, many hunt me perpetually; but I wish these borrowers and beggars to know that I am not rich. They argue that a man must be rich if he gives away large sums; but, in my case, this is just the reason why I am not rich. When I have a spare £5, the College, or Orphanage, or Colportage, or something else, requires it, and away it goes. I could very comfortably do with much more. Oh, that I could do more for

Christ, and more for the poor! For these, I have turned beggar before now, and shall not be ashamed to beg again. The outside world cannot understand that a man should be moved by any motive except that of personal gain; but, if they knew the power of love to Jesus, they would understand that, to the lover of the Saviour, greed of wealth is vile as the dust beneath his feet." *Autobiography* 2:128.

15. Charles's own mother played a significant role in his eventual conversion to Christ. He recalled her prayers during family worship even in his adult years: "Then came a mother's prayer, and some of the words of that prayer we shall never forget, even when our hair is grey. I remember, on one occasion, her praying thus: 'Now, Lord, if my children go on in their sins, it will not be from ignorance that they perish, and my soul must bear a swift witness against them at the day of judgment if they lay not hold of Christ.' That thought of a mother's bearing swift witness against me, pierced my conscience, and stirred my heart." *Autobiography* 1:68.

16. Cf. Prov 22:6. Charles elsewhere told the story of a villager in Waterbeach who refused to discipline his children: "There was another man, of that sort, who at one time frequently walked out with me into the villages where I was going to preach. I was glad of his company till I found out certain facts as to his manner of life, and then I shook him off, and I believe: he hooked himself on to somebody else, for he must needs be gadding abroad every evening of the week. He had many children, and they grew up to be wicked men and women; and the reason was, that the father, while he was constantly busy at this meeting and that, never tried to bring his own boys and girls to the Savior. He said to me, one day, 'I never laid my hand upon my children;' so I answered, 'Then I think it is very likely that God will lay His hand upon you.' 'Oh!' he said, 'I have not even spoken sharply to them.' 'Then,' I replied, 'it is highly probable that God will speak very sharply to you; for it is not His will that parents should leave their children unrestrained in their sin.'" *Autobiography* 1:259.

17. Charles struck through the word "most" and instead wrote "all." This change altered the meaning of his statement by emphasizing that common grace "habits of economy, order, temperance, and religion" always provide advantage to believers over unbelievers in day-to-day living.

18. Cf. 1 Tim 4:8.   19. Cf. 1 Tim 6:6.

Job. VI. 6. Can that which is unsavoury be eaten without salt. &c.

How foolish to take odd texts & make a meaning out of them, that never was intended
But what is taught here is plain enough.
There are some things so unsavoury in themselves that they need something else with them to make us willing to receive them.

1. *Reproofs* are never agreeable in themselves & when we administer them let us be careful to blend much love & kindness with them.

2. *Afflictions*, are not joyous but grievous they cause us sorrow, & we need & if true believers shall receive, much grace to help us through them safely.

3. *Our Doctrines* of grace, are unpalatable to our neighbours, let us put a holy & generous life with them, thus only will they gain ground.

4. *Thoughts of Death*, are disagreeable because men are unprepared for it & cannot take hold on the true salt &

5. *Death* itself cannot & ought not to be endured without the supporting grace of God — &c —

459.

CAN THAT WHICH IS UNSAVOURY BE EATEN WITHOUT SALT, ETC.[?]
Job 6:6[1]

"Can that which is unsavoury be eaten without salt?
or is there any taste in the white of an egg?"

How foolish to take odd texts and make a meaning out of them, that never was intended.[2] But what is taught here is plain enough. There are some things so unsavoury in themselves that they need something else with them to make us willing to receive them.

1. <u>Reproofs</u> are never agreeable in themselves and when we administer them let us be careful to blend much love and kindness with them.[3]

2. <u>Afflictions</u> are not joyous but grievous. They cause us sorrow, and we need and if true believers shall receive, much grace to help us through them safely.[4]

3. <u>Our Doctrines</u> of grace are unpalatable to our neighbours. Let us put a holy and generous life with them, thus only will they gain ground.[5]

4. <u>Thoughts of Death</u> are disagreeable because men are unprepared for it and cannot take hold on the true salt and

5. <u>Death</u> itself cannot and ought not to be endured without the supporting grace of God etc. etc.[6]

459.

SERMON 259

1. It appears that Charles preached a later sermon on this text, "A Cure for Unsavoury Meats: Or, Salt for the White of an Egg" (MTP 29, Sermon 1730). While the first two points contained original material, the third point of the later sermon contained significant overlapping content with this sermon. Under that heading, "III. The third point is, that THERE ARE CERTAIN THINGS IN THE WORLD WHICH NEED SOMETHING ELSE WITH THEM" (MTP 29:392, capitals in the original), Charles discussed the need to savor reproofs, doctrines, afflictions, and death with the salt of grace. Additional overlapping content will be noted below.

2. Charles once counseled his students in this way when it came to spiritualizing a text: "A great deal of real good may be done by occasionally taking forgotten, quaint, remarkable, out-of-the-way texts; and I feel persuaded that if we appeal to a jury of practical, successful preachers, who are not theorizers, but men actually in the field, we shall have a majority in our favour. . . . Within limit, my brethren, be not afraid to spiritualize, or to take singular texts." *Lectures* 1:102–3.

3. Cf. 2 Tim 2:25. "One of the first of these may read us a lesson of prudence; that is, reproof. It is a Christian duty to reprove a brother who is in a fault, and we should speak to him with all gentleness and quietness, that we may prevent his going farther into evil, and lead him back to the right way. But will you please remember, brothers and sisters, that the giving of reproofs is dainty work, and needs a delicate hand. . . . Rebuke, however kindly you put it, and however prudently you administer it, will always be an unsavoury thing: therefore, salt it well. Think over it. Pray over it. Mix kindness with it. Rub the salt of brotherly love into it. Speak with much, deference to your erring friend, and use much tenderness, because you are not faultless yourself. Speak acknowledging all the excellences and virtues of your brother which may, after all, be greater than your own; and try, if you can, to wrap up what you have to say in gentle words of praise for something else wherein the friend excels." MTP 29:392–93.

4. "Now, a third egg which cannot be eaten without salt is affliction. Afflictions are very unsavoury things. . . . What is to be done with them, then? Why, let us salt them, if we can. Salt your affliction with patience, and it will make a royal dish. By grace, like the apostle, we shall 'glory in tribulations also.' . . . Have you been forgetting that salt? Have you failed to ask of the Lord grace equal to your day? . . . Be forgetful no longer, but throw in a pinch of salt; then the tasteless

thing will go down comfortably enough, and you will bless the name of the Lord for it." *MTP* 29:394–95. Additionally, Charles's sentence should be read "They cause us much sorrow, and we need . . . much grace to help us through them safely." The conditional "and if we are believers shall receive" disrupts the flow of the sentence but is intended to provide assurance of divine aid.

5. "Now for other matters, which many people do not like by themselves; I mean, the doctrines of the gospel. The true doctrines of the gospel never were popular, and never will be; but there is no need for any of us to make them more distasteful than they naturally are. The human heart especially revolts at the sovereignty of divine grace. . . . It becomes us who preach this doctrine to take care that we do not add needless offensiveness to it. . . . Brothers and sisters, since we want people to receive these doctrines, what must we do? We must mix an abundance of salt with them. If the gospel be distasteful we must add a flavouring to it. What shall it be? We cannot do better than flavour it with holiness! Where there is a holy life men cannot easily doubt the principles out of which it springs. If it be so that men and women are kindly, generous, tender, affectionate, upright, truthful, Christlike, because of the doctrines they hold, then the world begins to think that there must be truth in those doctrines." *MTP* 29:393.

6. "But, lastly, there is the thought of death. Is not death an unsavoury thing in itself? The body dreads dissolution and corruption, and the mind starts back from the prospect of quitting the warm precincts of this house of clay, and going into what seems a cold, rarefied region, where the shivering spirit flits naked into mystery untried. . . . 'What salt,' say you, 'shall I mingle with my thoughts of death?' Why the thought that you cannot die: since because he lives you shall live also. Add to it the persuasion that though you be dead, yet shall you live. Thoughts of the resurrection and the swinging open of the pearly gates, and of your entrance there; thoughts of the vision of the Well-beloved's face; thoughts of the glory that shall be yours for ever and ever at his own right hand. These are the things with which to savor your meditations among the tombs." *MTP* 29:395–96.

260. Heb. III. 7. "The Holy Ghost saith Today"
The text deserves our serious attention since the Speaker is none other than the third person of the ever-glorious Trinity. The great quickener, supporter, purifier, comforter — without whom we are nothing.
Every word of Scripture is his word but this one most certainly so, since it is expressly ascribed to him

I. The advice of the Evil Spirit. —
Directly the contrary of my text is the advice suggested by Satan & laid hold on by the corrupt heart — tomorrow — is its burden.
It is hell's plaster for uneasy consciences. More have been damned by this than by any thing else, it has slain its millions.
Satan stood by the ear of Felix & Agrippa by the side of many of you.
Oh God, my God give me earnestness to combat this deadly error.
1. Help me to urge upon them the uselessness of procrastination — you will never be more fit to come than now & if you come at last you will always regret that you did not

"THE HOLY GHOST SAITH TODAY"
Hebrews 3:7¹

"Wherefore as the Holy Ghost saith, To day if ye will hear his voice . . ."

The text deserves our serious attention since the Speaker is none other than the third person of the ever-glorious Trinity. The great quickener,² supporter,³ purifier,⁴ comforter⁵ – without whom we are nothing.⁶

Every word of Scripture is his word⁷ but this one most certainly so, since it is expressly ascribed to him.⁸

I. THE ADVICE OF THE EVIL SPIRIT.

Directly the contrary of any text is the advice suggested by Satan and laid hold on by the corrupt heart – <u>tomorrow</u> – is its burden.⁹

It is hell's plaster¹⁰ for uneasy consciences. More have been damned by this than by any thing else[;] it has slain its millions.

Satan stood by the ear of Felix¹¹ and Agrippa,¹² by the side of many of you.

Oh God, my God give me earnestness to combat this deadly error.

1. Help me to urge upon them the uselessness of procrastination. You will never be more fit to come than <u>now</u>[,] and if you come at last you will always regret that you did not

come before. —
2. Consider sinner your own state a sinner condemned, under the wrath of God, how dare you say "tomorrow." —
3. Consider God may give you over to hardness of heart & final impenitence.
4. Consider again you may die to day at this moment you may drop into hell — beware th Procrastinator. —
Yet I know this is the advice you will all follow unless you hear within

II. The advice of the Good Spirit. —
When he awakens the sinner, all these empty dreams are gone "to day" "to day" becomes the hearty cry of the soul. —
Down on his knees he falls at once he dare not delay but to day.
For mercy he cries, not in a year or two but to-day. He cannot delay.
He runs, he hastens, now or never is his cry — the voice of Satan is hushed.
Oh may this cry sound in all our ears to-day — to-day.

463.476.

"THE HOLY GHOST SAITH TODAY"—*Hebrews 3:7*

come before.[13] –

2. Consider sinner your own state[,] a sinner condemned, under the wrath of God,[14] how dare you say "tomorrow." –

3. Consider God may give you over[15] to hardness of heart and final impenitence.[16]

4. Consider again you may die to day at this moment you may drop into hell[17] – beware Oh Procrastinator. –

Yet I know this is the advice you will all follow unless you hear within.

II. THE ADVICE OF THE GOOD SPIRIT.

When he awakens the sinner, all these empty dreams are gone "to day" "to day" becomes the hearty cry of the soul. Down on his knees he falls at once, he dare not delay, but to day. For mercy he cries, not in a year or two, but to-day. He cannot delay. He runs, he hastens, ["]now or never["] is his cry – the voice of Satan is hushed.

Oh may this cry sound in all our ears to-day—to-day.

463. 476.

SERMON 260

1. It appears that Charles preached two later sermons on this text, "The Entreaty of the Holy Ghost" (*MTP* 20, Sermon 1160) and "The Call of 'To-Day'" (*MTP* 55, Sermon 3160). There is some overlapping content, but there does not appear to be any structural similarity to this sermon. The overlapping content will be noted below.

2. Cf. John 6:63; Col 2:13.

3. Cf. Rom 8:26–27.

4. Cf. Acts 15:8–9; 1 Pet 1:22.

5. Cf. John 14:16, 26; 15:26.

6. "THE HOLY GHOST SAITH 'TO-DAY.' The Holy Ghost! That clothes it with deep solemnity. The Holy Ghost! That is, the Divine Person of the Godhead. . . . Remember how the Holy Ghost loves you—how he loves you! Jesus Christ loved men so that he came and lived amongst them, and the Holy Ghost loves men so that he comes and lives in them. I wonder which is the more admirable in condescension—the incarnation of the Son, or the indwelling of the Holy Spirit. They are both divinely merciful and gracious." *MTP* 55:426.

7. Cf. 2 Pet 1:19–21.

8. "I pray you ever remember whenever you read the Bible, that it is the Spirit of the living God who there admonishes you to immediate obedience. The calls of the inspired word are not those of Moses, or David, or Paul, or Peter, but the solemn utterances of the Holy Ghost speaking through them. With what a dignity does this truth invest Holy Scripture, and with what solemnity does it surround our reading of it! Cavilling [grumbling] at Scripture, trifling with it, disputing its doctrines, or neglecting its admonitions, we grieve the Spirit of God." *MTP* 20:122.

9. Cf. Jas 4:13–15. "A very large proportion of mankind, you will find, delight in dwelling upon the word 'tomorrow.' Oh what will they not do tomorrow! Sin shall be rejected tomorrow; the Savior shall be sought tomorrow. Clasped in the arms of faith, they will exult in the peace of Christ tomorrow; they will pray tomorrow; they will serve God tomorrow. Alas! Of all the nets of Satan as a

fowler for the souls of men, perhaps there is none in which he taketh more than in this big net of procrastination." *MTP* 55:421–22.

10. "A glutinous or adhesive salve." Johnson's *Dictionary*, s.v. "Plaster."

11. Cf. Acts 24:24–27.   12. Cf. Acts 26:28.

13. "Yesterday is also dwelt upon in lamentation and even in despair. Yesterday! alas, opportunities are past. 'The harvest is past, and the summer is ended, and we are not saved.' Yesterday we lived in sin; yesterday we rejected Christ; yesterday we stifled conscience; and therefore despair says that it is all over now. Time is gone. Closed for ever are the gates of mercy: the death warrant is signed: the gallows are erected for the execution. Now it is noteworthy that the Holy Ghost, neither that we may take comfort in it, nor despair about it, saith not 'yesterday'—he saith 'today.'" *MTP* 55:421.

14. Cf. John 3:36; Rom 1:18; 2:5; Eph 5:6; Heb 10:26–31. "The Lord also threatens as well as entreats. He warns you, 'If ye turn not, he will whet his sword: he hath bent his bow and made it ready.' He declares that the despisers shall wonder and perish. He asks, 'How shall we escape if we neglect so great salvation?' He says, 'The wicked shall be cast into hell with all the nations that forget God.' Though he hath no pleasure in the death of him that dieth, but had rather that he should turn unto him and live, yet [God] will by no means clear the guilty, but every transgression and iniquity shall have its just recompense of reward. If Christ be rejected, eternal wrath is certain." *MTP* 20:127.

15. Cf. Rom 1:24.

16. Charles appeared to be referring to the doctrine of "final impenitence" which, in Thomas Aquinas's use of Augustine, is articulated as a condition "when, namely a man perseveres in mortal sin until death." Augustine, quoted in Thomas Aquinas, *Summa Theologicae*, vol. 32 (London: Blackfriars in Conjunction with Eyre & Spottiswoode; New York: McGraw-Hill, 1975), 119. This is a condition marked by an indifference toward God and unrepentance. "Today, while yet you are not utterly hardened, while still there is a conscience left within you; today, while yet you are conscious of your danger in some degree, while yet there is a lingering look towards your Father's house, hear ye and live; lest, slighting your

present tenderness it should never come again, but you should be abandoned to the shocking indifference which is the prelude of eternal death." *MTP* 20:128.

17. "Do you not know that other people die? Why may you not die yourself? During these present services several have been taken from among us. I was surprised when I came home to find how many have died of late concerning whom I should have predicted a much longer life. Why may you not die speedily? 'I am robust and healthy,' says one. If you ever hear of a sudden death, does it not generally happen to the robust? It seems as if the storm swept over the sickly, and they bowed before it like reeds, and so escaped its fury, while the vigorous in health, like powerful forest trees, resist the storm, and are torn up by it. How often does sudden death come just where we least expected it." *MTP* 20:129.

261. Haggai. I. 5. Consider your ways.
The text turns us off from every other subject to ourselves — we need not consider the dead — but let the living look to themselves.
I. How does the Lord say this. —
He said it by a sacred impulse on the prophets mind. He said it by wars & famines to the ancient Israelites. He says it to us every Sabbath, yea every day in his word. The thunder storm speaks it in thunder, Pains & sickness whisper it in our ears. But loudest of all <u>death</u> cries out "Consider your ways."
II. What are we to consider in our ways.
1. Consider whether they have been conformed to the law of God & the example of Jesus Christ.
2. Consider whether you have had a thorough conversion, whether as a poor lost undone sinner you have ever cast yourself at the feet of Jesus.
3. Consider the end of your ways, are they downward, or upward, to heaven

CONSIDER YOUR WAYS
Haggai 1:5[1]

"Now therefore thus saith the Lord of hosts; Consider your ways."

The text turns us off from every other subject to ourselves. We need not consider the dead, but let the living look to themselves.[2]

I. HOW DOES THE LORD SAY THIS[?]

He said it by a sacred impulse on the prophet[']s mind.[3] He said it by wars and famines to the ancient Israelites.[4] He says it to us every Sabbath, yea every day in his word. The thunder storm speaks it in thunder. Pains and sickness whisper it in our ears.[5] But loudest of all <u>death</u> cries out "Consider your ways."[6]

II. WHAT ARE WE TO CONSIDER IN OUR WAYS[?]

1. Consider whether they have been conformed to the law of God and the example of Jesus Christ.[7]

2. Consider whether you have had a thorough conversion, whether as a poor[,] lost[,] undone sinner you have ever cast yourself at the feet of Jesus.

3. Consider the end of your ways, are they downward, or upward, to heaven

or hell. —
5. Mind that you consider them soberly & honestly. Do not mince the matter. Be wise & shun not to know the whole of it.
Give not a hasty look but diligently consider your ways & attend to the voice

III. To whom spoken.
To the father & mother of the deceased in particular — to each of you his brothers & sisters — To all young men & women. To all of you. To myself as well. — Oh that this Death might be <u>Life</u> to some. by leading you to
"<u>Consider your ways</u>"

464

CONSIDER YOUR WAYS—*Haggai 1:5*

or hell[?]

5. Mind[8] that you consider them soberly and honestly. Do not mince[9] the matter. Be wise and shun not to know the whole of it.

   Give not a hasty look, but diligently[10] consider your ways and attend to the voice.

III. TO WHOM SPOKEN.

To the father and mother of the desceased in particular, to each of you his brothers and sisters. To all young men and women. To all of you. To myself as well.[11] Oh that this <u>Death</u> might be <u>Life</u> to some by leading you to

"<u>Consider your ways.</u>"[12]

464

1. It appears that Charles did not preach another sermon on the text of Hag 1:5.

2. Cf. Jer 22:10; Matt 8:22; Luke 9:60.

3. Cf. 2 Pet 1:19–21.   4. Cf. Deut 30:1–5.

5. Cf. Ps 119:67.   6. Cf. Eccl 7:1–4.

7. Cf. Rom 8:29; 12:2.

8. "1. To mark; to attend. 2. To incline; to dispose." Johnson's *Dictionary*, s.v. "Mind."

9. "1. To cut into very small parts. 2. To speak with affected softness; to clip the words. 3. To speak small and imperfectly." Johnson's *Dictionary*, s.v. "Mince."

10. Cf. Jas 1:23.

11. The context of Charles's conclusion indicates that this sermon was preached at a funeral. It appears that the deceased passed away unexpectedly at a relatively young age.

12. Charles normally did not preach funeral sermons during his ministry. In his sermon "Heaven" (*NPSP* 2, Sermon 56), he wrote, "I never preach any funeral sermons for anybody, and never intend to. I have passed by many persons who have died in our church, without having made any parade of funeral sermons; but, nevertheless, three or four of our friends having departed recently, I think that I may speak a little to you about heaven, in order to cheer you, and God may thus bless their departure." *NPSP* 2:19. What bothered Charles with respect to preaching funeral sermons was the expectation of lavishing praise on the departed, when the goal of a sermon is to exalt Christ. He wrote, "Frequent funeral sermons I utterly abhor, and I believe they are not under God's sanction and approval. Of the dead we should say nothing but that which is good: and in the pulpit we should say very little of that, except, perhaps in the case of a very eminent saint; and then we should say very little of the man, but let the 'honor be unto him that sitteth upon the throne, and unto the Lamb for ever.'" *NPSP* 2:19. Given these views, it is not surprising that Charles gave no portion of this sermon to remembering the deceased but focused on calling the living to "look to themselves."

262. Rom. VIII. 15. The Spirits of Bondage & Adoption.

How marked the difference between the Unbeliever & the child of God; not only in their actions but also in their Spirit

I. The common Spirit of false Religions.

The Spirit of Bondage pervades Heathenism, Catholicism, Mormonism, Arminianism, Legalism, Phariseeism — these are all on the Bondage principle, we must, we are afraid to do otherwise. Even the true believer has a tendency to this.

II. The constant effect of false Religions.

"Fear" is the fruit of them all. They are never sure, never confident. Poor Slaves they fear. If we have fears they come from this source — but remember we have not rec^d this.

III. The true & peculiar Spirit of the Gospel.

Adoption, childlike, love, humble trust & joy in all trials, or afflictions

IV. Whence this Spirit comes.

Not from nature, but we have received this of pure grace. Can we see the true Spirit of the child, then we are the subjects of grace and have received mercy.

457.

THE SPIRITS *of* BONDAGE *and* ADOPTION
Romans 8:15[1]

"For ye have not received the spirit of bondage again to fear; but ye have received the Spirit of adoption, whereby we cry, Abba, Father."

How marked the difference between the Unbeliever and the child of God: not only in their actions but also in their Spirit.

I. THE COMMON SPIRIT OF FALSE RELIGIONS.

The Spirit of Bondage pervades Heathenism, Catholicism, Mormonism,[2] Arminianism,[3] Legalism, [and] Phariseeism. These are all on the Bondage principle, ["]we must.["] We are afraid to do otherwise. Even the true believer has a tendency to this.

II. THE CONSTANT EFFECT OF FALSE RELIGIONS.

"Fear" is the fruit of them all. They are never sure, never confident. Poor Slaves[,] they fear. If we have fears they come from this source, but remember we have not recd this.[4]

III. THE TRUE AND PECULIAR SPIRIT OF THE GOSPEL.

Adoption,[5] childlike,[6] love,[7] humble trust[8] and joy in all trials, or afflictions.[9]

IV. WHENCE THIS SPIRIT COMES.

Not from nature, but we have received this of pure grace. Can we see the true Spirit of the child[?][10] Then we are the subjects of grace and have received mercy.

457.

1. Charles preached a later sermon on this text, "The Spirit of Bondage and of Adoption" (*MTP* 30, Sermon 1759). However, while his later sermon does not appear to contain significant overlapping content, it is notable that Charles kept a nearly identical title for it. Furthermore, Charles adopted a different definition of the "Spirit of Bondage." In his original sermon, the "Spirit of Bondage" was associated with false religions such as "Heathenism, Catholicism, Mormonism, Arminianism, Legalism, [and] Phariseeism." In his later sermon, Charles identified this Spirit as the Holy Spirit, producing bondage in multiple senses. First, "*men are brought into bondage through being convinced of sin.*" *MTP* 30:16, italics in the original. Second, "he *made us feel the assurance that punishment must follow upon sin.*" *MTP* 30:16, italics in the original. Third, "to *feel the utter impossibility of their hoping to clear themselves by the works of the law.*" *MTP* 30:17, italics in the original. Lastly, Charles explained, "Our text reminds us that *the result of the spirit of bondage in the soul is fear,*" and "*. . . while this fear lasts it is intended to work us toward God.*" *MTP* 30:18–19, italics in the original. Charles then concluded that "in due time we outgrow this bondage, and never receive it again," meaning that once the conviction of sin by the Holy Spirit brings a person to repentance and belief in Christ, the fear departs as well. *MTP* 30:19. This is similar to what Charles wrote in his autobiography: "Neither in the Church militant nor in the host triumphant is there one who received a new heart, and was reclaimed from sin without a wound from Jesus. The pain may have been but slight, and the healing may have been speedy; but in each case there has been a real bruise, which required a Heavenly Physician to heal. With some of us, this wounding commenced in early life; for, as soon as infancy gave place to childhood, the rod was exercised upon us. We can remember early convictions of sin, and apprehensions of the wrath of God on its account. An awakened conscience in our most tender years drove us to the throne of mercy." *Autobiography* 1:79.

2. Charles was not hesitant to express his views concerning Mormonism. He claimed that there could never be a "delusion more apparent, or a counterfeit less skillful" than Mormonism. *NPSP* 2:182. Regarding the Book of Mormon, Charles wrote, "I could not blame you should you laugh outright while I read aloud a page from that farrago." *MTP* 37:45. In Charles's mind, Mormonism was a false religion that promoted deadly bondage.

3. "I will not say that the Arminian teaches that salvation is by works; this is so continually denied by the Arminian, that I will not charge a falsehood upon

him, at which he professes to shudder; but at the same time, I do say, that the tendency of Arminianism is towards legality; it is nothing but legality which lays at the root of Arminianism. . . . Do you not see at once that this is legality -- that this is hanging our salvation upon our work -- that this is making our eternal life to depend on something we do? Nay, the doctrine of justification itself, as preached by an Arminian, is nothing but the doctrine of salvation by works, after all; for he always thinks faith is a work of the creature, and a condition of his acceptance." MTP 6:304.

4. Cf. 2 Tim 1:7.

5. Cf. Gal 4:5; Eph 1:5. "Thus it is clear that the Spirit of adoption is a spirit of liberty, and a spirit of confidence. As a child is sure that its father will love him, feed him, clothe him, teach him, and do all that is good for him, so are we sure that 'No good thing will he withhold from them that walk uprightly;' but he will make all things to 'work together for good to them that love God.'" MTP 30:20.

6. Cf. Luke 18:15–17. "The Spirit of adoption is a spirit of *child-likeness*. It is pretty, though sometimes sad, to see how children imitate their parents. How much the little man is like his father! Have you not noticed it? Do you not like to see it, too? You know you do. Ay, and when God gives the Spirit of adoption, there begins in us, poor fallen creatures as we are, some little likeness to himself; and that will grow to his perfect image. We cannot become God; but we have the privilege and the power to become the sons of God." MTP 30:21; italics in the original.

7. Cf. 1 John 4:7–10. "The first thing is that he works in us great love to God. None love God but those that are born of him. There is no true love to God in Christ Jesus except in those that have been begotten again by God's own Spirit, so that our love to God is the witness of the Spirit that we are the children of God." MTP 30:23.

8. Cf. Jer 17:7–8; Gal 3:6–9. "In addition to this, the Spirit of God works in us a holy confidence. By his grace we feel in days of trouble that we can rest in God. When we cannot see our way we go on joyfully without seeing. What is the good of seeing with our own eyes when the eyes of the Lord are running to and fro in the earth to show himself strong in the behalf of all them that trust in him? Our faith feels a joy in believing seeming contradictions, a delight in accepting

apparent impossibilities. We have a belief in God's veracity so sure and steadfast that if all the angels in heaven were to deny the truth of God we would laugh them to scorn." *MTP* 30:23.

9. Cf. 2 Cor 4:16–18; Jas 1:2-4.

10. The meaning of the phrase "Can we see the true Spirit of the child" is ambiguous. It is possible that Charles was asking whether his hearers could see God with the perspective of their adoption (i.e., "Can we see with the true Spirit of the child?"). Another option is that Charles was calling for self-examination, asking whether his hearers could see the true Spirit of the child within themselves. Either reading fits in the context, and in order to clarify the meaning of the line, the question mark has been supplied.

Job. I. 1. Job the perfect man. 263

446.

JOB THE PERFECT MAN[1]
Job 1:1[2]

446.

1. It is unclear why Charles left this sermon blank, especially because he included a preaching occurrence number, 446, at the bottom left corner of the page. Previously, Charles has only left six sermons blank: "Son, Be of Good Cheer" (Notebook 4, Sermon 225); "He Filleth the Hungry with Good Things" (Notebook 4, Sermon 226); "He Will Bring Every Work into Judgment" (Notebook 4, Sermon 228); "As One Whom His Mother Comforteth" (Notebook 4, Sermon 229); "Text for Boys and Girls" (Sermon 239); and "Text for Young Unbelievers" (Sermon 240). For reasons on why "Text for Boys and Girls" (Sermon 239) and "Text for Young Unbelievers" (Sermon 240) were left blank, see the corresponding notes in those sermons. As for this instance, no immediate reason presents itself.

2. It appears that Charles did not preach another sermon on the text of Job 1:1.

264. II Kings XX. 15. What have they seen in thy house.

I. Let us consider Hezekiah's conduct.
He had been ill, the sun was sent back as a pledge of his recovery, the Babylonians probably wishing to hear more of so wonderful a phenomenon, sent ambassadors. Hezekiah proud of being so noticed shews them all his treasuries, but alas sin was in it.
1. Pride. He was proud of being so rich, so noble &c.
2. Vain Confidence. See said he I have power to fight any army your king may bring into the field
3. Neglect of a fine opportunity of preaching the truth to a heathen nation.
Mark how the punishment fitted the sin.

II. Let us consider the question as addressed to us.
Our house will be somewhat of an index to our heart. You may tell a man's trade by his house so ought you to tell a man's religion.
1. What never ought to be there.
A dusty bible — a cobwebbed hymn book — an idle song — a bad book — a bad picture — broken things looking like a fight &c &c.
2 What ought to be there.
A well read bible, some good books, family prayer, private devotion, good fathers, wives, sons &c —

Remember God seeth, angels visit you. Never let a person go out without some flour from your mill. & when this question is asked give a good answer.

468

WHAT HAVE THEY SEEN *in* THY HOUSE[?]

2 Kings 20:15[1]

"And he said, What have they seen in thine house? And Hezekiah answered, All the things that are in mine house have they seen: there is nothing among my treasures that I have not shewed them."

I. LET US CONSIDER HEZEKIAH'S CONDUCT.

He had been ill,[2] the sun was sent back as a pledge of his recovery.[3] The Babylonians[,] probably wishing to hear more of so wonderful a phenomenon,[4] sent ambassadors.[5] Hezekiah[,] proud of being so noticed[,] shews them all his treasuries, but alas sin was in it.

1. Pride. He was proud of being so rich, so noble, etc.[6]
2. Vain Confidence. ["]See["] said he, ["]I have power to fight any army your king may bring into the field[."]
3. Neglect of a fine opportunity of preaching the truth to a heathen nation.[7]

Mark how the punishment fitted the sin.

II. LET US CONSIDER THE QUESTION AS ADDRESSED TO US.

Our house will be somewhat of an index to our heart. You may tell a man's trade by his house[,] so ought you [be able] to tell a man's religion.

1. What never ought to be there[:]

    A dusty bible, a cobwebbed hymnbook, an idle song, a bad book,[8] a bad picture, broken things looking like a fight, etc. etc.[9]

2. What ought to be there[:]

    A well read bible, some good books, family prayer, private devotion, good fathers, wives, sons, etc.[10]

Remember God seeth,[11] angels visit you.[12] Never let a person go out without some flour from your mill. And when this question is asked give a good answer.[13]

468

1. It appears that Charles did not preach another sermon on this text.

2. Cf. 2 Kgs 20:1.

3. Cf. 2 Kgs 20:10–11.

4. Cf. 2 Kgs 20:12. Charles likely relied on Matthew Henry's exposition of 2 Kings. On this point, Henry wrote, "The kings of Babylon had hitherto been only deputies and tributaries to the kings of Assyria, and Nineveh was the royal city. We find Babylon subject to the king of Assyria, 2 Kgs. 17:24. But this king of Babylon began to set up for himself, and by degrees things were so changed that Assyria became subject to the kings of Babylon. This king of Babylon sent to compliment Hezekiah, and ingratiate himself with him upon a double account. 1. Upon the account of religion. The Babylonians worshipped the sun, and, perceiving what honour their god had done to Hezekiah, in going back for his sake, they thought themselves obliged to do honour to him likewise. It is good having those our friends whom we perceive to be the favourites of heaven." Matthew Henry, *An Exposition on the Old and New Testament*, vol. 2 (London: W. and J. Stratford, Holborn-Hill, n.d., The Spurgeon Library), II Kings. XX.15, n.1.

5. Cf. 2 Kgs 20:12–13.

6. Cf. 2 Chr 32:25. Matthew Henry wrote, "The sentence passed upon [Hezekiah] for his pride and vanity, and the too great relish he had of the things of the world, after that intimate acquaintance he had so lately been admitted into with divine things. The sentence is, ver.17,18. (1) That the treasures he was so proud of should hereafter become a prey, and his family should be robbed of them all. It is just with God to take that from us which we make the matter of our pride and in which we put our confidence." Henry, *An Exposition on the Old and New Testament*, II Kings. XX.15, n.3.

7. Henry wrote, "It is not said that [Hezekiah] showed them the temple, the book of the law, and the manner of his worship, that he might proselyte them to the true religion, which he had now a fair opportunity of doing; but in compliment to them, lest he should affront them, he waived that, and showed them the rich furniture of his closet, that house of his precious things, the wealth he had heaped up since the king of Assyria had emptied his coffers, his silver, and gold, and spices." Henry, *An Exposition on the Old and New Testament*, II Kings. XX.15, n.2.

8. In referring to "a bad book," Charles may have had in mind the developing genre of "sensation fiction," which burst onto the literary scene in the 1860s. According

WHAT HAVE THEY SEEN IN THY HOUSE[?]—2 Kings 20:15

to Winifred Hughes, these novels "desired to create a sensation in every sense of the word," and accordingly, the plots were filled with murder, divorce, and seduction. Winifred Hughes, "The Sensation Novel," *A Companion to the Victorian Novel*, ed. Patrick Brantlinger and William B. Thesing (Oxford: Blackwell, 2002), 260.

9. Charles described Waterbeach prior to his arrival in this way: "Did you ever walk through a village notorious for its drunkenness and profanity? Did you ever see poor wretched beings, that once were men, standing, or rather leaning, against the posts of the ale-house, or staggering along the street? Have you ever looked into the houses of the people, and beheld them as dens of iniquity, at which your soul stood aghast? Have you ever seen the poverty, and degradation, and misery of the inhabitants, and sighed over it? . . . I once knew just such a village as I have pictured, — perhaps, in some respects, one of the worst in England, — where many an illicit still was yielding its noxious liquor to a manufacturer without payment of the duty to the government, and where, in connection with that evil, all manner of riot and iniquity was rife." *Autobiography* 1:227–28.

10. Charles recounted these scenes of family prayer during his time in Waterbeach: "I was delighted, one Sabbath evening in the year 1853, when driving from the village where I had supplied for a minister, to see in one place a father, with four or five little ones about him, sitting on a small plot of grass before the cottage door. He had a large Bible on his knee, and the children also had their Bibles; and he in the midst was holding his finger up, with all solemnity and earnestness, in simple style endeavoring to enforce some sacred truth. . . . A little further was a house which had a small workshop adjoining it. The door was open, so I could see that no one was inside; but there stood a chest, and on it lay a Bible of the largest kind, and on the floor below was a cushion which still bore the impress of knees which, I trust, had been bent in wrestling prayer. Perhaps a Mother had there been begging at the Redeemer's hands the souls of her dearly-beloved children; or, possibly, some son, in answer to that Mother's prayer, had been secretly pouring out his heart, and crying for mercy from the hands of God. Yet once more, I saw a little girl spelling over to her parents the words of the Book of Truth. . . . Blest households, of which these things can be written! May you not be solitary instances, but may God raise up thousands like unto you!" *Autobiography* 1:285–86.

11. Cf. Matt 6:6.   12. Cf. Heb 13:2.   13. Cf. 1 Pet 3:15.

Prov. XIII. 7   Making ones-self rich yet having nothing. 265

Here we have an exposition of David's hasty speech "all men are liars" alas it was too true

I. Many temporally profess to be rich yet are poor. Some dress beyond their income, spend more than is proper for their circumstances, flash & turn out nothing.

Some on the other hand plead poverty when they are rich — cannot help their neighbours, subscribe to the cause, they are poor while truly they roll in money

II. Many men get rich & yet are truly poor. They sell their souls for gold & die poor, miserable wretches. He who gets money without Christ is a beggar still. Many have been made poor by religion & yet were truly rich as kings — he who loses all, gains all.

III. Many think themselves spiritually rich but are not so — see the Pharisee & many of his descendants in our day. So even the righteous think themselves prospering when they are declining — see the Laodoceans.

Again many persons are poor in spirit, full of fear and distrust yet these are the rich ones in the kingdom. Emptiness is fulness. Poverty is the road to wealth.

Can I comfort a poor and needy one.

Is there here a rich one, falsely so.

Admire the grace of Jesus our Lord.

Be poor & thus you shall be rich.

465

MAKING ONES-SELF RICH YET HAVING NOTHING
Proverbs 13:7[1]

"There is that maketh himself rich, yet hath nothing: there is that maketh himself poor, yet hath great riches."

Here we have an exposition of David's hasty speech "all men are liars[.]"[2] [A]las[,] it was too true.

I. MANY TEMPORALLY PROFESS TO BE RICH YET ARE POOR.

Some dress beyond their income, spend more than is proper for their circumstances, flash[,][3] and turn out nothing.[4]

Some on the other hand plead poverty when they are rich,[5] cannot help their neighbours, [and] subscribe to the cause [that] they are poor while truly they roll in money.

II. MANY MEN GET RICH AND YET ARE TRULY POOR.

They sell their souls for gold and die poor, miserable wretches.[6] He who gets money without Christ is a beggar still. Many have been made poor by religion and yet were truly rich as kings.[7] He who loses all, gains all.[8]

III. MANY THINK THEMSELVES SPIRITUALLY RICH BUT ARE NOT SO.

See the Pharisee and many of his descendants in our day. So even the righteous think themselves prospering when they are declining – see the Laodiceans.[9]

Again many persons are poor in spirit,[10] full of fear and distrust[,] yet these are the rich ones in the kingdom. Emptiness is Fulness. Poverty is the road to wealth.[11]

    Can I comfort the poor and needy one.

    Is there here a rich one, falsely so.

    Admire the grace of Jesus our Lord.

    Be poor and thus you shall be rich.[12]

465

SERMON 265

1. It appears that Charles did not preach another sermon on Prov 13:7.

2. Cf. Ps 116:11. Charles used David's phrase "all men are liars" to summarize the point of the proverb, namely that people's outward appearance does not truly reveal their inward condition.

3. "2. To glitter with a quick and transient flame. 3. To break out into wit, merriment, or bright thought." Johnson's *Dictionary*, s.v. "Flash."

4. Charles hated debt and sought to avoid it his entire life. He wrote, "I have hated debt as Luther hated the pope, and if I say some fierce things about it, you must not wonder.... Living beyond their incomes is the ruin of many of my neighbors; they can hardly afford to keep a rabbit, and must needs drive a pony and chaise. I am afraid extravagance is the common disease of the times, and many professing Christians have caught it, to their shame and sorrow. Good cotton or stuff gowns are not good enough nowadays; girls must have silks and satins, and then there's a bill at the dressmaker's as long as the winter's night, and quite as dismal. Show, and style, and smartness run away with a man's means, keep the family poor, and the father's nose on the grindstone." C. H. Spurgeon. *John Ploughman's Talk; or, Plain Advice for Plain People.* (New York: Sheldon, 1868, The Spurgeon Library), 73–75.

5. "If I were put in possession of great wealth, I do not say what I would do, for very frequently people's hearts get smaller when their means get greater; but where God has given us wealth, I am sure where there are necessitous children of God, we ought to remember them directly. How much of the superfluities might be given to their necessities! How many of our lavished luxuries might be bestowed on that which they crave for their very existence. Ye know not how poor this world is.... Go and see such cases, and if you do not put your hands in your pockets, and help the aged pilgrims, I am afraid there is not much Christianity in you; or if you do not help the one that you see has the greatest need, I am afraid the love of God dwelleth not in you." *NPSP* 2:366–67.

6. Cf. Matt 16:26.   7. Cf. Matt 19:29; Heb 10:34.

8. Cf. Matt 16:25; Phil 3:7–8.

9. Cf. Rev 3:14–22.

10. Cf. Matthew 5:3. Charles seems to have had the first beatitude in mind in his conclusion. The poverty he described here is not a material poverty but a spiritual poverty. In a sermon he preached on this beatitude ("The First Beatitude," *MTP* 55, Sermon 3156), he wrote, "Its first blessing is allotted to a characteristic, not of the outer, but of the inner man; to a state of soul, and not to a posture of body; to the poor in spirit, and not to the exact in ritual." *MTP* 55:276.

11. Charles believed that material poverty did not commend anyone to Christ. At the same time, he saw a particular burden in Scripture to preach to the materially poor, and he rejoiced at their response to the gospel. In his sermon "Preaching for the Poor" (*NPSP* 3, Sermon 114), Charles wrote, "True it is, the gospel affects all ranks, and is equally adapted to them all; but yet we say, 'If one class be more prominent than another, we believe that in Holy Scripture the poor are most of all appealed to.' 'Oh!' say some very often, 'the converts whom God has given to such a man are all from the lower ranks, they are all people with no sense; they are all uneducated people that hear such-and-such a person.' Very well, if you say so; we might deny it if we pleased, but we do not know that we shall take the trouble, because we think it no disgrace whatever; we think it rather to be an honor that the poor are evangelized, and that they listen to the gospel from our lips. I have never thought it a disgrace at any time. When any have said, 'Look, what a mass of uneducated people they are.' Yes, I have thought, and blessed be God they are for those are the very people that want the gospel most." *NPSP* 3:63.

12. "'Poor in Spirit;' the words sound as if they described the owners of nothing, and yet they describe the inheritors of all things. Happy poverty! Millionaires sink into insignificance, the treasures of the Indies evaporate in smoke, while to the poor in spirit remains a boundless, endless, faultless kingdom, which renders them blessed in the esteem of him who is God over all, blessed for ever." *MTP* 55:382.

266. I Thess. V. 6. Let us not sleep as do others.

The strongest buildings need repair, the best fields want manure & the best men want warning & advice.

I. To whom is the text directed? — "To the children of light" — how grand a title & one involving many duties, So far from having less to do we have even more than others. Compared with the Jews, the Catholics, heathens or our former selves we are children of light. Of joy, of knowledge, of holiness, of heaven.

II. What is the conduct forbidden. "Let us not sleep as do others".

1. Sleeping persons are insensible of even the most agreeable objects around them so are sinners.
2. Sleepers are inactive & move neither hand nor foot.
3. Sleepers dream idle things.
4. Sleepers are unable to protect themselves.
5. Sleepers such as sinners are can only be awakened by the trumpet either of peace or judgment.

Let us not in the least imitate these.

III. What conduct is commanded?

1. <u>Watch</u> against inward & outward foes in prosperity or adversity <u>watch</u>. For opportunities of doing good, for Jesus' coming.
2. <u>Be Sober</u> here something more than drunkenness is forbidden, vexing, carking cares are to be avoided.

Put these in practise Oh heirs of heaven

LET US NOT SLEEP AS DO OTHERS
1 Thessalonians 5:6[1]

"Therefore let us not sleep, as do others; but let us watch and be sober."

The strongest buildings need repair, the best fields want manure[,] and the best men want warning and advice.

I. **TO WHOM IS THE TEXT DIRECTED?** *"To the children of light"*[2]

How grand a title and one involving many duties. So far from having less to do we have even more than others.

Compared with the Jews, the Catholics, heathens or our former selves we are children of Light. Of joy,[3] of knowledge,[4] of holiness,[5] of heaven.[6]

II. **WHAT IS THE CONDUCT FORBIDDEN[?]** "*Let us not sleep as do others*."

1. Sleeping persons are insensible of even the most agreeable objects around them[,] so are sinners.[7]
2. Sleepers are inactive and move neither hand nor foot.[8]
3. Sleepers dream idle things.[9]
4. Sleepers are unable to protect themselves.[10]
5. Sleepers such as sinners are can only be awakened by the trumpet, either of grace or Judgment.

Let us not in the least imitate these[.]

III. **WHAT CONDUCT IS COMMANDED?**

1. <u>Watch</u> against inward and outward foes[.][11] [I]n prosperity[12] or adversity <u>watch</u>. For opportunities of doing good, for Jesus'[s] coming.[13]
2. <u>Be Sober</u> here something more than drunkenness is forbidden[;][14] vexing, carking[15] cares are to be avoided.[16]

   Put these in practise Oh heirs of heaven.[17]

466

SERMON 266

1. It appears that Charles preached three later sermons on this text: "The Enchanted Ground" (*NPSP* 2, Sermon 64); "Awake! Awake!" (*NPSP* 3, Sermon 163); and "Sleep Not" (*MTP* 17, 1022). Though they are structurally different, Charles's later sermons appear to have some overlapping content that will be noted below.

2. Cf. 1 Thess 5:5.   3. Cf. Ps 16:11; Phil 4:4.

4. Cf. John 10:14; 17:3; Phil 3:8; 1 John 2:3.

5. Cf. 1 Pet 1:15–16.   6. Cf. Eph 2:6; Phil 3:20.

7. "First, sleep is a state of *insensibility* and such is that state which too often is upon even the best children of God. When a man is asleep he is insensible. The world goes on, and he knows nought about it. The watchman calls beneath his window, and he sleeps on still. A fire is in a neighboring street, his neighbour's house is burned to ashes, but he is asleep and knows it not. . . . Christian, behold your condition, have you not sometimes been brought into a condition of insensibility? You wished you could feel; but all you felt was pain because you could not feel. You wished you could pray. It was not that you felt prayerless, but it was because you did not feel at all. You sighed once; you would give a world if you could sigh now. You used to groan once; a groan now would be worth a golden star if you could buy it. . . . Once if you thought of a man's being damned you would weep your very soul out in tears; but now you could sit at the very brink of hell, and hear its wailings unmoved." *NPSP* 2:82, italics in the original.

8. "Again, sleep is a *state of inaction*. No daily bread is earned by him that sleepeth. The man who is stretched upon his couch neither writeth books, nor tilleth the ground, nor plougheth the sea, nor doth aught else. His hands hang down, his pulse beateth, and life there is, but he is positively dead as to activity. Oh, beloved, here is the state of many of you. How many Christians are inactive! Once it was their delight to instruct the young in the Sabbath-school, but that is now given up. Once they attended the early prayer-meeting, but not now. Once they would be hewers of wood and drawers of water, but alas; they are asleep now. Am I talking of what may happen? Is it not too true almost universally? Are not the churches asleep?" *NPSP* 2:83, italics in the original.

9. "Then again, he that sleepeth is *subject to divers illusions*. When we sleep, judgment goeth from us, and fancy holdeth carnival within our brain. When we sleep,

dreams arise and fashion in our head strange things. Sometimes we are tossed on the stormy deep, and anon we revel in kings' palaces. We gather up gold and silver as if they were but the pebbles of the shore; and anon we are poor and naked, shivering in the blast. What illusions deceive us! . . . Christian, if thou art one of the sleepy brotherhood, thou art subject to divers illusions. Strange thoughts come to thee which thou never hadst before. Sometimes thou doubtest if there be a God, or if thou dost exist thyself. Thou tremblest lest the gospel should not be true; and the old doctrine which ones thou didst hold with a stern hand thou art almost inclined to let go. Vile heresies assail thee. . . . Or perhaps thy dreams are brighter, and thou dreamest that thou art somebody, great and mighty, a special favorite of heaven; pride puffs thee up; thou dreamest that thou art rich and hast need of nothing, whilst thou art naked, poor, and miserable. Is this thy state, O Christian? If so, may God wake thee up from it!" NPSP 2:82–83, italics in the original.

10. "Once more. The man who is asleep is in a *state of insecurity*. The murderer smiteth him that sleeps; the midnight robber plundereth his house that resteth listlessly on his pillow. . . . Christian, if thou art sleeping, thou art in danger. Thy life, I know, can never be taken from thee, that is hid with Christ in God. But oh! thou mayest lose thy spear from thy bolster; thou mayest lose much of thy faith; and thy cruse of water wherewith thou dost moisten thy lips may be stolen by the prowling thief. Oh! thou little knowest thy danger." NPSP 2:83, italics in the original.

11. Cf. 1 Pet 5:8; 2 Pet 1:10–11.

12. In "The Enchanted Ground," Charles listed three circumstances when Christians are most liable to sleep: "*when his temporal circumstances are all right. . . . when all goes well in spiritual matters. . . . when we get near our journey's end.*" NPSP 2:85–86, italics in the original.

13. Cf. Luke 12:36–39; Gal 6:10. "There are many that never watch. They never watch against sin; they never watch against the temptations of the enemy, they do not watch against themselves, nor against 'the lusts of the flesh, the lusts of the eye, and the pride of life.' They do not watch for opportunities to do good, they do not watch for opportunities to instruct the ignorant, to confirm the weak, to comfort the afflicted, to succor them that are in need; they do not watch for opportunities of glorifying Jesus, or for times of communion, they do

not watch for the promises; they do not watch for answers to their prayers; they do not watch for the second coming of our Lord Jesus. These are the refuse of the world: they watch not, because they are asleep. But let us watch: so shall we prove that we are not slumberers." *NPSP* 3:448.

14. Cf. Rom 13:13; Eph 5:18; 1 Pet 4:3.

15. "To be careful; to be solicitious; to be anxious. It is now very little used, and always in an ill sense." Johnson's *Dictionary*, s.v. "To Cark."

16. "There be many that are not sober; they sleep, because they are not so; for insobriety leadeth to sleep. They are not sober—they are drunkards, they are gluttons. They are not sober—they cannot be content to do a little business—they want to do a great deal. They are not sober—they cannot carry on a trade that is sure—they must speculate. They are not sober—if they lose their property, their spirit is cast down within them, and they are like men that are drunken with wormwood. If on the other hand, they get rich, they are not sober: they so set their affections upon things on earth that they become intoxicated with pride, because of their riches—become purse-proud, and need to have the heavens lifted up higher, lest their heads should dash against the stars. How many people there are that are not sober! Oh! I might especially urge this precept upon you at this time, my dear friends. We have hard times coming, and the times are hard enough now. Let us be sober." *NPSP* 3:448.

17. Cf. 1 Thess 5:9–10.

Rom. V. 10. The Believers certain Salvation. 267

Rich as the Bible is in promises, we shall find abundant need for them all — Sometimes we fear lest the work will never be completed, now this passage is written on purpose to allay such a fear.

Where the Arminian can find any way of escape or derive comfort if he should confute this verse is more than I can venture to guess. —

Here are two clauses with 3 opposite in them.

If when we were enemies / we were reconciled to God / by the death of his son
much more Being reconciled / we shall be saved / by his life.

Here are three proofs couched in one verse.

I. The First consists in the change of our relation once "enemies" now "reconciled"

You admit your ancient enmity to God, you humbly acknowledge it with tears. Now, consider he spared you then, he gave his son to die for you then, he looked in love & gave you his Spirit then. Will he serve you worse now, will he not treat a friend better than an enemy. Consider how utter and entire that enmity was, how vile you were, how obstinate in sin, yet he loved you, will he now desert?

You are now reconciled, sweetly, entirely reconciled & shall he treat as a foe one who desires him for a friend You enjoy communion with him and prayer to him what will he spurn you. Nay, nay.

THE BELIEVER[']S CERTAIN SALVATION

Romans 5:10[1]

"For if, when we were enemies, we were reconciled to God by the death of his Son, much more, being reconciled, we shall be saved by his life."

Rich as the Bible is in promises, we shall find abundant need for them all. Sometimes we fear lest the work will never be completed, now this passage is written on purpose to allay such a fear.

Where the Arminian can find any way of escape or derive comfort if he should confuse this verse is more than I can venture to guess.[2]

Here are two clauses with 3 opposite[s] in them.

| Much More | If when we were enemies
Being reconciled | we were reconciled to God
we shall be saved | by the death of his son
by his life |

Here are three proofs couched in one verse.

I. THE FIRST CONSISTS IN THE CHANGE OF OUR RELATION.

Once "enemies" Now "reconciled"

You admit your ancient enmity to God, you humbly acknowledge it with tears. Now, consider he spared you then,[3] he gave his son to die for you then,[4] he looked in love and gave you his Spirit then.[5] Will he serve[6] you worse now, will he not treat a friend[7] better than an enemy[?] Consider how utter and entire that enmity was, how vile you were[,] and how obstinate in sin, yet he loved you. Will he now desert?

You are now reconciled,[8] sweetly, entirely reconciled[,] and shall he treat as a foe one who desires him for a friend[?] You enjoy communion with him and prayer to him. What[,] will he spurn[9] you[?] Nay. Nay.[10]

we are not what we once were. If we were now enemies we might doubt but as now friends we need not fear.

our reconciliation is real, & eternal.

II. The Second consists in what he has already done for us.

He has "reconciled" — will he not "save."

1. The first seemed a very unlikely thing that he should be at trouble to reconcile us — but to save ~~enemies~~ friends is but a common thing.

2. As to the first it was undesired & unsought on our part — till he began the work — will he not much more give what we ever beg for.

3. As to reconciliation — it seems after the manner of men to be more difficult & to require more cost than after-salvation can require.

4. Would it be at all like our God — first to make a man reconciled & then slay him.

Remember this argument can be strengthened by other mercies already received. Election, Redemption, Adoption &c all forbid thee to think He'll leave thee at last in trouble to sink.

Unbelief is not only wicked, it is foolish too.

III. The third consists in the different means employed.

If by his "death", much more by "his life"

1. Christ's death was an exhibition of weakness

THE BELIEVER[']S CERTAIN SALVATION—*Romans 5:10*

We are not what we once were.¹¹ If we were now enemies we might doubt[,] but as now [we are] friends we need not fear.¹²

Our reconciliation is real, and eternal . . .¹³

II. THE SECOND CONSISTS IN WHAT HE HAS ALREADY DONE FOR US.

He has "<u>reconciled</u>" – will he not "<u>save</u>[?]"

1. The first seemed a very unlikely thing[,]¹⁴ that he should be at trouble to reconcile us – but to save ~~enemies~~ friends is but a common thing.
2. As to the first it was undesired and unsought on our part¹⁵ – till he began the work – will he not much more give what we ever beg for[?]
3. As to reconciliation – it seems after the manner of men to be more difficult and to require more cost than after-salvation can require.¹⁶
4. Would it be at all like our God – first to make a man reconciled and then slay him[?]

Remember this argument can be strengthened by other mercies already received. Election, Redemption, Adoption, etc. all forbid thee to think He'll leave thee at last in trouble to sink.¹⁷

Unbelief is not only wicked, it is foolish too.

III. THE THIRD CONSISTS IN THE DIFFERENT MEANS EMPLOYED.

If by his "<u>death</u>," much more by "<u>his life</u>."

1. Christ's death was an exhibition of weakness

or at least it was the bruising of his heel but his life is an exhibition of power.
2. Death was the act of his manhood, his life is by the omnipotence of his Godhead.
3. Christ's death had in it an awful manifestation of the wrath of God, his life is a declaration of the loving-kindness of the Father.
4. Since he loved us so much as to give up his soul to death will he not employ every hour of his life in our service
All these are as clear proofs as any mathematics can afford, if we had faith as a grain of mustard seed. Surely the two sights of Jesus Agonizing & Jesus Triumphant are enough to banish all doubts & fears.
1. Christian try to comfort thyself with these words — reflect — think whether thy doubts are not dishonouring to God & ruinous to thyself — Search lest there be something wrong.
2. Sinner — dost thou not admire the state of the heir of heaven? Dost thou desire to be one — then the way thou knowest. Believe on the Lord Jesus Christ.
    Father vouchsafe me thine aid

470.

THE BELIEVER['] S CERTAIN SALVATION—*Romans 5.10*

or at least it was the bruising of his heel[18] but his <u>life</u> is an exhibition of <u>power</u>.[19]

2. Death was the act of his manhood, his life is by the omnipotence of his Godhead.[20]
3. Christ's death had in it an awful manifestation of the wrath of God. His life is a declaration of the loving-kindness of the Father.[21]
4. Since he loved us so much as to give up his soul to death[,] will he not employ every hour of his <u>life</u> in our service[?][22]

All these are as clear proofs as any mathematics can afford, if we had faith as a grain of mustard seed.[23] Surely the two sights of Jesus Agonizing and Jesus Triumphant are enough to banish all doubts and fears.

1. Christian[,] try to comfort thyself with these words – reflect – think whether thy doubts are not dishonouring to God and ruinous to thyself. Search lest there be something wrong.[24]
2. Sinner, dost thou not admire the state of the heir of heaven? Dost thou desire to be one[?] Then the way thou knowest.[25]

Believe on the Lord Jesus Christ.

       Father vouchsafe[26] me thine aid[.]

470.

SERMON 267

1. It appears that Charles preached a later sermon on this text, "Much More" (*MTP* 44, Sermon 2587). The structure of this sermon is quite different, but the third point of this sermon had significant influence on the second point of the later sermon. Overlapping content has been noted below.

2. Adam Clarke, a Methodist commentator and Arminian foil to Charles, approached this passage differently. Regarding Rom 5:10, Clarke wrote, "The example also of the life of Christ is a means of salvation. He hath left us an example that we should follow his steps: and he that followeth him, shall not walk in darkness, but shall have the light of LIFE, John viii.12." Adam Clarke, *The Holy Bible Containing the Old and New Testaments: With Commentary and Critical Notes*, vol. 5 (London: William Tegg, 1854, The Spurgeon Library), Rom 5:10. Rather than focusing on the perseverance of the saints and assurance of salvation thanks to the death of Christ, Clarke pointed to a maintenance of salvation through following the example set forth by Jesus. While it is difficult to judge Clarke's entire theological system through this one commentary, it is safe to say that Charles could have seen this statement as a rejection of eternal security because of one's inability to follow Jesus's example perfectly.

3. Cf. Mic 7:18.

4. Cf. John 3:16.

5. Cf. 1 Thess 4:8.

6. "To treat; to requite; in an ill sense." Johnson's *Dictionary*, s.v. "To Serve."

7. Cf. John 15:15.

8. Cf. 2 Cor 5:18–19; Col 1:20.

9. "2. To reject; to scorn; to put away with contempt; to disdain." Johnson's *Dictionary*, s.v. "To Spurn."

10. "1. No; an adverb of negation." Johnson's *Dictionary*, s.v. "Nay."

11. Cf. 2 Cor 5:17.

12. Cf. 1 John 4:18.

13. "The soul becomes consciously reconciled to God, yet further, when peace flows into the soul as the result of the conviction that God is reconciled through Jesus Christ. My heart feels this morning perfect reconciliation with God, because I know that whatever my sins may have been, and I know they are far more than

I think them to be--they were all laid upon Christ's head upon Calvary, and whatever punishment was due to me for my sins Christ has borne on my behalf. How do I know that he bore my sins in particular? Is it because I think he bore the sins of all men? By no manner of means. That would give me no comfort, because some men are lost, and I might be among them, and if Jesus bore the sins of all men, it is clear that his bearing sin in that sense is not effectual; but, when I know that he so bore the sins of believers that they are clear, and am also certain that I am a believer, I feel the profoundest peace of mind." *MTP* 15:211.

14. Cf. Rom 5:6–8.

15. Cf. Ps 10:4; Rom 3:11.

16. In simpler language, Charles was making a point about how the reconciliation of enemies is costlier than the salvation of a reconciled friend.

17. This is a line from John Rippon's 1779 hymn "Begone, Unbelief." The stanza from which this line was taken reads: "His love in time past forbids me to think / He'll leave me at last in trouble to sink; / Each sweet Ebenezer I have in review, / Confirms His good pleasure to help me quite through." This hymn was evidently one that Charles held dear, since he included it in the Metropolitan Tabernacle hymnal that he published some thirty years later. C. H. Spurgeon, *Our Own Hymn-Book. A Collection of Psalms and Hymns for Public, Social, and Private Worship* (London: Passmore and Alabaster, 1885, The Spurgeon Library), Hymn 734.

18. Cf. Gen 3:15.

19. Cf. John 10:18. "*When our Savior reconciled us by his death, it was the time of his weakness.* See, he is nailed to the cross, the fever burns him up, he cries, 'I thirst;' he says, 'I am a worm, and no man;' weakness has come upon him to the uttermost; he closes his eyes in the last dread sleep of death. They take down his poor body, and wrap it in white linen, with sweet spices, and put it away in Joseph's tomb. There could not be greater weakness, could there, than in the crucified Christ? Yet, even then, he reconciled us: but now, he is clothed with power, Head over all things, Lord of angels, King of kings; all heaven resounds with his praises. Do you not see the drift of my argument? If, when he was in his uttermost weakness, he redeemed us by his death, 'much more,' now that he is in all his power and glory, he must be able to save his people by his life." *MTP* 44:438, italics in the original.

20. "Do you not see, then, that it is 'much more' that he can do for his people under such circumstances? If, when he took an inferior place, and condescended for our sake to be a servant, so that . . . he reconciled us, 'much more' can he now save us when he has taken to himself his great power, and with authority pleads before his Father's face. . . . If I can trust a dying Savior with my soul, and feel perfectly safe in doing so, how easy it is to trust a living Savior, and to roll myself upon his almighty love, and feel eternally secure!" MTP 44:438–39.

21. "According to the Word of God, Jehovah bruised him, Jehovah hid his face from him till Jesus cried, 'My God, my God, why hast thou forsaken me?' He came under the curse, for 'cursed is every one that hangeth on a tree.' For your sakes and mine, he bore the scourgings of infinite justice, and the frown of the offended majesty of heaven. This was diving very low; and if, even then, he was able to reconcile us to God, how 'much more' must he be able to save us now that the Father's well-beloved Son has come home again, and lives in the eternal sunlight of his dear Father's smile." MTP 44:439.

22. "For a while, it looked like defeat. He closed his eyes in death, saying, 'It is finished,' and he gave up the ghost. Those nail-prints, and that gory side, and that pallid countenance, looked as if death had won the victory, though it was not really so. Yet, beloved, he reconciled us even then! . . . Well now, if, when he lay there, all blood-bespattered and dead, defeated as it seemed, he reconciled us to God, my brothers, what can he not do now that he is in all the splendor of his majesty, the delight of heaven and of all holy beings?" MTP 44:439–40.

23. Cf. Matt 17:20; Luke 17:6.

24. Cf. 2 Cor 13:5.   25. Cf. John 14:4–6.

26. "To condescend to grant." Johnson's *Dictionary*, s.v. "To Vouchsafe."

268. Matt V. 20. A Righteousness better than the Pharisees.

We can imagine how startling these words must have been to the Jewish audience around — who most of them reverenced the Pharisees as the best of men. To us the words are not so strange since the hand of truth hath torn away their mask & we know their true character. —

These words are now come to us, let us seriously learn their meaning.

There are two kinds of righteousness necessary before we can enter the kingdom

Justification & Sanctification.

Unless we have (in both these senses) a better righteousness than the Pharisees we are undone.

I. <u>We need a better Justification than any the Pharisee trusted in</u>.

1. For the Law requires the utmost possible obedience, with all thy heart soul, strength & no Pharisee however free from sins of commission has ever done all his duties perfectly —

2. The Law requires a perfect obedience one sin violates the whole covenant now no Pharisee has ever kept

268

A RIGHTEOUSNESS BETTER THAN THE PHARISEES
Matthew 5:20[1]

"For I say unto you, That except your righteousness shall exceed the righteousness of the scribes and Pharisees, ye shall in no case enter into the kingdom of heaven."

We can imagine how startling these words must have been to the Jewish audience around, who most of them reverenced the Pharisees as the best of men. To us the words are not so strange since the hand of truth hath torn away their mask and we know their true character.

These words are now come to us. Let us seriously learn their meaning.

There are two kinds of righteousness necessary before we can enter the kingdom[:]

Justification and Sanctification.[2]

Unless we have (in both these senses) a better righteousness than the Pharisees we are undone.

I. WE NEED A BETTER JUSTIFICATION THAN ANY THE PHARISEE TRUSTED IN.

1. For the Law requires the utmost possible obedience, ["]with all thy heart, soul, strength[,"][3] and no Pharisee[,] however free from sins of commission[,] has ever done all his duties perfectly.

2. The Law requires a perfect obedience.[4] One sin violates the whole covenant. Now[,] no Pharisee has ever kept

the law perfectly, even though he might try to.

3. The law did not make mere ceremonies effectual for sin as Pharisees did. We must not rely on any ceremonies whatever.

4. Some of the Pharisee (+ but a few) did as well as they could & tried to render sincere obedience, thinking that sufficient; but we must have better than this.

To those who rely on their own goodness, to Churchmen trusting in forms or to Dissenters either this voice cries aloud Oh that ye might hear its thunders. Now this part of my subject is no doubt very pleasing to some of my congregation who have no right to be pleased. Saducees like to hear Pharisees beaten But now I will attack the Saducees through the ribs of the Pharisees.

II. <u>We need a better Sanctification than any the Pharisees possessed.</u>

Prate not oh Man about Imputed Righteousness & live without Inwrought righteousness. If so you are a mere prattler & no true son of God. Some of those who cry out loudest against good works are the greatest Pharisees alive.

the law perfectly[,] even though he might say so.⁵

3. The law did not make mere ceremonies effectual for sin as Pharisees did.⁶ We must not rely on any ceremonies whatever.

4. Some of the Pharisees (and but a few) did as well as they could and tried to render sincere obedience,⁷ thinking that sufficient, but we must have better than this.

To those who rely on their own goodness, to Churchmen trusting in forms or to Dissenters either[,]⁸ this voice cries aloud. Oh that ye might hear its thunders. Now, this part of my subject is no doubt very pleasing to some of my congregation who have no right to be pleased.

Sadducees like to hear Pharisees beaten.⁹ But now I will attack the Sadducees through the ribs of the Pharisees.¹⁰

II. WE NEED A BETTER SANCTIFICATION THAN ANY THE PHARISEES¹¹ POSSESSED.

Prate¹² not Oh Man¹³ about Imputed Righteousness and live without Inwrought righteousness.¹⁴ If so[,] you are a mere prattler¹⁵ and no true son of God. Some of those who cry out loudest against good works are the greatest Pharisees alive.

Unless ye are better men than the Pharisees ye cannot enter the Kingdom of heaven.

1. The Pharisees religion was merely <u>notional</u> ours must touch the heart. No pretended experience, no borrowed humility, no mere doctrinal knowledge will suffice.
  Heart must be really at work or in vain is it all

2. The Pharisees religion was merely <u>external</u> — to be seen of men & praised.
  Ours must have an influence on our secret as well as public life.

3. The Pharisees religion was <u>variable</u>.
  It was hot on Sabbaths, new moons & fasts but it was not constant. How many have this kind of stuff which is nothing more the toadstool of Hell.

4. The Pharisees religion was <u>partial</u>
  It only made him perform some duties others his sleepy conscience forgot. So some here keep one commandment & break others. They are sober but dishonest not Sabbath breakers but yet swearers.

5. The Pharisees religion consisted in <u>man's opinion of him</u>. So some keep right when our eye is on them

Unless ye are better men than the Pharisees ye cannot enter the kingdom of heaven.

1. The Pharisee[']s religion was merely <u>notional</u>[;][16] ours must touch the heart. No pretended experience, no borrowed humility, no mere doctrinal knowledge will suffice.[17]

   [The] Heart must be really at work or in vain is it all.

2. The Pharisee[']s religion was merely <u>external</u>, to be seen of men and praised.[18] Ours must have an influence on our secret as well as public life

3. The Pharisee[']s religion was <u>variable</u>. It was hot[19] on Sabbaths, new moons[,] and fasts[20] but it was not constant. How many have this kind of stuff which is nothing more the toadstool of Hell.[21]

4. The Pharisee[']s religion was <u>partial</u>.[22] It only made him perform some duties[,] others his sleepy conscience forgot.[23] So some here keep one commandment and break others. They are sober but dishonest,[24] not Sabbath breakers[25] but yet swearers.[26]

5. The Pharisee[']s religion consisted in <u>man's opinion of him</u>. So some keep right when our eye is on them

but go very wrong at other times. It should be what will God think & not what will man think.

Friends does this hit any of you, does it suit your case: then yours is a very bad case indeed, but not hopeless.

Repent & Believe still are the commands. And a kind Jesus openeth wide arms.

Great one touch my lips.

471

Matt V. 9.   Blessed are the peacemakers. 269
In one sense there is but one peacemaker even Jesus or Redeemer who hath reconciled us.

But this is peace between Man & Man.

I. Between nations let us labour to preserve peace. war is so horrible a thing, so demoralizing, bloody, fiendish that all who have ever been in it will say "blessed are the peacemakers". Spread the Gospel & thus you will spread Peace.

II. Between Individuals cultivate peace & for this purpose let us labour to get rid of Envy, pride, Anger, malice. for these will make us peacebreakers. Forgive. Forget.

III. Thus will you be blessed. The peculiar blessing is to be called Sons of God, to be esteemed to be so even by the world who see your father's likeness in you. 475.

but go very wrong at other times.

It should be what will God think and not what will man think.[27]

Friends does this hit any of you[?] Does it suit your case[?] Then yours is a very bad case indeed, but not hopeless.

Repent and Believe still are the commands and a kind Jesus openeth wide [his] arms.

Great one[,] touch my lips.

471

BLESSED ARE *the* PEACEMAKERS
Matthew 5:9[1]

"Blessed are the peacemakers: for they shall be called the children of God."

In one sense there is but one peacemaker[,] even Jesus as Redeemer[,] who hath reconciled us.[2]

But this is peace between Man and Man.

I. **BETWEEN NATIONS LET US LABOUR TO PRESERVE PEACE.**

War is so horrible a thing,[3] so demoralizing, [so] bloody, [so] fiendish that all who have ever been in it will say "blessed are the peacemakers." Spread the Gospel and thus you will spread Peace.

II. **BETWEEN INDIVIDUALS CULTIVATE PEACE.**

And for this purpose let us labour to get rid of Envy, Pride, Anger, Malice for these will make us peacebreakers. Forgive. Forget.[4]

III. **THUS WILL YOU BE BLESSED.**

The peculiar blessing is to be called sons of God, to be esteemed to be so even by the world who see your father's likeness in you.[5]

475.

SERMON 268

1. It appears that Charles did not preach another sermon on the text of Matt 5:20.

2. Charles believed that justification and sanctification are inseparable yet distinct within salvation. After examining Eph 5:25–27, Charles concluded, "When the text says, '[Christ] gave himself for [sin] that he might sanctify and cleanse it,' is there not allusion here to the double cure of sin? Here is Christ sanctifying by the Spirit, that is to say, taking away the propensity to sin, killing the power of sin in us, helping us to reign over our corruptions that we may in heart and life be pure, even as our Father which is in heaven is pure. And as to the cleansing, may not that allude to justification and pardon? . . . We are complete in him; we are perfect in Christ Jesus, and the design of Christ is, that sanctification shall be as perfect as justification, that the power of sin shall be as thoroughly slain as the guilt of it, that altogether sin shall cease to be in the Christian." *MTP* 11:259–60.

3. Cf. Deut 6:4–5; Luke 10:27.

4. Cf. Deut 27:26; Gal 3:10; Jas 2:10.

5. Cf. Rom 2:17–24; 3:23.

6. John Gill, who often influenced Charles's interpretation of Scripture, wrote, "[Jesus] mentions the Scribes, because they were the more learned part of the people, who were employed in writing out, and expounding the law; and the Pharisees, because they were the strictest sect among the Jews for outward religion and righteousness; and yet, it seems, their righteousness was very defective; it lay only in an external observance of the law; did not arise from a purified heart, or the principles of grace; nor was it performed sincerely, and with a view to the glory of God; but for their own applause, and in order to obtain eternal life: besides, they neglected the weightier matters of the law, and contented themselves with the lesser ones; and as they were deficient in their practice, so they were very lax in their doctrines, as appears from the foregoing verse." John Gill, *An Exposition of the New Testament* 1:38.

7. Cf. Mark 12:28–34; John 3:1–21; 7:50–51; 19:39–42.

8. "Either" referred to both Churchmen and Dissenters (i.e., "to [either] Churchmen trusting in forms or to Dissenters").

9. Cf. Acts 23:6–8.

10. The Sadducees were rivals of the Pharisees, and Charles used this to illustrate the "rivalry" between moralists and antinomians. In the first point, Charles went after the "Pharisee," the moralist who trusts in his own merit for salvation. In his second point, Charles will address the "Sadducee," the antinomian who claims to trust in Christ alone for salvation, and yet whose life gives no evidence to sanctification. For more on Charles's battle against antinomianism in his congregation, see Sermon 236, "The Nail in a Sure Place."

11. Charles continued to address the Pharisee, though in doing so, he was also attacking the Sadducee "through the ribs of the Pharisees."

12. "Talk carelessly and without weight; to chatter; to tattle; to be loquacious; to prattle." Johnson's *Dictionary*, s.v. "Prate."

13. Cf. Rom 2:1–6.

14. "Adorned with work." Johnson's *Dictionary*, s.v. "Inwrought."

15. "A trifling talker; a chatterer." Johnson's *Dictionary*, s.v. "Prattler." Cf. n. 12 just above; a prattler is one who prates.

16. "1. Imaginary. 2. Dealing in ideas, not realities." Johnson's *Dictionary*, s.v. "Notional."

17. In a sermon titled "The Great Liberator," Charles wrote, "There is another kind of freedom of which we must all be aware, it is a notional professional freedom. . . . a man may think himself free, and be a slave still. You know there are many in this world who dream themselves to be what they are not, and you have a faculty of dreaming in the same manner. Christ must have come to you and shown you your slavery, and broken your heart on account of it, or else you are not free; and you must have looked to the wounds of Jesus as the only gates of your escape, and have seen in his hand the only power which could snap your fetters, or else, though you have professed and re-professed, you are as much slaves of Satan as though you were in the pit itself." *MTP* 10:224.

18. Cf. Matt 6:1–6, 16–18; 23:5–7.

19. "5. Eager; keen in desire. 6. It is applied likewise to the desire, or sense raising the desire, or action excited; as, a hot pursuit." Johnson's *Dictionary*, s.v. "Hot."

20. Cf. Col 2:16.

21. "I delight not in the religion which needs or creates a hot head. Give me the Godliness which flourishes upon Calvary rather than upon Vesuvius. The utmost zeal for Christ is consistent with common-sense and reason: raving, ranting, and fanaticism are products of another zeal which is not according to knowledge." C. H. Spurgeon, *The Soul Winner* (Pasadena, TX: Pilgrim Publications, 2007), 16.

22. Cf. Matt 23:3–4, 23–26.

23. Cf. Rom 2:17–24; Jas 2:10–11.

24. Cf. Matt 23:25–28.

25. Cf. Matt 12:1–2.

26. Cf. Matt 5:33–37; 23:16–22.

27. Cf. Matt 23:5–12.

1. It appears that Charles preached a later sermon on this text, "The Peacemaker" (*MTP* 7, Sermon 422). The first two points of the later sermon follow the structure of this sermon, and the overlapping content is noted below. Charles began his first point in the later sermon by discussing how Christians are to be peacemakers in the nation and individually (the first two points of this sermon); in his second point, he discussed the blessing that comes to peacemakers (the third point of this sermon). The last two points of the later sermon do not contain overlapping content—they give more practical application and address the non-Christian.

2. Cf. 2 Cor 5:18; Col 1:20.

3. Charles's written record indicates that he was likely a pacifist. "The peacemaker, then, as a citizen, loveth peace. If he liveth in this land, he knows that he lives among a people who are very sensitive of their honour, and are speedily and easily provoked--a people who are so pugilistic in their character that the very mention of war stirs their blood, and they feel as if they would go at it at once with all their force[.] The peacemaker remembereth the war with Russia, and he recollecteth what fools we were that we should have meddled there, to bring to ourselves great losses both in trade and money, and no advantage whatever that is perceptible. He knoweth that this nation hath often been drifted into war for political purposes, and that usually the pressure and burden of it cometh upon the poor working man, upon such as have to earn their living by the sweat of their face. Therefore, though he, like other men, feeleth hot blood, and being an Englishman born, feeleth the blood of the old sea kings often in his veins, yet he represseth it, and saith to himself, 'I must not strive, for the servant of God must be gentle to all men, apt to teach, patient.'" *MTP* 7:593–94.

4. "But the peacemaker is not only a citizen, but a *man*, and if sometimes he letteth general politics alone, yet as a man he thinks that the politics of his own person must always be those of peace. There, if his honor be stained, he starteth not up for it: he counteth that it were a greater stain to his honor for him to be angry with his fellow than for him to bear an insult. . . . The peacemaker goes abroad also, and when he is in company he sometimes meets with slurs, and even with insults, but he learns to bear these, for he remembereth that Christ endured much contradiction of sinners against himself. . . . He doth not rush to defend himself, knowing that he whom he serves will take care that his good name

will be preserved, if only he himself be careful how he walketh among men. He goes into business, and it sometimes happens to the peacemaker, that circumstances occur in which he is greatly tempted to go to law; but he never doth this, unless he be straitly compelled to it, for he knoweth that law work is playing with edged tools, and that they who know how to use the tools yet cut their own fingers. . . . So he saith, 'Nay better that I be wronged by my adversary, and he get some advantage, than that both of us should lose our all.' So he letteth some of these things go by, and he findeth that on the whole, he is none the loser by sometimes giving up his rights. There be times when he is constrained to defend himself, but even then he is ready for every compromise, willing to give way at any time and at any season." *MTP* 7:594–95, italics in the original.

5. "[He is one of the children of God] by adoption and grace, but peacemaking is a sweet evidence of the work of the peaceful Spirit within. As the child of God, moreover, he hath a likeness to his Father who is in heaven. God is peaceful, longsuffering, and tender, full of lovingkindness, pity, and compassion. So is this peacemaker. Being like to God, he beareth his Father's image. Thus doth he testify to men that he is one of God's children. As one of God's children, the peacemaker hath access to his Father. . . . And still, there is a third word of commendation in the text. 'They shall be *called* the children of God.' They not only are so, but they shall be called so. That is, even their enemies shall call them so, even the world shall say, 'Ah! that man is a child of God.' Perhaps, beloved, there is nothing that so strikes the ungodly as the peaceful behavior of a Christian under insult." *MTP* 7:597, italics in the original.

270. Job. XXXVI. 18 "Beware".

Sometimes the young exceed the aged in understanding, if the Lord is pleased to teach them wisdom. When any are so gifted let them like Elihu pay due respect to age, & if compelled by a sense of duty let them not fear to speak the truth.

He reproves Job for justifying himself & murmuring at the providence of God – & now exhorts Job to be cautious in his words & thoughts, lest God should take him away with a stroke.

I. The Subject of Elihu's warning "Beware".
II. Three arguments to back it up — { Because "wrath" Sudden death Certain ruin

I. The Substance of Elihu's warning.
"Beware"

The words are few in fact but one single one. but suppose not hence that Elihu did not mean it. Strong exhortations are usually short. Captain in Battle. Short prayers are often the most earnest. When should we use this —

When people venture on unsafe ice.
When children sport on the margin of a river.
If a person had a bowl of poison about to drink it by mistake.
If we saw a fierce beast or serpent

"BEWARE"

Job 36:18[1]

"Because there is wrath, beware lest he take thee away with his stroke: then a great ransom cannot deliver thee."

Sometimes the young exceed the aged in understanding, if the Lord is pleased to teach them wisdom. When any are so gifted let them[,] like Elihu[,] pay due respect to age, and if compelled by a sense of duty[,] let them not fear to speak the truth.

He reproves Job for justifying himself and murmuring at the providence of God. And now exhorts Job to be cautious in his words and thoughts,[4] lest God should take him away with a stroke.

I. THE SUBJECT OF ELIHU'S WARNING *"Beware."* — Because wrath."
I. THREE ARGUMENTS TO BACK IT UP — Sudden death.
II. THE SUBSTANCE OF ELIHU'S WARNING. — Certain Ruin.

   "Beware."

   The words are few[,] in fact but one single one, but suppose not hence that Elihu did not mean it. Strong exhortations are usually short.[6] Captain in Battle.[7] Short prayers are often the most earnest.[8]

   When should we use this? When people venture on unsafe ice.

   When children sport on the margin of a river.

   If a person had a bowl of poison [and was] about to drink it by mistake

   If we saw a fierce beast or serpent

lurking. Surely none of the occasions are more dangerous than the danger of every sinner.
Young man venturing into sin. "Beware"
Man of business, dallying with the world "Beware"
Old man, on hell's margin "beware"
Beware of sinful thoughts, words or acts.
Beware of blaspheming or provoking God.
Beware of neglecting Salvation.
Beware! Beware! Beware! —

II. Three arguments to back it.
1. "Because there is wrath" God is angry on account of sin. Not as we are angry, but as a Judge he cannot endure sin. There is love but there is wrath too. And if an angry lion be dreadful what must an angry God be. — We have scarce need to turn to our Bibles to see that this is true for all Creation testifies it. — Look at the dreadful sufferings our race have endured from war, from plague, famine.
See the slave toiling, the freeman suffering, the holy dying, nature convulsed & torn.
If there were no wrath where would be the justice of God. But justice brings down wrath on the guilty. — Remember there is wrath now. He is at this present hour wrath with sin. Beware.

lurking. Surely none of the occasions are more dangerous than the danger of every sinner.⁹

Young man venturing into sin, "Beware."¹⁰

Man of business, dallying with the world, "Beware."

Old man on hell's margin, "beware."

Beware of sinful thoughts, words[,] or acts.

Beware of blaspheming or provoking God.

Beware of neglecting Salvation.

Beware! Beware! Beware!

II. THREE ARGUMENTS TO BACK IT.

1. "*Because there is wrath*." God is angry on account of sin.¹¹ Not as we are angry, but as a Judge he cannot endure sin. There is love, but there is wrath too. And if an angry lion be dreadful what must an angry God be[?] We have scarce need to turn to our Bibles to see that this is true[,] for all Creation testifies [to] it. Look at the dreadful sufferings our race have endured from war, from plague, [from] famine.

   See the slave toiling, the freeman suffering, the holy dying, nature convulsed and torn.

   If there were no wrath where would be the justice of God[?]¹² But Justice brings down wrath on the guilty. Remember there is wrath <u>now</u>. He sets the present hour wrath¹³ with sin. Beware.

2. "Lest he take thee away with his stroke"
So frail are we that one stroke is enough to sever our soul from our body. The tender grass needs but one touch of the scythe. God can thus take us away. He has done so to many — Sudden deaths. The flood, Egypt, Sodom & Gomorrah, Korah &c, Herod, Sapphira.

How vain are the hopes of men who postpone repentance. they may die suddenly. Sudden death is Sudden Glory to a Son of God. but Sudden Damnation to the wicked. How useful this fear.
To die dancing, swearing, cheating, this none desire to do. Oh Lord help.

3. "Then a great ransom cannot deliver thee"
Riches cannot bribe death, he is inexorable. Prayers are then too late. the man must die & when he is gone.
No well-paid masses can release the soul.
No money left to religion can atone.
No works are found there.
Jesus is no redeemer to the damned. None can escape who have neglected him. Lord help me to cry Beware after each of these reasons.

477.

2. "*Lest he take thee away with his stroke.*" So frail are we that one stroke is enough to sever our soul from our body.[14] The tender grass needs but one touch of the scythe.[15] God can thus take us away. He has done so to many. Sudden deaths.[16] The Flood.[17] Egypt.[18] Sodom and Gomorrah.[19] Korah etc.[20] Herod.[21] Sapphira.[22]

How vain are the hopes of men who postpone repentance. They may die suddenly. Sudden death is Sudden Glory to a [s]on[23] of God, but Sudden Damnation to the wicked. How useful this fear [is]. To die dancing, swearing, cheating, this none desire to do. Oh Lord help.

3. "*Then a great ransom cannot deliver thee.*" Riches cannot bribe death, he is inexorable.[24] Prayers are then too late, the man must die[,] and when he is gone.

No well-paid masses can release the soul.

No money left to religion can atone.[25]

No works are found there.

Jesus is no redeemer to the damned. None can escape who have neglected him. Lord help me to cry ["]Beware["] after each of these reasons.

477.

1. It appears that Charles did not preach another sermon on the text of Job 36:18.

2. Cf. Job 32:1–10.

3. Cf. Job 33–35.

4. Cf. Job 36:16–26.

5. "For this reason; in consequence of this. . . . From this cause; from this ground." Johnson's *Dictionary*, s.v. "Hence."

6. Cf. Matt 3:2; 1 Thess 5:14; 2 Tim 4:2.

7. Charles's phrase "Captain in Battle" was set off from its sentence by punctuation as an illustrative visual cue. Charles was likely referring to how a captain in battle will not give long-winded instructions but short, strong commands.

8. Cf. Matt 6:7–13. Charles believed in the power of brief prayers throughout his ministry. In an exposition of Matthew 15, written decades after this sermon, Charles reiterated this idea by writing, "I think that, when prayers grow shorter, they grow stronger. There is often more proof of earnestness in a short prayer than there is in a long one; glibness of speech is not prevalence in intercession." *MTP* 42:11–12.

9. "You cannot stop in an evil course just when and where you please. You cannot say to sin, 'Thus far shalt thou go, and no further.' The beginnings of evil are like the letting out of water, and when the dyke is once broken, and the pent-up flood is set free, it soon deluges the fields, and, perhaps, sweeps away multitudes of men and their habitations as well. Oh, that men could but realize that, while they are living in sin, they are always in danger of committing more sin, and yet more sin, going on from bad to worse, and from worse to the very worst of all!" *MTP* 51:172.

10. "Many a young man would shudder with horror if he could foresee what he will yet become unless the grace of God shall prevent it. You have often seen that familiar picture of the child, and the kind of man that he will yet become— either drunken or sober. If that child should be told that, one day, he would be like that red-faced old drunkard, he would not believe that he could ever grow to be as bad as that; neither will most young men, who are now living in sin, believe

that they can ever grow to be what they will be if they continue in their present course. Yet that is the danger to which they are continually exposed—the danger of sin ever producing yet more sin; and, to my mind, it seems to be punishment of a most grievous kind, even if these were no other, that sin should be allowed to breed within itself something yet more black and foul and filthy than it is itself—till, on the cancer of sin there comes yet another and another, more foul and loathsome, and yet another, and another, and another." *MTP* 51:172.

11. Cf. Rom 1:18; 2:5; Eph 5:6.

12. "The wrath of God is the anger of one who is never angry without a cause, one who is very patient and longsuffering. It takes much to bring the [color] into Jehovah's face, yet is he wroth with unbelievers. He is never wroth with anything because it is feeble and little, but only because it is wrong. His anger is only his holiness set on fire. He cannot bear sin; who would wish that he should? What right-minded man would desire God to be pleased with evil? That were to make a devil of God. Because he is God, he must be angry with sin wherever it is. This makes the sting of it, that his wrath is just and holy anger." *MTP* 27:538.

13. "Angry." Johnson's *Dictionary*, s.v. "Wroth." Charles likely meant "wroth" and mistakenly spelled this with an "a" instead of an "o."

14. Cf. Matt 10:28.   15. Cf. Isa 40:6–7.

16. Cf. Luke 12:13–21.   17. Cf. Gen 7:17–22.

18. Cf. Exod 12:29.

19. Cf. Gen 19:24–25. Additionally, it appears that in the manuscript Charles misspelled "Gomorrah" by writing "Gomorrha" instead. This has been corrected in the transcription.

20. Cf. Num 16:31–33.   21. Cf. Matt 2:19; Acts 12:20–23.

22. Cf. Acts 5:1–11.

23. In the manuscript, Charles capitalized the word "Son" in the phrase "Son of God," a title usually reserved for Jesus Christ. However, the context of the line

makes it clear that Jesus Christ was not in view but rather those who believe in him, "a son of God" (cf. 1 John 3:2).

24. "Not to be intreated; not be moved by intreaty." Johnson's *Dictionary*, s.v. "Inexorable."

25. Charles illustrated this point well during a sermon titled "A Free Salvation" (*NPSP* 4, Sermon 199): "Now, I see a man come up to the stall, and he says, 'Well, I will have salvation, sir; I have made in my will provisions for the building of a church or two, and a few almshouses; I always devote a part of my substance to the cause of God; I always relieve the poor, and such-like; I have a pretty good share of money, and I take care not to hoard it up; I am generous and liberal; I try to set up poor trades-people, and so forth. Won't that carry me to heaven?' . . . I must undeceive you. You cannot buy heaven with gold. Why, they pave the streets up there with it. . . . What Christ bought with blood you cannot buy with gold. He redeemed us not with corruptible things, as silver and gold, but with his precious blood; and there is no other price that can ever be allowed. Ah! My rich friend, you are just on a level with your poorest labourer." *NPSP* 4:277.

Rom. XII. 11. Not Slothful in Business &c.   271

The Ethics of the Bible are most complete. Duties hold their relative place, none being omitted.

I. Duty 1. Diligence in Business.
Every man must have some business to earn his bread by & so far from religion thwarting him in industry, it even bids him be diligent.
Laziness is a sin & a prolific parent of sins. The best men have been the most industrious. Time is too precious to be wasted.

II. Duty 2. Fervency in Spirit.
"Fervent", the word means burning hot, the greatest amount of heat. These must go together. This can only be maintained by much prayer. We must be fervent for every truth, in every duty, at every time, having in all a single eye to God's glory. This last will save us from being ruined by our business.

III. The Knot uniting the two. "Serving the Lord"
In both ways we may serve God. Our Daily labour honours God if it be done with a single eye to God's glory & if we maintain fervency of Spirit with it.
Remember we are his & ought to serve him with all our hearts.

481.

NOT SLOTHFUL *in* BUSINESS ETC.

Romans 12:11[1]

"Not slothful in business; fervent in spirit; serving the Lord."

The Ethics of the Bible are most complete.[2] Duties hold their relative place, none being omitted.

I. DUTY 1. DILIGENCE IN BUSINESS.

Every man must have some business to earn his bread by[3] and so far from religion thwarting him in industry, it even bids him be diligent.[4] Laziness is a sin and a prolific parent of Sins.[5] The best men have been the most industrious.[6] Time is too precious to be wasted.

II. DUTY 2. FERVENCY IN SPIRIT.

"Fervent." The word means burning hot,[7] the greatest amount of heat. These must go together. This can only be maintained by much prayer. We must be fervent for every truth, in every duty, [and] at every time, having in all a single eye to God's glory.[8] This last will save us from being ruined by our business.

III. THE KNOT UNITING THE TWO. "*Serving the Lord.*"

In both ways we may serve God. Our Daily labour honours God if it be done with a single eye to God's glory and if we maintain fervency of Spirit with it.

Remember we are his and ought to serve him with all our hearts[9]

481.

SERMON 271

1. It appears that Charles preached a later sermon on this text, "Serving the Lord" (*MTP* 15, Sermon 885). However, the later sermon focused entirely on expositing the third part of the verse, "serving the Lord," whereas this sermon deals with the entire verse. As a result, the later sermon does not appear to contain notable overlapping content.

2. Charles repeatedly asserted the value of the Christian ethic. He wrote, "If I were a secularist, I would wish to be a Christian. If there were no hereafter, yet were it better to have sin forgiven, even as a mortal man, so as to live at peace with the Eternal, and to feel a glow of gratitude to him impelling to self-sacrifice, and moving to intense love toward my guilty fellow-men. I am sure that it is so; Christianity is the noblest of all ethics, even for the present day, and much more for the eternal world whither we are hastening." *MTP* 43:139–40.

3. Cf. Eph 4:28; 2 Thess 3:10–12.

4. Cf. Prov 10:4; 21:5.

5. Cf. Prov 6:9–10; 24:33. Charles preached adamantly against the sin of laziness. He wrote, "The sin of doing nothing is about the biggest of all sins, for it involves most of the others. The sin of sitting still while your brethren go forth to war breaks both tables of the law, and has in it a huge idolatry of self, which neither allows love to God or man. Horrible idleness! God save us from it!" *MTP* 32:459.

6. "The ordinary duties of our calling we are not called upon to forget; we are not to neglect the shop for the sanctuary, or the counting-house for the class-meeting. The legs of a fool are not equal, but the holiness of a believer should always be well arranged. Whatever our position in life may be, we are so to order our conduct therein as to commend ourselves for diligence and uprightness both to the church and to the world. The Christian is not to be a worse tradesman because of his religion, but a better; he is not to be a less skilled mechanic, but he is to be all the more careful in his work. It were a pity indeed if Paul's tents were the worst in the store, and Lydia's purple of the poorest dye." *MTP* 15:445–46.

7. "1. Hot; boiling. 2. Hot in temper; vehement. 3. Ardent in piety; warm in zeal; flaming with devotion." Johnson's *Dictionary*, s.v. "Fervent." "*To be hot, fervent.*" John Parkhurst, *A Greek and English Lexicon to the New Testament* (London: printed

for William Baynes and Son, 1822, The Spurgeon Library), s.v. "ζεω," italics in the original.

8. "'Fervent in spirit.' We must not neglect the spiritual because of the pressing demands of the temporal. Perhaps we are more likely to forget this precept than the former, therefore let us lay it the more to heart. We are to maintain the holy fire within our souls constantly burning, for that is the meaning of 'fervent.' Our love to God must not merely be there in a small degree, but it must exist as a vigorous flame. Our spirit must be kept warmly zealous, burningly affectionate. Our spiritual nature is to glow like coals of fire. The keystone of the arch of life is to be a desire for God's glory; at this point the public and the private, the bodily and the spiritual, are to be as one; both in business diligence and spiritual fervency we are to set the Lord always before us. Our every-day labor is to be consecrated into priestly sacrifice, our inward fervor is to be like temple incense, and so, our bodies being temples of the Holy Ghost, we are ever to remain 'serving the Lord.'" *MTP* 15:446.

9. "To serve the Lord is the *highest honor*. How men pride themselves on being attached to the train of great men! How proud they are of wearing the livery of princes! But what must it be to have God, the Eternal, for your Master, to have Jesus Christ as your gracious helper, the Holy Spirit as your divine guide in all that you are called to do? To serve the Lord is to stand on a level with the angels; to worship the same Master as they do who are in the presence of the divine majesty. It is better to serve God than rule a kingdom; nay, he is both a king and a priest who has thoroughly entered into the service of the Most High." *MTP* 15:454, italics in the original.

272. Ps. 72.15. Prayer for Jesus.—

This Psalm is an interesting one as being probably the last David wrote. His death-song for Solomon or rather for a greater than Solomon, even our adorable Redeemer.

The kingdom which David foresaw would come to the Messiah was fraught with glories such as none other can possess. Its administration is perfectly righteous. Its state peaceful. Its poor exalted. Its subjects happy. Its state prosperous. Its extent universal. Its conquests glorious. Its duration eternal & ever blessed.

Now comes a prophecy concerning his subjects.

I. That Liberality towards their prince will distinguish all his subjects.

Every other kingdom is supported by forced taxation, so also is every false System of Religion but "gifts" in Christ's Kingdom altogether supersede all tax-gathering.

To Christ must be given of the gold of Sheba, as it was given to Solomon. Christ's cause has until now been opposed by gold, yet has it worked its way aided by omnipotence alone. Some of the richest countries are entirely heathen soon these shall bring their treasures &

PRAYER FOR JESUS
Psalm 72:15[1]

"And he shall live, and to him shall be given of the gold of Sheba: prayer also shall be made for him continually; and daily shall he be praised."

This Psalm is an interesting one as being probably the last David wrote.[2] His death-song for Solomon[,] or rather for a greater than Solomon, even our adorable Redeemer.

The kingdom which David foresaw would come to the Messiah was fraught with glories such as none other can possess.

> Its administration is perfectly righteous.[4] Its state peaceful.[5] Its poor exalted.[6] Its subjects happy.[7] Its state prosperous.[8] Its extent universal.[9] Its conquests glorious.[10] Its duration eternal and ever blessed.[11] Now comes a prophecy concerning his subjects:[12]

I. THAT LIBERALITY TOWARDS THEIR PRINCE WILL DISTINGUISH ALL HIS SUBJECTS.[13]

> Every other kingdom is supported by forced taxation, so also is every false System of Religion[14] but "gifts" in Christ's kingdom altogether supersede all tax-gathering.[15]
>
> To Christ must be given of the gold of Sheba, as it was given to Solomon.
>
> Christ's cause has until now been opposed by gold, yet has it worked its way aided by omnipotence alone. Some of the richest countries are entirely heathen. Soon these shall bring their treasures and

pour them into his coffers. The King can never die & living, he shall receive gifts.

Even now the countries richest in metals are most of them Protestant.

II. Prayer for the Prince shall be ever put up. We pray for our governors and for the Queen: good subjects are bound to pray for their monarch. But how can we pray for Jesus. He is ever praying for us but how can we pray for him. We know it to be our duty to pray for our Christian brethren, but how for Jesus.

1. This is one of the ways - viz. to intercede for his people, for they are his bone & his flesh.

2. Many poor penitents & distressed believers know what it is to pray for him, for him in all the plenitude of his atonement, as the great high-priest.

3. We pray for the spread of his cause in the world, we long to see him reign with wider sway, "thy <u>Kingdom come</u>".

4. We should daily pray for his second coming in triumphant might to reign spiritually with his saints. In the sacred ordinance of the Lord's Supper we are reminded of this "till he come".

Thus may we pray for Jesus, or if as some

pour them into his coffers.[16] The King can never die[,] and living, he shall receive gifts.

Even now the countries richest in metals are most of them Protestant.

II. PRAYER FOR THE PRINCE SHALL BE EVER PUT UP

We pray for our governors and for the Queen: good subjects are bound to pray for their monarch. But how can we pray for Jesus[?] He is ever praying for us[,][17] but how can we pray for him[?] We know it to be our duty to pray for our Christian brethren,[18] but how for Jesus[?]

1. This is one of the ways, viz. to intercede for his people, for they are his bone and his flesh.[19]

2. Many poor penitents and distressed believers know what it is to pray for him, for him in all the plenitude of his atonement as the great high-priest.[20]

3. We pray for the spread of his cause in the world, we long to see him reign with wider sway, "Thy Kingdom come."[21]

4. We should daily pray for his second coming in triumphant might to reign spiritually with his saints.[22] In the sacred ordinance of the Lord's Supper we are reminded of this[,] "till he come."[23]

Thus may we pray for Jesus, or if as some

read it, it means through Jesus then indeed our prayers do ever ascend by this medium only.

I believe that even the saints in heaven pray for Jesus, the souls under the altar cry aloud for vengeance, they ask for the fulfilment of the eternal promises.

III. The Praises of the Prince shall not be forgotten. "daily shall he be praised" Kings love praises from their subjects & Jesus as the best of Kings should receive double praise. So is he now daily praised, on the Sabbath especially, then a double offering ascends. Daily mercies demand daily praises. So from the tents of Jacob daily praises bring new honours to him. Rejoice believer in the promise that thine insulted, despised Lord will soon be daily praised.

These three together make an acceptable offering to Jesus, but if any one be left out it is no whole burnt offering.

Liberality, Prayer, & Praise are a sacred triumvirate & conquest will wait on their banners.

Help Oh King.

484.

read it, it means through Jesus then indeed our prayers do ever ascend by this medium only.[24]

I believe that even the saints in heaven pray for Jesus. The souls under the altar cry aloud for vengeance,[25] they ask for the fulfilment of the eternal promises.[26]

III. THE PRAISES OF THE PRINCE SHALL NOT BE FORGOTTEN. "[D]aily shall he be praised."

Kings love praises from their subjects[,] and Jesus as the best of Kings should receive double praise.

So is he now daily praised, on the Sabbath especially,[27] [for] then a double offering ascends.[28]

Daily mercies demand daily **praises**. So from the tents of Jacob daily praises bring new honours to him.[29] Rejoice believer in the promise that thine insulted, despised Lord will soon be daily praised.

These three together make an acceptable offering to Jesus, but if any one be left out it is no whole burnt offering.

Liberality, Prayer, and Praise are a sacred triumvirate[30] and conquest will wait on their banners.

Help. Oh King.

484.

SERMON 272

1. Charles preached two later sermons on this text, "Pray for Jesus" (*MTP* 12, Sermon 717) and "Homage Offered to the Great King" (*MTP* 54, Sermon 3100). An examination of "Pray for Jesus" reveals some overlapping content, but it focuses entirely on the second point of this sermon, namely "praying for Jesus." Charles's other later sermon, "Homage Offered to the Great King," appears to have a significant amount of overlapping material, and its general structure appears to have been influenced by this earlier sermon as well. Although differing in degree, both sermons appear to have been influenced by this one. The overlapping material is noted below.

2. This assertion may have been taken from John Gill's commentary. Gill wrote, "This psalm is thought by some to be the last that was written by *David*, though put in this place; and it is certain that the psalms are not always placed in the order of time in which they were written: this being, as is supposed, made by him in his old age, when *Solomon* his son was appointed and set upon his throne by his order; on account of which he composed it, with a view to the Messiah, the antitype of *Solomon*." John Gill, *An Exposition of the Old Testament* 3:773, italics in the original.

3. "1. Laden; charged. 2. Filled; stored; thronged." Johnson's *Dictionary*, s.v. "Fraught."

4. Cf. Isa 9:6–7; 32:1.   5. Cf. Rom 14:17; Phil 4:7.

6. Cf. Matt 5:3; 23:12.   7. Cf. Gal 5:22; Rev 21:4.

8. Cf. Eph 2:7; Rev 21:18–21.

9. Cf. Ps 145:13; Rev 5:9; 7:9.

10. Cf. Matt 28:18–20; Rev 19:11–21.

11. Cf. Dan 7:14; Heb 1:8; Rev 1:6; 11:15.

12. In his later sermon, "Homage Offered to the Great King" (*MTP* 54, Sermon 3100), Charles appears to have followed the outline of this sermon, though altering the wording of his headings: "Here are three things which are, throughout all time, even till the dawning of eternity, always to be bestowed on Christ. The first is *the gift of property*, the gold of Sheba; the second is *the gift of prayer*; and the third is *the gift of praise*." *MTP* 54:326, italics in the original.

13. "I think that this ought continually to be impressed upon the minds of all Christians. Since Jesus Christ is the Son of God and their Savior, and has given himself for them, they are not their own, but are bought with a price; their possessions as well as themselves are the absolute property of their Redeemer; they have, in fact, nothing whatever in their own private right; they have made over themselves to the Lord Jesus, to have and to hold them through life, and even till death, and for ever and ever. They are not to call their own their purse, their lands, their houses, nor anything that they have; but to give up everything to their Lord." *MTP* 54:326.

14. Charles vigorously opposed the use of a national tax to support the Church of England and saw this as a form of religious oppression. At one point he wrote, "Religious opinion . . . is not a thing of which the law can justly take cognizance. As far as the civil government is concerned, whether a man's sentiments be those of a Christian or an idolater, a Catholic, a Protestant, or a Mormonite, he is entitled to all civil rights. Be he who he may, he is oppressed if he be deprived of his liberty, or of any privilege, because of his thoughts. Be he who he may, he is injured if any one sect be rendered dominant, or be supported by a forced taxation drawn from the whole. Thought must be free, and it shall be acknowledged, by God's help, perfectly free as between man and man." *MTP* 57:3.

15. Rather than a forced tax, Charles adhered to the "voluntary principle" practiced by Nonconformists, namely personal giving. In a speech delivered prior to the opening of the Metropolitan Tabernacle, he emphasized that "we earnestly desire that we may open this place without a farthing of debt upon it." *NPSP* 6:359. This was not simply because Charles was worried about debt, but because "it would tell well for the whole body who rely upon the voluntary principle, if this temple can be completed without a loan or debt." *NPSP* 6:359–60. This was an urgent matter to Charles because his church was publicly prominent, indeed the "forefront of Nonconformity." *NPSP* 6:360. Charles wanted to prove to the Church of England that the humble gifts of God's people could surpass the compulsory taxation power of the state. "I believe in the might of the voluntary principle. I believe it to be perfectly irresistible in proportion to the power of God's Spirit in the hearts of those who exercise it." *NPSP* 6:360. In Charles's view, the Church had no king but Christ, and personal, sacrificial giving made sure that his congregation never became subject to a government authority with the power of the purse.

16. Cf. Rev 21:24, 26. "We may rejoice that Christ's cause will not stand still for want of funds; the silver and the gold are his, and if they are not to be found at home, far off lands shall hasten to make up the deficit. Would to God we had more faith and more generosity." TD 3:321.

17. Cf. Heb 7:25.   18. Cf. Eph 6:18; Heb 13:3; Jas 5:16.

19. Cf. 1 Cor 12:12–13. "Forget not to pray for the church of God that it may be knit together in one. Do not ask that it may be made uniform; that is neither desirable nor probable, but pray that all Christians may be one as the Father is one with the Son; that is, one in spirit; so that we, dividing as we always shall do as to our thoughts upon many points, may be one in the hope that animates us, in the spirit that actuates us, one in the life of God that pulsates in our souls. Pray that the churches may be knit together in holy love, and may strive together for nothing but for the advancement of the faith of Christ." MTP 12:595.

20. "I would ask you then to pray especially for *the conversion of many souls*. This is Christ's delight, his love, his heart's joy. You were told last Sunday morning, that there was 'joy in heaven over one sinner that repenteth.' The angels sing, but Christ is the choirmaster there. He is the chief musician, for he has the greatest joy. It is his joy, his heaven, to see sinners saved. Pray, pray for *him* then; you are praying for the Shepherd when you pray for the lost sheep. You are praying for the King when you ask that the lost jewels of his crown may be found and set therein. Oh that we loved souls as Christ loves them, then should we hunger and thirst after their salvation!" MTP 12:594–95, italics in the original.

21. Cf. Matthew 6:9–10. "When you have thus prayed *for Christ*—and I am sure it is all for Christ if you so pray—then ask that the kingdoms of this world may become the kingdoms of our Lord and of his Christ. Let no ideas of doctrine check you in such a prayer; you are bound to pray it. The example of prophets and of apostles urges you forward, your allegiance to King Jesus should constrain you to it. You believe that he will come, but believe also the truth, which is equally certain, that he shall have dominion from sea to sea and from the river even to the ends of the earth." MTP 12:595, italics in the original.

22. Cf. 1 Thess 4:16–18; 2 Tim 2:12; Rev 20:6.

23. Cf. 1 Cor 11:23–26.

24. Charles may have been echoing Jonathan Edwards's interpretation here, found in the *Treasury of David*. "It might have been rendered, 'Prayer also shall be made through him continually, and daily shall he be blessed.' The word is rendered 'blessed,' when speaking of an act of worship towards God and the word translated 'for' is sometimes used for 'through,' as Joshua 2 15, 'Through the window.' If we hold the translation 'for him,' then it must be understood of the saints praying for the Father's accomplishment of his promises, made to the Son in the covenant of redemption, that his kingdom may come, his name be glorified, and that he may see his seed, and that the full reward may be given him for his sufferings, and so that he may receive the joy that was set before him." *TD* 3:331.

25. Cf. Rev 6:9–11.

26. Cf. Heb 11:40. "People have said there is no faith in heaven, and no hope; they know not what they say--in heaven it is that faith and hope have their fullest swing and their brightest sphere, for glorified saints believe in God's promise, and hope for the resurrection of the body. The apostle tells us that 'they without us cannot be made perfect;' that is, until our bodies are raised, theirs cannot be raised, until we get our adoption day, neither can they get theirs." *MTP* 14:6.

27. "First, methinks, *Jesus daily shall be praised as long as there is a Christian ministry*. . . . Has there ever been a season when God has not sent his prophets throughout the land to speak in living words, from burning hearts and fervid souls, the very Word of God? No; and there never shall be." *MTP* 54:330–31, italics in the original. Additionally, Charles asserted: "*The ordinances that he has instituted will ever continue to perpetuate his praise*. There are two Scriptural ordinances, in both of which Jesus Christ is very much praised. There is, first, that holy ordinance of believers' baptism, in which Jesus Christ is much honoured, for it has especial relationship to him. . . . Nor less at the blessed supper of the Lord shall the name of Jesus be praised. I think the moments we are nearest to heaven are those we spend at the Lord's table." *MTP* 54:331–32, italics in the original.

28. "Double offering" here likely refers to the practice of having multiple church services on Sundays, a common phenomenon in Charles's day. In the case of

his church at Waterbeach, the congregation met twice on Sundays, once in the morning and again in the afternoon (see *Autobiography* 1:266).

29. "*While there is a family on earth where Christ's name is named, it shall be daily praised.* I trust there is no Christian man or woman here who has a house without a family altar. If I came into your house, and heard that you had no fireplace in the winter time, I should certainly advise you to build one; and if I heard that any of you had not a family altar, I should say, 'Go home and lay the first brick tonight: it will be a good thing if you do so, I am sure.' . . . Well, supposing we had no family prayer, suppose we had no ordinances in the house, and the altar did not smoke there; yet daily should Jesus Christ be praised, for still *there would be our own hearts, and we could praise Christ there.* If they put us in prison, and we could not speak to one another, we could still praise him; or if our tongues were dumb, there is a language of the heart which can be heard in heaven. With stammering words, or with actions which speak louder than words, our hearts shall always praise him. Beloved brethren and sisters, do you think you will ever have done praising Christ as long as you are alive?" *MTP* 54:332–34, italics in the original.

30. "A coalition or concurrence of three men." Johnson's *Dictionary*, s.v. "Triumvirate."

Job XIV.10. "Man dieth & where is he?"

Job commences at the beginning tracing us to our original — We are born of weak & sinful woman, we are of few days & full of trouble. We start from the same place, traverse different roads and come at last to the same end.

I. The Fact.

"Man dieth", the mighty man dieth. However great the man, he dieth. —

Some die in infancy, some in old age. The wise, the rich, the great, the good all die. The poor, unlearned, feeble all die. The wicked die, their sins demand it, there is a voice demanding their death. —

"He wasteth away". By diseases before death or by the natural infirmities of old age.

"He wasteth away", after death. When the body is in the coffin, it rots or becomes the food for worms. Soon it is all gone.

"He giveth up the ghost" This is the great difference between the deaths of men and animals. They die but they have no spirits to resign, no souls to yield up.

Man's spirit now caged, then seeks a wider circuit for her wing.

The thought of this fact will benefit us if we ask divine influences.

MAN DIETH *and* WHERE IS HE?
Job 14:10[1]

"But man dieth, and wasteth away: yea, man giveth up the ghost, and where is he?"

Job commences at the beginning [by] tracing us to our original. We are born of weak and sinful woman, we are of few days and full of trouble.[2] We start from the same place, traverse different roads[,] and come at last to the same end.

I. THE FACT.

"<u>Man dieth.</u>" The mighty man dieth. However great the man, he dieth.

Some die in infancy, some in old age. The wise, the rich, the great, [and] the good all die. The poor, unlearned, [and] feeble all die.[3] The wicked die, their sins demand it. There is a voice demanding their death.[4]

"<u>He wasteth away.</u>" By diseases before death or by the natural infirmities of old age.[5]

"<u>He wasteth away,</u>" after death. When the body is in the coffin, it rots or becomes the food for worms. Soon it is all gone.

"<u>He giveth up the ghost.</u>" This is the great difference between the deaths of men and animals. [Animals] die but they have no spirits to resign, no souls to yield up.[6] Man's spirit, now caged,[7] <u>then</u> seeks a wider circuit for her wing.

The thought of this fact will benefit us if we ask divine influences

II. The Question. "Where is He?"

A natural question enough. There is the body but that is not the person. Where is he? The shop, bedroom, field, chapel, road once could tell you but now they return no answer, save the echo of the question "where is He?"

Ask pale scepticism & it tells us that he is annihilated & dead. But our reason tells us that so grand a thing as the human soul was not born to die. Our innate ideas are repugnant to the thought. The universal world reject the black idea & every man of reason scouts the thought of the soul's death. The justice of God demands a future state to right the wrongs of the present.

And it shall come since the very constitution of the world requires it.

He must then be somewhere. Where is he comes again. The Heathen cannot tell, the Catholic will not know But we who believe in Gods revelation can answer this question.

Where is the soul the moment it leaves the body? The Bible informs

II. THE QUESTION. "*Where is He?*"

A natural question enough. There is the body, but that is not the person.[8]

Where is he? The shop, bedroom, field, chapel, [and] road once could tell you, but now they return no answer, save[9] the echo of the question "where is He?"

Ask pale scepticism and it tells us that he is annihilated and dead. But our reason tells us that so grand a thing as the human soul was not born to die.[10] Our innate ideas are repugnant to the thought. The universal world reject[s] the black idea and every man of reason scouts[11] the thought of the soul's death. The justice of God demands a future state to right the wrongs of the present.[12]

And it shall come since the very constitution of the world requires it.

He must then be somewhere. ["]Where is he[?"] comes again. The Heathen cannot tell, the Catholic will not know. But we who believe in God['s] revelation can answer this question.

Where is the soul the moment it leaves the body? The Bible informs us that then its state is settled. The spirit goes before its God & is tried for its sins done <u>without</u> the body. It is at once either acquitted or condemned. —

At the day of Judgment the soul will be reunited with the body, all will again be tried for the sins done <u>in</u> the body. Then body & soul shall enjoy eternal suffer endless woe. —

Now some will be asking this question of the deceased — do not — leave that alone, but think of what will one day be asked of yourself. — —

Our present conduct must decide our future condition. Are we believers? Do we rely on the blood of the Redeemer? Oh my Lord, I am not worthy to breathe, yet suffer me to ask thine aid So that I may be clear of the blood of my hearers. I beg it, give it me through the sweetest of all names Jesus Christ. —

485.

us that then its state is settled.[13] The spirit goes before its God and is tried for its sins done <u>without</u>[14] the body. It is at once either acquitted or condemned.[15]

At the day of Judgment the soul will be reunited with the body, all will again be tried fore the sins done <u>in</u> the body.[16] Then body and soul shall enjoy eternal ~~joy~~ extacy[17] or suffer endless woe.

Now some will be asking this question of the ~~di~~deceased. Do not. Leave that alone, but think of what will one day be asked of yourself.

Our present conduct must decide our future condition. Are we believers? Do we rely on the blood of the Redeemer?

Oh my Lord, I am not worthy to breathe, yet, suffer me ask thine aid. So that I may be clear of the blood of my hearers. I beg it. Give it [to] me

through the sweetest of all names,
Jesus Christ.

485.

SERMON 273

1. It appears that Charles did not preach another sermon on the text of Job 14:10.

2. Cf. Job 14:1–2.

3. In another sermon from Job 38:17, "The Doors of the Shadow of Death" (*MTP* 51, Sermon 2917), Charles described the unceasing stream of the dead: "If you will stop here a minute, and look, and have eyes strong enough in the shade to mark who they are that come, you will see there a man leaning on his staff. But did you notice that there also went by him little children that had not yet learnt to speak? You see the strong man come on a sudden, running away from life; and you see the invalid who had long waited for his summons: you may tell his bones as he passes down to his grave. Do you see yonder man? There is nothing special about him; he looks just like another. He was a king once; there is little royal about him now. Do you see that other man? He was once a beggar; he does not now seem a bit more beggarly than did the monarch. They have neither of them brought any store with them; they come here penniless—all of them, and they pass through with empty hands. Titles, grandeur, estates, position, fame, all are left behind. They came a great crowd in a liberty, equality, and fraternity of death[,] a common brotherhood that will never be realized in life." *MTP* 51:15–16.

4. Cf. Job 1:6–12; John 10:10; Rom 6:23a.

5. "When a man gets troubled with memory and fear, and his body is racked with pain, he is very ill-fitted to listen to the voice of Jesus. I would not discourage a dying man for a moment from looking to Jesus, if he desireth salvation, if he will but believe in the Christ of God, he shall have eternal life even at the last. But speaking from what I have seen, the most of men in the article of death are quite unfit for thought; quite unable to feel anything beyond the stabs of physical anguish, and quite incapable of faith. No man knoweth how far God's mercy goeth; but, if that mercy be given to faith, I cannot see how it can be extended to some dying men. Delirium, a wandering mind, an aching head—oh, these will give you quite enough to do in dying, without having to seek your peace with God then." *MTP* 51:20.

6. Cf. Gen 1:26–27.

7. Charles's remark is best understood in light of his previous sermon, "The Resurrection Body" (Notebook 3, Sermon 185), where he expounded on the better

blessing of the spiritual body that believers wait expectantly to receive. Indeed, Charles often spoke longingly of his anticipated spiritual body, which although of a different substance, was viewed as physical (*NPSP* 1:2; 2:402; *MTP* 19:140; 24:666; 27:488; 51:140). Charles often used the term "mortal clay" when talking about the physical body, but he did not view it as inherently evil. This can be seen in his frequent usage of the term in connection with the incarnation of Jesus Christ (*NPSP* 1:2; 2:402; *MTP* 19:140; 24:666). Charles was insistent on Christ's hypostatic union. He was careful to note that "[Christ's] essence did not undergo a change when it became united with manhood. When Christ in past years did gird himself with mortal clay, the essence of his divinity was not changed; flesh did not become God, nor did God become flesh by a real actual change of nature; the two were united in hypostatical union, but the Godhead was still the same." *NPSP* 1:2. Rather, Charles's concern here seemed to be the same as when he later said, "What with sin dwelling in our breast, and this vesture of mortal clay, we are glad that now is our salvation nearer than when we believed, and we long to enter into full enjoyment of it." *MTP* 27:488. Simply, the present body was a "cage" inasmuch as the fallenness of this creation inhibited communion with God, specifically the painful effects of indwelling sin. This did not cause Charles to reject the goodness of God's physical creation, but he nonetheless longed for the day when his enjoyment of Christ would no longer be inhibited by the fallenness of this world.

8. Charles's usage focused on the "person" as the inward, immaterial part of a human being, what Charles earlier referred to as "spirit," although they are not synonymous. Charles also clearly anticipated the coming return of a still incarnate Christ, and the attainment of a glorified body as illustrated in his previous sermon "The Resurrection Body" (Notebook 3, Sermon 185). With this in mind, the context suggests that a proper reading takes "person" as a functional synonym for "spirit" while recognizing that Charles understood new, glorified bodies to be indispensable, but not the sole aspect of a "person" in the age to come.

9. "Except; not including." Johnson's *Dictionary*, s.v. "Save."

10. "Look at your wife, man—you that believe all living men to be mere beasts. What of that dear body of your wife whom you have loved these many years? Well, principally so much water and so much gas; when that is taken away there is a small residuum of earthy ash—that is all. And that is what you have loved—so many pounds of water and gas and earth! No, sir, you have not. You have loved

a *woman*. You have loved a thing infinitely better than dead earth and water and gas. You know that. You do not believe that your mother is only mere water and gas and earth, nor your child, nor yet yourself. You cannot persuade yourself to accept such materialism as that. There is a something in this body that is better than this water, and gas, and earth, a something that will consciously exist when these have been dissolved: and there is that within all of us that makes us believe it whether we will it or not. Hence, at the portals of death there comes into the mind the question, 'Where am I going?'" *MTP* 51:20, italics in the original.

11. "To ridicule; to sneer. This is a sense unauthorized, and vulgar." Johnson's *Dictionary*, s.v. "To Scout." Worcester clarifies that this usage was "Unauthorized till of late years, but getting into good use." Worcester's *Dictionary*, s.v. "To Scout."

12. "One of the clearest proofs of the judgement to come is to be found in the present sufferings of the saints through persecutions and tribulations; for if they, for the very reason that they love God, have to suffer here, there must be a future state and time for rectifying all this that is now so wrong." *MTP* 56:95.

13. Cf. Eccl 12:7.

14. "In a state of absence from. . . . On the outside of. . . . Not within." Johnson's *Dictionary*, s.v. "Without."

15. Cf. Heb 9:27.   16. Cf. Matt 12:36–37; 2 Cor 5:10; Rev 20:11–15.

17. "1. Any passion by which the thoughts are absorbed, and in which the mind is for a time loft. 2. Excessive joy; rapture." Johnson's *Dictionary*, s.v. "Ectasy." Johnson recorded the spelling as "ectasy" rather than the modern "ecstasy." Charles misspelled the word regardless.

274.   James. I. 14.   The Parent & Child of Sin.

Like our first parents we are all too prone to lay our sins at the door of others. One would think that no man would be so dreadfully profane as to charge God with their sins, but some have done so. They have said they were fated to do it. They charge it on providence. & say if they had not been placed in certain circumstances they should not have done it. This is all foolish. We are the authors of our own sins & no one else is to blame for them.

James here tells us:
I. The Parent of Sin. "Lust."
II. The Offspring of Sin. "Death."

I. The true Parent of Sin. "Lust"
The greatest rivers often have very small sources so does Sin begin with little. Seeds are small but who knows how large the plant may be. Evil thoughts come easily into our minds, so long as we resist them they are not ours, but if we harbour them — then come

THE PARENT *and* CHILD *of* SIN
James 1:14[1]

"But every man is tempted, when he is drawn away of his own lust, and enticed."

Like our first parents we are all too prone to lay our sins at the door of others.[2]

One would think that no man would be so dreadfully profane as to charge God with their sins, but some have done so.[3] They have said they were fated to do it.[4] They charge it on providence and say if they had not been placed in certain circumstances they should not have done it.[5] This is all foolish. We are the authors of our own sins and no one else is to blame for them.

James here tells us:

I. THE PARENT OF SIN. *"Lust."*
II. THE OFFSPRING OF SIN. *"Death."*

I. THE TRUE PARENT OF SIN. *"Lust."*

The greatest rivers often have very small sources[;] so does Sin begin with littles.[6] Seeds are small but who knows how large the plant may be.[7] Evil thoughts come easily into our minds, so long as we resist them they are not ours,[8] but if we harbour them, then come evil imaginings, then looks, then words at last the monster is born. Sin is brought forth. This is the reason why some things are to be avoided that appear harmless. For they may be the precursors of ruin. Again let us remark how sin like a wedge makes room for itself. Little did the man who only thought evil, imagine that soon he should act it out.

Examine any man who has been guilty of great sins & you shall see that they were preceded by evil thoughts.

Lord help us to break the eggs of sin. Once brought forth to what a size sin will run. Adultery, Robbery, Murder.

He who would shun these must shun the beginnings of sin.

II. The Offspring of Sin "Death."

1. Natural death comes from this. How else could a benevolent God, put men to such suffering as death involves

2. Every sin we commit bears death in its bowels but some sins especially ruin the health of men & women bring on dire diseases & premature death.

evil imaginings, then looks, then words [and] at last the monster is born.[9] Sin is brought forth. This is the reason why some things are to be avoided that appear harmless. For they may be the precursors of ruin.[10] Again let us remark how sin like a wedge makes room for itself. Little did the man who only thought evil, imagine that soon he should <u>act</u> it out.

Examine any man who has been guilty of great sins and you shall see that they were preceded by evil thoughts.[11]

Lord help us to break the eggs of sin. Once brought forth to what a size sin will run. Adultery. Robbery. Murder.

He who would shun these must shun the beginnings of sin.

II. THE OFFSPRING OF SIN "<u>Death.</u>"

1. Natural death comes from this.[12] How else could a benevolent God put men to such suffering as death involves[?]

2. Every sin we commit bears death in its bowels[,][13] but some sins especially ruin the health of men and women, [and] bring on dire diseases and premature death.[14]

Little do we know the price of sin. It is dear even if this life closed the scene.
Oh may God help us to beware of sin.
3. But Death eternal is the great consequent of sin. Everlasting burnings Consuming fires — Oh my God may I do my duty though it be hard
Help. Help. Help — (one person joined Zion converted under this

486

275. Eccles. VIII. 13. A crook in every lot. Joy.
Ecclesiastes was written doubtless in Solomon's old age when his judgment was mature & strong.
I. Here is something implied. That our lot has a crook. In our persons, estate, relations, mind, heart, house, field, or somewhere we have a crook
II. Here is something expressed. God made the crook It is no chance, it is his ordination. We should look up to the great first cause & not repine at the channels of our troubles.
III. Here is something we are to do. Consider want of this is a sad want indeed.
 Consider — 1. That we cannot alter it.
    2. That others are worse
    3. That we have many good things.
    4. That all is wise & gracious.
Learn 1. Sin made the crook
  2. Fly from the creature to the Creator.
  3. Look for heaven.
480. 496.

Little do we know the price of sin. It is dear even if this life closed the scene.[15]

Oh may God help us to beware of sin.

3. But Death is eternal [and] is the great consequent of sin.[16] Everlasting burnings. Consuming fires.[17] Oh my God may I do my duty though it be hard.

Help. Help. Help.[18] — One person joined Zion Converted uncer this.

---

275   Jay.[1]

A CROOK[2] IN EVERY LOT
Ecclesiastes 7:13[3]

"Consider the work of God: for who can make that straight, which he hath made crooked?"

Ecclesiastes was written doubtless in Solomon's old age when his judgment was mature and strong.[4]

I. HERE IS SOMETHING IMPLIED. THAT OUR LOT HAS A CROOK.[5]

In our persons, estate,[6] relations, mind, heart[,] house, field, or somewhere we have a crook.[7]

II. HERE IS SOMETHING EXPRESSED. GOD MADE THE CROOK.[8]

It is no chance, it is his ordination.[9] We should look up to the great first cause[10] and not repine[11] at the channels of our troubles.

III. HERE IS SOMETHING WE ARE TO DO. CONSIDER WANT OF THIS IS A SAD WANT INDEED.[12]

Consider: 1. That we cannot alter it.[13]
       2. That others are worse.
       3. That we have many good things.
       4. That all is wise and gracious.[14]

Learn: 1. Sin made the crook.[15]
      2. Fly from the creature to the Creator.[16]
      3. Look for heaven.[17]

490. 496.

SERMON 274

1. It appears that Charles did not preach another sermon on the text of Jas 1:14.
2. Cf. Gen 3:12–13.   3. Cf. Jas 1:13.   4. Cf. Rom 9:19.
5. Charles may have been influenced by John Gill on this point. In his commentary on Jas 1:13, Gill wrote: "God is holy, and without iniquity, nor does he delight in sin, but hates and abhors it; nor can he commit it, it being contrary to his nature, and the perfections of it; whereas no one can tempt another to sin, unless he is sinful himself, and delights in sin, and in those that commit it, nor without committing it himself; and yet sinful men are apt to charge God with their sins, and temptations to them, in imitation of their first parent, Adam, when fallen, Gen iii.12 who, to excuse himself, lays the blame upon the woman, and ultimately upon God, who gave her to him; and suggests, that if it had not been for the woman, he should not have ate of the forbidden fruit, nor should he have had any temptation to it, had not God given him the woman to be with him, and therefore it was his fault; and in this sad manner do his sons and daughters reason, who, when, through affliction, they murmur against God, distrust his providence, or forsake his ways, say, if he had not laid his hand upon them, or suffered such afflictions to befall them, they had not been guilty of such sin: he himself is the occasion of them; but let no man talk at this wicked rate." Gill, *An Exposition of the New Testament* 3:468.
6. "A small part; a small proportion." Johnson's *Dictionary*, s.v. "Little." Cf. Jas 3:5.
7. Cf. Mark 4:31–32.
8. Charles described his own experience with this temptation: "Ah! I recollect a dark hour with myself when I, who do not remember to have even heard a blasphemy in my youth, much less to have uttered one, found rushing through my mind an almost infinite number of curses and blasphemies against the Most High God. I specially recall a certain narrow and crooked lane, in a country town, along which I was walking, one day, while I was seeking the Savior. On a sudden, it seemed as if the floodgates of hell had been opened; my head became a very pandemonium; ten thousand evil spirits seemed to be holding carnival within my brain. . . . Oh, how I groaned and cried before God! That temptation passed away; but ere many days, it was renewed again; and when I was in prayer, or when I was reading the Bible, these blasphemous thoughts would pour in upon me more than at any other time. I consulted with an aged godly man about it. He said to me, 'Oh, all this many of the people of God have proved before you! But,' he asked, 'do you hate these thoughts?' 'I do,' I truly answered. 'Then,' said he, 'they are not yours. . . . Groan

over them, repent of them, and send them on to the devil, the father of them, to whom they belong, for they are not yours.'" *Autobiography* 1:86–87.

9. Cf. Jas 1:14–15.

10. "Apostates and great backsliders do not reach their worst at one bound. The descent to hell is sometimes a precipice, but far oftener a smooth and gentle slope. It were hard to find out in the worst of men exactly when they were utterly given up to judicial blindness. It is often a long and laborious process by which conscience is completely seared." *MTP* 11:160.

11. Cf. Matt 15:18–19. 12. Cf. Rom 6:23a.

13. "The inner parts of anything." Johnson's *Dictionary*, s.v. "Bowels."

14. Cf. Prov 5:11; Jas 5:1–3.

15. "There are sins whose judgment hastens as a whirlwind—sins of the flesh, which eat into the bones and poison the blood; sins of appetite, that degrade and destroy the frame. If young men knew the price of sin, even in this life, they would not be so but to purchase pleasurable moments at the price of painful years. Who would coin his life into iniquity to have it returned to him in this life, red-hot from the mint of torment! Mark well the spendthrift, void of understanding! I have seen him at my door. I knew his relatives; people of reputable character and good estate. I have seen him in rags which scarcely covered him, piteously weeping for a piece of bread. Yet a few short years ago he inherited a portion which most men would have thought wealth. In a mad riot, into which he could not crowd enough of debauchery, he spent all that he had. He was soon penniless, and then loathsome and sore sick. He was pitied by his friends, but pity has been lost on him, and now none of his kith or kin dare own him." *MTP* 17:188.

16. Cf. Rom 6:23a. 17. Cf. Isa 33:14.

18. In the manuscript, Charles added the superscripted text "One person joined Zion Converted under this" and circled the text. This type of marking in the manuscript is unusual, but Charles's recording of conversions, while infrequent, has a precedent in his earlier Notebooks. For additional places where Charles recorded the conversion of a listener, see: "Sinners Must Be Punished" (Notebook 1, Sermon 9); "The Little Fire and Great Combustion" (Notebook 2, Sermon 54); and "Hew Down the Tree" (Notebook 4, Sermon 215).

1. In the upper left-hand corner of the manuscript Charles penned the last name "Jay." This marking signified his attribution of the sermon's material to William Jay, a preacher in Bath, England. Charles admired Jay's example in his earlier years. In his autobiography, Charles mentioned an occasion when he heard Jay preaching in Cambridge: "I remember with what dignity he preached, and yet how simply." *Autobiography* 1:208. On another occasion, Charles was struck by a number of Jay's pithy sayings, in particular the assertion, "Popery is a lie, Puseyism is a lie, and baptismal regeneration is a lie." *Autobiography* 1:208. Indeed, it appears that this appreciation resulted in the collecting of Jay's *Works and Sermons*. William Jay, *The Works of William Jay Collected and Revised by Himself*. Vols. 1–7 (London: C. A. Bartlett, 1842–1843, The Spurgeon Library); William Jay, *Sermons*. Vols. 1–2 (5th ed.; London: Hamilton, Adams, and Co., 1830, The Spurgeon Library). However, the original source that Charles consulted for his sermon outline is not contained in any of his copies of Jay's works in his personal library, now housed at Midwestern Baptist Theological Seminary, Kansas City, Missouri. Rather, a sermon skeleton attributed to Jay on the text of Eccl 7:13–14, titled "The Crooked in Life," can be found in Joseph S. Excell, *The Biblical Illustrator: Or, Anecdotes, Similes, Emblems, Illustrations; Expository, Scientific, Geographical, Historical, and Homiletic, Gathered from a Wide Range of Home and Foreign Literature, on the Verses of the Bible: Ecclesiastes* (New York: Fleming H. Revell, n.d.), 172–73. Hereinafter, *The Biblical Illustrator*. While Excell did not provide a primary source citation, a comparison of the attributed skeleton to Charles's sermon reveals a significant degree of structural and content overlap. The overlapping content is noted below.

2. "3. Any thing bent; a meander." Johnson's *Dictionary*, s.v. "Crook."

3. It appears that Charles did not preach another sermon on the text of Eccl 7:13.

4. This idea may have originated with John Gill. Gill wrote, "In short, what is said of the descent and dignity of the writer of this book, of his wisdom, wealth, riches, and grandeur, of his virtues and of his vices, agrees with none as with Solomon; to which may be added, that there is one passage in it, the same he used in his prayer at the dedication of the temple, chap. Vii.20 compared with 1 Kings viii.46. As to the time in which it was written by him, it seems to have been in his old age, as the Jewish writers observe; after his sin and fall, and recovery out of it, and when he was brought to true repentance for it: it was after he had made him great works, and built houses, his own house and the house of

God, which were twenty years in building; it was after he had acquired not only vast riches and treasures, which must require time, but had gotten knowledge of all things in nature; and had seen all the works that are done under the sun, and had made trial of all pleasures that were to be enjoyed; see chap. i. and ii. It was after he had been ensnared by women, which he confesses and laments, chap. vii.26; and his description of old age seems to be made, not merely upon the theory of it, but from a feeling experience of the evils and infirmities of it, chap. xii:1–6." Gill, *An Exposition of the Old Testament* 4:513.

5. Jay wrote, "I. What Is Here Implied? It is something crooked." Quoted in Excell, *The Biblical Illustrator: Ecclesiastes*, 172.

6. "2. Condition of life; with regard to prosperity or adversity. 3. Condition; circumstances in general. 4. Fortune; possession; generally meant of possessions in land, or realities. 5. Rank; quality." Johnson's *Dictionary*, s.v. "Estate."

7. "Who among us has not got some crooked thing or other to deal with? As they say that there is a skeleton somewhere in every house, so there is a crook in every lot, and none can make straight what God hath made crooked. Awkward embarrassments and anxious perplexities full often drive us to our wit's end, until we do not know which way to turn. To the right hand shall I go, or to the left? Both seem equally blocked up. Shall I go forward, or shall I go backward? Both ways seem equally hazardous. The judgment has lost chart and compass. And sometimes a child of God really does not know what he ought to choose." *MTP* 22:477.

8. Jay wrote, "II. What Is Expressed—namely, that God is the author of this." Quoted in Excell, *The Biblical Illustrator: Ecclesiastes*, 172.

9. Jay wrote, "There is no such thing as chance in our world. Nothing can befall us without the permission and appointment of the all-disposing providence of our Heavenly Father." Quoted in Excell, *The Biblical Illustrator: Ecclesiastes*, 172.

10. "Let me just probe you now for a while. You are in despondency about temporal affairs: what is the reason why you are in trouble? 'Because,' say you, 'I never was in such a condition before in my life. Wave upon wave of trouble comes upon me. I have lost one friend and then another. It seems as if business had altogether run away from me.... 'And, oh! sir, my enemies have conspired against me in

every way to cut me up and destroy me; opposition upon opposition threatens me. My shop must be closed; bankruptcy stares me in the face, and I know not what is to become of me.' . . . Now, what is all this but simply looking at second causes? You are looking at your trouble, not at the God who sent your trouble; you are looking at yourselves, not at the God who dwells within you, and who has promised to sustain you." *NPSP* 5:170–71.

11. "To fret; to vex himself; to be discontented." Johnson's *Dictionary*, s.v. "To Repine."

12. Jay wrote, "III. What Is Enjoined. It is to 'consider.'" Quoted in Excell, *The Biblical Illustrator: Ecclesiastes*, 172.

13. Jay wrote, "1. So consider the work of God as to be led to acknowledge that resistance to it is useless." Quoted in Excell, *The Biblical Illustrator: Ecclesiastes*, 172.

14. Jay wrote, "There is wisdom in the appropriating of your crook. . . . There is goodness in your crook." Quoted in Excell, *The Biblical Illustrator: Ecclesiastes*, 173.

15. Here, Charles deviated from Jay's outline. Jay wrote in his outline, "Let [the crook] embitter sin" (quoted in Excell, *The Biblical Illustrator: Ecclesiastes*, 173), whereas Charles focused on the effects of sin making the crook. At face value, Charles's statement here appears to contradict his previous assertion that "God made the crook." However, it is likely that Charles intended that sin is the instrumental cause, or second cause, of the "crookedness" of this life and creation. Such a reading also appears to be supported by his prior remark, "It is no chance, it is his ordination. We should look up to the great first cause and not repine at the channels of our troubles." For Charles, then, the tension between humanity's sin and God's providence did not create a contradiction but is resolved by avoiding sin and trusting in God.

16. Jay wrote, "You are to improve [the crook] by turning from the creature to the Creator." Quoted in Excell, *The Biblical Illustrator: Ecclesiastes*, 173. Charles wrote, "But I would remind you that you have forgotten to look to Christ since you have been in this trouble. Let me ask you, have you not thought less of Christ than you ever did? I will not suppose that you have neglected prayer, or have left your Bible unread; but still, have you had any of those sweet thoughts of Christ which once you had? Have you been able to take all your troubles to him and

say—'Lord, thou knowest all things; I trust all in thy hands?' Let me ask you, have you considered that Christ is omnipotent, and therefore able to deliver you; that he is faithful, and must deliver you, because he has promised to do so? Have you not kept your eye on his rod, and not on his hand? Have you not looked rather to the crook that smote you, than to the heart that moved that crook? Oh, recollect, that you can never find joy and peace while you are looking at the things that are seen, the second causes of your trouble; your only hope, your only refuge and joy must be to look to him who dwells within the veil." *NPSP* 5:171.

17. Jay wrote, "You are to improve [the crook], by its leading you from earth to heaven." Quoted in Excell, *The Biblical Illustrator: Ecclesiastes*, 173.

John III. 23. Baptism.

I select this text because it seems to in keeping with the occasion. One cannot help thinking of John Baptist standing clad in camel's hair baptizing in the river the disciples of the truth. We have in this a strong proof that Baptism by Immersion is the true mode.

In speaking of Baptism

I. I would speak of the Mode.

Properly speaking the "mode of Baptism" is a tautological expression for Baptism means dipping according to Greek Lexicons. So that we cannot speak of the Mode of dipping unless it be with an allowance for ignorance.

But that Dipping is the ordinance is proved

1. From the word βαπτίζω which is translated mergo or immergo in the lexicons of Constantine, Budæus &c. and those of Hadrian Junius, Plantinus, Scapula, Stephens, Schrevelius, Stockius & others — besides a great number of critics as Beza, Casaubon, Witsius &c. Our translators should have rendered it "dip" & then the question would have been settled

2. The places chosen were rivers or other places having abundance of water. The river Jordan, Enon our text, "See here is water" — Nor is the case of the

BAPTISM

John 3:23[1]

"And John also was baptizing in Aenon near to Salim, because there was much water there: and they came, and were baptized."

I select this text because it seems so in keeping with the occasion.[2] One cannot help thinking of John Baptist standing clad in camel's hair baptizing in the river the disciples of the truth.[3] We have in this a strong proof that Baptism by Immersion is the true mode.

In speaking of Baptism:

I. I WOULD SPEAK OF THE MODE.

Properly speaking[,] the "mode of Baptism" is a tautological[4] expression,[5] for Baptism means dipping according to Greek Lexicons, so that we cannot speak of the Mode of dipping unless it be with an allowance for ignorance.

But that Dipping is the ordinance is proved[:]

1. From the word βαπτιζω which is translated mergo or immergo in the lexicons of Constantine, Budaeus etc. and those of Hadrian Junius, Plantinus, Scapula, Stephens, Schrevelius, Stockius and others – besides a great number of critics as Beza, Casaubon, Witsius etc.[6]

    Our translators should have rendered it "dip" and then the question would have been settled.[7]

2. The places chosen were rivers or other places having abundance of water. [i.e.] The river Jordan,[8] Aenon[9] [in] our text, "See here is water."[10] Nor is the case of the

jailer who was baptized at night at all to be mentioned for is it not likely that there was a bath in the prison or if not the river was near at hand.

3. Descriptions of Baptisms given in the Testament are rendered more intelligible if dipping be the proper mode.

See Mark. I. 8-10 where Baptizing with the Holy Ghost is mentioned & cannot mean sprinkling

Jesus came to John why not John to him since he was the superior & ought to be waited upon — but the river was near John. "in Jordan", why need stand there to sprinkle Besides it says "coming up out of the water"

The Eunuch came unto the water then went down into it & then was baptized now why should it be "unto" twice. Is not the other rightly rendered "into"?

4. In Rom. VI. 4. Burial by baptism is spoken of which must suppose immersion.

Col. II. 12 shews baptism to be an emblem of the death, burial and resurrection of Jesus & how can sprinkling represent this.

But in closing this let me remark that we ought not to have the burden of proving this but our opponents

Jailer who was baptized at night[11] at all to be mentioned for is it not likely that there was a bath in the prison or if not[,] the river was near at hand.[12]

3. Descriptions of Baptisms given in the [New] Testament are rendered more intelligible if dipping be the proper mode. See Mark. I. 8–10[13] where Baptizing with the Holy Ghost is mentioned and cannot mean sprinkling. Jesus came to John[.] [W]hy not John to him since he was the superior and ought to be waited upon[?] But the river was near John. "In Jordan," why need stand there to sprinkle[?] Besides it says "coming up out of the water."[14]

   The Eunuch came unto the water then went down into it and then was baptized.[15] Now, why should it be "unto" twice[?] Is not the other rightly rendered "into["]?[16]

4. In Rom. VI. 4.[17] Burial by baptism is spoken of, which must suppose immersion.

   Col. II. 12[18] Shews baptism to be an emblem of the death, burial[,] and resurrection of Jesus. And how can sprinkling represent this[?]

But in closing this let me remark that we ought not to have the burden of proving this but our opponents are bound to prove to the contrary. for Churchmen themselves can read in their own prayer-book that dipping is to be preferred, unless the child be a weakling. —

The Greek Churches practise trine immersion It is said that John Wesley practised immersion of children & the majority of honest ingenuous divines agree that this was the ancient mode though they say that change of climate alters it. But if this be allowed how can we be sure that other matters are not altered too. Some say the practise cannot be universal but we think no one can prove this fancy.

II. Let me speak of the Subject.
The Prayer-book declares faith & repentance to be necessary before Baptism. & certainly there is no instance of any being baptized who did not profess to have each of these things. — Men & women were baptized & none else. If thou believest with all thine heart thou mayest. Many people now a days believe this though they still stand aloof & hide their heads in other denominations. Some drag in the Abrahamic covenant to prove infant sprinkling but how the circumcision of infants

are bound to prove to the contrary, for Churchmen themselves can read in their own prayer-book that dipping is to be preferred, unless the child be a weakling.[19]

The Greek Churches practise trine immersion.[20] It is said that John Wesley practised immersion of children[21] and the majority of honest ingenuous divines agree that this was the ancient mode[,] though they say that change of climate alters it.[22] But if this be allowed, how can we be sure that other matters are not altered too[?] Some say the practise cannot be universal but we think no one can prove this fancy.

II. LET ME SPEAK OF THE SUBJECT.

The Prayer-book declares faith and repentance to be necessary before Baptism,[23] and certainly there is no instance of any being baptized who did not profess to have each of these things. Men and women were baptized and none else. If thou believest with all thine heart thou mayest.[24] Many people now a days believe this though they still stand aloof and hide their heads in other denominations. Some drag in the Abrahamic covenant to prove infant sprinkling, but how the circumcision of infants can prove that under a new covenant they are to be baptized is indeed mysterious.

If so then tithes paid to the Levites ought still to be paid to the clergy which Dissenting Poedoes will not allow. If so how inconsistent are those who do not allow all baptized persons to come to the Lord's table — for surely as circumcision gave a right to the passover so will baptism give a right to the Lord's Supper.

Again some say it was anciently so done but this we deny for there is no mention of Infant Baptism earlier than the third century when Tertullian mentions it only to condemn it. —

Some again say "Suffer little children &c" but these were not babes for he called them which he would not have done had they been infants. They were brought to be touched not to be baptized

The subjects of it are true believers in our Lord Jesus Christ.

III Let me now speak of its meaning. It is not to regenerate them & cause them to be changed in heart. It is a solemn profession of attachment can prove that under a new covenant they are to be baptized is indeed mysterious.[25] If so, then tithes paid to the Levites ought still be paid to the clergy which Dissenting Paedoes will not allow.[26] If so[,] how inconsistent are those who do not allow all baptized persons to come to the Lord's table, for surely as circumcision gave a right to the passover[27] so will baptism give a right to the Lord's supper.[28]

Again some say it was anciently so done but this we deny for there is no mention of Infant Baptism ~~later~~ earlier than the third century when Tertullian mentions it only to condemn it.[29]

Some again say "Suffer little children etc.,"[30] but these were not babes for he called them[,] which he would not have done had they been infants. They were brought to be touched not to be baptized.

The subjects of it are true believers in our Lord Jesus Christ.

III. LET ME NOW SPEAK OF ITS MEANING.

It is not to regenerate them and cause them to be changed in heart.[31] It is a solemn profession of attachment to our Lord & master & is an imitation of him in his death, burial & resurrection.

1. To the candidates for Baptism. You my friends have good ground for being baptized. Now fear not; look up to heaven. Beg for more grace & boldly follow your Master. God be with you.

2. You who have been baptized. Remember the day, renew your vows. walk worthy of your high vocation. Watch & pray.

3. You who are Christians why stay from this ordinance, rather come bravely on. Obey your Lord & fear not. Read & see if we are right.

4. You who are ungodly. Baptism would do you no good. Believe is our exhortation to you; that must come first. Oh God of the weak help thou me.

491.

to our Lord and master and is an imitation of him in his death, burial[,] and resurrection.[32]

1. To the candidates for Baptism. You my friends have good ground for being baptized. Now fear not, look up to heaven. Beg for more grace and boldly follow your Master[.] God be with you.

2. You who have been baptized. Remember the day, renew your vows, [and] walk worthy of your high vocation.[33] Watch and pray.[34]

3. You who are Christians[,] why stay from this ordinance, rather come bravely on. Obey your Lord and fear not. Read and see if we are right.[35]

4. You who are ungodly. Baptism would do you no good. ["]Believe["] is our exhortation to you; that must come first.

Oh God of the weak help thou me.

491.

1. It appears that Charles did not preach another sermon on the text of John 3:23.

2. Charles's comment here indicates that he preached this sermon at a baptismal service. Although the date of this occasion is unknown, it does appear that Charles practiced baptismal services at Waterbeach Chapel. In a letter to his mother dated November 1852, Charles remarked, "Our anniversary passed off grandly: six were baptized; crowds on crowds stood by the river; the chapel was afterwards crammed, both to the tea and the sermon." *Autobiography* 1:248–49. Charles's autobiography, however, does not reveal the frequency of such services.

3. Cf. Matt 3:1–10; Mark 1:2–6; Luke 3:1–9; John 1:19–28.

4. "Repeating the same thing." Johnson's *Dictionary*, s.v. "Tautological."

5. In Charles's mind, to say "baptism by immersion" was the same as saying "baptism by baptism" or "immersion by immersion." This thought may have come to him through John Gill, who wrote, "Custom, and the common use of writing in this controversy, have so far prevailed, that for the most part immersion is usually called the mode of baptism; whereas it is properly baptism itself; to say that immersion or dipping is the *mode* of baptism, is the same thing as to say, that dipping is the mode of dipping. . . . And as for sprinkling, that cannot, with any propriety, be called a mode of baptism; for it would be just such good sense as to say, sprinkling is the mode of dipping, since baptism and dipping are the same. . . . That baptism is immersion, or the dipping of a person in water, is to be proved, 1. From the proper and primary signification of the word baptize, which in its first and primary sense, signifies to *dip* or *plunge into*: and so it is rendered by our best *Lexicographers, mergo, immergo*, dip or plunge into." John Gill, *A Body of Practical Divinity*, vol. 3 (London: printed for the author and sold by George Keith, 1770, The Spurgeon Library), 332, italics in the original. Hereafter *BPD*.

6. This list of lexicographers is a direct quote from the chapter concerning baptism in Gill, *BPD* 3:332.

7. Gill wrote, "Had our translators, instead of adopting the *Greek* word *baptize* in all places where the ordinance of baptism is made mention of, truly translated it, and not have left it untranslated, as they have, the controversy about the manner of baptizing, would have been at an end, or rather have prevented; had they used

8. Cf. Matt 3:5–6; Mark 1:5; Luke 3:3; John 1:28.

9. Cf. John 3:23.

10. Cf. Acts 8:36. Gill wrote, "That baptism was performed by immersion, appears by the places chosen for the administration of it; as the river *Jordan* by *John*, where he baptized many, and where our Lord himself was baptized by him. Matt. iii. 6, 13, 16. . . . *John* also, it is said, *was baptizing in Aenon, near Salim, because there was much water.*" Gill, BPD 3:333, italics in the original.

11. Cf. Acts 16:33.

12. Gill wrote, "Another instance is that of the jailer and his household, Acts xvi. 33. In which account there is nothing that makes it improbable that it was done by immersion; for it seems to be a clear case, that the jailer, upon his conversion, took the apostle out of prison into his own house, where they preached to him and his family, verse 32. And after this they went out of his house, and he and his were baptized, very probably in the river without the city, where the oratory was, verse 13, for it was certain, that after the baptism of him and his family, he brought the apostles into his house again, and set meat before them, verse 33, 34, upon the whole, these instances produced, fail of shewing the improbability of baptism by immersion; which must appear clear and manifest to every attentive reader of his Bible, notwithstanding all that has been opposed unto it." Gill, BPD 3 338.

13. Mark 1:8–10, "I indeed have baptized you with water: but he shall baptize you with the Holy Ghost. And it came to pass in those days, that Jesus came from Nazareth of Galilee, and was baptized of John in Jordan. And straightway coming up out of the water, he saw the heavens opened, and the Spirit like a dove descending upon him."

14. Gill wrote, "That this was the way in which it was anciently administered, is clear from several instances of baptism recorded in scripture, and the circumstances attending them; as that of our Lord, of whom it is said, *That when he was baptized, he went up straightway out of the water*, which supposes he had been in it." Gill, BPD 3:333, italics in the original.

15. Cf. Acts 8:36, 38.

16. Gill wrote, "The baptism of the eunuch is another instance of baptism by immersion; when he and *Philip* were *come unto a certain water,* to the water-side, which destroys a little piece of criticism, as if their going into the water, after expressed, was no other than going to the brink of the water, to the water-side, whereas they were come to that before; and baptism being agreed upon, *they went down both into the water,* both *Philip* and the eunuch, *and he baptized him; and when they were come up out of the water,* etc. Now we do not reason merely from the circumstances of *going down into, and coming up out of the water;* and we know that persons may go down into water, and come up out of it, and never be immersed in it; but when it is expressly said, upon these persons going down into the water, that *Philip* baptized, or dipped, the eunuch; and when this was done, that both came up out of it, these circumstances strongly corroborate, without the explanation of the word *baptized,* that it was performed by immersion." Gill, *BPD* 3:334, italics in the original.

17. Romans 6:4, "Therefore we are buried with him by baptism into death: that like as Christ was raised up from the dead by the glory of the Father, even so we also should walk in newness of life."

18. Colossians 2:12, "Buried with him in baptism, wherein also ye are risen with him through the faith of the operation of God, who hath raised him from the dead."

19. According to *The Book of Common Prayer*, at the point in the "rite" when the parish priest names the child, the following text is included in subscript, "*And then naming it after them (if they shall certify him that the Child may well endure it) he shall dip it in the Water discreetly and warrily. . . . But if they certify that the Child is weak, it shall suffice to pour Water upon it.*" "The Ministration of Publick Baptism of Infants, to Be Used in the Church," *The Book of Common Prayer, and Administration of the Sacraments, and Other Rites and Ceremonies of the Church, According to the Use of the United Church of England and Ireland: Together with the Psalter or Psalms of David, Pointed as They Are to Be Sung or Said in Churches* (Cambridge: John Smith, sold by John W. Parker, 1832, The Spurgeon Library), n.p., italics in the original. Hereinafter, *The Book of Common Prayer*.

20. "Trine immersion" is the practice of immersing a baptismal candidate three times in the names of the members of the Trinity. Charles's comment about the Greek Churches practicing trine immersion possibly came from the *Didache*. In

his critical edition, Philip Schaff later noted that "the normal and favorite mode of Baptism is threefold immersion 'in living [running] water,' i.e. fresh, running water, wither in a stream or a fountain, as distinct from standing water in a pool or cistern." Philip Schaff, *The Oldest Church Manual Called the Teaching of the Twelve Apostles: ΔΙΔΑΧΗ ΤΩΝ ΔΩΔΕΚΑ ΑΠΟΣΤΟΛΟΝ: The Didache and Kindred Documents in the Original. with Translations and Discussions of Post-Apostolic Teaching, Baptism, Worship, and Discipline, and with Illustrations and Fac-similes of the Jerusalem Manuscript* (New York: Funk and Wagnall, 1885, The Spurgeon Library), 32. Charles's library also contained William Cathcart's work, *The Baptism of the Ages and of the Nations*, which gave an account of trine immersion being practiced by Greek churches throughout history. William Cathcart, *The Baptism of the Ages and of the Nations* (Philadelphia: American Baptist Publication Society, 1878, The Spurgeon Library), 163–84.

21. This point by Charles appears to have been confirmed by the work of a writer known only as "An Old Methodist" in his work, *John Wesley: In Company with High Churchmen*, 2nd ed. (London: Church Press, 1870). Notably, the "Old Methodist" cited Whitehead's *Life of Wesley*, saying, "When Mr. Wesley baptized adults, professing faith in Christ, he chose to do it by *Trine Immersion*, if the persons would submit to it; judging this to be the Apostolic method of baptizing" (Old Methodist, *John Wesley: In Company with High Churchmen*, 98); see also John Whitehead, *The Life of the Rev. John Wesley, M.A. With Some Account of His Ancestors and Relations; and the Life of the Rev. Charles Wesley, M.A. Complete in One Volume* (Toronto: William Briggs, n.d.), 131. Charles also likely drew this point from *The Book of Common Prayer*. It is likely that Charles found a source similar to the "Old Methodist" or drew an analogy based on the Wesleys' background in the Church of England.

22. Charles's comment here resembles one made by Conybeare and Howson in their work, *The Life and Epistles of St. Paul*. There they noted, "It is needless to add that baptism was (unless in exceptional cases) administered by immersion, the convert being plunged beneath the surface of the water to represent his death to the life of sin, and then raised from this momentary burial to represent his resurrection to the life of righteousness. It must be a subject of regret that the general discontinuance of this original form of baptism (though perhaps necessary in our northern climates) has rendered obscure to popular apprehension some very important passages of Scripture." W. J. Conybeare and J. S. Howson, *The Life and Epistles of St. Paul. In Two Volumes*, vol. 1 (New York: Charles Scribner, 1854), 439.

23. Here Charles was probably referring to the brief catechism found in *The Book of Common Prayer*. In response to the question "What is required of persons to be baptized?" the catechism states, "Repentance, whereby they forsake sin; and Faith, whereby they stedfastly believe the promises of God made to them in that Sacrament." "A Catechism, that is to say, An Instruction to Be Learned of Every Person, Before He Be Brought to Be Confirmed by the Bishop," *The Book of Common Prayer*.

24. Cf. Acts 8:37.

25. Here Charles may have been referring to what Robinson called "Reformed Baptism" or "Baptism by Calvinist Congregational Churches Not Established." Robert Robinson, *The History of Baptism* (London: printed by Couchman and Fry for Thomas Knott, 1790, The Spurgeon Library), 536. In his work, Robinson outlined the covenantal view—common to Reformed theology—where God made two primary covenants, a Covenant of Works with Adam and a Covenant of Grace with Abraham, although Robinson also asserted that the New Covenant of Christ was a new "dispensation" of the Covenant of Grace. Robinson, *The History of Baptism*, 537. Robinson then noted that the Abrahamic covenant "had been administered under the law by sacrifices, circumcision, the passover, and other types, and that it was now administered under the gospel by preaching, baptism, and the Lord's supper." Robinson, *The History of Baptism*, 537. Robinson described the benefits of the covenant as "inheritable," such that "if any one of [an infant's] ancestors had been a believer the infant might claim as the seed of the faithful the benefit of the contract made with Abraham." Robinson, *The History of Baptism*, 538. Thus, the theological position argued for an analogy between circumcision and baptism.

26. Charles argued here that if circumcision corresponds to baptism via analogy, then it follows that tithes paid to Levites, by analogy, must be paid to clergy. However, the "tithe to the clergy" should be understood as referring to the State Church Tax that England imposed on the public for the maintenance of the Church of England. In this instance, Charles was critiquing Dissenting denominations such as Presbyterians or Independent Congregationalists, who, while opposed to the state church tax, nonetheless practiced infant baptism. The core issue at stake, then, was the tension produced by analogies to Old Testament law and the impact those analogies had upon the relationship between church

and state. In this respect, Charles was opposed to the concept of a "National Church" because he viewed it as an "unhallowed institution," asserting, "No National Church is possible on the principle of believer's baptism. . . . A State Church *must* hold to infant baptism; necessarily it must receive all the members of the State into its number – it *must*, or else it cannot expect the pay of the state." *MTP* 13:128, italics in the original. Thus in Charles's view, denominations that affirmed infant baptism but opposed the State Church tax were "limping between two opinions" (1 Kgs 18:21), as it were.

27. Cf. Exod 12:43–45.

28. Paedobaptists typically withheld the Lord's Supper until the individual baptized as an infant had gone through confirmation at an older age. Baptists, on the other hand, believed that believer's baptism granted access to the Lord's Supper. Gill wrote, "None but penitent sinners, and true believers, and those baptized, upon a profession of their repentance and faith are to be allowed communicants at this ordinance." Gill, *BPD* 3:571.

29. Here Charles appears to allude to the Latin Father Tertullian's work, *On Baptism*. In chapter 18, Tertullian advocated against the baptism of little children, saying, "And so, according to the circumstances and disposition, and even age, of each individual, the delay of baptism is preferable; principally, however, in the case of little children. For why is it necessary—if (baptism itself) is not so necessary—that the sponsors likewise should be thrust into danger." Tertullian, "On Baptism," in *The Ante-Nicene Fathers: Translations of the Writings of the Fathers down to A.D 325. Volume III. Latin Christianity: Its Founder, Tertullian. I. Apologetic; II. Anti-Marcion; III. Ethical*, ed. Alexander Roberts and James Donaldson; rev. A. Cleveland Coxe (Grand Rapids: Eerdmans, 1956), 678.

30. Cf. Matt 19:14; Mark 10:14; Luke 18:16.

31. Here Charles drew attention to the doctrine of baptismal regeneration, which he despised. For other instances in his Notebooks where Charles repudiated the doctrine, see "Salvation in God Only" (Notebook 1, Sermon 24); "More for Us Than Against Us" (Notebook 3, Sermon 180); "The Baptism of the Spirit" (Notebook 3, Sermon 181); "The Downfall of Pride" (Notebook 4, Sermon 200); and "Linsey-Woolsey Forbidden" (Notebook 4, Sermon 210).

32. Gill wrote, "The end of baptism, which is to represent the burial of Christ, cannot be answered in any other way than by immersion, or covering the body in water; that baptism is an emblem of the burial of Christ, is clear from *Rom.* vi. 4. *Col.* ii.12. It would be endless to quote the great number, even of *paedobaptist* writers, who ingeniously acknowledge that the allusion of these passages, is to the ancient rite of baptism by immersion; as none but such who are dead are buried, so none but such who are dead to sin, and to the law, by the body of Christ, or who profess to be so, are to be buried in and by baptism, or to be baptized; and as none can be properly said to be buried, unless put under ground, and covered with earth; so none can be said to be baptized, but such who are put under water, and covered with it; and nothing short of this can be a representation of the burial of Christ, and is ours with him; not sprinkling, or pouring a little water on the face; for a corpse cannot be said to be buried, when only a little earth or dust is sprinkled or poured on it." Gill, *BPD* 3:334, italics in the original.

33. On the day of his baptism, Charles recorded in his diary a vow he made to the Lord: "I vow to glory alone in Jesus and His cross, and to spend my life in the extension of His cause, in whatsoever way He pleases. I desire to be sincere in this solemn profession, having but one object in view, and that to glorify God." *Autobiography* 1:135.

34. Cf. Matt 26:41; Mark 14:38; Luke 21:36.

35. Though Charles grew up in a paedobaptist context, he became convinced of the Baptist position through his own study of Scripture. "I would that all churchmen were better churchmen; if they would be more consistent with their own articles of faith, they would be more consistent with Scripture; and if they were a little more consistent with some of the rubrics of their own Church, they would be a little more consistent with themselves. I became a Baptist through reading the New Testament, — especially in the Greek, — and was strengthened in my resolve by a perusal of the Church of England Catechism, which declared as necessary to baptism, repentance and the forsaking of sin." *Autobiography* 1:150.

277. Mal. I. 7. The table of the Lord not contemptible.

In Malachi's days the table of the Lord was the table of shewbread & the tables of the priests. Now the people would not pay tithe, they brought maimed beasts for sacrifice, the priests offered them contrary to law & thus did they in effect say the table of the Lord is contemptible. Now we have the Lord's table & some do say that this is contemptible.

I. I will try & show who treat this as if it were contemptible. —
1. All those who laugh at those who sit down at it.
2. All those who sit down at it for gain or without true conversion.
3. All Christian members who abstain from it.
4. All persons who refuse to come out from the world & remember their dying Lord.

II. I will try & show the sinfulness of despising the table of the Lord.
1. It is the ordinance of God & not of man. what man invents you may despise

THE TABLE *of the* LORD NOT CONTEMPTIBLE
Malachi 1:7[1]

"Ye offer polluted bread upon mine altar; and ye say, Wherein have we polluted thee? In that ye say, The table of the Lord is contemptible."

In Malachi's day the table of the Lord was the table of shewbread and the tables of the priests.[2] Now the people would not pay [their] tithe,[3] they brought maimed beasts for sacrifice,[4] the priests offered them contrary to Law[,][5] and thus did they in effect say the table of the Lord is contemptible. Now we have the Lord's table[6] and some do say that this is contemptible.

I. I WILL TRY AND SHOW WHO TREAT THIS AS IF IT WERE CONTEMPTIBLE.

1. All those who laugh at those who sit down at it.
2. All those who sit down at it for gain[7] or without true conversion.[8]
3. All Christian members who abstain from it.
4. All persons who refuse to come out from the world and remember their dying Lord.

II. I WILL TRY AND SHOW THE SINFULNESS OF DESPISING THE TABLE OF THE LORD.

1. It is the ordinance of God and not of man[;] what man invents you may despise

but God's ordinances you must not.
2. It is the last dying request of the Redeemer
3. It is a memorial of the means of our salvation, the ground of our hope, it is a solemn thing therefore.
4. It is the means of much grace to our souls.

III. I will try & speak to those about to partake of it.
1. You sit down at a _solemn_ table, requiring deep searchings of heart, & tryings of soul.
2. You sit down at a _loving_ table, where everything speaks of love, let your lives be an exposition of love.
3. You sit down at a _public_ table looked on by many eyes, seen by enemies.
4. You sit down at an _honorable_ table at which kings & prophets could not sit down, the table of God. —
5. You sit down at a _joyful_ table, one of festivity, a feast, an antepast.

Forgive & help. Oh my God.
Amen

THE TABLE OF THE LORD NOT CONTEMPTIBLE—*Malachi 1:7*

   but God's ordinances you must not.
2. It is the last dying request of the Redeemer.
3. It is a memorial of the means of our salvation, the ground of our hope, it is a solemn thing therefore.
4. It is the means of much grace to our souls.[9]

III. I WILL TRY AND SPEAK TO THOSE ABOUT TO PARTAKE OF IT.
1. You sit down at a <u>solemn</u> table,[10] requiring deep searching of heart and tryings of soul.[11]
2. You sit down at a <u>loving</u> table, where everything speaks of love. Let your lives be an exposition of love.[12]
3. You sit down at a <u>public</u> table looked on by many eyes, seen by enemies.[13]
4. You sit down at an <u>honorable</u> table at which kings and prophets could not sit down, the table of God.
5. You sit down at a <u>joyful</u> table, one of festivity, a feast, an antepast.[14]

Forgive and Help. Oh my God.

Amen

492

SERMON 277

1. It appears that Charles did not preach another sermon on the text of Mal 1:7.

2. Cf. Lev 24:8–9.   3. Cf. Mal 3:8–10.

4. Cf. Mal 1:8. Charles misspelled "sacrifice" as "sacrafice" in the manuscript. This has been corrected, and "sacrifice" has been supplied in the transcription.

5. Cf. Mal 2:8.

6. With the previous sermon being for a baptismal service, it is likely that this sermon was written for a communion service, which could have been the first communion service for those who had been recently baptized. Like many Baptists, Charles believed that baptism was a prerequisite for participating in the Lord's Table. "When I had been accepted as a member of the Congregational Church at Newmarket, I was invited to the communion table, although I had not been baptized. I refused, because it did not appear to me to be according to the New Testament order: 'Then they that gladly received his word were baptized: and the same day there were added unto them about three thousand souls. And they continued steadfastly in the apostles' doctrine and fellowship, and in breaking of bread, and in prayers.' I waited until I could go to the Lord's table as one who had believed, and who had been baptized." *Autobiography* 1:148.

7. An example of "[sitting] down at it for gain," which Charles may have had in mind, are the Corporation and Test Acts enacted in Britain in 1661 and 1678 respectively. In his work *English Constitutional History*, Taswell-Langmead noted that the abolishment of the Corporation and Test Acts in 1828 removed the "civil disabilities of Dissenters," namely "the sacramental test previously required as a qualification for civil, military, and corporate offices, [was] replaced by a declaration, upon the true faith of a Christian." Thomas Pitt Taswell-Langmead, *English Constitutional History from the Teutonic Conquest to the Present Time*, 2nd ed. (London: Stevens and Haynes; Boston: Houghton, Mifflin, 1881), 752. As a result, many Dissenters took Communion in the Church of England once per year to pass the Acts, while not possessing genuine Anglican conviction. Taswell-Langmead also alluded to this when he noted, "These monuments of bygone bigotry were not only unjust to a large and worthy section of the community, but hurtful to the

8. "What multitudes of professors are quite content with the outward sign! I fear that the Lord's supper, through being so grossly misused, has deceived many. See how eagerly they send for a clergyman when they lie dying! Men, who have scarcely ever entered a church or chapel in their lives—men, who fear not God, and have no saving interest in the death of Christ—desire to have this bread in their mouths at the last. Let them know that, dying impenitent, this bread shall be a swift witness against them. Not being born of God, and having no right whatever to this ordinance, they ate and drank unworthily, and so ate and drank condemnation to themselves. If any of you have imagined that this ordinance can save your souls, let me correct that error at once; it may ruin them, but it cannot save them. You must get right away to Christ, right away from this ordinance. It is not as unrenewed sinners, but as saints, as Christ's disciples, as his saved ones, that you are to partake of this feast." *MTP* 50:104.

9. "The two ordinances of Baptism and the Lord's Supper . . . are both made a rich means of grace. But let me ask you, . . . with regard to the eating of bread and the drinking of wine at the Lord's Supper, can it by any means be conceived by any rational man that there is anything in the mere piece of bread that we eat, or in the wine that we drink? And yet doubtless the grace of God does go with both ordinances for the confirming of the faith of those who receive them, and even for the conversion of those who look upon the ceremony." *NPSP* 5:211.

10. "Brethren, it is a solemn thing to think that, every time we come to the communion table, we bring before the Eternal Father the memorial of the death of his only-begotten and well-beloved Son." *MTP* 50:105.

11. Cf. 1 Cor 11:27–29.   12. Cf. 1 Cor 10:17; 11:20–22, 33.

13. "Besides showing forth Christ's death to ourselves, to our God, and to our fellow-Christians, *we also show it to the world*. We do, in effect, say to the world, 'Here we show that we believe in him whom you crucified. He who went without the

camp, the Man of Nazareth, despised and rejected of men, is our Master. You may trust in your philosophies; we trust in him. You may rely upon your own merits, sacrifices, and performances; but, as for us, his flesh and his blood are our dependence. As we eat this bread, and drink of this cup, Christ Jesus is set forth to you as being All-in-all to us—the bread which sustains our spiritual life, and the wine which gives us joy and sacred exhilaration and delight.'" *MTP* 55:319–20, italics in the original.

14. "A foretaste; something taken before the proper time." Johnson's *Dictionary*, s.v. "Antepast." Cf. Matt 26:29; Mark 14:25; Luke 22:18.

278. Jer. XXXVI. 18. 19.   The Rechabites.
God's ministers & prophets even more than other men must carry their eyes in their heads, being observant of every thing occuring around them.

Hobab or Raguel the father in law of Moses came from his desert home &, persuaded by Moses, staid with the Israelites & shared their toilsome marches, battle & deliverances.

His descendants appear to have had no inheritance in the promised land but led a nomadic life in & around Palestine. In Judges. I. 16. we find them living in the deserts of the tribe of Judah. The noble Jael was one of this race. Judg. IV In I Sam. XV. 6. They are found dwelling among Amalekites yet God spareth them all. In II Kings. X. 15. Jonadab first appears riding with royalty, honoured as a man of God. One whose good opinion Jehu desired.

Once more they are honorably mentioned their escutcheon is without a stain — a race every way renowned.

I. We would try to discover the reasons of their parent's advice

Not because it is wrong to drink wine,

THE RECHABITES
Jeremiah 35:18–19[1]

"And Jeremiah said unto the house of the Rechabites, Thus saith the Lord of hosts, the God of Israel; Because ye have obeyed the commandment of Jonadab your father, and kept all his precepts, and done according unto all that he hath commanded you: Therefore thus saith the Lord of hosts, the God of Israel; Jonadab the son of Rechab shall not want a man to stand before me for ever."

God's ministers and prophets even more than other men must carry their eyes in their heads, being observant of every thing occurring around them.

Hobab or Raquel[,] the father in law of Moses[,] came from his desert home and, persuaded by Moses, staid[2] with the Israelites and shared their toilsome marches, battles[,] and deliverances.[3]

His descendants appear to have had no inheritance in the promised land but led a nomadic life in and around Palestine. In Judges. I. 16.[4] we find them living in the deserts of the tribe of Judah. The noble Jael was one of this race. Judg IV.[5] In I Sam. XV. 6.[6] They are found dwelling among Amalekites yet God spareth them all. In II Kings X. 15.[7] Jonadab first appears riding with royalty, honoured as a man of God. One whose good opinion Jehu desired.

Once more they are honorably mentioned[,] their escutcheon[8] is without a stain. A race every-way renowned.

I. WE WOULD TRY TO DISCOVER THE REASONS OF THEIR PARENT'S ADVICE.

Not because it is wrong to drink wine,[9]

live in houses, or plant fields but because he thought it good policy for them not to do so.—

1. That they might ever remain a distinct race, separate from all the world.
2. That the people of Israel might not be jealous of them & attempt to destroy them.
3. That they might not be corrupted by evil example & fall into drunkenness & other vices of settled life.
4. That they might be lowly, unaspiring gentle, pastoral, simple in their habits.
5. That they might learn to practise self-denial — which is a noble virtue
6. That they might be ever reminded of the better land where the portion was & might remember that this is not our rest.

It were well for us if by any means we could gain some of these good things

II. The children's observance of it & their blessing from God.

They did not violate their ancestor's rules & 300 years after his death they held them sacred. Their being in Jerusalem was no violation of it since it is

THE RECHABITES—*Jeremiah 35:18-19*

live in houses, or plant fields[,] but because he thought it good policy for them not to do so.

1. That they might ever remain a distinct race, separate from all the world.[10]
2. That the people of Israel might not be jealous of them and attempt to destroy them.[11]
3. That they might not be corrupted by evil example and fall into drunkenness and other vices of settled life.[12]
4. That they might be lowly, unaspiring, gentle, pastoral, [and] simple in their habits.[13]
5. That they might learn to practise self-denial, which is a noble virtue.[14]
6. That they might be ever reminded of the better land where the portion was and might remember that this is not our rest.[15]

It were well for us if by any means we could gain some of these good things.

II. THE CHILDREN'S OBSERVANCE OF IT AND THEIR BLESSING FROM GOD.

They did not violate their ancestor[']s rules, and 300 years after his death they held them sacred.[16] Their being in Jerusalem[17] was no violation of it since it is possible that even in Jerusalem they lived in tents & Jonadab did not intend that they should needlessly destroy themselves he would himself have sanctioned this act. — They were doubtless often asked to drink & refusing became the drunkards scorn, they had a strong temptation coming from so good a man as the prophet & at free cost, but they refused.

Their father was dead but not their reverence to him. — God approved their obedience by promise of a perpetual name to their race & that a pious name.

Some affirm that the Rechabites still dwell in Arabia Felix as a distinct race.

III. Let us learn from their example. If they obeyed their earthly father, much more we our heavenly one.

1. The Rechabites obeyed a man in ordinances of his own invention & ought not we to obey a God.

2. They owed not so much to Jonadab

possible that even in Jerusalem they lived in tents, and Jonadab did not intend that they should needlessly destroy themselves[.] [H]e would himself have sanctioned this act. They were doubtless often asked to drink, and refusing became the drunkard's scorn[.] [T]hey had a strong temptation[,] coming from so good a man as the prophet, and at free cost, but they refused.[18]

Their father was dead but not their reverence to him.[19] God approved their obedience by promise of a perpetual name to their race and that a pious name.[20]

Some affirm that the Rechabites still dwell in Arabia Felix[21] as a distinct race.[22]

III. LET US LEARN FROM THEIR EXAMPLE.

If they obeyed their earthly father, [how] much more we our heavenly one.

1. The Rechabites obeyed a man in ordinances of his own invention[,] and ought not we to obey a God[?][23]

2. They owed not so much to Jonadab

as we to our best friend & Saviour.
3. They were not reminded of their duty as we.
4. His commands were harder than our Lord's — Oh can it be that the sons of Jonadab served their father & we the sons of Israel's God refuse to obey.
  Father aid me in pleading thy cause.
498

Zech XIII.1. A fountain opened.   279
How well do the various sacred writers, living at various periods, in diverse countries all agree. They unanimously point to the bleeding Lamb.
I. The Fountain. Jesus is so called as refreshing the thirsty, irrigating the barren, curing the sick. a Fountain from his unfailing supply. Open so that every needy sinner has a large welcome.
II. The time of opening. In Election's eternal covenant — In Redemption. In the applied world.
III. The reason of it's opening. For sin & for uncleanness to wash it away, to remove it from us. Not works, but sin it is opened for.
IV. For whom. The House of David. All who have experience somewhat like his. "the people of Jerusalem" the murderers of Jesus, the vilest scum of the earth.
493. 494. 495. 515.

as we to our best friend and Saviour.²⁴

3. They were not reminded of their duty as we.²⁵
4. His commands were harder than our Lord's.²⁶ Oh can it be that the sons of Jonadab served their father and we[,] the sons of Israel's God[,] refuse to obey.

Father aid me in pleading thy cause.

498

A FOUNTAIN OPENED
Zechariah 13:1¹

"In that day there shall be a fountain opened to the house of David and to the inhabitants of Jerusalem for sin and for uncleanness."

How well do the various sacred writers, living at various periods, in diverse countries all agree. They unanimously point to the bleeding Lamb.²

I. THE FOUNTAIN.

Jesus is so called as refreshing the thirsty,³ irrigating the barren,⁴ [and] curing the sick.⁵ A Fountain from his unfailing supply.⁶ <u>Open</u> so that every needy sinner has a large welcome.⁷

II. THE TIME OF OPENING.

In Election's eternal covenant. In Redemption.⁸ In the applied word.⁹

III. THE REASON OF ITS OPENING.

For sin and for uncleanness[,] to wash it away, to remove it from us.¹⁰ Not works, but sin it is opened for.¹¹

IV. FOR WHOM.

The House of David. All who have experience somewhat like his. "The people of Jerusalem,"¹² the murderers of Jesus,¹³ [and] the vilest scum of the earth.

493. 494. 495. 515.

SERMON 278

1. It appears that Charles did not preach another sermon on the text of Jer 35:18–19. Charles originally wrote "Jer. XXXVI.18.19" for his Scripture reference. However, the text Charles actually taught here is Jer 35:18–19, not 36:18–19. This correction has been supplied in the transcription.

2. An alternate past tense of "stayed." "To continue in a place; to forbear departure. . . . To dwell; to belong." Johnson's *Dictionary*, s.v. "To Stay."

3. Cf. Num 10:29–34.

4. Judges 1:16, "And the children of the Kenite, Moses' father in law, went up out of the city of palm trees with the children of Judah into the wilderness of Judah, which lieth in the south of Arad; and they went and dwelt among the people."

5. Judges 4:17, "Howbeit Sisera fled away on his feet to the tent of Jael the wife of Heber the Kenite: for there was peace between Jabin the king of Hazor and the house of Heber the Kenite."

6. First Samuel 15:6, "And Saul said unto the Kenites, Go, depart, get you down from among the Amalekites, lest I destroy you with them: for ye shewed kindness to all the children of Israel, when they came up out of Egypt. So the Kenites departed from among the Amalekites."

7. Second Kings 10:15, "And when he was departed thence, he lighted on Jehonadab the son of Rechab coming to meet him: and he saluted him, and said to him, Is thine heart right, as my heart is with thy heart? And Jehonadab answered, It is. If it be, give me thine hand. And he gave him his hand; and he took him up to him into the chariot."

8. "The shield of the family; the picture of the ensign's armorial." Johnson's *Dictionary*, s.v. "Escutcheon."

9. Though Waterbeach was a village marked by drunkenness (*Autobiography* 1:227–28), Charles was clear here that drinking wine is not a sin in itself.

10. Cf. 1 Pet 1:14–17.
11. Cf. Rom 12:18.
12. Cf. 1 Pet 2:11.
13. Cf. 1 Tim 2:1–2.

14. Cf. 1 Pet 1:13.

15. Cf. Heb 11:13–16.

16. Although neither of Charles's influences on Jeremiah 35 mentioned the "300 years" explicitly, his comments about the Rechabites appear similar to the analysis of John Gill and Matthew Henry, whose respective commentaries Charles used widely. Gill, *An Exposition of the Books of the Prophets of the Old Testament*, 1:569; Matthew Henry, *An Exposition on the Old and New Testament, Wherein Each Chapter is Summed up in Its Contents; The Sacred Text Inserted at Large in Distinct Paragraphs; Each Paragraph Reduced to Its Proper Heads; The Sense Given; and Largely Illustrated with Practical Remarks and Observations. Forming the Most Complete Family Bible Ever Published. Illustrated with Upwards of One Hundred Elegant Engravings, Descriptive of the Material Translations Recorded in the Sacred Writings*, vol. 2 (London: printed by W. and J. Stratford, n.d., The Spurgeon Library), Jer 35:18–19.

17. Cf. Jer 35:11.

18. Cf. Jer 35:1–6.

19. Cf. Jer 35:6–10.

20. Cf. Jer 35:18–19.

21. "Arabia Felix" was the Latin name given to the southern and fertile section of the Arabian Peninsula, now associated with modern-day Yemen. *Encyclopædia Britannica*, 11th ed. (1910), s.v. "Arabia Felix." This region "has been famous from all antiquity for the richness and fertility of its soil, the salubrity of its climate, the number and wealth of its inhabitants, the magnificence of its public buildings, and the splendor of its court." R. L. Playfair, *A History of Arabia Felix or Yemen, from the Commencement of the Christian Era to the Present Time; Including an Account of the British Settlement of Aden* (Bombay: printed for the government at the Education Society's Press, Byculla, 1859), 3.

22. It is possible that Charles was referring to Benjamin of Tudela, a traveler and adventurer whose journals have been preserved. Charles frequently studied Gill's commentary, which referenced this source. Gill wrote, "And if any credit could be given to *Benjamin Tudelensis*, there were *Rechabites* in the twelfth century, since the times of Christ; for he tells us, that in his travels he found a place where *Jews* dwelt, who were called *Rechabites*." Gill, *An Exposition of the Books of the Prophets of the Old Testament* 1:569. It is debatable, however, whether or not Benjamin of Tudela intended to refer to these individuals as Rechabites. Benjamin's translator and commentator, Marcus Nathan Adler, responded to a critic's charge

against Benjamin's report of the Rechabites as "wild," arguing that it was based on a misunderstanding. "Does Benjamin say so? There is no such reading in the MS. of the British Museum. The student, it is thought, will by this time have come to the conclusion that it is the oldest and most trustworthy of our available authorities. The whole misconception has arisen from the fact that the unreliable MS. E and all the printed editions have transposed the letters of רב׳כ and made בכר of it. Rapoport, in the article already referred to, seems to suspect the faulty reading: to justify it, he connects the men of Kheibar with the Rechabites and the sons of Heber the Kenite, basing his argument upon Jer. xxxv, Judges i. 16, I Sam. xxvii. 10, and I Chron. ii. 55." Marcus Nathan Adler, *The Itinerary of Benjamin of Tudela* (London: Henry Frowde, Oxford University Press, 1907), 49. Additionally, a missionary named Joseph Woolf testified to Rechabites in Arabia in 1836, but Adler wrote, "No weight, however, can be attached to his fantastic stories." Adler, *The Itinerary of Benjamin of Tudela*, 47.

23. Cf. Acts 5:29.
24. Cf. John 15:15.
25. Cf. 2 Pet 1:12–15.
26. Cf. Matt 11:28–30.

1. Charles preached two later sermons on this text, "The Open Fountain" (*MTP* 17, Sermon 971) and "The Double Cleansing" (*MTP* 41, Sermon 2431). The first of those later sermons, "The Open Fountain," appears to have a notable amount of overlapping content, as it dealt with the same portion of the verse as this one ("a fountain opened"). The other later sermon, "The Double Cleansing," contains less overlapping content, as it dealt primarily with the last part of the verse ("for sin and for uncleanness"). The overlapping content will be noted below.

2. The following quote is often misattributed to Charles, who was actually quoting another preacher. Still, Charles used the quote more than once and applied it accordingly. Charles wrote, "A Welsh minister who was preaching last Sabbath at the chapel of my dear brother, Jonathan George, was saying, that Christ was the sum and substance of the gospel, and he broke out into this story: . . . 'Well,' said the young man, 'Christ was not in the text; we are not to be preaching Christ always, we must preach what is in the text.' So the old man said, 'Don't you know, young man, that from every town . . . there is a road to London?' 'Yes,' said the young man. 'Ah!' said the old divine 'and so from every text in Scripture, there is a road to the metropolis of the Scriptures, that is Christ. And my dear brother, your business is when you get to a text, to say, "Now what is the road to Christ?" and then preach a sermon running along the road towards the great metropolis -- Christ. And,' said he, 'I have never yet found a text that had not got a road to Christ in it, and if I ever do find one that has not a road to Christ in it, I will make one; I will go over hedge and ditch but I would get at my Master, for the sermon cannot do any good unless there is a savour of Christ in it.'" *NPSP* 5:140.

3. Cf. John 4:13–14.   4. Cf. Ps 105:41; Isa 35:6; 41:18.

5. Cf. Isa 35:6; Mark 1:32–34.

6. Cf. John 7:37–38; Rev 21:6. "According to the verse before us this provision is inexhaustible. There is a *fountain* opened; not a cistern nor a reservoir, but a fountain. A fountain continues still to bubble up, and is as full after fifty years as at the first; and even so the provision and the mercy of God for the forgiveness and the justification of our souls continually flows and overflows." *MTP* 17:40, italics in the original.

7. "For sinners in the last days the fountain is as full, as cleansing, and as free, as for sinners in the first ages of the world. Thus I have testified to you that for

the great necessity of men in this double form, there is a divinely appointed and inexhaustible supply, and it is intended for high and low, rich and poor, for the royal and the ragged, the prince and the pauper." *MTP* 17:40.

8. "When was this fountain opened? When was this divine and inexhaustible supply revealed to men? The answer may be given thus. The fountain was opened for sin and for uncleanness when the Lord Jesus died. God, the everlasting Word, was made flesh and dwelt among us, and in the fulness of time the weight of human sin was laid on him. In order to put away he must die, for death was the penalty for guilt; up to the cross he went through agonies unspeakable, and at the last he yielded up his soul; and when he did so sin was put away, and the fountain for the cleansing of sin was effectually opened." *MTP* 17:40.

9. "Furthermore, the fountain may be said to be opened to each one of us when the gospel is preached to us. 'In that day there shall be a fountain opened,' means secondarily, that whenever the gospel of Jesus Christ is fully and faithfully preached, then the cleansing efficacy of the atonement of Jesus which aforetime was as a sealed fountain, is opened to those who hear. And best of all, according to the connection of the text, this fountain is opened in the day when men repent of sin." *MTP* 17:40.

10. "The text says, not that the filthiness is concealed, that the transgression is excused, but that there is a fountain opened for the effectual removal of sin and uncleanness. In the gospel God never trifles with human sin. We proclaim full, free, immediate forgiveness to the very chief of sinners, but it is not in a way which makes men think that sin is trivial in God's esteem, for there is coupled with the declaration of pardon a description of the way in which God by the sacrifice of his Son renders it possible for him to be merciful without being unjust." *MTP* 17:38.

11. Charles's point here was that the fountain of Christ's cleansing blood is intended to wash away the "uncleanness" of sin, not to discourage works of holiness.

12. Cf. Acts 2:14–39.   13. Cf. Acts 2:23; 3:13–15.

280.   Jer. XXXIII. 13. The telling of the flocks.

This text lays so upon my mind, that contrary to my usual custom I must spiritualize.

The meaning of the text literally is that such peace should prevail that the forsaken plains should be covered with sheep & the tellers should count them.

They were counted in order that the tenth might be the Lord's. —

Now if common flocks be counted, much more shall the flock of God's inheritance.

I. Why they are counted?

1. Because he is so fond of them that never is he more pleasantly employed than when he is counting them.

2. Because he is accountable to his father for them & he desire to see them right.

3. Because they have cost him such a price for purchase & such pains for recovery —

4. He knows they are most apt to stray & forsake him.

THE TELLING *of* THE FLOCKS
Jeremiah 33:13[1]

"In the cities of the mountains, in the cities of the vale, and in the cities of the south, and in the land of Benjamin, and in the places about Jerusalem, and in the cities of Judah, shall the flocks pass again under the hands of him that telleth them, saith the Lord."

This text lays so upon my mind, that contrary to my usual custom[,] I must spiritualize.[2]

The meaning of the text literally is that such peace should prevail that the forsaken plains should be covered with sheep[,] and the tellers should count them.

They were counted in order that the tenth might be the Lord's.[3]

Now if common flocks be counted, [how] much more shall the flocks of God's inheritance.[4]

I. WHY THEY ARE COUNTED?

1. Because he is so fond of them that never is he more pleasantly employed than when he is counting them.[5]
2. Because he is accountable to his father for them and he desires to see them right.[6]
3. Because they have cost him such a price for purchase and such pains for recovery.[7]
4. He knows they are most apt to stray and forsake him.[8]

II. When are they counted?
1. Their first counting was in the day of Election when the Father gave them to the Son.
2. Their second counting was when the price being paid, the Son claimed them as his by purchase
3. At the day of conversion they are told out again
4. Every Sabbath the census of heaven is taken, when they appear in Zion.
5. Death is a dreary hour but it a day of counting, as they emerge from that black Baptism they are recognized as Christ's.
6. At the Consummation of all things they shall once more be counted & none shall be found absent.

Question yourselves whether you have been converted, if not then sad is your condition. but if we can say this then if we have many sheepwashings of trouble, we shall be re-counted in the dreary hour.

Blessed be God, he helped me more in this than I anticipated.

497

THE TELLING OF THE FLOCKS—*Jeremiah 23:13*

II. WHEN ARE THEY COUNTED?

1. Their first counting was in the day of Election when the Father gave them to the Son.[9]
2. Their second counting was when[,] the price being paid, the Son claimed them as his by purchase.[10]
3. At the day of conversion they are told[11] out again.[12]
4. Every Sabbath the census of heaven is taken when they appear in Zion.[13]
5. Death is a dreary hour but is a day of counting[;] as they emerge from that black Baptism they are recognized as Christ's.[14]
6. At the Consummation of all things they shall once more be counted and none shall be found absent.[15]

Question yourselves whether you have been converted; if not then sad is your condition. But if we can say this then if we have many sheepwashings of trouble, we shall be re-counted in the dreary hour.[16]

> Blessed be God, he helped me more in this than I anticipated.[17]

497

SERMON 280

1. It appears that Charles did not preach another sermon on the text of Jer 33:13.

2. Charles urged his students to seek a moderate spiritualized interpretation if it could benefit their congregations. The plain reading, however, should remain in the forefront, as Charles demonstrated here. Charles wrote, "Within limit, my brethren, be not afraid to spiritualize, or to take singular texts. Continue to look out passages of Scripture, and not only give their plain meaning, as you are bound to do, but also draw from them meanings which may not lie upon their surface." *Lectures* 1:103. Charles expressed these limitations through five warnings: "1. *Do not violently strain a text by illegitimate spiritualizing.* 2. *Never spiritualize upon indelicate subjects.* 3. *Never spiritualize for the sake of showing what an uncommonly clever fellow you are.* 4. *Never pervert Scripture* to give it a novel and so-called spiritual meaning. 5. Once more, *in no case allow your audience to forget that the narratives which you spiritualize are facts*, and not mere myths or parables." *Lectures* 1:103–8, italics in the original.

3. Cf. Lev 27:32.   4.   Cf. Deut 32:9; Ps 74:2.

5. Cf. John 10:14–16. Charles was not alone in his spiritualization of this text. John Gill, who Charles may have turned to for commentary, wrote, "This is not to be understood literally, but mystically. So *Jarchi*, *Kimchi*, and *Abarbinel* interpret it of the *Israelites* going in and out under the hands of their king, that goes at the head of them; and the *Targum*, of the King Messiah, and who is no doubt meant. The elect of God, who are intended by the *flocks*, were in eternal election considered as sheep, and by that act of grace were distinguished from others; and so when an exact account was taken of them, their names were written in heaven, and in the Lamb's book of life; and had this seal and mark put upon them, *the Lord knows them that are his*; also in the gift of them to Christ; in the covenant of grace, when they were brought into the bond of that covenant, they were likewise considered as sheep, distinct from others; and were told into the hands of Christ, where they are kept, and who has a most perfect knowledge of them; and in the effectual calling they will again pass under his hands; they are then as sheep that had gone astray, returned to the Shepherd and Bishop of their souls; and when they are separated from others, and special knowledge is taken of them, and Christ's mark, the sanctification of the Spirit, is put upon them; and at the last day, when Christ shall deliver them up to the Father, he will say, lo, I and the children, or sheep, whom thou hast given me; and they will

all be numbered, and not one will be wanting." Gill, *An Exposition of the Books of the Prophets of the Old Testament* 1:558–59, italics in the original.

6. Cf. John 6:37–39; 10:29.   7. Cf. Luke 15:4; John 10:11, 15.

8. Cf. Isa 53:6.   9. Cf. John 10:29.

10. Cf. John 10:14–15; 1 Cor 6:20.

11. "To count; to number." Johnson's *Dictionary*, s.v. "To Tell."

12. Cf. Rev 7:4.   13. Cf. Rev 14:1–3.

14. Cf. 2 Cor 5:8.   15. Cf. Rom 8:29–30; Phil 1:6.

16. "The fact is, that this world is not the place of punishment. There may now and then be eminent judgments; but as a rule God does not in the present state fully punish any man for sin. He allows the wicked to go on in their wickedness.... And, on the other hand, he casts the Christian down; he gives the most affliction to the most pious; perhaps he makes more waves of trouble roll over the breast of the most sanctified Christian than over the heart of any other man living. So, then, we must remember that as this world is not the place of punishment, we are to expect punishment and reward in the world to come; and we must believe that the only reason, then, why God afflicts his people must be this; -- 'In love I correct thee, thy gold to refine, to make thee at length in my likeness to shine.'" *NPSP* 3:453.

17. This unusual autobiographical aside, when the context of the entire sermon is considered, appears to express Charles's thanks to the Lord in helping him to faithfully "spiritualize" his text. Charles once acknowledged the danger of the practice, saying, "An allowable thing carried to excess is a vice, even as fire is a good servant in the grate, but a bad master when raging in a burning house." *Lectures* 1:103. However, Charles's remark indicates that, in his view, he heeded the advice he would later give his students when he said, "[John Bunyan] was a swimmer, but we are mere waders, and must not go beyond our depth." *Lectures* 1:114.

281. Eph. II. 13. The far off made nigh.

Many beautiful & wonderful changes occur in our world but none so great or wonderful as the change when a sinner becomes a saint.

In contemplating the change let us notice

I. Our Distance. "afar off"

Not a little way off but far away. How far none can tell. So far that not one ray of the Sun of Righteousness could be seen, or one word of Jehovah heard.

By nature & practise, by open or covert sin, in words & actions in some way we were far.

II. Our Nearness. "brought nigh"

Living at a distance is truly death. But God would not suffer us to remain so. As we would not come nigh, he brought us nigh.

We are now by relationship, love & communion made nigh to God. & to his people. How near true christians are to one another. Members of the same body. Heirs of the same inheritance.

III. The bond. "the blood of Christ" "in Christ Jesus"

Without this we should still remain at the same awful distance, but this attracted us. This too is the bond of union between all true followers of the Lamb. This cement unites the living stones.

My soul bathe thyself wholly in his blood.

500. 501. 502. 503.

THE FAR-OFF MADE NIGH
Ephesians 2:13[1]

"But now in Christ Jesus ye who sometimes were far off are made nigh by the blood of Christ."

Many beautiful and wonderful changes occur in our world[,] but none so great or wonderful as the change when a sinner becomes a saint. In contemplating the change Let us notice[:]

I. OUR DISTANCE, *"afar off"*

Not a little way off but far away. How far none can tell. So far that not one ray of the Sun of Right.[2] could be seen or one word of Jehovah heard.[3]

By nature and practise, by open or covert sin, in words and actions in some way we were far.[4]

II. OUR NEARNESS, *"brought nigh"*

Living at a distance is truly death. But God would not suffer us to remain so. As we would not come nigh, he brought us nigh.

We are now by relationship, love[,] and communion[5] made nigh to God, and to his people.[6] How near true Christians are to one another. Members of the same body.[7] Heirs of the same inheritance.[8]

III. THE BOND, *"the blood of Christ" "in Christ Jesus."*

Without this we should still remain at the same awful distance, but this attracted us.[9] This too is the bond of union between all true followers of the Lamb. This cement unites the living stones.[10]

> My soul bathe thyself wholly in his blood.

500. 501. 502. 503.[11]

SERMON 281

1. It appears that Charles preached a later sermon on this text, "Nearness to God" (*MTP* 15, Sermon 851). While there is some overlapping content, the later sermon is structured differently and does not appear to have been influenced by this former one. Overlapping content will be noted below.

2. Abbr., "Righteousness." Cf. Mal 4:2.

3. Cf. Amos 8:11.

4. In his later sermon "Nearness to God" (*MTP* 15, Sermon 851), Charles illustrated humanity's distance from God with three illustrations: the fall of Adam, "You and I were farther gone than Adam outside of Eden, with a gospel promise newly given him. We were not on the threshold of Paradise, but we were far off by wicked works. Our natural position as Gentile sinners was not with Adam outside the gate, but with the nations that knew not God, when they had wandered farthest away from Paradise, had become most estranged from God and had set up gods many, and lords many, and had polluted and defiled themselves with all manner of uncleanness" (*MTP* 15:40); the unclean placed outside Israel's camp, "Outside the camp of Israel altogether, you would have seen a company of miserable wretches who herded together as best they could—lepers, unclean, driven without the camp. This is more like our position" (*MTP* 15:42); and Israel trembling at Mount Sinai, "At the base of Mount Zion you have stood trembling while we have warned you of the judgment to come, and told you of the indignation of God against sin . . . but alas! what has been the result of your fear and your vow? You have gone back farther from God, and have plunged anew into the world's idolatry, and are today worshipping yourselves, your pleasures, your sins, or your righteousness; and when the Lord cometh, the nearness of opportunity which you have enjoyed will prove to have been to you a most fearful responsibility, and nothing more." *MTP* 15:43–44.

5. "We see our nearness to God in the act of praise. Oftentimes in praising him, we have taken the wings of seraphs, and passed up into the glory and magnified the Lord, but it has always been through him who by his precious blood makes our praises acceptable to the Most High. We who have believed, come very near to God in the act of baptism, for we are baptised into the name of the Father, and of the Son, and of the Holy Ghost. Wicked and base is he who has dared to touch that ordinance, unless he sincerely desired fellowship in the Lord's death.

The nearness we get to God in baptism by faith, depends upon whether or no we see the blood there, and behold Jesus as buried for us. Then in the Lord's-supper, what nearness is there! but it all lies in the blood. We get no nearness through the wine, no nearness through the bread; the elements are nothing of themselves; it is only when we get to feel that our Lord's flesh is meat indeed, and his blood drink indeed, that we draw near to him." *MTP* 15:47–48.

6. Cf. 1 Pet 2:9–10. 7. Cf. Rom 12:5; Eph 2:14–19.

8. Cf. Rom 8:17.

9. "Beloved, you thus see that we are made nigh because the blood of Christ has sealed a covenant between us and God, and has for ever taken away the sin which separated us from God. Experimentally, we are brought nigh by the application of the blood to our conscience. We see that sin is pardoned, and bless the God who has saved us in so admirable a manner, and then we who hated him before come to love him; we who had no thought towards him desire to be like him. We are experimentally and in our own souls, drawn and attracted to God by the blood of Jesus. The great attracting loadstone of the gospel is the doctrine of the cross. To preach the atoning sacrifice of Jesus is the shortest and surest way, under God's Holy Spirit, to draw those that are far off, mentally and spiritually, very near unto God." *MTP* 15:39.

10. Cf. 1 Pet 2:5.

11. Interestingly, the preaching occasion numbers in the bottom left corner of the page indicate that Charles preached this sermon four times in a row, and that he did not repeat it afterwards.

Ephes. V. 2.   Walk in Love.

We can scarcely conceive what would have been the state of society in our world if Adam had retained his first estate. Supposing that there had been, as now, the same distinctions of rich & poor, of old & young, nation & tribe & family, how different would it yet have been. There would be no jail, no punishments. Men on the exchange would easily transact their business, the poor would not be slighted the rich would not be envied. But this pleasing picture is but a mere dissolving view, the reality is different.

Is there no means of restoring this earth to her former state. Come let us see. Here we have it, Here it is in these few words,

"Walk in love, as Christ also hath loved us.

By divine Help I shall speak.

I. Of the heavenly precept.
II. Of the heavenly exemplar.
III. I will endeavour to back the precept with a few arguments.

WALK *in* LOVE
Ephesians 5:2[1]

> "And walk in love, as Christ also hath loved us, and hath given himself for us an offering and a sacrifice to God for a sweet smelling savour."

We can scarcely conceive what would have been the state of society in our world if Adam had retained his first estate.[2] Supposing that there had been, as now, the same distinctions of rich and poor, of old and young, nation and tribe and family, how different would it yet have been. There would be no jail, no punishments. Men on the exchange would easily transact their business, the poor would not be slighted, the rich would not be envied. But this pleasing picture is but a mere dissolving[3] view[;] the reality is different.

Is there no means of restoring this earth to her former state[?] Come let us see. Here we have it. Here it is in these few words,

"Walk in love, as Christ also hath loved us.["]

By divine Help I shall speak:

I. OF THE HEAVENLY PRECEPT.

II. OF THE HEAVENLY EXEMPLAR.[4]

III. I WILL ENDEAVOUR TO BACK THE PRECEPT WITH A FEW ARGUMENTS.

I. A Heavenly Precept. "Walk in love".
I call this heavenly because it is practised in heaven & because all heaven's commands, precepts & sermons to man are epitomized in these few words. The ten commands are all here. Both tables are here in one line.
Let us for the sake of better understanding the text look at it more closely.
1. It mentions a cardinal grace. "Love"
2. It tells us our behaviour to it, "walk in
1. It mentions a cardinal grace called "love". A word too often vilely misplaced on things whose proper name is lust. Natural love between relations & friends is pleasant to the eye & helps to smooth the roughness of our earthly journey, but that is but as water when compared with Christian love which is as heavenly wine.
It is the brightest of the train — it does not say walk "in faith" for though this is to be our rule between God & ourselves, it cannot lead us with respect to our fellow-creatures. "Love" is opposed to all "anger" "hatred", "envy", "selfishness", & "neglect".
It is that grace which combined with faith enabled so many martyrs to endure the fire, gave strength & eloquence to many

WALK IN LOVE—*Ephesians 5:2*

I. A HEAVENLY PRECEPT. "*Walk in love.*"

I call this heavenly because it is practised in heaven[5] and because all heaven's commands, precepts[,] and sermons to man are epitomized in these few words.[6] The ten commands are all here. Both tables[7] are here in one line.

Let us for the sake of better understanding the text look at it more closely.

1. It mentions a cardinal grace.[8] "Love"

2. It tells us our behaviour to it. "Walk in" it[.]

   1. It mentions a cardinal grace called "love." A word too often vilely misplaced on things whose proper name is lust.[9] Natural love between relations and friends is pleasant to the eye and helps to smooth the roughness of our earthly journey, but that is but as water when compared with Christian love which is as heavenly wine.[10]

   It is the brightest of the train.[11] It does not say walk "in faith," for though this is to be our rule between God and ourselves, it cannot lead us with respect to our fellow-creatures. "Love" is opposed to all "anger,"[12] "hatred,"[13] "envy,"[14] "selfishness,"[15] or "neglect."[16]

   It is that grace which combined with faith enabled so many martyrs to endure the fire,[17] gave strength and eloquence to many a faithful minister, flaps the wings of angels, fires the souls of Christians, guides us to the sick-chamber, the distressed house, the dying bed. Love sends out its arms as far as the world's wide bounds extend & links the most distant lands into one family.

2. It tells us our behaviour to it. "Walk in" it. Many men know not the meaning of this word, to get, to keep, to revenge, to suspect, these they daily practise but to bear love on their forehead is a thing with them either Utopian or Contemptible.

Others again affect to love this precept, it is often in their mouth, it sits on the tip of the tongues but unhappily while they can talk of love they cannot "walk in" love. Some again are loving by starts & practise this heavenly grace in fits longer or shorter according to occasion. Now this is not the idea meant by "walk" in love. it means a constant & steady course of love.

Walk not with it, but in it. Not as a Companion to you but as a part of the very texture of your soul. To all whether friend or foe, whether good or evil "walk in love."

WALK IN LOVE—*Ephesians 5:2*

a faithful minister, flaps the wings of angels, fires the souls of Christians, [and] guides us to the sick-chamber, the distressed house,[18] [or] the dying bed. Love sends out its arms as far as the world's wide bounds extend[19] and links the most distant lands into one family.

2. It tells us our behaviour to it. "Walk in" it[.]

Many men know not the meaning of this word[.] [T]o get, to keep, to revenge, to suspect, these they daily practise, but to bear love on their forehead is a thing with them either Utopian or Contemptible.

Others again affect[20] to love this precept[.] [I]t is often in their mouth, it sits on the tip of the tongues[,] but unhappily while they can talk of love[,] they cannot "walk in["] love.[21]

Some again are loving by starts[,][22] and practise this heavenly grace in fits longer or shorter according to occasion. Now this is not the idea meant by "walk" in love. [I]t means a constant and steady course of love.[23]

Walk not <u>with</u> it, but <u>in</u> it. Not as a companion to you but as a part of the very texture of your soul. To all whether friend or foe, whether good or evil[24] "walk in love."

Did we practise this in the church, what peace, harmony & unity would exist. Did we use it in daily life how many trials we should avoid, Could we look on sinners thus, how often would our eyes run with tears for their sins & our hearts yearn for their conversion — Sweet precept. "Walk in love."

II. A heavenly Exemplar "As Christ also hath loved us."

The Holy Scriptures do not give us bare commands & demand obedience, but they act most wisely by supplying us with examples of the virtues they inculcate.

If faith be commanded, Abraham, Moses, Joshua, Gideon, David, Daniel &c rise up and set us a high standard.

Is decision recommended, the 3 Jews, Daniel, Joseph &c commend it.

Job advises patience, Moses meekness. Habbakuk trust in Providence, Peter boldness. Paul zeal, Dorcas charity. But who shall stand as the great example of love. So heavenly a precept

WALK IN LOVE—*Ephesians 5:2*

Did we practise this in the church, what peace, harmony and unity would exist.[25] Did we use it in daily life how many trials we should avoid. Could we look on sinners thus,[26] how often would our eyes run with tears for their sins and our hearts yearn for their conversion. Sweet precept. "Walk in love."

II. A HEAVENLY EXEMPLAR "*As Christ also hath loved us*'

The Holy Scriptures do not give us bare commands and demand obedience[,] but they act most wisely by supplying us with examples of the virtues they inculcate.

If faith be commanded, Abraham,[27] Moses,[28] Joshua,[29] Gideon,[30] David,[31] Daniel,[32] and [etc.] rise up and set us a high standard. Is decision recommended, the 3 Jews,[33] Daniel,[34] Joseph,[35] etc. commend it.

Job advises patience,[36] Moses meekness,[37] Habbakuk trust in Providence,[38] Peter boldness,[39] Paul zeal,[40] [and] Dorcas charity.[41] But who shall stand as the great example of love[?] So heavenly a precept demands a heavenly pattern who shall it be? Christ, the Son of God. No one else will be suitable. If we say love as David loved Jonathan that would be a pattern of friendship but not of love of enemies, love of those who provoke us to anger. —

Jesus Christ alone suffices for our example. If we think of the amazing extent & unparralleled intensity of Jesus love, we shall indeed be forced to cry out, "We can never equal this."

We cannot love in the same measure as Jesus — therefore it means let us love as much as possible, let us not be afraid lest we should be too loving for we can never outstrip infinity or excel Christ.

But as to the manner we are to love in the same manner as Christ loves. This is spoken to saints, to whom Jesus has a peculiar regard. Let us think how Christ hath loved us.

1. He loved us disinterestedly, we had done nothing to deserve his love, nor were we worth loving — so should we love even those who deserve it not & those whom we think never will be of service to us.

demands a heavenly pattern[.] [W]ho shall it be? Christ, the Son of God.[42]

No one else will be suitable. If we say love as David loved Jonathan[43] that would be a pattern of friendship but not of love of enemies, love of those who provoke us to anger.[44]

Jesus Christ alone suffices for our example. If we think of the amazing extent and unparalleled intensity of Jesus['s] love, we shall indeed be forced to cry out, "We can never equal this."

We cannot love in the same measure as Jesus, therefore it means let us love as much as possible, let us not be afraid lest we should be too loving for we can never outstrip infinity or excel Christ.

But as to the manner[,] we are to love in the same manner as Christ loves.[45] This is spoken to saints, to whom Jesus has a peculiar regard. Let us think how Christ hath loved us.[46]

1. He loved us disinterestedly.[47] We had done nothing to deserve his love, nor were we worth loving. So should we love even those who deserve it not and those whom we think never will be of service to us.[48]

2. He loved us constantly. His love is unchangeable — so let ours be ever the same — let us always love the brethren.
3. He loved us so much as to die, he loved us really. So let our love be self sacraficing.
4. He loved us sympathetically for we cannot suffer alone — he feels at his heart all our sighs and our groans.

Consider he loved us & we are the worst of all, let us then love —

III. Let me urge this upon you.
1. Because thus you will derive very much benefit to your self. You will recieve love again into your own soul. You will never regret it.

If you would be happy, Love.
2. Because in proportion as you do this, will you be truly what you profess to be. A Christian.
3. Because Religion can only be spread by love, or at least by nothing so much. —
4. Love the brethren for their own

WALK IN LOVE—*Ephesians 5:2*

2. He loved us constantly.[49] His love is unchangeable. So let our [love] be ever the same[,] let us always love the brethren.[50]

3. He loved us so much as to die,[51] he loved us really, so let our love be self sacrificing.[52]

4. He loved us sympathetically for we cannot suffer alone[;] he feels at his heart all our sighs and our groans.[53]

Consider he loved <u>US</u> and we are the worst of all,[54] let us then love.

III. LET ME URGE THIS UPON YOU.

1. Because thus you will derive very much benefit to your self. You will receive love again into your own soul. You will never regret it.

   If you would be happy, Love.

2. Because in proportion as you do this, will you be truly what you profess to be. A Christian.[55]

3. Because Religion can only be spread by love or at least by nothing so much.[56]

4. Love the brethren for their own

sakes, love them for Jesus' sake, love them because you all are hated by the world, & love will comfort.

5. Love, because thus will you be fit to be the companion of angels & perfect saints in heaven.

6. Love because Jesus loved, "as" may mean since, or because he hath loved us. Now oh how I wish I had eloquence that I might in telling words let all the wounds of Jesus speak & put a tongue into each drop of his blood that should cry aloud. "Walk in Love as Christ also hath loved you." —

Give me oh Father thy smile
oh Son thy love
oh Spirit thine influences.

504. 506. 542. 563.

sakes, love them for Jesus'[s] sake,[57] love them because you all are hated by the world,[58] and love will comfort.[59]

5. Love because thus will you be fit to be the companion of angels and perfect saints in heaven.[60]

6. Love because Jesus loved, "<u>as</u>" may mean since, or because he hath loved us.[61] Now Oh how I wish I had eloquence that I might in telling words let all the wounds of Jesus speak[,] and put a tongue into each drop of his blood that should cry aloud, "Walk in Love as Christ also hath loved you."

> Give me Oh Father thy smile[,]
>   Oh Son thy love[,]
>   Oh Spirit thine influences.

504. 506. 542. 563.

1. It appears that Charles did not preach a later sermon on this text.

2. "Rank; quality . . . A person of high rank." Johnson's *Dictionary*, s.v. "Estate."

3. "To fall to nothing. To melt away in pleasures." Johnson's *Dictionary*, s.v. "To Dissolve."

4. "A pattern; an example to be imitated." Johnson's *Dictionary*, s.v. "Exemplar."

5. Cf. 1 Cor 13:8–13. 6. Cf. Matt 22:34–40; Mark 12:28–34.

7. The two "tables" of the Ten Commandments refer to the first four commands (love for God) and the following six commands (love for neighbor). Charles saw both tables reflected in this one command.

8. Cf. 1 Cor 13:1–3, 13.

9. "Counterfeited love is one of the vilest things under heaven. That heavenly word, *love*, has been trailed in the mire of unclean passion and filthy desire. The licentiousness, which comes of the worship of Venus, has dared to take to itself a name which belongs only to the pure worship of Jehovah. Now, the works which counterfeit love are these: '*adultery*, fornication, uncleanness, lasciviousness.' To talk of 'love' when a man covets his neighbour's wife, or when a woman violates the command, 'Thou shalt not commit adultery,' is little less than sheer blasphemy against the holiness of love. It is not love, but lust; love is an angel, and lust a devil." *MTP* 30:291, italics in the original.

10. Cf. Gal 6:10; 1 Pet 3:8.

11. "A series; a consecution; either local or mental." Johnson's *Dictionary*, s.v. "Train."

12. Cf. Eph 4:25–27. 13. Cf. Gal 5:19–20; 1 John 4:20.

14. Cf. 1 Cor 13:4; Gal 5:21. 15. Cf. Rom 12:10; 1 Cor 13:5.

16. Cf. Rom 12:13; Jas 1:27.

17. "Let me bring thee down through the ages of the rack and the wheel, the times of stocks and inquisitions; let me tell thee of martyrs who clapped their hands in the

flames, and while their limbs were burning at the stake, could yet sing a carol, as if it were Christmas-day in their hearts, though it was Ash-day to their bodies. How often you find those who are foremost in suffering, foremost in joy!" MTP 11 629.

18. At the end of one of his sermons, Charles called for a collection for St. Thomas Hospital. Charles wrote, "I have done when I have said this — if our Lord was thus sympathetic, let us be tender to our fellow-men. Let us not restrain our tenderer feelings, but encourage them. Love is the brightest of the graces, and most sweetly adorns the gospel. Love to the sorrowing, the suffering, the needy, is a charming flower, which grows in the garden of a renewed heart. Cultivate it! Make your love practical! Love the poor, not in word only, but in actual gifts to them! Love the sick, and help them to a cure!" MTP 36:324.

19. "Sit down and listen to that sorrowful yet majestic demand, 'Whom shall I send, and who will go for us?' and then respond, 'Ready, aye ready; ready for anything to which our Redeemer calls us.' Let those who love him, as they perceive all around them the terrible token of the world's dire need, cry in an agony of Christian love, 'Here am I; send me.'" MTP 23:252.

20. "To aim at; to endeavour after; spoken of persons. . . . To make a shew of something; to study the appearance of any thing; with some degree of hypocrisy." Johnson's *Dictionary*, s.v. "To Affect."

21. Cf. Jas 2:14–16.

22. "Sudden fit; intermitted [*sic*] action." Johnson's *Dictionary*, s.v. "Start."

23. Cf. 1 Cor 13:7.   24. Cf. Matt 5:44–47.

25. "Whatever be the enmity without, we must love one another. If we do not walk in love we certainly cannot have prosperity. God alone can give peace to a church, and he only gives it by sanctifying its members, stirring them up to good works, keeping them in sacred activity, making them fit to labor for him, and working in them to do that which is well-pleasing in his sight. When you hear of disturbances in churches you need not so much seek to compose the differences among the members as to amend the men themselves." MTP 23:450

26. "Oh, how we ought to love sinners, since Jesus loved us, and died for us while we were yet sinners! We must care for drunkards while they still pass round the

cup; swearers even while we hear them swear; and profligates while we mourn to see them polluting our midnight streets. We must not wait till we see some better thing in them, but feel an intense interest for them as what they are—straying and lost. When the sheep is torn with the thorns of the waste places, and is sick, and worn to skin and bones with long wanderings and hungerings, we must seek its restoration, though we see in it no desire to submit itself to the Shepherd's care and rule. Such was our Saviour's love to us: such be our love to lost ones." *MTP* 35:244.

27. Cf. Gen 15:6; 22:1–18; Heb 11:8–10, 17–19.

28. Cf. Heb 11:24–29.   29. Cf. Josh 5:13–6:27; Heb 11:30.

30. Cf. Judges 6; Heb 11:32.   31. Cf. 2 Sam 7; Heb 11:32.

32. Cf. Daniel 6; Heb 11:33.   33. Cf. Dan 3:16–18.

34. Cf. Dan 6:10.   35. Cf. Gen 39:12; Heb 11:22.

36. Cf. Jas 5:10–11.   37. Cf. Num 12:3.

38. Cf. Hab 3:17–18.   39. Cf. Acts 4:13.

40. Cf. 2 Cor 11:23–29.   41. Cf. Acts 9:36–42.

42. Cf. John 13:34; 15:12; Eph 5:25–27; 1 Pet 2:21–22.

43. Cf. 1 Sam 18:1.   44. Cf. Matt 5:43–48; Rom 5:8.

45. "What a path to walk in! 'Walk in love.' What a well-paved way it is! 'As Christ also hath loved us.' What a blessed Person for us to follow in that divinely royal road! It would have been hard for us to tread this way of love, if it had not been that his blessed feet marked out the track for us. We are to love as Christ also hath loved us; and the question which will often solve difficulties is this, 'What would Jesus Christ do in my case?' What he would have done, that we may do: 'Walk in love, as Christ also hath loved us.' And if we want to know how far that love may be carried, we need not be afraid of going too far in self-denial; we may even make a sacrifice of ourselves for love of God and men, for here is our model: 'As Christ also hath loved us, and hath given himself for us, an offering and a sacrifice to God for a sweet-smelling savour.'" *MTP* 41:94.

46. Charles may have been influenced by Charles Simeon in this section of the sermon. Simeon wrote, "In the circumstance before notice, we cannot resemble (Christ); for 'no man can redeem his brother, or give to God a ransom for him.' Nevertheless in the love which instigated him to this we may resemble him. Our love, like his, should be, disinterested . . . generous . . . self-denying . . . (and) constant." Charles Simeon, *Horae Homileticae or Discourses Upon the Whole Scriptures*, vol. 10 (London: printed by Richard Watts, 1820, The Spurgeon Library), 70–71.

47. Samuel Johnson defined "interest" as "Concern; advantage; good," or as "Share; part in any thing," denoting benefit. Johnson's *Dictionary*, s.v. "Interest."

48. Cf. Luke 14:12–14. Simeon wrote, "In the exercise of our love we should not consider whether the objects of it will ever be able to make us any suitable return: we should shew love in every possible way, without so much as desiring any return from man, or even desiring that our exercise of it should be known; yea, even though we knew that it would only be requited with evil. We should love our very enemies." Simeon, *Horae Homileticae* 10:70.

49. Cf. Jer 31:3; Rom 8:35–39. Simeon commented, "'Whom our Lord loved, he loved to the end.' There were many occasions whereon his immediate Disciples displeased him: but he did not therefore 'withdraw his mercy from them, or shut up his loving-kindness in displeasure.' There are occasions also whereon we shall be called to exercise forbearance and forgiveness one towards another; and we ought to meet those occasions with love proportioned to them." Simeon, *Horae Homileticae* 10:71.

50. Cf. Heb 13:1.   51. Cf. John 3:16.

52. Simeon wrote, "Our blessed Lord 'emptied himself of all the glory of heaven,' and endured all the wrath of an offended God; and became a curse for himself, in order to deliver us from the curse which our iniquities had deserved. And shall we decline exercising our love, because it may be attended with some pain or difficulty on our part? No: we should not hesitate even to lay down life itself, if by so doing we may promote the eternal welfare of our brethren." Simeon, *Horae Homileticae* 10:71. Additionally, it appears that Charles misspelled "sacrificing" and instead wrote "sacraficing." The correct spelling has been supplied in the transcription.

53. Cf. Heb 4:15.

54. Cf. 1 Tim 1:15–16. "The chief of sinners comprises so numerous a body, I believe every one of us must come in the list in some shape or other, and I know this—if ever you and I are saved, if God shall give us very great mercy, we shall feel that we were the greatest sinners. When Paul saw how kindly his Master treated him, it seemed to break his heart—'What! did I ever curse that Christ who has blessed me? He that is so rich in lovingkindness, did I ever spurn him?' Verily now I do think I have had the blackest sight of sin when I have had the brightest sight of mercy. . . . It is great mercy that sets forth our great sin, for we only come to reckon ourselves the chief of sinners when we see the great love of God." *MTP* 9:524.

55. Cf. 1 John 3:16–20.

56. Charles believed that a Christian's character was a crucial aspect of evangelism. He wrote, "Take it for granted, dear friends, as a truth which your own observation and experience will make every day more and more clear, that your power to spread religion in the world must mainly depend upon your own personal character, of course, in absolute reliance upon the Holy Spirit. . . . Your power to achieve this noble purpose [of winning souls] must largely depend upon your own personal consistency. It little availeth what I say if I do the reverse. The world will not care about my testimony with the lip, unless there be also a testimony in my daily life for God, for truth, for holiness, for everything that is honest, lovely, pure, and of good report. There is that in a Christian's character which the world, though it may persecute the man himself, learns to value." *MTP* 42:278. One of the most powerful aspects of a Christian's character is a deep love for sinners. "O beloved, I pray you, love the sons of men! Somebody has asked, 'How are we to convert sinners?' That is not our work; it is only the Spirit of God who can do that; but what we can do is this, we can love sinners to Christ." *MTP* 52:227.

57. Cf. John 13:34.   58. Cf. John 15:18.

59. Cf. 2 Cor 7:5–7.

60. "What shall I say to those of you, my friends, who have no acquaintance with God? You certainly cannot be fitted for heaven. Your cause is not committed to

him. He is doing nothing for you. He has not begun the good work in you. You live in this world as if there were no God. The thought, the stupendous thought of his 'Being' does not affect you. You would not act any differently if there were twenty Gods, or if there were no God.... If thou breathe but a desire towards him, that desire shall be accepted and fulfilled. He will yet begin to work in thee that gracious preparation which shall make thee meet to be a partaker of the inheritance of the saints in light." *MTP* 62:549.

61. Cf. 1 John 4:19.

283. Matt IV. 19. Fishers of Men.
This is an Ordination Sermon by Jesus Christ for thus Peter & Andrew were called and ordained to the Ministry.

It is a good plan to try & speak to every man in some way with an observation on his work or trade. Let us learn like Jesus to take our text from our hearers.

This was a special call and was most readily obeyed by both.

Let us see wherein ministers are fishermen.

I. They have a very wide sphere. The sea is the fisherman's water & the world is a minister's parish. The fisherman cannot fish in the whole of the ocean, nor can we preach in the whole world. Yet let us try. These are our Marching orders.

2. Fisherman have an opportunity of exploring the wonders of the Lord in the deep.— They from the nature of their calling must search the Scriptures, must meditate on divine things & must sound the depth

FISHERS *of* MEN
Matthew 4:19[1]

"And he saith unto them, Follow me, and I will make you fishers of men.'

This is an Ordination Sermon by Jesus Christ for thus Peter and Andrew were called and ordained to the ministry.[2]

It is a good plan to try and speak to every man in some way with an observation on his work or trade. Let us learn[,] like Jesus[,] to take our text from our hearers.

This was a special call and was most readily obeyed by both.

Let us see wherein ministers are fishermen[:]

1. They have a very wide sphere. The sea is the fisherman's water and the world is a minister's parish.[3] The fisherman cannot fish in the whole of the ocean, nor can we preach in the whole world. Yet let us try. These are our Marching orders.

2. Fisherman have an opportunity of exploring the wonders of the Lord in the deep. They[,] from the nature of their calling[,] must search the Scriptures, must meditate on divine things, and must sound the depth

of subjects other can but partially understand.

3. Fishermen must be prepared for storms. He that regardeth the clouds will not fish. Stormy weather is the lot of every faithful minister.

4. Fishermen cast their nets for fish. We want souls, not stones nor gold. Let us be applauded by all the world, if no fish are taken we reckon our day to be lost.

5. Fishermen have need of skill & study is required. So must we keep our eyes open to watch every opportunity of catching fish — we must know what bait to use, what are the signs of the heavens.

6. A fisherman's life is laborious. So should every minister's be. He must all the week long be diligent & ever gleaning for the Sabbath & be ever ready for every good word & work.

7. Fishermen need patience. they often toil for nothing but they must

FISHERS OF MEN—*Matthew 4:19*

of subjects other[s] can but partially understand.

3. Fishermen must be prepared for storms. He that regardeth the clouds will not fish. Stormy weather is the lot of every faithful minister.[4]

4. Fishermen cast their nets for fish. We want souls, not stones nor gold. Let us be applauded by all the world, if no fish are taken we reckon our day to be lost.[5]

5. Fishermen have need of skill and study is required. So must we keep our eyes open to watch every opportunity of catching fish. We must know what bait to use, what are the signs of the heavens.[6]

6. A fisherman's life is laborious. So should every minister's be. He must all the week long be diligent and ever gleaning for the Sabbath[,] and be ever ready for every good word and work.[7]

7. Fishermen need patience. They often toil for nothing but they must

put down the net again & again.
 We are not responsible for success but for our labour we must still persevere,
8. The Fisherman's success depends upon God & so does ours. We can catch none unless we have his aid
 But, blessed be his name, he helpeth us.
Christ must <u>make</u> fishers of men. No one else can <u>make</u> a minister — though man can <u>make</u> a scholar,
1. Pray for the fishermen,
2. Sinner behold all this trouble is about you, yet you think Christ is not worth a moment's trouble.
3. Toiling brother, be of good cheer soon shall we gain port & receive a hearty welcome.
 Lord <u>make</u> me a fisher of men.

505

put down the net again and again.

We are not responsible for success[,] but for our labour we must still persevere.⁸

8. The Fisherman's success depends upon God and so does ours. We can catch none unless we have his aid.⁹

But, blessed be his name, he helpeth us.

Christ must <u>make</u> fishers of men.¹⁰ No one else can <u>make</u> a minister, though man can <u>make</u> a scholar.¹¹

1. Pray for the fishermen.
2. Sinner behold all this trouble is about you, yet you think Christ is not worth a moment's trouble.
3. Toiling brother, be of good cheer[.] Soon shall we gain port and receive a hearty welcome.

Lord <u>make</u> me a fisher of men.

505

1. It appears that Charles preached two later sermons on this text, "Peter's Three Calls" (*MTP* 12, Sermon 702) and "How to Become Fishers of Men" (*MTP* 32, Sermon 1906). The first of these, "Peter's Three Calls," is structurally different and has little, if any, overlapping content. The second later sermon contains significant overlapping content in its third point, as Charles meditated on the figure of the fisherman, which is the substance of this sermon. The overlapping content is noted below.

2. Charles may have been influenced by Matthew Henry on this point. As Henry explained this passage, "It was an instance of *ordination*, and appointment to the work of the ministry. When Christ, as a Teacher, set up his great school, one of his first works was to appoint ushers, or under masters, to be employed in the work of instruction. Now he began to give gifts unto men, to put the treasure into earthen vessels. It was an early instance of his care for the church." Matthew Henry, *An Exposition of the New Testament* 1:65. While Charles rejected any ideas of human ordination beyond the local church, he did recognize a divine ordination to preach, and this is likely what he was referring to in this sermon. "Is not the Divine call the real ordination to preach, and the call of the church the only ordination to the pastorate? The church is competent, under the guidance of the Holy Spirit, to do her own work; and if she calls in her sister-churches, let her tell them what she has done, in such terms that they will never infer that they are called upon to complete the work." *Autobiography* 1:356.

3. Cf. Matt 28:18–20. The Church of England divided its regions by parishes for their priests, but here Charles made the point that the whole world is to be the sphere of ministry for the minister of the gospel.

4. "The fisherman is a *daring man*. He tempts the boisterous sea. A little brine in his face does not hurt him; he has been wet through a thousand times, it is nothing to him. He never expected when he became a deep-sea fisherman that he was going to sleep in the lap of ease. So the true minister of Christ who fishes for souls will never mind a little risk. He will be bound to do or say many a thing that is very unpopular; and some Christian people may even judge his utterances to be too severe. He must do and say that which is for the good of souls. It is not his to entertain a question as to what others will think of his doctrine, or of him; but in the name of the Almighty God he must feel, 'If the sea roar and

the fullness thereof, still at my Master's command I will let down the net.'" *MTP* 32:347, italics in the original.

5. "Well, if any person in the world said to you, 'I am a fisherman, but I have never caught anything,' you would wonder how he could be called a fisherman. A farmer who never grew any wheat, or any other crop—is he a farmer? When Jesus Christ says, 'Follow me, and I will make you fishers of men,' he means that you shall really catch men—that you really shall save some; for he that never did get any fish is not a fisherman. He that never saved a sinner after years of work is not a minister of Christ. If the result of his life-work is nil, he made a mistake when he undertook it." *MTP* 32:347–48.

6. "The fisherman in his own craft is *intelligent and watchful*. It looks very easy, I dare say, to be a fisherman, but you would find that it was no child's play if you were to take a real part in it. There is an art in it, from the mending of the net right on to the pulling it to shore. How diligent the fisherman is to prevent the fish leaping out of the net! I heard a great noise one night in the sea, as if some huge drum were being beaten by a giant; and I looked out, and I saw that the fishermen of Mentone were beating the water to drive the fish into the net, or to keep them from leaping out when they had once encompassed them with it. Ah, yes! and you and I will often have to be watching the corners of the gospel net lest sinners who are almost caught should make their escape. They are very crafty, these fish, and they use this craftiness in endeavoring to avoid salvation. We shall have to be always at our business, and to exercise all our wits, and more than our own wits, if we are to be successful fishers of men." *MTP* 32:346–47, italics in the original.

7. "The fisherman is a *very laborious person*. It is not at all an easy calling. He does not sit in an armchair and catch fish. He has to go out in rough weathers. If he that regardeth the clouds will not sow, I am sure that he that regardeth the clouds will never fish. If we never do any work for Christ except when we feel up to the mark, we shall not do much. If we feel that we will not pray because we cannot pray, we shall never pray, and if we say, 'I will not preach today because I do not feel that I could preach,' we shall never preach any preaching that is worth the preaching." *MTP* 32:347, italics in the original.

8. "A fisherman who gets his living by it is *a diligent and persevering man*. The fishers are up at dawn. At day-break our fishermen off the Doggerbank are fishing, and

they continue fishing till late in the afternoon. As long as hands can work men will fish. May the Lord Jesus make us hard-working, persevering, unwearied fishers of men! "In the morning sow thy seed, and in the evening withhold not thine hand; for thou knowest not whether shall prosper, either this or that." *MTP* 32:346, italics in the original.

9. "A fisher is a person who is *very dependent, and needs to be trustful.* He cannot see the fish. One who fishes in the sea must go and cast in the net, as it were, at a peradventure. Fishing is an act of faith. I have often seen in the Mediterranean men go with their boats and enclose acres of sea with vast nets; and yet, when they have drawn the net to shore, they have not had as much result as I could put in my hand. . . . Nobody is so dependent upon God as the minister of God. Oh, this fishing from the Tabernacle pulpit! What a work of faith! I cannot tell that a soul will be brought to God by it. I cannot judge whether my sermon will be suitable to the persons who are here, except that I do believe that God will guide me in the casting of the net. I expect him to work salvation, and I depend upon him for it." *MTP* 32:346, italics in the original.

10. "When [Christ's] dear servants are following him, he says, 'I will make you fishers of men;' and be it never forgotten that *it is he that makes us follow him;* so that if the following of him be the step to being made a fisher of men, yet this he gives us. 'Tis all of his Spirit. I have talked about catching his spirit, and abiding in him, and obeying him, and hearkening to him, and copying him; but none of these things are we capable of apart from his working them all in us. 'From me is thy fruit found,' is a text which we must not for a moment forget. So, then, if we do follow him, it is he that makes us follow him; and so he makes us fishers of men." *MPT* 32:344, italics in the original.

11. "A true minister is a creation of the God of heaven. It is no more in the power of the Church than it is in the power of the bishops to make ministers. Independency is as weak as Episcopacy on this point. God alone ordains ministers; all that the Church can do is recognise them. We cannot make them at our colleges; we cannot make them by the laying on of hands, nor even by the choice of the Church. God must make them; God must ordain them; it is only for the Church to perceive God's work and cheerfully to submit to his choice." *MTP* 8:459.

Eph. III. 8 Less than the Least.   284

The Bible is not like an Almanack, soon used up, or as other books whose interest dies, but it is the same to us now, as in days of yore.

I. A great Subject. Christ with all his riches of loving, redeeming, pardoning, quickening, helping grace. Riches unsearchable by men, angels, or glorified Spirits.

II. A great Commission "to preach" these riches, not to read, or merely talk of them, but to preach. To cry aloud, frequently, earnestly, affectingly &c — this is an art God alone can teach us.

III. An Unworthy preacher. Such Paul felt himself. What are we to say of ourselves. Good men will be humble men. Abraham, Moses, David, Isaiah — we are little indeed.

IV. An Unworthy Congregation. The Gentiles sunk in lust, cruelty & idolatry. Dead to the voice of truth in their conscience, yet even these must hear the glad news.

Preachers then may preach to all classes & may rejoice that none are beyond the pale of hope or the reach of mercy. None is excluded but the self excluded.

507. 509.

LESS THAN THE LEAST
Ephesians 3:8[1]

"Unto me, who am less than the least of all saints, is this grace given, that I should preach among the Gentiles the unsearchable riches of Christ."

The Bible is not like an Almanack soon used up, or as other books whose interest dies, but it is the same to us <u>now</u>, as in days of yore.

I. A GREAT SUBJECT.

Christ with all his riches of loving, redeeming, pardoning, quickening, helping grace. Riches unsearchable by men, angels, or glorified [s]pirits.[2]

II. A GREAT COMMISSION.

"To preach" these riches, not to read, or merely talk of them, but to preach.[3] To cry aloud, frequently, earnestly, affectingly etc. This is an art God alone can teach us.

III. AN UNWORTHY PREACHER.

Such Paul felt himself.[4] What are we to say of ourselves[?] Good men will be humble men. Abraham.[5] Moses.[6] David.[7] Isaiah.[8] We are little indeed.[9]

IV. AN UNWORTHY CONGREGATION.

"The Gentiles." Sunk in lust, cruelty[,] and idolatry.[10] Dead to the voice of truth in their conscience,[11] yet even these must hear the glad news.[12]

Preachers then may preach to all classes and may rejoice that none are beyond the pale of hope or the reach of mercy.[13]

None is excluded but the self excluder.[14]

507. 509.

1. It appears that Charles preached two later sermons on this text: "The Unsearchable Riches of Christ" (*MTP* 13, Sermon 745) and "A Grateful Summary of Twenty Volumes" (*MTP* 20, Sermon 1209). The first of these focused almost entirely on Christ and his riches, and so contains little overlapping content. The second later sermon, "A Grateful Summary of Twenty Volumes," has more overlapping content, as it was structured around the four headings of this sermon, although with different wording and order, and with one additional point. "*Paul thought very little of himself. . . . Paul thought very much of his brethren. . . . Paul thought very highly of his work. . . . Paul thought very lovingly of his congregation. . . . Paul thought most of all of his subject.*" *MTP* 20:709–15, italics in the original. Overlapping content is noted below.

2. In "A Grateful Summary of Twenty Volumes" (*MTP* 20, Sermon 1209), having expounded the unsearchable riches of the person of Christ, Charles described the riches of Christ's redemption: "Oh, the unsearchable love which led him to give his hands to the nails and his heart to the spear! What love unspeakable is centred in the cross! What riches of grace that he should deign to die a malefactor's death for his enemies! Can any of us conceive the unsearchable riches of merit which must lie in the holy life and painful death of our beloved Lord[?] If the Son of God himself deigns to die, the just for the unjust, surely no limit can be set to the virtue of that death, neither indeed can we calculate how precious it must be in the Father's sight. O thou bleeding Savior, when thou hadst become poorest of all in thine own glory, surely thou didst also become richest of all for the redemption of the sons of men! None shall ever know, nor even eternity itself fully declare, the infinite value of thy tears, and bloody sweat, and agony and death!" *MTP* 20:717.

3. "Paul does not claim to be sent to regenerate the Gentiles by sprinkling them, to hear their confessions of secret sin, to pry into their private lives with filthy questions, and to absolve them on the fulfillment of appointed penances; he has not a word to say about playing the priest; he does not glory in the grace which enabled him to display a comely ritual, or restore a pompous ceremonialism; he boasts not of carrying a crucifix or a banner in a procession up and down the aisles to delight the Gentiles; nor, in a word, does he set himself up as a sort of demi-god, able to kill and to make alive, to distribute pardons and to regenerate babes. . . . he is to preach among the Gentiles the unsearchable riches of Christ." *MTP* 20:712.

4. Cf. 1 Cor 15:9.   5. Cf. Gen 18:27.

6. Cf. Exod 3:11.   7. Cf. 2 Sam 7:18.

8. Cf. Isa 6:5.

9. "Was Paul really less than the least of all saints? Was not this too low an estimate of himself? Brethren, I suppose he meant that he felt this to be the case when he looked at himself from certain aspects. He was one of the late converts, many of his comrades were in Christ before him, and he yielded precedence to the older ones. He had been aforetime a persecutor and injurious, and, though God had forgiven him, he had never forgiven himself; and when he recollected his share in the sufferings and martyrdom of the saints, he felt that, though now numbered among them, he could only dare to sit in the lowliest place Besides, any devout man, however eminent he may be in most respects, will find that there are certain other points in which he falls short, and the apostle, instead of looking at the points in which he excelled, singled out with modest eye those qualities in which he felt he failed, and in those respects he put himself down as 'less than the least of all saints.'" MTP 20:710.

10. Cf. Eph 4:17–19; 1 Thess 4:5.   11. Cf. Rom 1:21–32.

12. "Paul was sent to preach to the Gentile dogs, who were despised by the Jews as uncircumcised and unclean.... They were such an ignorant crew—these Gentiles, ignorant of the true God and eternal life; though they were some of them wise in their own conceits, yet were they sunk in spiritual ignorance There were the Greeks, proud of their learned folly, the Romans, boasting of brute force and despising a merely spiritual kingdom, the Scythians, barbarous and uncouth, and the bondsmen, sunk in vice and degradation; but he who was sent to labor among them preferred them to any other audience.... Dear brethren and sisters, wherever you and I are called to labor we ought to be thankful that God has given us that particular place to labor in." MTP 20:714.

13. Cf. Luke 18:25–27.

14. Planted in between High Calvinism and Arminianism, Charles was an adamant Calvinist as well as a persistent evangelist. He did not see a contradiction between God's electing love and man's responsibility to respond. He wrote, "I

am quite certain that God has an elect people, for he tells me so in his Word; and I am equally certain that everyone who comes to Christ shall be saved, for that also is his own declaration in the Scriptures. When people ask me how I reconcile these two truths, I usually say that there is no need to reconcile them, for they have never yet quarrelled with one another. Both are true, and both relate to the same persons, for those who come to Christ are those who were from eternity given to Christ by his Father." *MTP* 56:631. Charles's strong commitment to Scripture allowed him to break away from the traditional High Calvinism that lay at the root of his congregation's antinomianism. Whereas High Calvinists neglected, if not ignored, the call to evangelism, Charles frequently concluded his sermons with an evangelistic call. Charles wrote, "Invitations of the most general character, nay, invitations which shall be universal in their scope, are perfectly consistent with the election of God. I have preached here, you know it, invitations as free as those which proceeded from the lips of Master John Wesley. Van Armin himself, the founder of the Arminian school, could not more honestly have pleaded with the very vilest of the vile to come to Jesus than I have done. Have I therefore felt in my mind that there was a contradiction here? No, nothing of the kind; because I know it to be my duty to sow beside all waters, and like the sower in the parable, to scatter the seed upon the stony ground, as well as upon the good land, knowing that election does not narrow the gospel call which is universal, but only affects the effectual call, which is and must be particular; which effectual call is no work of mine, seeing that it cometh from the Spirit of God. My business is to give the general call, the Holy Spirit will see to its application to the chosen." *MTP* 10:79–80. In this sermon, Charles displayed his evangelistic zeal, calling his hearers to respond to the free offer of the gospel and holding them responsible if they refused.

THE LORD IS MY BANNER

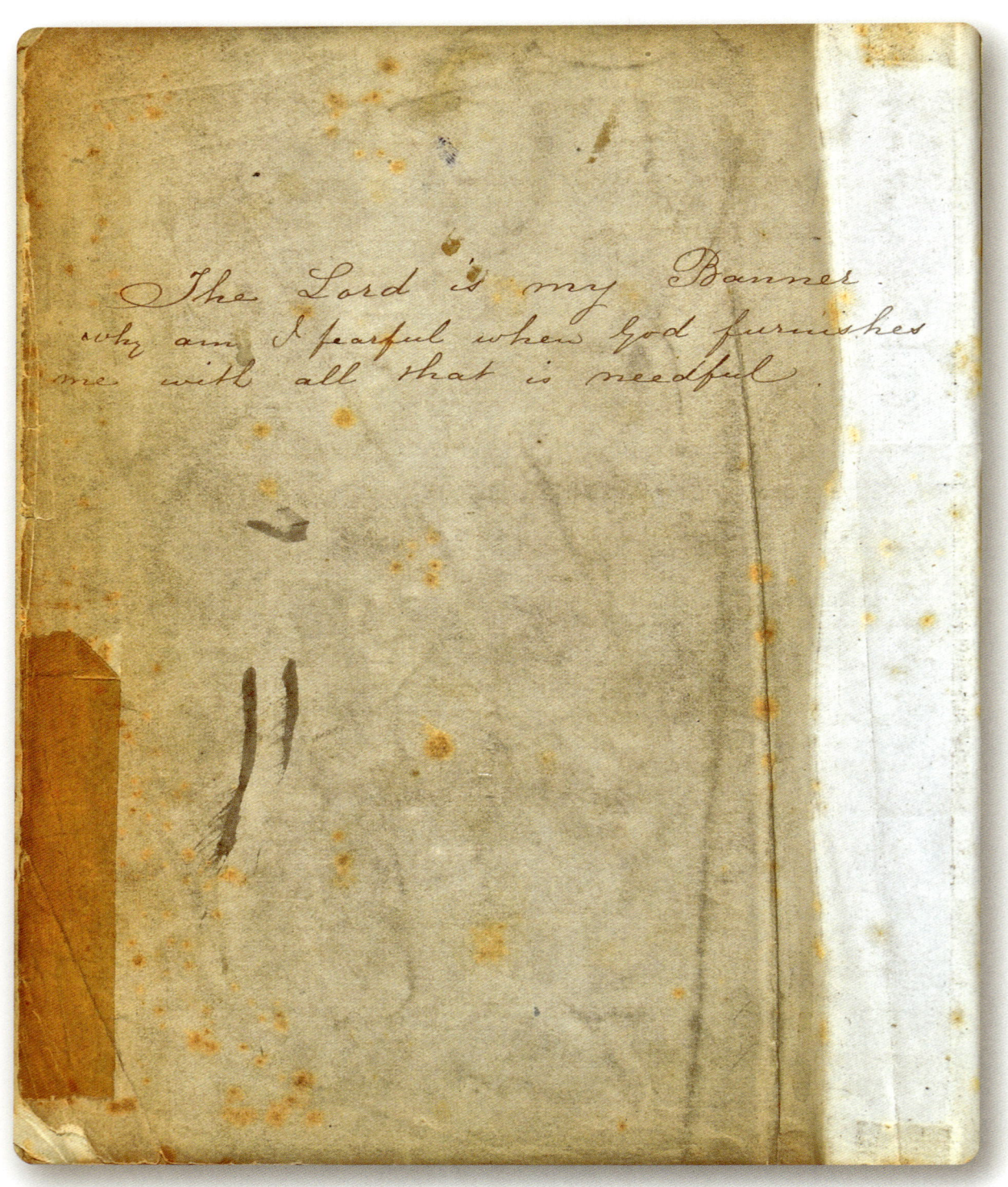

The Lord is my Banner. why am I fearful when God furnishes me with all that is needful.

THE LORD IS MY BANNER

The Lord is my Banner[1]
why am I fearful when God furnishes
me with all that is needful.[2]

1. Cf. Exod 17:15.

2. Cf. Matt 6:26–34. A search of Charles's frequently cited hymnals indicates that this poetic fragment was probably original to him. Charles's practice of writing hymns began in these early years. At times the young pastor would write hymns for special occasions, such as his Jubilee service at Waterbeach Chapel on June 26, 1853. For that occasion, Charles penned two hymns to be sung that morning: "The One Request" and "Immanuel." *Autobiography* 1:293–95. The hymns are unique in that they provide a view into Charles's mind and reveal to an extent how he sought to personally shape his congregation's worship of God. This desire to shepherd the worship of his congregation did not stop at Waterbeach, as is evidenced by the hymnal that Charles personally compiled for his London church, the Metropolitan Tabernacle. See C. H. Spurgeon, comp., *Our Own Hymn-Book. A Collection of Psalms and Hymns for Public, Social, and Private Worship* (London: Passmore and Alabaster, 1885, The Spurgeon Library).

INSIDE BACK COVER OF NOTEBOOK 5

INSIDE BACK COVER OF NOTEBOOK 5

[blank][1]

1. Due to being attached to the back cover, the majority of this page is missing from Notebook 5. This page appears to have been torn off when the rear cover was torn.

BACK COVER OF NOTEBOOK 5

*The Lord is my Banne[r]
why am I fearful when God furni[shes]
me with all that is needful.*

BACK COVER OF NOTEBOOK 5

[Back page/cover has been torn from the book][1]

1. Similar to the front of Notebook 5, the back cover has been removed, likely with an edged instrument of some kind. Due to the removal of the cover, most of Charles's benediction can be read.

ABOUT THE PROJECT AT MIDWESTERN SEMINARY

In 1857, Charles Spurgeon—the most popular preacher in the Victorian world—promised his readers that he would publish his earliest sermons. For almost 160 years, these sermons were lost to history. But with these volumes, these rediscovered sermons can finally be read, studied, and enjoyed by the millions around the world who admire Spurgeon's spiritual insights and literary grace.

This multi-volume set includes full-color facsimiles of Spurgeon's original handwriting, transcriptions of his outlines and sermons, biographical introductions, and editorial commentary that further illuminates Spurgeon's work. Taken together, *The Lost Sermons of C. H. Spurgeon* will add approximately 10 percent more material to Spurgeon's total body of literature, making it a must-have for pastors and scholars as well as the multitude of Spurgeon enthusiasts around the world.

The Lost Sermons project is overseen by a team of scholars and researchers at Midwestern Baptist Theological Seminary in Kansas City, Missouri, home of The Spurgeon Library, which houses nearly 6,000 volumes from Charles Spurgeon's personal library. Managers of spurgeon.org, Midwestern Seminary, under the leadership of President Jason K. Allen, are honored to steward these early works of Spurgeon as they seek to contribute to Spurgeon scholarship and research for the next generation.

ABOUT SPURGEON'S COLLEGE

Spurgeon's College was founded by the great Victorian preacher and philanthropist Charles Haddon Spurgeon in 1856. He recognised the injustice and frustration faced by those who desired to serve churches as ordained ministers but who had not benefited from the academic education required to gain entry for professional training. Charles Spurgeon wanted to embrace natural talents and abilities and looked for potential and passion, rather than academic privilege and family connections, when recruiting his students. The college remains thoroughly committed to these principles.

Today Spurgeon's College continues to prepare candidates for ordination to Baptist ministry within the Baptist Union of Great Britain. It also trains pastors from other denominations and those called to pioneer ministry and missional work. Since its foundation, more than 5,000 churches worldwide have been served by Spurgeon's ministers, and its trained ministers are active in more than thirty-five countries. The college has an exciting postgraduate program and a thriving postgraduate research community composed of students from around the world.

Charles Spurgeon derived the college's motto from a book by nineteenth-century poet and essayist Dora Greenwell: "We labour to hold forth the Cross of Christ with a bold hand among the sons of men, because that Cross holds us fast by its attractive power. Our desire is that every man may both hold the Truth, and be held by it; especially the truth of Christ crucified." *Et Teneo Et Teneor*—"I hold and I am held"—is embedded in the crest of Spurgeon's College. To find out more please visit www.spurgeons.ac.uk.

SCRIPTURE INDEX

GENESIS
1:26–27   360
2:1   37
2:21   208
2:21–22   209
3   221
3:11   128
3:12   370
3:12–13   128, 370
3:15   311
4:9   128
6   52
6–8   53
7:17–22   335
15:6   442
15:12–21   208
15:17   208
18:23–33   183
18:27   459
19:1–25   242
19:24   54
19:24–25   335
22:1–18   442
22:2   174
22:14   26
28:12   208
28:12–17   208
30:31–33   119
32:9–13   209
32:24–29   183
32:24–31   208–9
32:30   209
37:5–11   209
39:12   442
43:8–10   119
43:9   119
49:24   232

EXODUS
3:11   459
9:16–18   36
12:29   208, 335
12:43–45   391
13:21–22   208
14:19–20   208
15:1–21   176
15:23–26   154
17:15   464
28   222
29:12   153
33:12–23   183
33:20   36

LEVITICUS
6:13   222
8:15   153
10:1–2   54
17:6   222
24:8–9   398
27:32   420

NUMBERS
6:10–11   222
6:14   222
10:29–34   410
12:3   442

15:27 222
16:27–33 54
16:31–33 335
20:27–28 224
21:17–18 176
29:11 222
35:1–29 142
35:12 143, 145
35:14 144
35:15 143
35:19 145
35:25–28 144
35:28 145
35:29 142

DEUTERONOMY

4:24 36
6:4–5 322
12:27 222
18:15 222
27:26 322
29:18 80
29:29 52
30:1–5 278
32:9 420
33:27 26

JOSHUA

2:15 351
5:13 247
5:13–6:27 442

JUDGES

1:16 410, 412
4 403
4:17 410
5 176
6 442
6:36–40 183
7:9–22 208
9:15 233

14:8–9 44
14:14 44
16:2–3 208

RUTH

1:1 259

1 SAMUEL

3:1–14 209
15:6 403, 410
18:1 442
18:6–7 176
18:8–9 259
19:10–11 259
21:1–6 259
23:7–8 259
27:10 412

2 SAMUEL

5:17–25 183
7 442
7:18 459
22:1–50 176
24:10–25 183

1 KINGS

3:5–15 209
5:6–9 233
6–8 174
8:46 372
18:21 391
18:30–38 183
18:37–38 54
18:41–46 183
19:19 224

2 KINGS 292

1:9–12 54
2:21–22 154
6:16–17 37
6:25 259

SCRIPTURE INDEX

8:1 259
10:15 403, 410
14:9 233
17:24 292
19:4 41, 44
19:14–37 183
19:35–36 208
20:1 292
20:1–11 183
20:10–11 292
20:12 292
20:12–13 292
20:15 291–92
25:1–21 242
25:3 259

1 CHRONICLES
2:55 412

2 CHRONICLES
32:25 292
33:12–13 183

EZRA
3:11 176
6:14–15 174

NEHEMIAH
9:6 37

JOB
1:1 287–88
1:6–12 360
1:16 54
4:12–21 209
6:6 263
14:1–2 360
14:10 355
32:1–10 334
33–35 334
36:16–26 334
36:18 329, 334
38:17 360

PSALMS
7:1–4 278
9:16 36
10:4 311
16:11 300
18:2 222
30:5 161
37:25 253, 258
46:4 152
50:3 51, 55
51:5 250
51:10 250
56:15–16 55
69:9 165
72:15 343
74:2 420
91 232
94:14 259
97:2–5 51, 55
103:12 67
105:41 413
110 66
110:1 175, 220
115:1 175
116:11 296
118:8–9 26
119:60 229, 232
119:67 278
119:122 111, 116
145:13 348

PROVERBS
5:11 371
6:9–10 340
8:13 166
10:4 340
13:7 295
16:18 166

SCRIPTURE INDEX

21:5 *340*
22:6 *260*
24:33 *340*

ECCLESIASTES
7:13 *369, 372*
7:13–14 *372*
12:7 *362*
12:12 *166*

SONG OF SOLOMON
2:1 *161*
2:10–13 *157*

ISAIAH
2:4 *144*
6:4–5 *36*
6:5 *459*
8:20 *100*
9:6 *221, 224*
9:6–7 *348*
22:20–24 *64*
22:23–24 *59*
22:25 *64*
26:1–4 *66*
28:16 *227*
28:17 *67*
32:1 *348*
33:14 *371*
35:6 *413*
40:2 *145*
40:6–7 *335*
40:8 *233*
40:29–31 *154*
40:31 *209*
41:18 *413*
43:19–20 *153*
45:19 *26*
45:22 *10*
49:5 *119*
49:6 *119*
51:11 *209*
53:3–7 *44*
53:4–6 *222*
53:5–6 *119*
53:6 *421*
53:10 *64*
55:1–3 *144*
56:12 *55*
56:15 *51*
56:16 *51*
60:11 *143*
61:7 *145*
64:6 *160*

JEREMIAH
17:7–8 *283*
17:9 *107*
22:10 *278*
23:15 *233*
31:3 *443*
33:13 *417, 420*
35 *411, 412*
35:1–6 *411*
35:6–10 *411*
35:11 *411*
35:18–19 *403, 410–11*
36:18 *410*
36:18–19 *410*
36:19 *410*
42:11 *26*
45:5 *xv*

LAMENTATIONS
5:1–21 *259*

EZEKIEL
1 *36*
1:1 *152*
1:1–3 *36*
1:3 *152*
1:4 *36*

SCRIPTURE INDEX

1:5 29, 36–37
1:6 38
1:7 38
1:8 37–38
1:9 39
1:10 37, 39
1:13 35, 39
1:14 39
3:15 152
3:23 152
5–7 242
7:2 37
8 242
9 237
9:2 242
9:2–4 242
9:4–6 243
9:8–10 242
9:11 242
10:15 152
10:20 152
10:22 152
36:26 80
36:26–27 250
43:3 152
47:1 153
47:1–12 147, 152
47:3–5 153
47:5 152
47:8 152, 153
47:8–9 154
47:8–11 153
47:9–10 154
47:12 155

DANIEL

3:16–18 442
5:30 208
6 442
6:10 442
6:16–22 208
7:14 348

HOSEA

7:9 187

JOEL

1:4 192

AMOS

1:1 224
8:11 424

JONAH

2:1–10 183
2:2 67

MICAH

7:18 310

NAHUM

1:3 51
1:3–5 56
1:4 51
1:5 51

HABAKKUK

2:14 153
3:17–18 442

HAGGAI

1:5 275, 278
1:13 26
2:4 26

ZECHARIAH

3:1–5 106
3:2 105
9:11–12 142
9:12 137, 142
13:1 409
14:8 155

SCRIPTURE INDEX

MALACHI
1:7   395, 398
1:8   398
2:8   398
3:8–10   398
4:2   424

MATTHEW
2:19   335
3:1–10   386
3:2   334
3:5–6   387
3:6   95, 100, 387
3:12   56
3:13   95, 100, 387
3:16   387
4:19   447
5:3   297, 348
5:9   144, 321
5:11–12   44
5:16   38
5:20   315, 322
5:33–37   324
5:43–44   44
5:43–48   442
5:44–47   441
6:1–6   323
6:3–4   38
6:6   293
6:7–13   334
6:9–10   350
6:16–18   323
6:19–21   166
6:24   251
6:26–34   464
7:7   179
7:12   182
7:22   121, 128
8:22   278
8:23–27   208
9:20–22   143
10:28   335
11:28   144
11:28–30   412
12:1–2   324
12:36–37   362
13:8–9   135
13:31–32   133, 134
13:40   56
13:43   39
14:25   208
15:18–19   371
15:33   209
16:25   296
16:26   296
17:20   312
18:15–21   166
19:14   84
19:21–22   166
19:27–29   145
19:29   296
21:6–11   174
21:12–13   174
21:16   83
22:12   121
22:13   130
22:34–40   440
23:3–4   324
23:5–7   323
23:5–12   324
23:12   348
23:16–22   324
23:23–26   324
23:25–28   324
23:44   209
25   121, 129
25:1–13   129, 233
25:14–30   129
25:30   38
25:31–46   129
26:29   400
26:41   392

27:45   209
27:45–50   209
28:18–20   348, 452
28:20   26

MARK

1:2–6   386
1:5   387
1:8–10   379, 387
1:12–13   44
1:32–34   413
4:8–9   135
4:31–32   370
4:37–41   208
6:48   208
7:21–23   166
9:7   36
10:28–31   145
10:45   222
11:4–10   174
11:15–17   174
12:28–34   322, 440
14:25   400
14:38   392
15:33–37   209
16:16   95, 100

LUKE

1:68   222
2:6–7   209
2:41–52   174
3:1–9   386
3:3   387
6:12   209
7:29   95
7:29–30   100
7:30   95
8:8   135
8:23–25   208
9:60   278
10:27   322

12:2   209
12:13–21   331
12:36–39   301
14:12–14   445
15   143
15:4   421
17:6   312
17:10   38
18:15–17   281
18:25–27   457
18:28–30   145
19:32–38   174
19:45–46   174
20:36   36
21:36   392
22:18   400
23:34   250
23:44–46   209

JOHN

1:16   225
1:19–28   386
1:28   387
3:1–2   209
3:1–21   322
3:2–6   251
3:16   310, 443
3:23   377, 387
3:36   271
4:1   95, 100
4:13–14   413
5:22–23   271
6:17–19   208
6:27   166
6:35   144
6:37   143
6:37–39   421
6:63   270
7:37–38   413
7:50–51   322
8:34–36   251

9:4 *210*
10:7–9 *153*
10:10 *360*
10:11 *222, 421*
10:14 *300*
10:14–15 *421*
10:14–16 *420*
10:15 *421*
10:18 *311*
10:28–29 *224*
10:29 *421*
12:15 *223*
13:30 *209*
13:34 *442, 444*
14:4–6 *312*
14:6 *144*
14:9–11 *116*
14:16 *270*
14:16–18 *161*
14:26 *161, 270*
15:12 *442*
15:15 *222, 310, 412*
15:18 *444*
15:26 *270*
16:7–15 *161*
16:14 *153*
17:3 *300*
18:37 *223*
19:34 *153*
19:39–42 *322*
20:19 *209*

ACTS

1:12 *152*
2:8 *153*
2:14–39 *414*
2:19 *56*
2:23 *64, 414*
2:33 *143*
2:36 *44*
2:41 *95, 100, 153*
3:13–15 *414*
3:22–23 *222*
4:13 *442*
4:27–28 *64*
5:1–11 *335*
5:29 *412*
6:1–7 *76*
8:5–8 *77*
8:6–8 *79*
8:12 *95, 100*
8:13 *69, 76, 79*
8:14–17 *78*
8:15–16 *77*
8:20 *79*
8:20–24 *79*
8:21 *69, 76, 79–80*
8:22 *80*
8:23 *80, 233*
8:26–39 *232*
8:35 *100*
8:36 *95, 100, 387–88*
8:37 *95, 100–101, 390*
8:38 *388*
9:36–42 *442*
12:6–12 *208*
12:20–23 *335*
15:8–9 *270*
16:13 *387*
16:25–26 *208*
16:25–34 *232*
16:32 *387*
16:33 *95, 387*
16:33–34 *101*
16:34 *95, 387*
20:26 *130*
20:28 *66*
23:6–8 *323*
24:24–27 *271*
26:28 *271*

SCRIPTURE INDEX

ROMANS

1:18   271, 335
1:21–32   459
1:24   271
2:1–6   323
2:5   271, 335
2:14–19   425
2:17–24   322, 324
3:11   311
3:19   130
3:22–24   66
3:23   322
4:5   143
5:4   392
5:6   222
5:6–8   311
5:8   442
5:10   305
5:12–21   224
5:20   153
6:3   95
6:3–4   101
6:4   95, 101, 379, 388
6:5   66
6:16   233
6:23   233
6:23a   360, 371
7   12
7:24   12
8:11   251
8:15   281
8:17   425
8:26–27   270
8:29   278
8:29–30   421
8:34   66, 221
8:35–37   66
8:35–39   259, 443
8:37   222
9:19   370
10:8–9   144

11:33–36   176
12:2   278
12:5   425
12:10   440
12:11   339
12:13   440
12:17–21   44
12:18   410
13:13   166, 192
14:10   67
14:17   348
15:7   67

1 CORINTHIANS

1:30   222
1:31   65
3:1–3   192
6:9–10   166
6:20   421
7:23   222
10:17   399
11:20–22   399
11:23–26   357
11:27–29   399
11:33   399
12:12–13   350
12:13   95, 101
13:1–3   440
13:4   440
13:5   440
13:7   441
13:8–13   440
13:11–12   209
13:12   37, 209
13:13   135, 440
15   66
15:9   459
15:20–28   224
15:26   210
15:54–55   210

SCRIPTURE INDEX

2 CORINTHIANS
2:16   *154*
3:18   *67*
4:6   *67*
4:16–18   *284*
4:17–18   *44*
5:8   *421*
5:10   *67, 362*
5:17   *310*
5:18   *325*
5:18–19   *310*
5:21   *119, 222*
7:5–7   *444*
7:10   *80*
11:3   *7*
11:23–29   *442*
13:5   *312*

GALATIANS
1:4   *222*
1:8–9   *44, 92, 100*
3:6–9   *283*
3:10   *322*
3:13–14   *222*
3:23–25   *142*
3:27   *95, 101*
4:5   *283*
5:17   *167*
5:19–20   *440*
5:19–21   *166*
5:21   *440*
5:22   *348*
5:22–23   *135, 161*
6:10   *301, 440*

EPHESIANS
1:3–5   *66, 153*
1:3–14   *176*
1:5   *283*
1:7   *66, 222*
1:13–14   *243*
2:1–3   *142, 210*
2:5–6   *154*
2:6   *300*
2:7   *348*
2:8–10   *65, 233*
2:13   *423*
3:8   *457*
4:5   *95, 101*
4:17–19   *459*
4:25–27   *440*
4:28   *340*
5:2   *427*
5:6   *271, 335*
5:8   *251*
5:18   *302*
5:23   *66*
5:25–27   *322, 442*
6:18   *350*

PHILIPPIANS
1:6   *421*
2:6–11   *176*
2:9–11   *66, 143*
3:7–8   *296*
3:8   *300*
3:9   *66*
3:10–11   *66*
3:20   *300*
4:4   *300*
4:7   *348*

COLOSSIANS
1:13   *251*
1:13–14   *222*
1:14   *66*
1:15–20   *176*
1:18   *66, 220*
1:19   *213*
1:20   *310, 325*
2:12   *95, 101, 379, 388, 392*
2:13   *270*

2:16   324
4:6   44

1 THESSALONIANS
1:10   222
4:5   459
4:8   310
4:13–18   154
4:16–18   350
4:17   53
5:2   53
5:4–8   161
5:5   300
5:6   299
5:7   209
5:9–10   302
5:14   334

2 THESSALONIANS
1:7   51
1:7–8   56
1:8   51
3:10–12   340

1 TIMOTHY
1:15–16   444
2:1–2   410
2:14   44
4:8   260
6:6   260
6:10   166
6:15   223
6:15–16   37

2 TIMOTHY
1:7   283
2:12   350
2:23   44
2:25   264
4:2   334
4:7–8   66

PHILEMON
18–19   113

HEBREWS
1:2   44
1:4–14   221
1:8   348
1:14   36
2:10   222
3:1–6   65
3:7   267
4:1–10   209
4:15   44, 442
4:16   66
5:11–14   142
6:13–18   56
6:18   142
6:20   222
7:11–28   222
7:18–22   113
7:22   111, 161
7:25   66–67, 350
8:6–13   55
9:6–10   222
9:11–12   144
9:14–15   221
9:26–27   222
9:27   210, 312
10:8–14   222
10:12   222
10:26–27   103
10:26–31   271
10:34   295
11:8–10   442
11:13   44
11:13–16   111
11:17–19   442
11:22   442
11:24–29   442
11:30   442
11:32   442

11:33   442
11:35–38   259
11:40   351
12:2   243
12:29   36
13:1   443
13:2   37, 293
13:3   350
13:5   259
13:8   224

JAMES

1:2–4   284
1:12   66
1:13   370
1:14   365
1:14–15   371
1:23   278
1:27   440
2:10   322
2:10–11   324
2:14–16   441
3:5   370
4:13–15   270
5:1–3   371
5:10–11   442
5:16   350
6:23a   371

1 PETER

1:3   66
1:3–5   53
1:13   411
1:14–17   410
1:15–16   300
1:22   270
2:2   192
2:4–6   232
2:5   425
2:9   251
2:9–10   66, 425

2:10   251
2:11   410
2:19–20   44
2:21–22   442
2:23–25   222
2:24   119
3:8   440
3:9   44
3:15   293
3:18   119
4:3   302
5:8   301

2 PETER

1:10–11   301
1:12–15   412
1:19–21   270, 278
1:21   153
3:1–10   44
3:3–7   52
3:7   56
3:10   53
3:10–11   47
3:11–13   53

1 JOHN

2:1–2   221
2:3   300
2:16   166
2:23   116
3:2   336
3:16–20   444
4:7–10   283
4:18   310
4:19   445
4:20   440
5:11–13   233

JUDE

3   44, 92, 100

REVELATION

1:5 175
1:6 348
1:8 67
3:14–22 296
3:21 66
4:6–8 37
4:8 209
5:6 175
5:9 348
5:11 37
5:11–14 224
5:12 66
6:9–11 351
7:1 37
7:2–3 243
7:4 421
7:9 175, 348
7:15 209
7:16–17 38
8:5–8 56
9:17–18 56
11:15 348
14:1 175
14:1–3 169, 421
14:13 209
17:14 223
19:11 222
19:11–16 129
19:11–21 348
19:16 223
20:6 350
20:11–15 362
20:12 53
20:15 53
21:1–2 53
21:4 348
21:6 67, 413
21:18–21 348
21:23 38
21:24 350
21:26 350
21:27 209
22:1–2 152
22:2 155
22:4 176
22:5 199
22:13 67
22:17 152

SUBJECT INDEX

A

Abihu   49
Abraham   26, 79, 169, 174, 181, 199, 201, 390, 433, 457
Acts   44, 56, 64, 66, 69, 76–80, 95, 100–101, 130, 143, 152–53, 208, 222, 232–33, 270–71, 323, 331, 335, 387–88, 390, 398, 412, 414, 442
Adam   84, 121, 173, 213, 219, 370, 390, 424, 427
adoption   281–84, 307, 326, 351
adultery   367, 440
Aenon   377, 387
affliction   45, 167, 191, 263–64, 281, 370, 421
agony   441, 458
Agrippa   78, 267
Alpha   61, 77, 221
altar   147, 194, 215, 237, 347, 352, 395
Amalekites   403, 410
Amen, saying   127
angels   31, 37–39, 56, 123, 127, 130, 223, 284, 291, 311, 341, 350, 431, 439, 457
anger   56, 321, 335, 429, 435
anxiety   xiv, 189
apostles   69, 71, 77, 79, 147, 153, 350, 387, 389, 398
Arabia Felix   407, 411
Arminianism   220, 281–83, 459
atheism   47, 52
atonement   147, 169, 243, 345, 414
authority   39, 55, 241, 253, 312, 349

B

Babylonians   237, 291–92
baptism   78, 81, 97, 100–103, 159, 351, 377, 379, 381, 383, 385–92, 398–99, 419, 424–25

Baptist denomination   75
Baptists   100, 103, 176, 247, 391, 398
Bashan   56, 63
Bath (England)   153, 154, 372
Battle of Dunbar   277
believers   69, 71, 77, 78, 95, 97, 99, 113, 195, 229, 231–32, 260, 263, 265, 311, 345, 351, 359, 361, 383, 391
Belshazzar   201
Benjamin   113, 118, 411–12, 417
Beza   377
Bible   53, 83, 135, 139, 143, 147, 155, 174–75, 220, 253, 258, 272, 291, 293, 305, 310, 339, 357, 370, 372, 374, 387, 411, 457
bitterness   75, 80
blasphemies   370
blessing   36, 69, 144, 182, 193–94, 255, 297, 321, 325, 361, 405
blood   61, 84, 129, 142, 147, 169, 175, 195, 244, 312, 325, 336, 359, 371, 400, 414, 423–25, 439
boast; boasting   33, 61, 231, 233, 459
boldness   433
bondage   142, 281–82
books   47, 65, 142, 144, 160, 232, 291, 300, 412, 421, 457
boys and girls   95, 260, 288
brothers   83, 264–65, 277, 312
Budeaeus (Guillaume Budé)   377
business   56, 111, 165, 189, 191, 193, 302, 326, 331, 339, 341, 373, 413, 427, 453, 460

C

Cain   121

calm *36*
Calvinism *459, 460*
Calvinists *247, 460*
Cape [of Good Hope] *61, 66*
captain *167, 215, 329, 334*
care *336, 442, 452*
carefulness *193*
cares *29, 159, 193*
Casaubon, [Isaac] *377*
Catholicism *281–82*
celebration *173*
ceremonies *317, 388*
character *35, 41, 54, 78, 101, 106, 174, 181, 215, 237, 241–42, 249–50, 315, 325, 371, 444, 460*
charity *41, 133, 433*
Chebar *29, 152*
children *53, 56, 81, 83–85, 88, 92, 102, 113, 127, 189, 193–95, 239, 253, 255, 258, 260, 283, 293, 296, 299, 300, 321, 326, 329, 360, 383, 391, 405, 410, 420*
Christ
    our surety *111–15*
Christian *43, 57, 65–66, 78, 97, 107, 117–18, 155, 161, 210, 213, 229, 232, 234, 264, 300–301, 309, 322, 325, 326, 340, 345, 349, 351–52, 395, 398, 411, 421, 429, 437, 441, 444, 452*
church, the (body of Christ) *16, 44, 52, 76, 80, 99, 102–3, 128, 134, 142, 147, 181, 183, 187, 195, 217, 223, 227, 232, 250, 282, 340, 349–50, 433, 452, 454*
Church of England *80, 155, 183, 223, 349, 388–90, 392, 398, 452*
churchmen *317, 322, 381, 389, 392*
circumcision *381, 383, 390*
cities *53–54, 137, 142–45, 417*
city of God *147*
Clarke, Adam *253, 258, 310*
clouds *29, 54–56, 203, 207, 449, 453*
comfort *39, 41, 135, 141, 143, 192, 232, 271, 295, 301, 305, 309, 311, 439*
communion *135, 162, 301, 305, 361, 398, 399*

condemnation *127, 399*
confidence *25, 44, 133–34, 160, 167, 195, 223, 283, 291, 292*
confirmation *71, 77–78, 391*
conflagration, the great *47, 49, 54, 57*
conquest *61, 107, 108, 347, 398*
conscience *127, 160, 191, 195, 249, 260, 271, 282, 319, 371, 425, 457*
Constantine *377*
conversion *51, 76, 77, 105, 108, 134, 160, 166, 191–92, 195, 250, 260, 275, 350, 371, 387, 395, 399, 419, 433*
corner stone *227*
courage *35, 133*
covenant *49, 59, 64–65, 113, 116, 147, 199, 220, 243, 315, 351, 381, 383, 390, 409, 420, 425*
Creator *37, 52, 166, 222, 369, 374*
crime *127*
Cromwell, Oliver *173, 177*
cruelty *457*
cure *83, 322, 441*
curse(s) *73, 118, 196, 312, 370, 443*

D

daily life *433, 444*
damned, the *181, 333*
Damon *113, 118*
danger *67, 105, 108, 116, 271, 301, 331, 334–35, 391, 421*
Daniel (prophet) *201, 433*
darkness *29, 55, 160, 183, 205, 223, 249, 310*
David *171, 181, 229, 253, 255, 258–59, 270, 295–96, 343, 409, 433, 435, 457*
day of judgment *8, 260*
day of the Lord *47, 56*
deacons *69, 76*
Dead Sea *149, 152*
death *29, 31, 41, 101, 105, 115, 118, 139, 144, 151, 195, 207, 210, 219, 221, 223, 237, 239, 243, 251, 264–65, 271–72, 275, 305, 307, 309–12, 333, 343, 349, 355, 357, 360, 362, 367,*

SUBJECT INDEX

379, 385, 388–89, 399, 405, 414, 423–24, 458
Deborah 173
debt 64, 76, 113, 116–18, 296, 349
decline, spiritual 187–92
delight 76, 189, 194, 283, 300, 312, 350, 400
delirium 360
Deliverer 215
denial 99, 405, 442
depravity 105, 107, 137, 166, 258
desire(s) 142, 165, 440, 442, 445, 464
destruction 49, 56–57, 174, 239, 242–43
devil 12, 45, 193–94, 234, 335, 371, 440
devotion 7, 8, 13, 144, 187, 194, 257, 291, 340
diligence 35, 339–41
discernment 29, 55, 203, 241
discipleship 95, 100, 377, 399, 443
discontent 189, 374
Dissenters 247, 317, 322, 398
divine work 241
doctrine(s) 41, 44, 49, 61, 100, 152, 154, 213, 220, 222, 232, 263–65, 270–71, 283, 301, 322, 350, 391, 398, 425, 452
Dorcas 433
Drusilla 71, 78, 79
Dunbar 173, 177

E

earnestness 75, 267, 293, 334
earth 29, 31, 38, 47, 49, 51–56, 76, 83, 102, 121, 157, 159, 167, 169, 174, 176, 199, 208, 220, 223, 283, 302, 350, 352, 361–62, 375, 392, 407, 409, 427, 429
Ecclesiastes 369
effectual calling 232, 247, 420
Egypt 78, 144, 162, 199, 333, 410
election 61, 84, 220, 224, 241, 247, 307, 409, 419–20, 460
Eliakim 59, 64
Elijah 49, 181
Eliphaz 201
encouragement 43, 85, 141

England 61, 80, 154–55, 167, 177, 183, 223, 293, 349, 372, 388–90, 392, 398, 452
envy 78, 321, 429
Established Church 176, 247
Establishment 75
eternity 53, 115, 167, 195, 210, 213, 221, 348, 418, 460
eunuch 95, 229, 379, 388
Euphrates 29
evangelists 69, 458
Eve 121
evil 43, 162, 166, 189, 264, 334–35
evil company 139, 250
evil example 205
evil love 127
evil nature 215
evil spirit(s) 267, 370
evil thoughts 365, 367
Exemplar 427, 433, 440
exhortation 137, 329, 385
eye 36, 43, 244, 301, 319, 339, 375, 429, 459
Ezekiel (prophet) 29, 147, 152, 242

F

faith 41, 65–67, 69, 73, 75–77, 80, 95, 97, 101–3, 111, 115, 133–34, 139, 143, 153, 169, 174, 195, 231–33, 258, 273, 283, 301, 309, 350–51, 360, 381, 388–92, 398–99, 425, 429, 433, 454
fallenness 361
fame 73, 107, 135, 360
family 59, 61, 118, 143, 189, 192, 194, 253, 258, 260, 291–93, 295, 352, 387, 410–11, 427, 431, 473
family prayer 135, 194, 291
far-off, the 429
farthing 111, 116–17, 349
fathers 8, 85, 29
Father's name 169, 171, 176
fear(s) 99, 102–3, 115, 184, 205, 217, 220, 258, 281–82, 293, 305, 309, 333, 360, 424
Felix 71, 78, 257, 407, 411
final conflagration 47

SUBJECT INDEX

fire   29, 31, 36, 47, 49, 51—56, 105—8, 135, 215, 221, 234, 243, 300, 335, 341, 369, 371, 421, 429, 431
fisherman   447, 449, 451—53
fishers of men   447, 451—54
flesh   56, 129, 162, 166, 195, 207, 301, 345, 361, 371, 400, 414, 425
flood   47, 102, 333—34
folly   203, 459
foolishness   115, 250, 263, 307, 365
foreigners   41, 137
forgiveness   102, 413—14, 443
freedom   115, 142, 323
friendship   118, 162, 435
future, the   44, 52, 65, 357, 359, 362

G

Galatians   101
Gaza   199, 201
gentleness   264
Gideon   181, 199, 201, 433
gifts   71, 77, 152, 201, 213, 259, 343, 345, 349, 441, 452
glory   29, 36, 38, 52, 59, 61, 65, 76, 84, 101, 113, 118—19, 129, 147, 169, 203, 209, 220—21, 224, 231, 243, 257, 264—65, 311, 322, 333, 339, 341, 388, 392, 424, 443, 458
Godhead   59, 219, 222, 270, 309, 361
godliness   47, 192—93, 257, 324
gold   292, 295, 301, 336, 343, 348, 350, 421, 449
Gomorrah   49, 333, 335
good   41, 43, 299, 355
good men   253, 255, 258, 457
good works   38, 317, 441
gospel   56, 65, 69, 73, 77, 134—35, 143—44, 147, 152—54, 182, 194, 223, 265, 281, 297, 301, 321, 390, 413—14, 424—25, 441, 452—53, 460
grace   7, 11—12, 69, 73, 83, 85, 105, 107—8, 118, 128, 133—35, 144, 147
greed   73, 108, 260
Greek (language)   392
Greek churches   381, 388—89
Greeks   459
grief   9, 11, 80
guilt   108, 160, 221, 322, 414
guilty, the   139, 271, 331

H

Habakkuk   433
Hadrian Junius   377
Hallelujah   173
heart   38, 45, 69, 73, 75—76, 80, 83, 95, 101, 105, 107—8, 118, 129—30, 133—35, 149, 159, 161, 166, 179, 191, 194—95, 209, 220, 229, 232, 234, 243—44, 249, 260, 265, 267, 269, 282, 291, 293, 296, 310, 315, 319, 322—23, 339, 341, 349—52, 369, 375, 381, 383, 397, 410, 421, 433, 437, 441, 444, 458
heathenism   281—82
heaven   29, 31, 33, 36, 44—45, 47, 52—56, 63, 65, 83—84, 99, 102, 123, 133, 135, 157, 160, 169, 175—76, 182, 193, 199, 203, 205, 207, 209, 220, 222, 275, 278, 284, 292, 299, 301—2, 309, 311—12, 315, 319, 322, 326, 336, 347, 350—52, 369, 375, 385, 387, 419—20, 429, 439—40, 443—44, 449, 454
Hebrews   116, 267
heirs   299, 423
hell   45, 63, 83, 102, 113, 123, 125, 160, 244, 257, 267, 269, 271, 277, 300, 319, 331, 370—71
help   33, 71, 121, 177, 179, 349
helpmate   199
Herod   333
Hezekiah   41, 181, 291—92
High Priest   106, 144
Hindostan   61
history   154, 177, 199, 389, 390, 398—99, 411, 471
Hobab   403
holiness   36, 115, 128, 193, 223, 258, 265, 299, 335, 340, 414, 440, 444
holy, the   331
Holy Ghost; Holy Spirit   35, 69, 71, 76—78, 159, 182, 267, 270—71, 282, 341, 379, 387, 424—25, 444, 452, 460

SUBJECT INDEX

Holy Scriptures   152, 433
holy waters   147
honour   33, 61, 167, 213, 219–20, 224, 258, 292, 325, 347
hope   43, 53, 66–67, 84, 107, 118, 127, 133, 137, 142, 159, 166, 192, 221, 232, 239, 333, 350–51, 375, 397, 457
hour   51, 53, 101–2, 106, 193, 199, 201, 205, 229, 309, 331, 370, 419
House of David   409
house of God   107, 147, 372
human heart   265
humanity   374, 424
human nature   221
humans   38
human sin   414
human soul   53, 357
humility   133, 159, 161, 319
husband   65, 71, 78–79, 81, 161
hypocrisy   108, 441

I

immersion   97, 377, 379, 381, 386–89, 392
immortality   207
immutability   215, 221, 224
imputed righteousness   183, 317
indulgence   189
infants   84, 102, 381, 383, 388
infidelity   41
infinity   215, 435
inheritance   49, 84, 119, 139, 403, 417, 423, 445
iniquity   80, 130, 271, 293, 370–71
intelligence   33
intercession   61, 66, 334
inwrought righteousness   317
Isaac   26, 169
Isaiah (prophet)   154, 457
Israel   119, 144, 187, 199, 237, 403, 405, 409–10, 424

J

Jacob   113, 119, 177, 181, 199, 201, 347

Jael   403, 410
Jehovah   147, 312, 335, 423, 440
Jehu   403
Jerusalem   45, 135, 142, 147, 152–53, 155, 174, 237, 242–43, 339, 405, 407, 409, 417
Jesus
    fulness in   223–25
    prayer for   343–47
Jews   54, 101, 137, 258, 299, 322, 411, 433, 459
Job (patriarch)   43, 54, 209, 263, 287–88, 329, 354, 355, 360, 433
John (apostle)   152, 195, 221
John the Baptist   79, 100, 174, 377, 379, 387
Jonadab   403, 407, 409
Jonah   65, 67, 81, 183
Jonathan   435
Jordan   100, 377, 379, 387
Josephus, Flavius   71, 78–79, 174
Joshua   106, 247, 250, 351, 433
joy   67, 102, 129, 134, 159, 173, 195, 205, 207, 210, 221, 224, 281, 283, 299, 350–51, 359, 362, 375, 400, 441
Judah   113, 118, 403, 410, 417
Judas   205
Judges   144, 175, 403, 410, 412, 442
judgment   6, 55–56, 61, 88, 99, 107, 123, 125, 127, 194, 242–43, 257, 260, 288, 299, 300, 359, 369, 371, 373, 421, 424
justice   31, 56, 59, 113, 142, 227, 239, 312, 331, 357
justification   61, 115, 119, 183, 283, 315, 322, 413

K

king(s)   43, 119, 121, 123, 127, 129–30, 217, 223, 291, 292, 331, 341, 345, 347–50, 360, 410, 420
kingdom, the kingdom of heaven   65, 83, 130, 132, 133–34, 295, 297, 315, 319, 341, 343, 345, 351, 459
knowledge   39, 67, 76–77, 108, 127, 133, 143, 155, 205, 215, 258, 299, 319, 324, 373, 420
Korah   41, 433

SUBJECT INDEX

L
Lamb   61, 102, 169, 174–76, 278, 409, 420, 423
Laodiceans   295
last day(s)   413, 420
law   59, 78, 95, 100, 101, 105, 108, 113, 117–18, 137, 144, 220, 275, 282, 292, 315, 317, 322, 326, 340, 349, 390, 392, 395, 403, 410
laziness   339–40
learning   165
legalism   281–82
Levites   139, 143–44, 383, 390
light   33, 38, 54, 84, 106, 161, 189, 194, 199, 203, 205, 207, 210, 243, 299, 310, 360, 445
lion   35, 39, 41, 201, 205, 331
Lord's Supper   345, 383, 390–91, 399
love   31, 59, 73, 78, 127–28, 133, 147, 153, 161, 167, 183, 189, 195, 209, 215, 220, 231, 244, 250, 260, 263–64, 281, 283, 296, 305, 311, 312, 331, 340, 341, 350, 423, 427–44, 458–59
lust   365, 429, 440, 457

M
Maker   229
Malachi   65, 395
malice   321
man   25, 29, 31, 39, 45, 48, 53, 106, 111, 142, 184, 199, 205, 221, 307, 321, 340, 349, 355–62, 395, 451
man with the inkhorn   237–43
Manasseh   181
Man of Sorrows   45
martyrs   429, 440
Master   41, 43, 52, 134, 153, 194, 205, 222, 237, 249, 341, 350, 385, 400, 413, 444, 452–53
Mediator   65, 215, 232, 243
Melchizedek   215
men, fishers of   447–51
mercy   31, 36, 101, 135, 182, 192, 208, 217, 231, 233, 243, 244, 269, 271, 281–82, 293, 360, 413, 443–44, 457
merit   213, 221, 233, 323, 400, 458
Messiah   71, 78, 142, 343, 348, 420
Midianites   201

might   35, 175, 217, 345, 349
Miklat   141, 145
mind(s)   8, 16, 33, 47, 52, 118, 160, 203, 205, 220, 221, 265, 275, 349, 360, 365, 369
ministry   44, 55, 69, 76, 77, 79, 84–85, 154, 167, 187, 223, 242, 247, 250, 259, 278, 334, 351, 447, 452, 473
miracles   69, 77
Miriam   173
missions   6, 243
money   73, 111, 116, 165, 259, 295, 325, 333, 336
Mormonism   281–82
mortality   59, 271, 340, 361
Moses   78, 181, 270, 403, 410, 433, 457
mother's prayers   9, 255
mountains   53, 56, 149, 417
Mount Zion   169, 174, 424
murder   293, 367
murderers   409
mystery   51, 142, 265

N
Nadab   49
nature (character or natural condition)   12, 29, 31, 37–38, 105, 107, 119, 121, 135, 165–66, 213, 221, 225, 341, 361, 370, 423
nature (the external world)   53–54, 56, 281, 373
New Birth   12, 249
new earth   47
new heaven   47
new moons   319
New Testament   51, 54, 77–79, 130, 134, 143–44, 174, 258, 292, 310, 322, 340, 370, 392, 398, 411, 452
Nicodemus   201
night   47, 57, 76, 101, 125, 137, 159–61, 193, 199, 201–7, 229, 250, 296, 379, 453
Noah   47, 56

O
oath(s)   59, 64, 111, 196

494

SUBJECT INDEX

obedience 35, 39, 66, 118, 129,
    222, 270, 315, 317, 407, 433
offices 215, 398
old age 105, 187, 348, 355, 369, 372–73
Omega 61, 77, 221
omnipotence 105, 213, 221, 309, 343
omniscience 43, 213, 221
Onesimus 113, 116
opposition xvi, 41, 44, 374
ordinances 65, 351–52, 397, 399, 407
ordination 71, 77, 369, 374, 447, 452, 473
oxen 35, 39

P

Paedobaptists 97, 391
pain 113, 141, 208, 275, 282, 300, 360, 417, 443
Palestine 403
parables 121, 129, 135, 420
parents 85, 127, 194, 253, 260, 283, 293, 365
Paul 45, 77, 113, 116, 201, 270, 340,
    389, 433, 444, 457, 458, 459
peace 69, 108, 115, 139, 161, 189, 195, 201, 220, 270,
    310–11, 321, 325, 340, 360, 375, 410, 417, 433, 441
Peniel 201
perishing, the 255
persecuted, the 41–43
persecution 165, 167, 255, 259, 362
perseverance 61, 66, 220, 232, 247, 310
Peter 47, 51, 71, 75, 196, 201, 270, 433, 447, 452
Pharaoh 173
Pharisee 100, 193, 295, 315, 317, 319, 322–23
Phariseeism 281–82
Philemon 113
Philip 69, 73, 76, 100–101, 388
piety 41, 340
Plantinus 377
poor, the 195, 260, 297, 336, 355, 427, 441
pope 217, 296
popery 213, 220, 372
power 38, 49, 53, 55, 56, 69, 118, 134, 149, 166–67,
    210, 213, 217, 221, 224, 241, 260, 283, 291, 309,
    311–12, 322–23, 334, 349, 444, 454, 473
praise(s) 83, 131, 176, 213, 249, 264,
    278, 311, 347–48, 351–52, 424
prayer 41, 102, 115, 133, 135, 149, 157, 162,
    175, 177, 179, 183–84, 187, 189, 191, 193,
    195, 201, 247, 249, 255, 260, 293, 300, 302,
    305, 329, 333–34, 339, 343, 345, 347–48,
    350–52, 370, 372, 374, 381, 388–90, 398
preaching 6, 10, 12–13, 69, 76,
    135, 192, 223, 396, 453
pride 53, 165–65, 189, 239, 291,
    292, 301, 302, 321, 341, 391
priest 65, 106, 139, 144, 215, 217, 219, 223,
    239, 242, 245, 341, 345, 388, 395, 452, 458
Primitive Methodist 11, 75
princes 25, 341
procrastination 267, 271
profession 80, 103, 130, 193, 247, 383, 391–92
progress 4, 43, 67
promise(s) 116, 151, 179, 183, 229, 253,
    257, 302, 305, 347, 351, 390, 424
proofs 305, 359, 362
prophecy 7, 54, 242, 343
prosperity 75, 195, 299, 373, 441
Protestant 349
Providence xiv, xvi, 10, 133, 143,
    167, 315, 355, 370, 373–74, 433
public life 319
punishment 36, 53, 113, 118, 237,
    282, 291, 311, 335, 421, 427
purity 109
Pythias 115, 118

Q

Queen [of England] 61, 345

R

ransom 105, 119, 241, 329, 333, 443
Raquel 403
reason (intellectual power) 127,
    142, 195, 324, 357

SUBJECT INDEX

Rechabites   *403, 407, 411–12*
reconciliation   *307, 310–11*
Redeemer   *65, 215, 220, 232, 293, 321, 333, 343, 349, 359, 397, 441*
redemption   *61, 84, 171, 220, 307, 351, 409, 458*
Reformed theology   *390*
refuge   *63, 137, 139, 142–45, 177, 239, 375*
rejection   *310*
religion   *35, 41, 43, 47, 108, 149, 165, 189, 192–93, 195, 210, 220, 249, 257, 260, 281–82, 291–92, 295, 319, 322, 324, 333, 339–40, 343, 399, 437, 444*
remembrance   *43*
repentance   *75, 80, 97, 102, 130, 139, 161, 195–96, 231, 282, 333, 372, 381, 390–92*
resurrection   *61, 125, 265, 351, 360–61, 379, 385, 389*
rich, the   *208, 219, 355, 427*
righteous man   *255, 258*
righteousness   *52, 55, 61, 64–65, 97, 108, 113, 118, 119, 129, 142, 160, 183, 257, 315, 317, 322, 389, 424*
right hand   *65, 265, 373*
robbery   *367*
Romans (army)   *459*
rule(s)   *129, 210, 258, 405, 429, 442*

S

Sabbath   *76, 189, 193, 275, 293, 300, 319, 347, 413, 419, 449*
sacrifice   *26, 54, 142, 222, 340–41, 390, 395, 398, 400, 414, 425, 427, 442*
Sadducees   *317, 323*
safety   *51, 61, 67, 143, 237*
saints   *41, 45, 63, 84, 105, 153, 160–61, 181, 220, 232, 310, 345, 347, 351, 362, 399, 435, 439, 445, 457, 459*
salt   *155, 187, 263–65*
Salt Sea   *151, 154*
salvation   *64, 80, 83–85, 102, 108, 128, 134, 166, 181–83, 195, 213, 223, 229, 231, 232–33, 237, 239, 244, 271, 282–83, 305, 307, 310–11, 322–23, 331, 336, 350, 360–61, 391, 397, 453–54*

Samson   *199, 201*
Samuel (prophet)   *201, 410*
sanctification   *77, 97, 315, 317, 322–23, 420*
Sapphira   *333*
Satan   *45, 71, 105, 107, 108, 137, 207, 267, 269–70, 323*
Saul   *255*
Saviour   *65, 103, 108, 137, 160, 175, 205, 223–24, 231–32, 241, 260, 409, 442*
Scapula   *377*
Schrevelius   *377*
Scripture   *44, 51, 55, 84–85, 88, 97, 100, 111, 116, 135, 152, 157, 193, 233, 267, 270, 297, 322, 387, 389, 392, 410, 413, 420, 433, 443, 447, 460*
self-denial   *405, 442*
Sennacherib   *201*
service (benefit, or the work of serving)   *118, 153, 309, 341, 435*
serving the Lord   *339, 340–41*
Sheba   *343, 348*
sheep   *49, 113, 119, 129, 350, 417, 419–20, 442*
Simon Magus   *69, 71, 77–79*
sin   *47, 63–64, 71, 80, 97, 107, 125, 130, 142, 149, 159–60, 165–66, 189, 191, 194–95, 205, 221, 233, 237, 241, 243, 250–51, 260, 270, 271, 282, 291, 301, 305, 311, 315, 317, 322, 331, 334–35, 339–40, 361, 365, 367, 369–72, 374, 389–90, 392, 409–10, 413–14, 410, 413, 414, 421, 423–25, 444, 458*
  the parent and child of   *365–67*
singing   *157, 159, 171, 176*
Sisera   *173, 410*
Socinianism   *213, 220*
Sodom   *49, 149, 153–54, 239, 333*
Solomon   *157, 174, 201, 343, 348, 369, 372*
Son of God   *101, 244, 317, 335–36, 349, 435, 458*
sons of God   *283, 321*
sorcerer   *71*
sorrow   *144, 160, 205, 221, 265, 296*
soul   *37, 53, 64, 160–61, 192, 203, 219, 221, 223–24, 233–34, 260, 269, 282, 293, 297, 300,*

SUBJECT INDEX

309–10, 312, 315, 333, 357, 359, 397, 414, 423, 431, 437, 454
spirits   31, 37–39, 71, 167, 281, 355, 370
spiritual decline   187
spring   157–60
Stephen   69
Stephens, Henry   377
storms   29, 127, 130, 449
strangers   41, 143, 187
strength   33, 35, 39, 64–65, 67, 123, 143, 166, 187, 199, 221, 232, 315, 429
Substitute   215
suffering(s)   43, 45, 59, 119, 169, 195, 221, 331, 351, 362, 367, 441
sun   31, 157, 160, 177, 199, 207, 221, 291–92, 373, 423
Sunday   8, 10, 12, 83, 85, 106, 250, 350
sweetness   41, 107, 127, 133, 161, 171, 193, 209, 220, 311, 326, 374, 427, 433
sword   13, 51, 56, 221, 243, 247, 271
sympathy   41, 43, 45

T

teachers   77, 127
tears   35, 79, 115, 215, 244, 300, 305, 433, 458
temperance   257, 260
temple   142, 147, 169, 174, 243, 292, 341, 349, 372
temptation   250, 370, 407
terror   115, 129, 205
Tertullian   383, 391
thought (intellectual product/views)   35, 49, 386
thoughts   29, 38, 102, 193, 217, 220, 247, 263, 265, 301, 329, 331, 349, 350, 362, 365, 367, 370, 374
throne   55, 59, 61, 65, 119, 169, 174, 175–76, 203, 278, 282, 348
Titus (Roman general)   169, 174
toil, toils   76, 199, 229
tortures   41, 160
treasure   11, 56, 61, 452
trials   41, 105, 281, 433

Trinity   267, 383
triumph   169, 273–75
Triune God   59
trouble, troubles   36, 63, 76, 106, 133, 141, 159, 229, 283, 297, 307, 311, 355, 369, 373–75, 419, 421, 451
trust   59, 281
truth   31, 53, 67, 73, 76, 165, 177, 181, 187, 193, 195, 221, 233, 253, 270, 284, 291, 293, 315, 329, 339, 350, 377, 444, 457, 460, 473

U

unbelief   67, 111, 134, 233, 307, 311
ungodly, the   5, 56–57, 127, 326
unity   433
usefulness   59, 76, 191, 195, 232

V

vengeance   76, 229, 347
vileness   125
virtue   76, 143, 193, 405, 458
vows   196, 365

W

walk (one's conduct)   41
warning   7, 141, 299, 329
water   49, 55, 147, 149, 151–52, 154, 232–34, 244, 300, 301, 334, 361–62, 377, 379, 386–89, 392, 429, 447, 453
weak, the   301
weakness   95, 192, 307, 311
Wesleyan   75
wicked, the   56, 123, 130, 271, 333, 355, 421
Wesley, John   6, 381, 389, 460
wickedness   138, 421
wife   361, 440
wisdom   35, 58, 64, 215, 221, 329, 372, 374
witness, witnesses   3, 8, 125, 127, 193, 260, 283, 399
Witsius, [Hermann]   377
woman   71, 78–79, 201, 251, 352, 355, 362, 370, 440
wonders   73, 201, 215, 244, 447

497

SUBJECT INDEX

Word of God   *xv, 9, 65, 97, 135–36, 162, 193, 232, 275, 312, 351, 414, 460*
words (of one's mouth)   *329, 331, 367, 423*
work (one's vocation)   *340, 447*
work of grace   *133–34, 234*
work of the ministry   *77, 452*
works (deeds)   *12, 38–39, 47, 54, 77, 80, 108, 128, 133, 166, 215, 282–83, 317, 333, 409, 414, 441*
works of holiness   *128, 414*
works of men   *54*
world, the   *36, 38, 41, 52–57, 63, 80, 84, 111, 133–34, 144, 167, 171, 179, 191, 193, 195, 199, 203, 207, 221, 243, 250, 257–58, 260, 264–65, 292, 296, 300, 302, 321, 323, 326, 331, 340, 345, 350, 357, 361, 373, 395, 399, 405, 413, 421, 423–24, 427, 431, 439, 441, 444–45, 447, 449, 452–53, 471, 473*
worship   *41, 174, 194, 260, 292, 351, 440, 464*
worshippers   *169, 174*
wrath   *29, 80, 239, 243, 269, 271, 282, 309, 329, 331, 335, 443*

Y

young, the   *300, 329*

Z

zeal   *67, 165, 191, 195, 324, 340, 433, 460*